Bogowie

A Study of Eastern
Europe's Ancient Gods

Bogowie

A Study of Eastern Europe's Ancient Gods

T.D. Kokoszka

Winchester, UK
Washington, USA

JOHN HUNT PUBLISHING

First published by Moon Books, 2023
Moon Books is an imprint of John Hunt Publishing Ltd., No. 3 East Street, Alresford
Hampshire SO24 9EE, UK
office@jhpbooks.net
www.johnhuntpublishing.com
www.moon-books.net

For distributor details and how to order please visit the 'Ordering' section on our website.

ISBN: 978 1 80341 285 6
978 1 80341 286 3 (ebook)
Library of Congress Control Number: 2022939756

A CIP catalogue record for this book is available from the British Library.

Design: Matthew Greenfield

UK: Printed and bound by CPI Group (UK) Ltd, Croydon, CR0 4YY
Printed in North America by CPI GPS partners

Contents

Dedicated to the free peoples of Eastern Europe,
and to indigenous peoples everywhere who
still cling to their culture.

Acknowledgements

I must thank Jeff S. Wilson, Ph.D, of Texas State for freely providing many of the resources cited in this book. I must also thank my friends and family who have supported me through the production of this book. You were all indispensable in many ways. I must also give special thanks to the neopagan organization Ar nDraiocht Fein (ADF), for showing me how to bring ancient traditions into the present. Without the influence of ADF, the spiritual elements of this book would be far less developed.

Slava Dazhbog!

Introduction

Europe occupies a position of interest in many people's minds, and research on European history is heavily represented in a number of fields. Research on the origins of Europe has recently been invigorated by ancient DNA sequencing, which has revealed how modern Europeans arose from hunter-gatherers, Anatolian farmers, and people from the steppes of modern-day Russia. If you have European ancestry, then a significant portion of your ancestry can probably be traced back to the Yamnaya and Sredny Stog cultural horizons, 5000+ years ago, in Eastern Europe.

Despite its historical and prehistoric significance, Eastern Europe is a footnote for many, particularly in the west. It is not unusual to encounter educated westerners who do not even know who the Slavs are, despite the fact that they occupy almost the entire eastern half of Europe. The three main language groups in Europe are (in order of size) Slavic, Romance, and Germanic. Speakers of Slavic languages such as Russian, Polish, and Ukrainian number approximately 250 million as of 2022. For comparison, the Latin-derived Romance languages have approximately 225 million speakers (In Europe), and the Germanic languages have about 200 million. If we identify "Slavs" by language, then they constitute just over a third of Europe by population. Furthermore, the maximum extent of the Slavic tribes in the 7th century CE included much of modern-day Austria, Hungary, and Eastern Germany. These countries no longer host a Slavic-language speaking majority today, but we know that Slavic tribes once had a significant presence within their modern-day territories. Yet despite the historical and present-day significance of the Slavs, many English speakers will ask "who are they?" The Slavic peoples of Europe have a long history of being sidelined.

The term Slav is related to the word "Slovo" which in many languages like modern-day Russian simply means "word." The term for "German" in many Slavic languages simply means "mute" or "dumb" (e.g. someone without words). The term "Slav" likely referred to an ethnolinguistic identity originally, which helps explain how they managed to assimilate such a vast swath of eastern and central Europe during the early Middle Ages. Assimilation undoubtedly happened in the south, where many Romanized Balkan peoples originally lived. In ancient times, the Balkans were inhabited by the now extinct Illyrian, Thracian, and Dacian languages. The only survivor of this group is modern-day Albanian, although its exact relationship to the ancient languages of the Balkan region is uncertain. Some consider it a descendant of Thracian, but others find Illyrian to be a more likely source. The Serbs and the ostensibly related Sorbs of eastern Germany are an interesting case. In Roman sources, the "Sorboi" were identified as a Sarmatian group, yet at some point, they evidently joined the Slavic ethnolinguistic identity. The Bohemians today speak the West Slavic language known as Czech, yet they are named after an eastern Celtic tribe that was known as the Boii.

The Slavs, therefore, should not be treated as a racial group. Indeed, such flawed racial ideology nearly led to a mass genocide of Europe's Slavic peoples during World War II. The Nazi plan for the East (termed Generalplan Ost) anticipated mass extermination and deportation of people from Poland, Czechia, Ukraine, and Russia, in order to make room for "Aryan" settlers from Germany. The Slavs were regarded as inferior and ultimately rescued themselves from genocide on the eastern front by crushing the German Wehrmacht at Stalingrad and Kursk.

It is therefore highly disappointing that much of the interest in ancient Slavic culture comes from Russian and Ukrainian Neo-Nazis and other related far-right nationalist groups. It would seem that these people cannot appreciate the absurdity of following in the footsteps of an ideology that nearly exterminated them. The neopagan movement in Russia and Ukraine, often called Rodnoverie (literally "native faith") has a decidedly political nature. In the 2014 conflict between Russia and Ukraine, numerous Rodnovers fought on both sides. The infamous Azov Battalion (numbering approximately 400 people) combined Ukrainian Rodnoverie with Neo-Nazi and white supremacist ideology.

By contrast, the interest in Paganism in western countries like the U.S. is generally left-wing overall. It has its roots, at least partially, in the counter-cultural movements of the 1960s and 1970s. However, there are some similarly far-right elements associated with Germanic and Norse paganism in the West. Overall, however, we are fortunate in that the interest in European paganism in the U.S. and other western countries is generally not of a nationalist nature. I would argue that this western perspective has enhanced our ability to understand our history, not diminished it.

Many Rodnovers in Eastern Europe, on the other hand, actually have a very poor understanding of history. The pseudo-historical religion Ynglism, for example, claims to be based on hypothetical tablets that the founder discovered in Siberia. These hypothetical tablets are the so-called "Slavic Aryan Vedas." A ridiculous name if ever one existed. Ironically, it's partially due to the sorry state of reliable information that I felt called to Slavic paganism. If I didn't try to reconstruct it with rigorous research, then who would? The answer is that there are very few of us. As near as I can tell, there aren't many who are truly dedicated to the task. To be fair, I have no doubt that there are others like me in Eastern Europe, but they often seem to be drowned out by nationalists with no real desire for knowledge on the ancient culture they claim a connection to.

On the other hand, Western countries sometimes seem so cautious about ideology that they almost discourage people from seeking an identity. We are so timid about ideology that we've allowed an ideological vacuum to form in the West. And this is part of a broader trend, one that has left much of the world in need of a cultural revolution in order to reinvigorate itself spiritually and recover from its current disorder.

If our society was enlightened, or even halfway functional, we would now be responding rapidly to meet the challenges we face in the modern world, such as climate change. The reasons we fail to respond are not for lack of science or evidence. It's not even for lack of intelligence: The average person is perfectly capable of understanding the situation. The roadblocks are irrational and ideological. Consequently, only an ideological and psychological realignment in our culture can solve this problem. Logic is precious, but I no longer have faith that logic alone is sufficient to create an enlightened society. Obviously, there are no simple solutions to this dilemma. However, I believe that neopaganism is one movement that might revive an appreciation for our connection to the planet.

In short, the neopagan movement can be a force for positive change in our society. One that gives people a sense of belonging and values. Yet it must be a movement not based on racial hatred or the rejection of pluralism. The European neopagan movements should have deep solidarity with others who are attempting to revive / preserve their native faith in the Americas, Asia, and Africa. I believe that neopaganism should seek the rebuilding of a pre-racial and pre-colonial worldview. It must be against the outright destruction of native culture anywhere, which we must recognize as a birthright inherited by all human beings. This book is, in fact, written by a half-Jewish, half Polish-American author (from Texas of all places!) Even so, it represents an urgent call for Slavic Paganism and "Rodnoverie" to turn away from the darkest impulses of humankind.

Ideology aside, the main purpose of this work is to address the lack of English language sources that deal with the subject of Slavic pagan beliefs comprehensively. The view of many conventional scholars seems to be that Slavic mythology is destroyed beyond all recognition, and that it is also uninteresting compared to that of other cultures. I hope to challenge both of these views. While the end of this book does explain my own spiritual views, I will try to focus on the factual, history-based reconstruction of Slavic paganism. I will also include research on the broader subject of comparative mythology.

I will wander a bit beyond the cut-and-dried facts because I do embrace paganism on a religious and spiritual level. However, my main focus has always been to try and present the material in a fairly objective manner. I take the liberty of interpreting resources, to be sure, but always while specifying what is interpretation and what is not. I hope that my readers will understand that this cut-and-dried factual approach is driven by a deep spiritual desire to seek the truth in all things. In that sense, this is a very scholarly attempt at reconstructing Slavic paganism, but one driven by a single-minded desire to arrive at the historical truth of its origins.

One obvious thing that should be stated up-front is that I am questioning the conclusions of many scholars on this topic, though always with a fair representation of the various scholarly positions. Many would likely question what qualifies me to do this, but my hope is that the dedicated research will speak for itself. It is obvious that a spiritual love of Slavic folklore has motivated me to pursue this topic single-mindedly and passionately. Again, however, this passion is primarily oriented towards finding out the truth of the topic in question (historical Slavic paganism).

Additionally, the state of the research on Slavic paganism is fairly difficult to praise currently. There are still significant barriers preventing the type of research that needs to happen from taking place. One that remains in effect to this day is ethnic and national boundaries. The most logical approach to this topic is to analyze traditions from all 13 Slavic countries, and reconstruct a body of shared elements. It is precisely these shared elements that are most likely to represent old traditions from the Common Slavic or Proto-Slavic period. However, one of the primary motives for studying folklore in Eastern Europe has always been nationalism, and the goal to put forward a narrative of national or ethnic exceptionalism. While there are indeed many exceptional cultures in Eastern Europe, this book will attempt to show the incredible benefits that come with an international approach to understanding the ancient culture of Eastern Europe. There is a general principle that folklore concepts found in multiple isolated communities are more likely to be ancient than those found in a single location. Based on this, a localized approach to understanding Slavic paganism - or even one focused on material from just one nation - is unnecessarily limited.

Another circumstance that has stymied the field is obviously the environment of the Soviet Union. It's no secret that scholarship in this period could be incredibly narrow in its aims, and the discourse was not always a free-flowing one. This was definitely true for the topic of religion and Russian history during the Soviet Union. Furthermore, the scholarship of the USSR was often narrowly focused on "Russian" identity, if it was focused on cultural identity at all. This meant limited support for academic research on, say, Bulgarian folklore or Ukrainian folklore. At least not in an even-handed fashion that would do justice to all ethnic groups.

This also holds true for non-Slavic ethnic groups in Eastern Europe. It is not always appreciated how interconnected the various ethnic groups of the region are. In particular, we know that the Slavs probably assimilated a conglomeration of various ethnic groups from the fragments of the Hunnic empire during their expansion in the 5th century CE. This would have included Scytho-Sarmatian, Hunnic, Gothic, Baltic, and Romanized Balkan elements from an early date. As such, the mythology of the early Slavs is perhaps uniquely qualified to be analyzed under the comparative approach - precisely because the early Slavic culture is likely to have had mixed origins. Despite a strong resistance to this idea among many modern Slavic peoples, the comparison of Slavic folklore to various traditions across Eurasia makes a lot of methodological sense. We should expect to find a matrix of connections anchoring Slavic folklore into the crossroads of the Eurasian continent, and as this book will demonstrate, that is exactly what I have found.

In particular, I will stress the Scytho-Sarmatian elements in the Slavic religion. The word for "Gods" in most Slavic languages is derived from the root "Bog" which in Proto-Slavic denoted any deity. The title of this book "Bogowie" (Pronounced BO - GOV-YEH) references the Polish word for "Gods." This term, which is found in all Slavic languages, implies a huge influence from Iranian language-speaking cultures. Specifically, it is a direct borrowing from the nomads known as the Scythians and Sarmatians. This book is in part an acknowledgement of Slavic paganism's "eastern" or Asiatic inheritance. Disappointingly, I have encountered many Slavic pagans who are actually offended at the idea of a cultural connection with the Iranian and Indian cultures, despite the fact that their very language attests to a rich spiritual inheritance from Iranian nomads of the Eurasian steppe.

In one of the chapters of this book, we will discuss the giant Svyatogor, from the Russian Bylina (Epic Song) tradition. This bylina has great symbolic meaning to me. The song of Svyatogor looks like a swan song to Slavic paganism, probably composed orally by East Slavic peasants during the glory days of Kievan Rus (the predecessor state of Russia and Ukraine). In this bylina, the giant Svyatogor is laid to rest in a coffin. He accepts his fate, and before he falls silent, he transfers a portion of his strength to the Christian bylina hero Illya Muromets. In a way, this mythological death of Svyatogor accomplishes two things; It bids farewell to paganism, yet ironically preserves a great deal of it as well. The pagan symbolism is generally not contested. In fact, the giant's name literally translates to "Holy Mountain." It is clear that Svyatogor is not just a giant person, but rather that he personifies the strength and majesty of the land itself. As I hope to show, Slavic paganism is a lot like this sleeping giant who was sealed within a coffin. It may appear dead, yet in many ways the symbolic eulogies to paganism carefully preserved in folk tradition contain the secret to resurrecting it again.

I would like to begin this book with a message to the giant Svyatogor; Wake up! You are not dead. The rumors of your death have been greatly exaggerated. And so has the "death" of Slavic paganism. Like a dead "Prince Ivan" from Russian wonder tales, I hope to show that Slavic paganism has not really died at all. It has merely been sleeping for a long time. With the help of like-minded individuals, I believe that we can pour the water of life upon this sleeping giant, and thus raise it once more from the oaken coffin of modernity. The giant is already stirring, but with your help, dear reader, we can awaken it again!

This is, of course, a very dramatic way to open a book that is primarily research-based. But the burning desire for a believable and credible reconstruction of Slavic mythology has been a powerful motivator to scour all available evidence on this topic. Additionally, while many might roll their eyes at the idea of professed neopagan attempting research on Slavic prehistory, this does not make me inherently more biased than a devout Christian studying Slavic history. (Of which there have been many). Additionally, there is always some difficulty in explaining why paganism would be spiritually meaningful in today's day and age. To be inspired by the beauty of nature, and the simplicity of pre-industrial culture is often deemed sentimental or foolish. We rarely associate this sentimentality with morality or values. However, I would argue that the ability to venerate a mountain or a sunrise is not so unrelated to our sense of values. As Greek philosophers argued, the ability to appreciate beauty is not unrelated to our sense of right and wrong.

Of course, these two impulses are not the same. Just because you feel awe at a sunrise does not automatically mean you live by noble principles. But it is necessary to recognize that there is a connection between these two impulses, even if they are not identical to one another. Spiritually and psychologically, they both come from the same place - *namely, the fiery and irrational nucleus of the human soul.* All values require some sentimentality in order to become more than just words. For an increasing number of us in the modern world, the poetic beauty of mythology and folklore is intimately connected with our passion for our principles.

Chapter 1

The Ancient Origins of Europe up to the Early Slavs

It may puzzle some people that I am a student of Biology. Yet in many ways, the booming field of ancient genetics has given great clarity to speculations about our ancient origins that archaeologists and linguists have debated for over a century. Undoubtedly, we live in an era that heralds the revival of Indo-European studies. However, in order to understand what has been revived by ancient DNA, we must first understand the origins of Indo-European studies. What does "Indo-European" mean?

The Indo-European language family is often cited as having been "discovered" by the British Lawyer William Jones. As an English Lawyer, he spoke Greek and Latin. Once deployed to India, it became necessary for him to learn the ancient Indian language of Sanskrit. In 1786, he discovered something incredible about Sanskrit. His discovery is often summarized with the following quote, and for good reason. In 1786, William Jones wrote the following:[1]

> *The Sanskrit language, whatever may be its antiquity, is of a wonderful structure; more perfect than the Greek, more copious than the Latin, and more exquisitely refined than either… No philologer could examine the Sanskrit, Greek, and Latin, without believing them to have sprung from some common source, which perhaps no longer exists.*

While it is debatable whether he was the sole "discoverer" of Indo-European commonalities, he was definitely the first to present the case for it so succinctly and academically.

This book is not intended to be the definitive book on Indo-European studies, though I find them to be critical for interpreting the Pre-Christian culture of Europe. That distinction most likely goes to one of a handful of scholarly publications. Most recently, *"The Horse the Wheel and Language"* by David Anthony, which also cites the same exact quote by William Jones.

In his book, David Anthony examines the linguistic and archaeological evidence for the origins of the Indo-European language family. Using archaeology and linguistics, he presents a fairly up-to-date case for placing the original Indo-European language (Called Proto-Indo-European, or "PIE") in the Ukrainian and Russian steppes, or grasslands. The Indo-European languages are today found from the U.S. to India, not to mention Europe, Kurdistan, Iran, and Afghanistan. However, the majority of scholars - even in 2008 - saw Eastern Europe as the most likely homeland for the original PIE language.

David Anthony was far from the first to propose such a homeland for the Indo-European language family. Another excellent text on the subject is the book *"In Search of the Indo-Europeans"* by J.P. Mallory, published in 1989.[2] Together, these two texts probably present most of the linguistic and archaeological research that can be obtained by the casual English-speaking reader.

The story of the Indo-European language family is being unraveled in our lifetimes. Yet who really deserves the credit for placing the Indo-European homeland correctly in the Pontic-Caspian steppes of modern-day Ukraine and Russia? The first person to truly perceive the plausibility of this model was none other than a Lithuanian woman, born in 1921, by the name of Marija Gimbutas.

Today, Gimbutas is sometimes dismissed because of her extreme tendency to idealize the pre-Indo-European Neolithic farmers of Europe. According to her, the Neolithic farmers were a peaceful and matriarchal society which was violently destroyed by the so-called "Kurgan" nomads of the steppe region.[3] Modern genetic evidence adds some nuance to this picture. The nomads apparently arrived with plague. DNA research has clearly shown evidence of a plague epidemic during this migration. On one hand, they probably did not shy from violence. They also ended up fathering an uncomfortable number of children with the local women. But whatever aggression they displayed, the plague was a significant part of their expansion into Europe.[4]

Additionally, it's now apparent that the Neolithic farmers themselves had displaced the earlier hunter-gatherer population. Many earlier archaeologists assumed hunter-gatherers were assimilated in large quantities by incoming farmers from the Near East, but it's now clear that such assimilation was rare, and little ancestry from the original hunter-gatherer population ended up surviving through the late Neolithic. Therefore, the Neolithic farmers of the Middle East displaced much of the earlier hunter-gatherer population in Europe and were themselves then displaced by people with steppe ancestry.

Whatever you say about Gimbutas though, she deserves credit for getting the Proto-Indo-European homeland right. As Mallory argued in his book from the '80s, linguistics and archaeology alone were sufficient to craft a solid argument for the steppe origin model. In particular, the Tocharian languages of the Tarim Basin in northwest China were always nearly impossible to explain without the steppe model. The Tocharian languages are among the most archaic in structure (second only to Anatolian languages, which are the most basal branch of the family), and Tocharian is unambiguously of steppe origin. With ancient DNA bolstering the steppe model, it seems the writing is on the wall.

The other often touted model for the spread of Indo-European languages is the Anatolian model, which claims the Indo-European languages spread from Anatolia way back in the Neolithic, and began fragmenting around 7,000 BCE. There are some issues with this purely on linguistic grounds: Wheels were invented no earlier than 4,000 BCE, and all Indo-European languages other than the Anatolian branch have significant shared terminology for wheels and wagons. There was a high-profile study by biologists Atkinson and Gray, who decided to perform phylogenetic analysis on the language family. Basically, they constructed a linguistic family tree.[5]

Obviously, the tree in question comes from two proponents of the Anatolian model for the spread of Indo-European languages. Even so, it is informative, because it shows something that both sides of the debate have tended to agree on: Anatolian languages like Hittite split off first. Then the Tocharian branch. Then all the others. However, in their family tree they show Tocharian splitting off around 6,000 BCE, which is about 2,000 years before the wheel / wagon terminology of the Tocharian languages could have existed.

The wheeled vehicle simply didn't exist before 4,000 BCE. In his book "*The Horse, the Wheel, and Language*" David Anthony uses this argument with devastating effect to show the flaws of the Anatolian model - even just on linguistic grounds. He includes a map of the wheel/ wagon terminology in his book[6], which highlights the dilemma for the Anatolian model.

In one of the two Tocharian languages "Kukal" means wagon. This is cognate to Ancient Greek Kukla (literally plural of "wheels). It's also cognate to Russian "Kolo" (meaning wheel) and Indo-Iranian terms like Sanskrit "Cakra." Significantly, however, the Tocharian word "Kukal" has an "L" instead of an "R" thus proving that it is not a loan word from the neighboring Indo-Iranian branch. (Switching Proto-Indo-European "L" for "R" is a characteristic of all Indo-Iranian languages.)[7] This is actually the origin of the Sanskrit word "Chakra."

The fact that the Tocharian term "Kukal" has an "L" instead of an "R" is very telling. Indo-Iranian language speakers appear to have been the only neighbors of the Tocharians who also spoke Indo-European languages. The fact that the Tocharian wheel / wagon terminology is clearly not borrowed from any Indo-Iranian source means that this word was almost certainly inherited directly from Proto-Indo-European (i.e. prior to the divergence of Tocharian and Indo-Iranian languages). This supports David Anthony's assertion, which is that all of these terms for "wheel", "wagon", "axle" and "thill" belong to the early vocabulary of Proto-Indo-European from the very beginning of its expansion.

As I have mentioned, we don't just have to rely on linguistic and archaeological evidence anymore to support an expansion from the steppe starting around 4,000 BCE. Ancient DNA has provided this smoking gun beyond any shadow of a doubt, in some cases showing that as much as 70% of the ancestry in bronze age Europe was replaced by people with Eurasian Steppe ancestry.[8]

Even so, it is remarkable that scholars were able to construct the basics of this model long before 2015, without any genetic data whatsoever. One final caveat on the brutal expansion of people with steppe ancestry - there is an unfortunate trope that nomads are "bad" and violent whereas farmers are "good" and peaceful. Even Marija Gimbutas, as much as I admire her as an archeologist and as a pioneering woman of the mid-20th century, fell into this preconception.

As an avid follower of this research, however, I would submit that history shows land-grabbing agriculturalists to be the most invasive and genocidal type of people on earth. That was certainly the case in the Americas. Furthermore, the idealized Neolithic farmers that Gimbutas extolled performed a very similar erasure of the European Hunter-Gatherers who existed before them.

Finally, there are still many questions about the context of these population shifts. It is by no means clear that the elimination of Neolithic farming populations was carried out by nomads. We know that the people who replaced them had steppe ancestry, but there are still significant questions about how "nomadic" the Corded Ware individuals actually were. Agriculture appears to have continued in some capacity during this time period.

It may still turn out that the steppe nomads abandoned their wandering way of life, and adopted agriculture - and only then did they begin to obliterate their neighbors. Nomadic pastoralism is not a viable way of life throughout most of Europe - not on its own. Nomadic pastoralism essentially requires a limitless supply of grassland that allows massive herds of livestock to graze one area until it is bare and then move on to a new pasture. Once nomads leave the grassy steppes behind, this lifestyle tends to fade.

Sure enough, when we look at history, we almost always see that steppe nomads in Eastern Europe are dependent on farmers to provision them. Far from exterminating them, they actually require them. This was certainly the case for the 6th-7th century Avars, a nomadic people from Central Asia. Once they left the Pontic steppe behind, they were heavily dependent on provisions from Slavic and Byzantine farmers in Europe. After conquering cities in the Balkans, the Avars are recorded as imploring the natives "go out, sow and reap" so that the Avars could obtain food from them as tribute.[9]

While the Avars would eventually become more settled and agrarian, this does not seem to have happened under the first generation of "actual" Central Asian nomads from the 6th century. Perhaps the Proto-Indo-Europeans, like the Avars, established themselves as an elite group who demanded tribute in the form of agricultural produce. Over time, however, they may have evolved into a rival farming population - but one who carefully preserved a sense of "otherness" based on ancestry.

Thus, while it may be impossible to defend the actions of Proto-Indo-Europeans from a modern standpoint, we can also argue that agriculture was the main driver of population displacement from about 6000 BCE to 2000 BCE - and the Indo-Europeans were just the final wave of this 4,000-year long disruption precipitated by farming. Agriculturalists started the era of population displacement across Eurasia: the Proto-Indo-Europeans simply finished it.

As fascinating as the Proto-Indo-Europeans are, there is some unfairness in glorifying them alone, without thinking about the other major "builders" of European culture. The Indo-Europeans were the victors, who succeeded in winning sovereignty over the largely agrarian peoples they came into contact with. Yet most of our ancestors for the past 4,000 years have been simple farmers, continuing the agrarian tradition that was initiated during the Neolithic.

Additionally, we should not assume that the steppe nomads of the Pontic region remained "pure" in any sense of the word during their migrations. For one thing, the Corded Ware culture that carried an influx of steppe ancestry largely missed southern Europe. While it would certainly exert influence on its southern neighbors, the massive shift in ancestry associated with the Corded Ware culture did not necessarily happen to such an extent in the south. For instance, in Spain, it looks like about 40% of the total ancestry is from the steppe region.[10] That's still a lot - perhaps more than we would like to think about. Still, it shows that we should not dismiss the Pre-Indo-European element of Europe either. It may have been heavily diluted, but it didn't vanish altogether.

Furthermore, all populations must have been hunter-gatherers at some point. Even the people of Anatolia and the Steppe, at one time, probably lived in simple hunter-gatherer communities. Indeed, it's quite likely that many spirits and supernatural beliefs of these pagan cultures had continuity from the Mesolithic to the Neolithic, and possibly even up to the Bronze Age. One of the most beautiful things about paganism is that it maintains continuity with the past, rather than rewriting it completely. A river might be venerated in the Mesolithic as a disembodied power, and much later as a humanoid idol carved from marble - but in paganism there is generally little real reason to abandon earlier objects of worship altogether. Instead, I believe that paganism evolves without losing continuity - and in that sense, it will always be timeless, even if the outward forms morph.

Marija Gimbutas wrote a lot about what she saw as "Old European" beliefs hidden within paganism - that is, relics of the old matriarchal culture which she thought the Indo-European nomads had replaced. While she may have been more liberal than most in this pursuit, I don't think she was altogether wrong that some traditions can be traced back to the Neolithic.

In the ruins of Knossos, on the Greek island of Crete, archaeologists have found evidence of a domestic Snake goddess cult, one associated both with the dead ancestors, and with the household. This has parallels with the domestic snake cult that is well attested on mainland Greece.[11]

This is despite the fact that the Minoans apparently spoke a non-Greek (and most likely non-Indo-European language). The Minoans were almost exclusively descended from Neolithic farmers, and were isolated from the Proto-Greek speaking Mycenaeans on the Greek mainland for much of their history. So the Minoan religion is as good a proxy as any for the "Neolithic" religion of Europe. Marija Gimbutas certainly thought so.

As mentioned, the mainland Greeks practiced a very similar household snake cult to the Minoans. This is well known among scholars. In fact, multiple Slavic countries have a folk tradition involving a domestic guardian in the form of a snake. This cult may even be associated with the Russian folktale Witch, Baba Yaga.[12] Similar concepts show up as far north as Lithuania, where the domestic snake is often a feminine spirit or household Goddess called "Aspelenie" who dwells behind the stove.[13]

If there is one thing we have learned about Gimbutas, it's that we should never assume she was right, and never assume that she was wrong either! Because of her intense interest in the Neolithic European culture, she could be remarkably insightful about their mythology. Particularly what she saw as the Neolithic Goddess Cult. The one caveat is that the survival of a major Neolithic Goddess does not necessarily imply a matriarchal culture. Rather, this could simply reflect the fact that Neolithic maternal ancestry survived more successfully than Neolithic paternal ancestry - and hence most Neolithic traditions that survived did so via the oral transmission from mothers. It's not hard to see how this "maternal transmission" could bias the types of traditions that were most likely to survive past the Neolithic. This hypothesis is strengthened by the fact that the Neolithic snake Goddess seems to have a domestic character. So what should we think of when we think of "Indo-European" mythology? Ironically, and perhaps not coincidentally, it is the serpent-slayer or dragon-slayer who seems to have dominated many Indo-European mythologies. Scholars discovered this very shortly after they realized Sanskrit was an Indo-European language. Once they began to delve into the "Vedic" religion of ancient India, they noticed that the most popular deity seemed to be the thunder god Indra, who used his thunderbolt to slay the dragon Vritra, thus releasing the waters. This has an abundance of parallels in Europe, most famously the struggle between Thor and the Midgard Serpent in Norse Mythology.[14] As we will see, these old dragon- slaying narratives clearly survived in Slavic folk tradition.

When we talk about the cultural origins of the Slavs, in Northeastern Europe, we must start by understanding the Corded Ware Culture. As we have discussed, this culture arose from a mixture of influences. In their 2015 paper, Haak and Lazaridis estimated that the Corded Ware culture carried approximately 79% Steppe ancestry, 4% Western Hunter-Gatherer, and 17% Early Neolithic Farmer ancestry.[15]

Unfortunately, there's a long sequence of history that's missing between when the Proto-Indo-European language spread throughout Europe (approximately 4,000 BCE to 2,500 BCE) and when the "Slavs" suddenly appear in recorded history. A people identifiable as the "Slavs" first appears during the 6th century CE, initially only in Byzantine chronicles. Mentions of "Slavs" from the Germanic and Carolingian sphere show up somewhat later.

On the surface, we can say that the Proto-Slavic language spoken by these 6th-century tribes was an Indo-European language. The Proto-Slavic language gave rise to modern-day Russian, Ukrainian, Polish, Czech, Slovak, Slovene, Serbian, Bulgarian, and many others as well. Their exact relationship to the other Indo-European languages is a complex one. All scholars agree that the closest relative of the Slavic language branch is the Baltic branch (today represented only by Lithuanian and Latvian). In fact, "family trees" constructed around the Indo-European language family sometimes just have a "Balto-Slavic" branch on them, which then forks into Slavic and the much smaller Baltic branch.

This is significant because Baltic paganism is somewhat better preserved than Slavic paganism. The chief irony here is that there are far more people who would identify as "Slavic" than "Baltic" alive today. As mentioned, there are some 250 million Slavic language speakers in Europe alone. If we include diasporic communities living outside of Europe, that number increases to about 315 million - nearly the population of the United States of America. By contrast, there are under 5 million speakers of Lithuanian and Latvian combined, making the Baltic branch less than 1/60 times the size of the Slavic branch.

So, the tradition that more people would relate to is the tradition that is less well preserved. This is something that I will attempt to address somewhat in this book. To an extent, we can rely on Baltic material to help interpret the available material on Slavic paganism. However, there is some caution warranted in drawing parallels between the two. One thing we know for certain is that the Balts had a Sun Goddess[16], whereas the Slavs seem to have worshipped a fairly widespread male Sun God.[17] Therefore, anywhere that we encounter traces of the Slavic solar cult, it is likely that we have to look beyond a simple linear connection to Baltic mythology. On the other hand, it seems there's little reason to doubt the connection between the Lithuanian thunder God, Perkunas, and the Slavic Perun.[18]

The Balto-Slavic languages are also classified as "satem" languages. This requires some explanation. The satem isogloss is one of the major divisions within the Indo-European language family. The Balto-Slavic and Indo-Iranian languages are today the two major groups of satem languages. By contrast, all Romance, Germanic, and Celtic languages are classified as "centum." In modern times, there is very much an East-West divide between satem and centum languages respectively. (Though this has not always been the case.)

The satem isogloss seems to be characteristic of Corded Ware Culture populations who existed outside of the Bell Beaker sphere of influence. The Germanic languages are considered "centum" despite originating from the western territory of the bronze age Corded Ware Culture. The most obvious explanation for their exclusion from the satem language category seems to be that they arose from an "overlap-zone" between Corded Ware and Bell Beaker cultures. I've included a map showing this relationship (See Figure 1 below for illustration of these 3rd millennium BCE European cultures.)

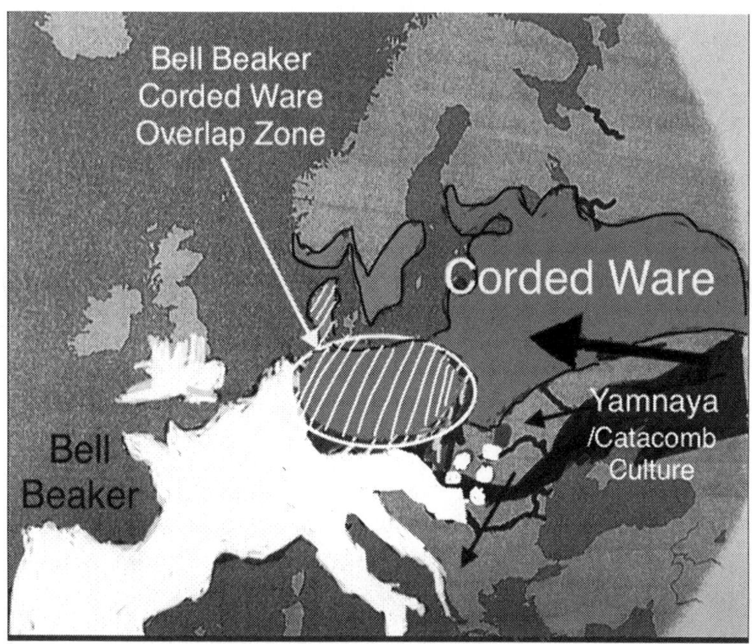

Figure 1: Three Cultural Zones in Europe during the 3rd millennium B.C, drawn by the author with guidance from Heyd, 2019.[19] *Black arrows indicate gene flow from the Pontic Steppe region. The black shows the actual "source" of Eurasian steppe ancestry, first coming from the Sredny Stog and Yamnaya cultures, later perhaps from the Catacomb Culture. The Bell-Beaker culture is shown in white, and the Corded Ware Culture is in grey. Stripes denote an overlap zone.*

It's likely that all three cultures portrayed in Figure 1 were heavily populated with Proto-Indo-European language speakers by the mid-3rd millennium BCE. However, the divisions between the different zones do help us interpret the variations present in different language groups. As I mentioned, the satem languages seem to be languages derived from the Corded Ware culture. Specifically, regions of the Corded Ware Culture that were outside of the Bell-Beaker overlap zone. It has been proposed that Proto-Germanic interactions with the Bell-Beaker folk caused them to "reject" or avoid the spread of the satem isogloss from further east. However, it appears that all other Corded Ware-derived groups adopted "Satemization" as a late innovation of Proto-Indo-European. This included not only the Balto-Slavs, but also the Indo-Iranians, who appear to have been descended from the easternmost branch of the Corded Ware Culture. This eastern branch of the Corded Ware culture is sometimes referred to as the "Fatyanovo-Balanovo" culture. By about 2,000 BCE the genetic signature of the Fatyanovo-Balanovo people had spread like wildfire from the Corded Ware periphery, eventually reaching as far as modern-day Kazakhstan. The telltale Y-DNA marker "R1a-Z93" clearly shows the spread of eastern Corded Ware ancestry from the Fatyanovo-Balanovo, all the way to modern-day South Asia and Central Asia.[20] Oddly enough, my Jewish side of the family also has this marker associated with the expansion of Indo-Iranian language speakers from the Eurasian steppe.

It should be noted that claiming East European origins for the Indo-Aryans is still a politically inflammatory topic in some circles, even though the genetic data obviously does not advocate for any political view. DNA is simply a polymer compound that stores information and is not inherently political until human beings make it so. The Nazis were infamous for claiming that Germany was the original homeland of the Indo-Europeans, thus appropriating the title of "Aryan" from the Sanskrit language in India. As a half-Jewish, half Polish-American man myself, I'm very familiar with these pitfalls, and I will attempt to navigate them as ethically as possible. Suffice to say, the Nazis would be horrified by much of the data that has been gained over the past several years. Not only would they have hated the idea of placing the Proto-Indo-European homeland in Ukraine, which they intended to colonize with German settlers, but they would also have probably rejected the revelation that only about half of their genome comes from the original Early Bronze Age steppe population. (The percentage has decreased since the time of the Corded Ware Culture!)

As strange as it may sound, the Balto-Slavic languages of Eastern Europe share a unique kinship with the Indo-Iranian languages like Hindi, Bengali, Farsi, Pashto, and Kurdish. Not only do they belong to the Indo-European language family, but these languages all seem to have shared the satem isogloss - a linguistic innovation that altered the way that sounds like *k, *g, and q* were pronounced. And the place where this innovation took place was apparently Northeastern Europe, during the 3rd millennium BCE. This has long been suspected on linguistic grounds, but the genetic data from the Fatyanovo-Balanovo culture seems to confirm it.

Throughout this book, you will see me frequently referencing comparative mythology as a means of interpreting the sources available on Slavic paganism. Most especially, the pagan folktales that have been passed down from word of mouth, only to be recorded in the 19th century by scholars like Afanasev. Some may ask - why reference ancient Vedic texts from India to interpret such material?

The truth is, the data supporting a connection between these cultures is stronger than it has ever been. I believe that with added insight from ancient DNA, now is the perfect time to present the case for reviving comparative mythology as a tool for understanding Slavic folklore. To be sure - folklore is not easy to interpret. The people who recited Russian Wonder Tales to be recorded by folklorists in the 19th century often only dimly understood the origins of their own tales. In order to interpret this material, you might argue that we need a time machine. Except we do have a sort of time machine now, thanks to the combined efforts of linguists, archaeologists, and geneticists.

However, the tale of the origin of the Balts and Slavs does not end with the Corded Ware culture. In order to understand the history of Eastern Europe over the 2nd and 1st millennia BCE - we must talk about a couple of other groups. The first of these are the Scythians.

The Scythians were the Indo-Iranians who came back home. Recall that the Proto-Indo-Iranians were offshoots of the eastern Corded Ware culture, who eventually migrated eastward into Central Asia. Obviously, a subset of the Indo-Iranians migrated south, into the Middle East and South Asia. This gave rise to the Old Persian and Sanskrit languages, and their many modern descendants.

The Scythians were different, however. They were a culture of Iranian nomads who had spent roughly a millennium in Asia before eventually finding their way back to Eastern Europe. As they rode across the Pontic grasslands into modern-day Ukraine, it's possible they did not even realize they were returning to the land of their Proto-Indo-European forefathers.

The Scythians left numerous loan words in Proto-Slavic. Perhaps the most important of these was "Bog" meaning "God" or "Deity" in all Slavic languages. This is a direct cognate to Iranian "Baga" of the same meaning. The loan of the word for "deity" from Iranian suggests significant cultural influence in the sphere of religion.[21] I have already mentioned that Baltic mythology and Slavic mythology differ in some key areas. This Iranian influence on the early Slavs is one likely cause of the difference. Therefore, we cannot simply treat Slavic mythology as a slightly different version of Baltic mythology - even though the Baltic languages are closely related. Early Slavic culture obviously had other influences as well that must be considered.

Also of Iranian origin is Proto-Slavic "Topor'' meaning "axe." This is cognate to Persian 'Tabar." This seems to imply that the Slavs were quite familiar with the light, single-handed battle axes used by Scythian warriors. The Scythian men and women were both renowned for their ferocity in warfare, and quite a few Scythian skeletons have skulls broken by axes.[22]

In many ways, the Scythians who extended from Eastern Europe to Mongolia were the last true nomads of the Indo-European language-speaking world. When all other Indo-European language speakers had settled down, and become sedentary, the Scythians were the only ones who still roamed the grasslands with their herds, much as the Yamnaya had done back in 3,000 BCE. Things changed in the 4th century CE, however; The Huns put an end to the Scythian era throughout much of Central Asia and modern-day Russia.

The successors to the "Scythian" or nomadic way of life were the non-Indo-European Huns, and their relatives - the Gokturks and Mongols. Evidently, the Huns and Mongols adopted the Scythian bow, which was a composite of animal horn, and ideal for use on horseback due to its compact size. In fact, the Mongol bow of the 13th century had the same basic design as a Scythian bow over a millennium earlier.[23] The Huns and Mongols also may have adopted their horses from the Scythians. In many ways, the Huns learned all of the tricks that the Scythians had depended on for success and beat them at their own game. However, it is quite likely that many Asiatic nomads today are partially descended from Scythians, even if they no longer speak an Indo-European language. The genetic evidence supports a strong Indo-Iranian element among the Huns and Avars, both nomads thought to have "East Asian / Siberian" roots from the Mongolian steppe. Thus far, one of the most common Y-Chromosomal haplotypes (showing paternal ancestry) sequenced from the remains of Huns and Avars is R1a-Z93.[24] If you recall, this is the same paternal lineage associated with the Eastern Corded Ware (Fatyanovo-Balanovo) expansion into Central Asia and India.

On the other hand, it is hard to deny that these East Asian nomads from the Mongolian steppe brought many East Asian and Siberian elements that had previously been absent or marginal among the Scythians. As I will discuss, these "Siberian" influences from the Mongolian Steppe are significant as well. However, the most significant source of Siberian influence in Europe was not the Huns or Mongols. The most significant influence from Siberia was the Uralic languages. Specifically, the Finno-Ugric languages of the broader Uralic language family. Today these "Uralic" languages can be found from Finland to Siberia, and they are definitely not related to Indo-European languages in any meaningful way.

Today the Finno-Ugric languages have a significant presence in Europe, despite also being present in Siberia. They include not only Finnish and Sami in Scandinavia, but also some minority languages in the modern-day Russian Federation. Among the Uralic languages in "European Russia" are Mordvinic, Komi, and Udmurt.

Moving even further east, into the Siberian side of Russia, we encounter Khanty and Mansi - not to mention the Samoyedic languages as well. How did a Siberian language family expand into Northeastern Europe? The most likely timing for the arrival of Siberian ancestry in the Eastern Baltic seems to be approximately the 8th century BCE. There is no evidence of non-Corded Ware Siberian ancestry in modern-day Estonia earlier than this period. However, modern Finno-Ugric language speakers have a very detectable genetic signature from a Ngansan-like Siberian population. Therefore, genetics seems to say that the Uralic language family spread from Siberia to the Baltic region around 800 BCE or right around the Bronze Age / Iron Age transition. This matches very well with linguistic attempts to date the "Proto-Finno-Ugric" language.[25] How exactly did Siberian Hunter-Gatherers and reindeer herders expand into former Corded Ware territory? That's a trickier question. But it appears that is what happened.

The legacy of these Siberian migrants is evident in much of Northeastern Europe. Especially in Y-DNA (DNA from the Y-Chromosome, which is passed from father to son). As is so often the case, male ancestry seems to have changed more than female ancestry with each subsequent migration! In the case of the hunter-gathering, reindeer-herding Finno-Ugrians from Siberia, it seems unlikely that this was due to any kind of pronounced aggression. It may simply be that some of these men were very successful, and successful men had many surviving children and grandchildren. Indeed, it's not unlikely that these were factors at play in the earlier steppe migrations as well - rapid expansions of foreign male ancestry clearly do not always involve an "invasion" of heavily armed warriors.

Finnish men have Y-Chromosomal haplogroup N at a frequency of about 59%, and it is similarly high among many Finno-Ugric language speakers.[26] However, this haplogroup appears to have been absent in most of Europe until almost 3,000 years ago, when it arrived with a general influx of Siberian ancestry. However, we also see the Siberian haplogroup N at a frequency of approximately 4.29% in Polish men[27], 9.6% among Ukrainians[28], and 21.6% among Russians.[29] Therefore, the Finno-Ugric peoples are noteworthy for understanding the heritage of Eastern Europe, even in Slavic countries.

In many ways though, studying the Finno-Ugric mythologies brings us full circle. That's because researchers of these traditions have repeatedly drawn attention to what they see as Indo-Iranian and Scythian influences from the steppe. Numerous scholars have observed this Indo-Iranian influence in the beliefs of the Khanty, from Siberia. Furthermore, even Finnish contains Indo-Iranian loan words, which were inherited from Proto-Finno-Ugric itself. Evidently the very first Finno-Ugrians borrowed words from Indo-Iranians during the Bronze Age. Proto-Finno-Ugric words adopted from an Indo-Iranian source include words for honey, horn, boar, piglet, sickle, axe, orphan, man, lord, seven, ten, hundred, God, and heaven - among many others.[30]

Thus in many ways, the patterns of influence throughout Eastern Europe are an endless loop. And it may be impossible to fully understand them - but if we are to reconstruct Slavic paganism, we cannot be entirely unaware of this complexity. This is also one reason why this book focuses so much on comparative analysis to interpret Slavic folklore - because the ancient history of Eastern Europe is one of continual, often circular mixing of influences. It seems there was a constant circulation of cultural influences and migrations between the Ukrainian steppe, and those living further east - reaching even as far as the Mongolian steppe, and as far north as the Volga. As we will see, the results are still evident in many myths and folk traditions.

Where do the Slavs come in, after all of this? Unfortunately, quite late. Thanks to Byzantine chronicles, we know they existed as a recognizable ethnic group by the 6th century. With some work, we can perhaps push their origins back a little earlier than this. The story of the Slavs probably starts with two major fragments of the Corded Ware culture - the Komarov culture and the Trzciniec culture - in modern day Poland and Ukraine. These are thought to be associated with the earlier Balto-Slavic languages.[31]

One likely offshoot of this group is the Chernoles culture around modern day Western Ukraine. This culture overlaps with a group described in Classical times by Herodotus. Herodotus referred to them as "Scythian farmers" obviously recognizing them as closely related to or influenced by the Scythians, despite not living their nomadic lifestyle. It is plausible that he was describing Iron Age Proto-Slavs, or perhaps it would be more accurate to call them "Pre-Proto-Slavs", since this would technically predate the classical "Proto-Slavic Language" by at least a few centuries. In any case, the main strength of this proposed Slavic "homeland" is that it overlaps quite well with the oldest Slavic hydronyms. There are other regions with archaic Slavic hydronyms, but by far the largest concentration of them is in modern-day Western Ukraine.

This is illustrated in Figure 2 below, based on a discussion of Slavic origins written by J.P. Mallory.[32]

Figure 2: The estimated territory of the Proto-Slavic homeland based on the archaeological record of the Chernoles Culture and the distribution of archaic Slavic hydronyms. Drawn by the author with Guidance from J.P. Mallory's book, "In Search of the Indo-Europeans."

It has often been noted that river names can stick for thousands of years, even when the language changes in a region. As we will see, Poland still has Celtic river names in places. So it makes sense to look for where the archaic Slavic ones seem to originate. Much of this region later got absorbed into the Zarubintsy culture. As we will discuss later, it is likely that Proto-Slavic spread from the Zarubintsy culture - although pushing it back to before that period gets tricky.

There is a school of thought that tries to place the Proto-Slavic homeland further west, in modern day Poland. The Poles have coined this as the "autochthonous" or Polish school. They generally attempt to link the Slavs with the Lusatian culture - and it's not entirely convincing. The Lusatian culture extended from the Urnfield complex around the Odra River. The early epicenter of this archaeological culture included most of Silesia, which is Southwestern Poland.[33] If we are discussing the homeland of the Proto-Slavs, this presents some issues for the so-called "Polish" or autochthonous school of thought. It seems doubtful that any satem language was spoken in Silesia, near the source of the Lusatian culture.

It's important to emphasize how isolated Proto-Slavic was from most western influence during the Iron Age. As I mentioned above, satem languages like Slavic pronounce a number of velar sounds differently from centum languages. Germanic is typically considered a centum language, but it's a very unique type: According to Grimm's law, where most centum languages have a hard "K", Germanic has an "H" sound. For comparison, see Latin "Kentum" and Old English "Hunda." Still, it's generally considered that these substitute "H" sounds in Germanic are derived from an earlier pronunciation that was more "centum" than "satem."[34] The "centum" character of Germanic is also apparent in the Proto-Germanic treatment of the "g" sound, which would be palatized into a "z/zh" in satem languages. There is absolutely no hint of this sound shift in Proto-Germanic, or in any language of the centum category.However, the presence of Grimm's law means we can not only identify centum loanwords in Proto-Slavic, but we can also identify Germanic vs Non-Germanic centum loanwords. As it turns out, Proto-Slavic has few if any non-Germanic centum loans. This is an issue for the Polish school, and for a number of reasons - and not just on the grounds that the Lusatian culture seems to be a product of the earlier Urnfield complex from Central Europe.

With the rise of the Hallstatt culture in the 1st millennium BCE, archaeologists start to see evidence of a recognizably "Celtic" culture, one that would eventually evolve into the so-called "La Tene" style. These cultures track amazingly well with the Celtic languages. They obviously are linked with the Celtic languages of Gaul, in modern day France. Even in Southern Poland, we see that a river bearing a Celtic river name "San" is associated with La Tene style artifacts during the Iron Age. Thus, we have some good evidence that the Celts had a presence in modern day Southern Poland, at least as far north as the San River.[35]

Therefore, if the Proto-Slavic homeland was truly in southern Poland, we should truly expect it to be reasonably rich in Celtic (or at least Non-Germanic centum) loan words. However, the evidence for such loans in Proto-Slavic seems to be nonexistent - or nearly so.

There is another issue for the "Polish School" of Slavic origins. Baltic hydronyms are attested at least as far south as the Bug river. Hydronyms show that the original territory of Baltic language speakers was vast, and covered much of the modern territory of Belarus and northwest Russia, not to mention northeastern Poland.[36] However, it is estimated that Proto-Slavic separated from the Baltic languages around 1,000 BCE.[37] It's not clear how such an early separation would be possible if Proto-Slavic coexisted with the West Baltic languages within this area. Furthermore, the Old Prussian West Baltic language in this region survived long after the expansion of the early Slavs, which would be surprising if the Old Prussians lived near the very epicenter of the Slavic migrations. Proposing a northern Polish homeland for the Slavs raises an important question- why were the Old Prussians not among the first to be Slavicized? Therefore, the Proto-Slavic homeland probably could not have been in northern Poland either.

I will obviously be arguing for an "eastern" homeland for the Proto-Slavs. Moving farther east, we do see evidence of Baltic languages once being spoken in modern day Belarus as well. However, the Baltic languages of this region are attested only via hydronyms. Unlike in Prussia (Northeast Poland) we cannot substantiate that Baltic languages survived throughout this region up to the Middle Ages. Here, the geographical barrier of the Pripyet marshes in Southern Belarus is significant. It is not hard to imagine Proto-Slavic becoming "split" or separated from Balto-Slavic languages north of the Pripyet marshes as early as 1,000 BCE. Geographically, however, it is not clear why such a split would have taken place in Poland.

On the subject of Slavic origins, a Balkan origin for the Slavs is probably the most ridiculous option. The Paleo-Balkan languages like Dacian largely died out as a result of Romanization. If Proto-Slavic had been among them, it likely would have shared in this fate. Also, the earliest references to the Slavs by Byzantine historians writing about them in the 6th and 7th centuries clearly depict them as outsiders from beyond the Danube.[38]

In the 5th century CE the presence of "Slavic" (Prague-Korchak) type artifacts in the Balkans seems mainly limited to modern day Romania, and is contemporaneous with similar material from Western Ukraine. This material in Western Ukraine finds its clearest precursors even further north, in the region of the "Kiev Culture" as early as the 3rd century CE. For instance, the "baggy" pottery of the Kiev culture is similar-looking to that of later Slavic cultures using the Prague-Korchak type pottery. Where early Prague-Korchak pottery occurs in Romania, it is often associated with a total break in continuity from the previous material culture. By contrast, the presence of early Prague-Korchak artifacts in Western Ukraine seems to reflect some kind of link with the nearby Kiev Culture. This may be due to the fact that the Kiev culture was just up the Dnieper River from where the typically "Slavic" Prague-Korchak culture seems to originate.[39] It's worth noting that the apparent "source" of the Prague-Korchak culture in Western Ukraine and the neighboring Kiev culture both covered territories formerly linked by the Zarubintsy culture in the archaeological record.

There is something of a dilemma about the cultural identity of the Zarubintsy culture. To be sure, it is not an easy thing to assign. The Zarubintsy culture lay within the territory of Baltic hydronyms. Therefore, some researchers like P.M Barford have suggested that they could have been Baltic.[40] On the other hand, some scholars have noted Scythian influences on the Zarubintsy culture from the south, and even La Tene influences associated with iron age Celts (and their neighbors) from the west.[41]

With that said, however, even the "mixed" nature of the Zarubintsy culture has significant implications for its ethnolinguistic character. For one, the assumption that the maximum range of Baltic languages (as preserved by hydronyms) survived from the 2nd millennium BCE all the way up to the common era seems unlikely.

The presence of intrusive elements in the Zarubintsy culture during the dawn of the common era appears to imply that the Baltic period of isolation was at an end, and therefore this era is unlikely to have allowed the Baltic languages to maintain their maximum range of territory. Simply based on the presence of both "southern" and "western" elements in the archaeological record, we can probably infer that the Baltic languages were already undergoing displacement at this time. To an extent, this is common sense, simply due the broader dynamics of the migration period. In general, by the migration period, we can generalize that most European linguistic identities were either expanding or declining. And it seems unlikely that the Baltic languages were expanding at this time.

Secondly, the hydronyms don't only tell us about where the Balts were. Hydronyms also indicate that the Proto-Slavs existed directly south of the Baltic territories. However, this raises questions about "Scythian" influences from even further south/

southeast. Presumably, the Slavs lived north of the Scythian nomads of the Pontic steppe. If that's the case, however, then how could Scythian influences have simply "leapfrogged" over the Slavs into formerly Baltic territory? It seems that the Scythian influences in the Zarubintsy culture hint at Slavic influence by proxy, simply due to the fact that the area of archaic Slavic hydronyms forms a "bridge" or bulwark between Scythian and Baltic territories.

Evidence of blending between two cultures that existed on opposite sides of the Proto-Slavs must presumably have been mediated (at least in part) by Proto-Slavs. The Scythian influences intruding into the Zarubintsy culture provide us evidence of just that; as many scholars have acknowledged, the Zarubintsy culture has Scythian influences, yet based on hydronyms, it also intrudes into the formerly Baltic territories.

In short, the location of early Slavic hydronyms from Figure 2 matches very well with the apparent point of origin for the early Slavic Prague-Korchak culture, as shown in the archaeological record. Additionally, this is approximately the correct location to explain the pattern of loan-words in Proto-Slavic; not just the presence of Iranian loan words from the Scythians, but also the apparent lack of centum loan words (aside from Gothic words).

The evidence for Latin, Celtic, or even "Italo-Celtic" influence on the Proto-Slavic language is extremely weak, which probably precludes a Polish or Balkan origin. As we discussed way back in the map from Figure 1, modern day Poland fell firmly within the Corded-Ware / Bell Beaker overlap zone during the 3rd millennium BCE (typically a region associated with Proto-Germanic). And in general, the archaeological record confirms that this region was closely connected with the west for most of prehistory. Additionally, the archaeological record of the migration period shows an intrusive culture spreading throughout the region.

If this interpretation of "intrusive" Slavs in former Baltic and Germanic territories seems forced, it's only because numbers are required in order to explain the Slavic migrations. Certainly, the Proto-Slavs could not have assimilated the Eastern half of Europe if they were only a comprised of a handful of villages.

Neither is there a compelling economic or military reason for the simple agrarian Slavs to have prospered in the absence of significant numbers. In order for the Slavic language to become a popular language in the aftermath of the migration period, a significant number of early Slavic peoples is required. An early expansion into formerly Baltic territories is one of the few explanations for how significant numbers of Slavic tribes could have been generated just prior to the arrival of the Huns.

Conversely, if the Slavs were not at all numerous on the eve of the Hunnic invasion, then it's unclear why they even survived as an ethnolinguistic group. (Much less how they expanded!) Therefore, the early expansion of the Slavs within the Zarubintsy culture seems to be a necessary fact in order to explain their significant numbers in the 6th century CE, and the loss of formerly "Baltic" territory is a prerequisite for this early expansion.

These three lines of evidence are probably sufficient to trace the Proto-Slavs to this approximate location, which today would be Western Ukraine and parts of Southern Belarus. This also includes much of the Pripyet marshes, which has been cited by some scholars as a Proto-Slavic homeland based on terms for flora and fauna in the early Slavic language.[42] While there are reasons to think that the Proto-Slavic homeland overlapped with the Pripyet marshes, limiting the early Slavs to this region alone has its issues. (Again, see my arguments that there must have been a significant Proto-Slavic population already existing in the 4th century CE.)

Still, the flora / fauna-based arguments behind the "Pripyet Marshes Homeland' hypothesis do bolster the general idea that the Proto-Slavs were at least familiar with this swampy region, even if they did not all exclusively live there. On the other hand, attempts to place this homeland further west, or worse still, further south, seem to be grounded mainly in nationalism and wishful thinking. Overall, the various types of evidence converge on a homeland around Western Ukraine.

This will likely be the driest and most technical chapter, but it is important for defending the comparative methodology that I use to revive the cryptic fragments of Slavic paganism found in folklore. Without this technical context, a lot of comparative mythology can look like random dot-connecting. However, as I hope I have shown, my methodology is anything but that.

Endnotes

1. Anthony, David W. The Horse, the Wheel, and Language: How Bronze-Age Riders from the Eurasian Steppes Shaped the Modern World. Princeton University Press, 2010. Page 7
2. Mallory, J P. In Search of the Indo-Europeans: Language, Archaeology, and Myth. New York, N.Y: Thames and Hudson, 2003.
3. Anthony, David W. The Horse, the Wheel, and Language: How Bronze-Age Riders from the Eurasian Steppes Shaped the Modern World. Princeton University Press, 2010. Pages 83, 214
4. Reich, David. Who We Are and How We Got Here: Ancient DNA and the New Science of the Human Past. OXFORD UNIV Press, 2019. Pages 112-114
5. Gray, Russel D, and Quentin D. Atkinson. "Language-tree Divergence Times Support the Anatolian Theory of Indo-European Origin." Nature. (2001): 435-439.
6. Anthony, David W. The Horse, the Wheel, and Language: How Bronze-Age Riders from the Eurasian Steppes Shaped the Modern World. Princeton University Press, 2010. Pages 63-64
7. Wenthe, Mark, Jared Klein, Brian Joseph, and Matthias Fritz. Handbook of Comparative and Historical Indo-European Linguistics, 2018. Internet resource. Pages 444-445

8. Reich, David. Who We Are and How We Got Here: Ancient DNA and the New Science of the Human Past. OXFORD UNIV Press, 2019. Pages 112-114
9. Pohl, Walter. The Avars: A Steppe Empire in Europe, 567-822. 2018. Pages 243-246
10. The Genomic History of the Iberian Peninsula Over the Past 8000 Years. American Association for the Advancement of Science, 2019. Internet resource.
11. Nilsson, Martin P. A History of Greek Religion. Westport: Greenwood Press, 1980. Pages 12-27
12. Johns, Andreas. Baba Yaga: The Ambiguous Mother and Witch of the Russian Folktale. Page 127, 2004.
13. Monaghan, Patricia. Encyclopedia of Goddesses and Heroines. 2014. Pages 168-169
14. Winn, Shan M. M. Heaven, Heroes, and Happiness: The Indo-European Roots of Western Ideology. Lanham: University Press of America, 1995. Pages 328, 117
15. Haak, et al. "Massive Migration from the Steppe Was a Source for Indo-European Languages in Europe." Nature. 522.7555 (2015): 207-211. Print
16. Monaghan, Patricia. Encyclopedia of Goddesses and Heroines. 2014. Page 170
17. Rosik, Stanislaw, and Anna Tyszkiewicz. The Slavic Religion in the Light of 11th and 12th-Century German Chronicles (Thietmar of Merseburg, Adam of Bremen, Helmold of Bosau): Studies on the Christian Interpretation of Pre-Christian Cults and Beliefs in the Middle Ages. 2020. Pages 124-125
18. West, Morris. Indo-European Poetry and Myth. Oxford: Oxford University Press, 2007. Pages 241-243
19. Heyd, V. (2019). Yamnaya – Corded Wares – Bell Beakers: or how to conceptualize events of 5000 years ago that shaped modern Europe. In T. Valchev (Ed.), Studia in honorem Iliae Iliev: A jubilee collection dedicated to the 70th anniversary of Ilia Iliev (page 136). (Bulletin of Regional Historical Museum in Yambol; Vol. 9). Regional Historical Museum of Yambol.

20. Genetic ancestry changes in Stone to Bronze Age transition in the East European plain, Lehti Saag, Sergey V. Vasilyev, Liivi Varul, Natalia V. Kosorukova, Dmitri V. Gerasimov, Svetlana V. Oshibkina, Samuel J. Griffith, Anu Solnik, Lauri Saag, Eugenia D'Atanasio, Ene Metspalu, Maere Reidla, Siiri Rootsi, Toomas Kivisild, Christiana Lyn Scheib, Kristiina Tambets, Aivar Kriiska, Mait Metspalu bioRxiv 2020.07.02.184507
21. Birnbaum, Henrik, and Peter T. Merrill. Recent Advances in the Reconstruction of Common Slavic (1971-1982). Columbus, Ohio: Slavica, 1985. Pages 8, 53
22. Mayor, Adrienne. The Amazons: Lives and Legends of Warrior Women Across the Ancient World. Princeton: Princeton University Press, 2016. Page 221
23. Haskew, Michael E, Christer Jorgensen, Chris McNab, Eric Niderost, and Rob S. Rice. Fighting Techniques of the Oriental World, Ad 1200-1860: Equipment, Combat Skills, and Tactics. 2013. Pages 104-105
24. Neparáczki, E, Maróti, Z, et al. Y-chromosome haplogroups from Hun, Avar and conquering Hungarian period nomadic people of the Carpathian Basin. Sci Rep 9, 16569 (2019). https://doi.org/10.1038/s41598-019-53105-5
25. Saag, Lehti et al. "The Arrival of Siberian Ancestry Connecting the Eastern Baltic to Uralic Speakers further East." Current biology: CB vol. 29,10 (2019): 1701-1711.e16. doi:10.1016/j.cub.2019.04.026
26. Rootsi, S, Zhivotovsky, L, Baldovič, M. et al. A counter-clockwise northern route of the Y-chromosome haplogroup N from Southeast Asia towards Europe. Eur J Hum Genet 15, 204–211 (2007).
27. Grochowalski, Łukasz et al. "Y-Chromosome Genetic Analysis of Modern Polish Population." Frontiers in genetics vol. 11567309.23Oct. 2020, doi:10.3389/fgene.2020.567309
28. Khar'kov VN et al. Struktura genofonda vostochnykh Ukraintsev po gaplogruppam Y-khromosomy [Structure of the gene pool of eastern Ukrainians from Y-chromosome haplogroups]. Genetika. 2004 Mar;40(3):415-21. Russian. PMID: 15125258.

29. Balanovsky, Oleg et al. "Two sources of the Russian patrilineal heritage in their Eurasian context." American journal of human genetics vol. 82,1 (2008): 236-50. doi:10.1016/j.ajhg.2007.09.019
30. Dani, Ahmad H, and V M. Masson. History of Civilizations of Central Asia. Paris: UNESCO, 1998. Page 366
31. Mallory, James P, and Douglas Q. Adams. Encyclopedia of Indo-European Culture. London: Fitzroy Dearborn, 1997. Pages 338, 526
32. Mallory, J P. In Search of the Indo-Europeans: Language, Archaeology, and Myth. New York, N.Y: Thames and Hudson, 2003. Pages 80-81
33. Abstracts of Works Published by the Staff of Jagiellonian University: Mathematics and Natural Sciences. Cracow: Univ, 1965. Page 120
34. Anthony, David W. The Horse, the Wheel, and Language: How Bronze-Age Riders from the Eurasian Steppes Shaped the Modern World. Princeton University Press, 2010. Page 29
35. Dzięgielewski, Karol. (2010). Expansion of the Pomeranian Culture in Poland during the Early Iron Age: Remarks on the mechanism and possible causes.
36. Grünthal, R. (2012). Baltic loanwords in Mordvin. In R. Grünthal, & P. Kallio (Eds.), A Linguistic Map of Prehistoric Northern Europe (pp. 297-343). (Mémoires de la Société Finno-Ougrienne). Suomalais-Ugrilainen Seura.
37. Mallory, James P, and Douglas Q. Adams. Encyclopedia of Indo-European Culture. London: Fitzroy Dearborn, 1997. Pages 145-146
38. Barford, Paul M. The Early Slavs: Culture and Society in Early Medieval Eastern Europe. Ithaca, N.Y: Cornell University Press, 2001. Pages 45-56
39. Barford, Paul M. The Early Slavs: Culture and Society in Early Medieval Eastern Europe. Ithaca, N.Y: Cornell University Press, 2001. Pages 41-43
40. Barford, Paul M. The Early Slavs: Culture and Society in Early Medieval Eastern Europe. Ithaca, N.Y: Cornell University Press, 2001. Page 101

41. Macmillan, Palgrave, and Andrew Bell-Fialkoff. The Role of Migration in the History of the Eurasian Steppe: Sedentary Civilization Vs. 'barbarian' and Nomad. New York: Palgrave Macmillan, 2016. Internet resource. Pages 137-138
42. Kulikowski, Michael. The Tragedy of Empire: From Constantine to the Destruction of Roman Italy. United States, Harvard University Press, 2020.

Chapter 2

Baba Yaga and Mokosh the Great Mother

As you may have guessed, this book will involve a lot of folklore analysis. That's simply because folklore is the most significant medium in which Slavic paganism has survived. I want to warn you all that folklore is inherently high-volume. Folklore texts are notoriously dry at times. The field of folklore often involves numerous fables and beliefs collected and compiled by an avid enthusiast. It is easy to say that two fairy tales are related, for example, but without reading both of them you cannot get a feeling for how related they are.

This is one reason why the Aarne-Thompson Classification system of fairy tales exists. If you're unfamiliar, it's a system that catalogues various international fairy tale types. In the context of the Russian Baba Yaga and German Frau Holle, for example, it is known that both of these figures appear in Aarne-Thompson Type 480: The Spinning Woman by the Spring. This is also known as "The Kind Girl and the Unkind Girl."[1] This is a story type that is especially relevant to the discussion of Baba Yaga, and as I hope to show, the Slavic Goddess Mokosh. However, the story type (AT 480) is extremely widespread, and exploration of the deeper meaning of these tales has implications well outside of Slavic paganism

On the Term "Sovereignty Goddess"

The concept of the "Sovereignty Goddess" is often wrapped up in the story motif of the loathly lady. In Irish lore, it is closely associated with the story known as Echtra Mac nEchach. In this tale, the protagonist willingly kisses an old hag who then transforms into a beautiful woman and bestows kingship upon him.[2] This is far from the only appearance of this motif. It is common in British folklore, the most famous parallel often being drawn to Queen Guinevere of the Arthurian Romances. There's also an old English Folk Song titled "King Henry" which features a loathly lady. The folk-rock band Steeleye Span has a great version of it for modern audiences.

The harder one looks though, the more so-called "sovereignty" connections pop up around a number of Celtic Goddesses. According to Irish lore, the ancient King of Munster, known as Ailill, tried to force himself on the Goddess Aine. In response to this rape, she bit off his ear. As Ruth Marshall writes in *"Limerick Folk Tales"*.[3]

> *As sovereignty guardian, Aine could grant or take away the right to rule. Under the ancient laws, a king had to be unblemished and whole in himself. Now that he was disfigured in the damage to his ear, Ailill was no longer fit to be king... As a result of the rape, Aine gave birth to a son, Eogan, who later became king of Munster. From him, the Eoganacht lineage claimed its descent.*

The last portion of the narrative mentioning the royal line of Munster helps cement her status as a sovereignty Goddess. As we shall see, stories about noble lineages going back to Goddess or fairy ancestors are fairly standard in Indo-European cultures.

Another Celtic Goddess who appears to be associated with sovereignty is the Cailleach. Legend says that a saint once struck the hag Cailleach with her own staff, turning her to stone. She became a pile of stones overlooking Coulagh Bay, which are now referred to as Ard na Cailli (The Hag's Height.) According to Kate Corkery, she embodies the strength of the land, and contains within her all ages and seasons.[4] Her association with the land is one reason why she is sometimes thought to embody sovereignty. A more explicit link is provided by an 8th century poem in which the Cailleach laments that she was once beautiful and powerful and slept with kings.[5] This strongly suggests that the "hag" aspect of the sovereignty Goddess is tied to Cailleach.

No discussion of the sovereignty Goddess would be complete without the Morrigan, however. One thing at issue here is that the Morrigan is often described as a triple Goddess. As such, it would almost be surprising if none of her aspects had sovereignty functions. These three are sometimes listed as Badb, Macha, and Neamain. The triad varies between sources, however, and the land Goddess Anu or Anan is also frequently included. This link is well demonstrated by the two hills known as the Paps of Morrigan. This links her to the Irish land Goddess Anu, who has a similar place in Ireland's geographical nomenclature.[6] The triad known as the Morrigan is clearly linked to the triad of Goddesses whose names were used to refer to the land of Ireland itself. Of these three, only Eriu is still used in the modern term for "Ireland."[7]

However, few would deny that the primary associations with the Morrigan are those of war, death, and destiny. Even here, we see some possible hints of a sovereignty function. For instance, when the Dagda finds her straddling a river and has sex with her on Samhain, she agrees to assist him and the Tuatha de Danaan in the fight against the Fomorians, which leads to the rule of the Tuatha de Danaan over Ireland. On the other hand, when the hero Cu Chulainn scorned Morrigan's advances, he sealed his doom. He would later see her in the form of the washer at the ford, an ominous woman of Celtic mythology who washes the clothing of the doomed. Her appearance was considered an omen of death. As we will see, this "washerwoman" aspect of Morrigan is one with deep roots going back to mainland Europe.

Kissing Dragons and Marrying Snakes

In the Irish tale of Echtra Mac nEchach, the sovereignty Goddess transforms into a beauty and then bestows kingship after being kissed. There seems to be a general agreement that this is one of the classic examples of the sovereignty Goddess. Yet there is an obvious parallel just across the sea, in northern Spain, which is often overlooked. I am speaking of the Spanish sovereignty myths involving fairies called xanas. Many Spanish nobles traced their descent back to a xana, often with a very peculiar type of animal-bride myth. In some of these narratives, the xana is actually cursed to take the form of a dragon and must be kissed by the noble ancestor in order to revert back to her true form. Upon having her beauty restored, the xana then marries the noble ancestor and the two found an aristocratic Spanish lineage together.[8]

This has all of the hallmarks of an Indo-European sovereignty myth. Not just because the frightening supernatural female transforms into a beautiful woman after being kissed, but also because it is a myth about the origins of a noble bloodline, much like the story of Aine and Ailill. What's more, the antiquity of this snake-woman or dragon ancestry myth is fairly easy to verify. There are numerous versions of this tale in the Indo-European language-speaking world.

One of the more famous examples of the snake-woman ancestor myth comes from Herodotus. Specifically, I am referring to his writings about the traditions of the Scythians, who lived north of the Black Sea in modern day Ukraine.

The story recounted by Herodotus is enigmatic, in part because it is viewed through a Greek perspective. In particular, the Scythian ancestor is referred to as "Herakles" which is obviously an interpolation by Herodotus. In this story, "Herakles" goes to sleep while driving cattle, and awakes to find his horses stolen. To quote Herodotus:[9]

> *When Herakles awoke, he searched for them, visiting every part of the country, until at last he came to the land called the Hylaien (Woodland), and there he found in a cave a creature of double form*

> *[i.e. the Skythian Drakaina] that was half maiden and half serpent (ekhidna); above the buttocks she was a woman, below them a snake. When he saw her he was astonished, and asked her if she had seen his mares straying; she said that she had them, and would not return them to him before he had intercourse with her; Herakles did, in hope of this reward.*

This culminates in the birth of three sons, one of whom goes on to found the line of Scythian kings. So this myth is also a sovereignty myth, explaining how a royal lineage acquired its divine mandate to rule by way of a sacred marriage with a supernatural woman. This account from Herodotus places the myth considerably farther east than Spain, and considerably farther back in time than the era in which most folklore was recorded. Yet the same basic myth extends even farther east, as far as India, where the royal line of Uddiyana once claimed descent from a naga (that is, a snake woman).[10] In fact, even as far as Cambodia, we can find stories in which certain dynasties claim descent from a naga.[11] This distribution from Spain to Cambodia is difficult to explain, short of attributing it directly to the Proto-Indo-European mythology.

One minor nuance in this theory is that the narrative also shows up in Basque folklore. The Basques, of course, do not speak an Indo-European language. According to Basque tradition, the Goddess Mari married the Lord of Biscay. She placed a condition upon their union that he was free to practice Christianity, but not within the household and away from Mari. Yet when her husband sees that one of her legs resembles that of a black goat, he makes the sign of the cross and she disappears.[12] This story has great significance for the Indo-European sovereignty myth. It clearly fits the criteria. Not only do we have a divine animal bride who contributes to the ancestry of a noble line (the Lords of Biscay) but as we will see, the image of a fairy woman or Goddess with an animal leg is also widespread.

We see this "taboo-breaking" element in the French tale of Melusine, for instance. In this story, the progenitor of the French Lusignan noble house marries a fairy woman named Melusine. She marries him, but makes him promise not to ever watch her bathe on Saturday. When he violates this taboo, he sees that she turns into a serpent from the waist down during this time period. He later gives himself away by calling her an "odious serpent" in anger, and she leaves him.[13]

Another tale that will be important for this discussion is "The Snake Wife" from Ukraine.[14] In this story, a farmer obeys the advice of a talking snake in the woods, and magical events unfold. Following the serpent's instructions, he harvests all but the last sheaf of his master's corn and asks only for the last sheaf as payment. He then throws the last sheaf into the fire, and a beautiful woman leaps out. He marries her, but she cautions him "Beware, for Heaven's sake, of ever calling me a serpent. I will not suffer thee to call me by that name, and if thou dost thou shalt lose thy wife." As expected for this story type, the man violates the taboo, and the wife transforms into a snake before leaving him. Before she departs, however, he kisses her three times. With each kiss, he gains new knowledge about the world. The story ends with the following dialogue.

> *"Go now," said she, "to the Tsar, and he will give thee his daughter for the knowledge thou hast. But pray to God for poor me, for now I must be and remain a serpent forever."*

The man goes on to marry the Tsar's daughter, and the snake wife vanishes.

The tale has obvious parallels to Spanish and French counterparts, as well as some stories that I have left out like the "Travels of Sir John Mandeville." Suffice to say, it fits the bill of an Indo-European sovereignty / animal bride myth. The protagonist must kiss a snake wife three times, much as in some

Spanish stories. It even ends with the protagonist marrying into royalty. There is one element of this story which is immensely significant, but which many readers might overlook; the element of the last sheaf of grain. Why does the peasant burn the last sheaf of grain in order to summon the snake wife? This brings us to our next section.

Grain Goddesses and Stone Goddesses

The last sheaf of grain holds significance in the folk traditions of many European countries. The tradition is perhaps best known from Scotland, where the last sheaf is often dedicated to the Cailleach. The Cailleach has been interpreted as the hag aspect of the loathly lady paradigm. According to Patricia Monaghan, the king had to kiss or have intercourse with her in order to "transform" her into a splendid young woman. This has been interpreted as a metaphor for the blossoming of the land itself under the rule of a just king. Like the snake wife of Ukrainian fairy tales, however, she also was closely tied to the last sheaf of grain in Scottish folklore. As each field was harvested, the field workers would shout "drive the Cailleach into the next field!" Finally, the last sheaf of grain was harvested and dressed up in woman's clothes. This last sheaf was given the name of the Goddess herself.[15]

If we turn our focus slightly further east, we encounter the grain mother of German folklore. Here too, a doll was often formed from the last sheaf, and it was named the corn mother or wheat-bride.[16] Here the figure changes slightly, however. The German grain spirits seem to be more frequently treated as a sort of bogeyman or ghost story to frighten children. So, for example, some Dutch stories portray the Ruggenmoeder (Rye Mother) as an old hag with red eyes and a black nose who carries a whip and pursues children.[17]

Another trait that will be significant in this chapter is the association with spinning and Christmas time. The Rye Aunt was believed to punish maidservants who were not fully spinning on their distaffs until the Twelfth Night of Christmas.[18] As we will see, this is very much like Frau Holle, another German folklore figure.

Still farther east, in Poland, the last ears or sheaves were fashioned into the shape of the Pszena Baba (Wheat Woman), Baba (Old Woman) or Dziad. (Old Man).[19] In Russia, the traditions of the field are complex. Much as with the German Rye mother, Russian children were told to avoid trampling fields or gardens so that the "Reaper", "Noon Woman", or "Iron Woman" did not get them. In the folklore of the Pskov region bordering Latvia and Estonia, a supernatural woman lives in the rye field, and during harvest is driven into a neighboring unharvested field or into the forest.

A number of phrases and songs accompanied the harvest rituals in Russia. Field workers would speak of "chasing away the old woman" or "cutting down the old woman" or the old woman was told to "marry our old man." Sometimes a small patch of rye stalks were left in the corner of the field, and braided for Baba Yaga. As they did this, people would say "Baba Yaga, you harvested our grain for us, and this is all that we have left for you."[20] This association between Baba Yaga and the harvest is not an isolated incident. There is also a folk riddle which claims Baba Yaga "Feeds the world, but is herself hungry!"

The association of the last sheaf with an old woman or hag is clearly widespread in Europe. Another tradition which intersects with this is found in Central Europe, where one can find narratives about an old hag getting ground up by a mill and coming out as a maiden, with her youth restored. Alternatively, stories from some Central European countries speak of a magic mill that destroys evil women, but turns other old women into young maidens.[21] This offers some striking parallels to the fearsome hag of Irish folklore, the Cailleach. In an Irish folktale titled "The Hag and the Long Leather Bag" we see a typical Aarne-Thompson 480 story (the same type associated with Frau Holle and Baba Yaga). The tale ends with the hag being destroyed by a mill.[22]

In Aukstaitija, Lithuania, there was a belief in a Gelezine Boba (Iron Woman) who lived under a stone at the edge of a swamp. The story about her says that she once went under the earth and then turned to stone or iron. Villagers scared their children with stories about her, saying that late at night she comes out to catch children and take them under her stone. Nijole Laurinkiene connects this "Iron Boba" with the German grain woman, who is also associated with iron. He notes that "Goddess stones" were also kept in granaries in Lithuania. He equates her with the Lithuanian Goddess "Zemyna."[23]

It is worth noting that "Zemyna" simply means "earth," and is cognate to the equivalent Slavic word. For instance, in Russian folklore, peasants would sometimes address a personified "Mat Syra Zemlya" or "Moist Mother Earth."

It is also extremely interesting that the Boba mentioned by Laurinkiene is said to "turn to stone" after going underground. This seemingly contradicts her status as an "iron woman", yet it is reminiscent of the stories about Cailleach who is also turned to stone. According to the narrative listed at the beginning of this chapter, the Cailleach was turned to stone when a Saint grabbed her staff from her hand and struck her, thus transforming her into the stone known as "Ard na Cailli" (The Hag's Height).[24] This is reminiscent of one Slovak tale, where Jenzibaba (the Slovak Baba Yaga) also strikes people with a stick which turns people into stone.[25]

Some Ukrainian folklore did feature an 'Iron Woman" as a kind of bogey to scare children, and keep them from wandering into gardens and forests. A similar Iron Woman appears in Belarus as well, although she appears to merge with Baba Yaga in many cases. In Hungarian fairy tales, her counterpart is the iron-nosed woman who lives in a hut that turns upon a goose leg. This is a slight variation on the chicken-legged hut of her Russian counterpart.[26] Sometimes even the Russian Baba Yaga is said to have iron teeth or an iron nose. This is oddly similar to the black nose of the Dutch Ruggenmoeder.

Petrification also features in the stories about Baba Dochia, in Romanian folklore. Interestingly, the name "Dochia" has been interpreted as an etymological deformation of "Dacia" which was the name for the land roughly corresponding to Romania and Moldova in ancient times.[27] This is tantalizingly similar to the Irish land Goddesses like Eriu, whose names were applied to Ireland itself. According to a legend recounted by Andreas Johns in his book "*Baba Yaga: The Ambiguous Mother and Witch of the Russian Folktale*" Baba Dochia insulted the month of March, who then enlisted February to freeze her to death. According to the legend, the frozen Baba Dochia then turned to stone.

Sacred stones named "Mokas" also show up throughout the country of Lithuania, and oftentimes are associated with a legend. In at least some cases, the stones are explained as being the body or bodies of a person or family that was turned to stone. The Mokas families usually consist of three stones: "Mokas" (the father), "Mokiene" (the mother), and "Mokiukas" (the child). Sometimes Mokas and Mokiukas are next to each other, but the mother, Mokiene, is said to be located under the water of the nearby lake. One of the more practical beliefs associated with the Mokas stones is their association with childbirth. Specifically, childless women would journey to these stones with offerings in order to become pregnant.[28]

Some have connected the name "Mokas" with Proto-Balto-Slavic *Mok meaning "wet." This makes sense, because the stones are often associated with stories featuring lakes and rivers. Recall that the stone of the Lithuanian "Iron Woman" was similarly located under a stone near a swamp. In all likelihood, this was also a kind of "Mokas" at one time.

The three stones grouped as a "Mokas family" have parallels in Scotland. In the valley of Glen Lyon, there is a place called Tigh nam Bodach, where a pile of stones is looked after by the locals. The stones are eroded sandstone in the rough shape of people, and they represent the hag Cailleach with her family. The largest stone represents Cailleach, and the second largest is her husband Bodach (meaning "Old Man"). The third largest is her daughter Nighean - although there are a number of small ones as well, representing additional children.[29]

However, the most interesting connection that can be drawn from the Mokas stones lies in the similarity of their names to "Mokosh," or "Mokosha" a Slavic Goddess. Scholars have speculated about the nature of the Slavic Goddess Mokosh, but in general they tend to link her with "Moist Mother Earth" of Russian folklore. The rationale behind her name is generally thought to be the association with wetness (Mokri in Russian). However, this doesn't explain the "-osh" ending, and it's not entirely clear why "Wet" would become the proper name of a Goddess. The Lithuanian sacred stone known as the "Mokas" offers a tempting intermediary by which this "Mok-" root could have acquired such significance.

However, when it comes to the Slavic Goddess Mokosh, we have a little bit more to go off of than her name. Our clearest glimpse of a Slavic pantheon comes from the Russian Primary Chronicle. In the year 980 CE, it tells us that Prince Vladimir of Kiev "...Placed idols on a hill, outside of the palace yard, a wooden Perun with a silver head and a golden moustache, and Khors, and Dazhbog, and Stribog, and Simargl, and Mokosh." These names should not be taken as evidence for a uniform pantheon across the entirety of the Slavic population. Not only do we hear some different names from West Slavic sources, but there is also evidence that different East Slavic deities such as Rod, Rozhanitsy, and Iarilo were worshipped on the countryside, outside of Kiev. Even so, it is noteworthy that

Mokosh seems to be the only Goddess listed among the six idols erected by Prince Vladimir.[30]

As to what sort of Goddess Mokosh is, we have only a few references from folklore. One of particular interest to this discussion comes from Slovenia, in the 19th century. It is obviously modernized, but it offers some tantalizing hints:[31]

> *Lamwaberl (a.k.a. Lamia, Lama-Baba) used to live in Grunau, a marshy place not far away from Saint Florian Square, near the Loznica, which often overflowed its banks. Archaeological artifacts confirm that in the olden times the place had been cultivated. A lone farming estate is situated there now, but once upon a time there stood the castle of Mokoshka, a heathen princess who lived in it. The castle was surrounded by gardens that were always green. She occasionally helped people, but sometimes also harmed them; she was especially wont to taking children with her. At long last, God punished her. On a stormy night, the castle and all its gardens sank into the ground. But Mokoshka was not doomed. She continued to appear, disguised in different female forms. She still carries off children, especially those who have been neglected by a parent.*

The similarity of this narrative to the Gelezine Boba (Iron Woman) in Lithuania is no coincidence, in my opinion. Here we have not only the narrative of a Goddess being "cast down" beneath the earth, but also taking children away. The two-sided nature emphasized here is also telling: Sometimes she helped people, and sometimes she hurt them. We see something oddly similar to this in fairy tales of Aarne-Thompson type 480, which are associated with Frau Holle and Baba Yaga. Finally, the remark that she could appear "disguised in different female forms" seems to reference something along the lines of the loathly lady motif. Presumably, she could appear as a fair young woman or as a hag.

The Spinner by the Well: Holle, Perchta, and the Baba Yaga:

As mentioned in my discussion of the grain woman, the Rye Aunt of German folklore sometimes punishes maidservants who have not been busy spinning. I'm not certain how widespread this connection was. More typically in German folklore, Frau Holle and Perchta were the ones who judged spinners, punishing the lazy and rewarding the industrious. Frau Holle may appear as a grey-haired woman with long teeth who makes sure women finish their spinning before Christmas or New Year's.[32]

Frau Holle and Frau Perchta often appear in tales featuring the motifs of Aarne-Thompson Type 480: "The Spinning Woman by the Spring" (abbreviated: AT 480) which is also associated with Baba Yaga and Baba Dochia.[33] The previously mentioned story from Donegal, Ireland, that ends with the hag getting ground to death by a mill is also AT 480. I believe this story type is actually more often referred to as the "Kind Girl and the Unkind Girl." However, it is worth asking where the other title comes from. Why is this story type called "The Spinning Woman by the Spring?"

This story often begins with a young girl who is abused by her stepmother, whereas her stepsister is treated very well. Her stepmother forces her to work hard, and in particular forces her to spin thread. In the Grimm's tale about Frau Holle, the poor girl subsequently drops the spindle into a well or a spring, and must dive in to retrieve it. Once she goes in, however, she suddenly finds herself in the abode of Frau Holle. She subsequently performs tasks for Holle, and is rewarded for her good work. When she gets back, this makes her stepmother jealous. The lazy stepsister is sent to do the same, but ultimately gets "rewarded" with a bucket of hot tar.[34] The story type is incredibly widespread, and doesn't always conform perfectly to the Grimm's fairy tale. However, you will recognize it if you see it.

Some versions cast the hag in a purely malevolent light. In the Donegal Irish story, the "reward" comes from animals that the young girl is kind to along the way, who help stop the hag from getting her. This can also be seen in some Russian stories about Baba Yaga. On the other hand, Baba Yaga also features in some tales that are almost identical to the Grimm's story about Holle (where she gives both punishments and rewards). A common element, however, is the hag acting as a stern taskmistress. In fact, one common task shared from Ireland to Eastern Europe is washing a colored piece of cloth white.

In Romania, it is Baba Dochia who directs the poor girl to wash wool until it is white, which she accomplishes only with outside help. A nearly identical motif is found in Ireland, where the Cailleach forces the young Goddess Bride to wash dark fleece until it is white.[35] This is the second major link between Cailleach and Dochia, the other striking parallel being an association with landmark stones (resulting from magical petrification).

In Southern Germany and the Alpine regions of Europe, Frau Perchta has a very striking appearance that is very familiar to anyone from Eastern Europe. In early written sources, there is a 1411 reference to Frau Perchta which denounces pagan beliefs in "Precht with an iron nose" another trait she shares in common with Baba Yaga.

Frau Perchta may also have a single goose leg, whereas Baba Yaga is often described as having a single "bony leg." Arguably the stronger connection is the one displayed by Baba Yaga's hut, however, which apparently "walks" on chicken legs. Additionally, witches of Carpatho-Ukrainian folk belief often have chicken feet. There was even an odd tradition in Toulouse, France of all places, in which people would swear by "the distaff of the goose footed queen." Most of these parallels are beautifully summarized in Andreas John's book on Baba Yaga (cited below, and numerous times throughout this book).

In Romania, a single chicken foot is attributed to Mother Friday, who is similarly associated with spinning. In reality, "Mother Friday" is probably a product of Slavic paganism and

Orthodox Christianity. This female personification of "Friday" has a significant place in Eastern European folk tradition, and she deserves some brief explanation.

The Russian scholar Rybakov strongly connected the Russian Orthodox Saint Paraskeva-Friday with the Slavic Goddess Mokosh, who is listed among the idols of Pre-Christian Kiev in the Russian Primary Chronicle. The key piece of evidence for this was a folk tradition from the Russian North, where the name "Mokusha" survived into the 20th century. Evidently, the Mokusha was a spirit who punished women for violating prohibitions on spinning.[36]

There were canon Saints named "Paraskeva" (Greek for "Friday"). However, in Eastern Europe this figure simply came to be referred to as Pyatnitsa (Russian for Friday) or St. Vineri (St. Friday in Romanian).[37] In the process, this saint acquired folkloric traits similar to the German Holle and Perchta, including an association with taboos related to spinning.[38] There is even a Romanian tale which inserts St. Vineri into a story of AT 480. The chicken leg associated with St. Vineri is also significant. Stories of a single animal leg should also remind the reader of the Basque Mari, who had a single goat leg. (Refer back to "Kissing Dragons" above.)

It is tempting to link the association with "Friday" to the Goddess Freyja, whom Friday is named after in most Germanic languages. The idea of identifying weekdays with Gods was transmitted throughout Europe by the Romans, but indirect transmission to Eastern Europe via the Germanic tribes is difficult to rule out.

Unfortunately, there are issues with this explanation, at least if we apply it as a complete explanation of the motif. Week-Day fairies show up in numerous folktales, and no summary of this idea would be complete without the Iranian / Central Asian Bibi Seshanbe (literally, "Queen of Tuesday"). In the deeply Islamic country of Uzbekistan, in Central Asia, she appears as one of the popular female "Saints" whom women can turn to for aid. Similarly, Tajik women perform a ritual involving flour, and which requires them to recite a story about Bibi Seshanbe. This story is categorized as AT 480 + AT 510 (The Kind Girl and the Unkind Girl + Cinderella). After the ritual is complete, chicken feet are believed to sometimes appear in the flour as an omen.[39]

Bibi Seshanbe belongs to a broad category of female "Saints" in Central Asian folk tradition, often associated with childbirth. While the names vary, many of the rituals are similar. Oftentimes these rituals center around a stone with a hole in it. One of these stones is found in Shakhimardan (Uzbekistan). During a ritual treatment procedure, childless women either sit on the stone or lay down on it, positioning their belly directly over the indentation.[40] This is very reminiscent of the Mokas stones of Lithuania, which also are utilized to facilitate pregnancy and childbirth. Parallels can also be drawn to certain landmarks associated with Frau Holle in Germany. Typically, newborn babies are said to come from Frau Holle's Pond. There are also many narratives about landmark stones involving Frau Holle (although it's not clear if these also were associated with childbirth).

In Slovenia as well, there is an analogous figure associated with Tuesday. This is Baba Torka (named after "Torek" which is "Tuesday" in Slovene). Like Paraskeva-Friday, she punishes women who break taboos around spinning. She doesn't differ much from the folklore figures already mentioned, except to illustrate that not all of them are associated exclusively with "Friday." However, there is another element that shows up in association with all of these fate spirits - and that's the domestic element.

Fates and Domestic House Spirits

Fates are an often-misunderstood concept in European folklore, and the western obsession with Greek mythology is partially to blame. We tend to conceptualize the three fates as just three major Goddesses, like the Greek Moirae. Similar figures are found throughout Europe, but the situation in other European traditions tends to be more complex. The word "fairy" in many European languages, including English and Italian (fata), and French (fée) actually comes from the Latin word "fata" or "fate." This implies that Vulgar Latin speakers of the late Roman Empire somehow associated fates with the fairies. But why would they?

The Prose Edda has some illuminating things to say about the fates of Norse mythology - the Nornir. It states that there are indeed three "main" Norns who weave at the well of Urd, but it also claims that there are many others who appear when a child is born. In one Eddic passage, Gangleri concludes:[41]

Most sundered in birth I say the Norns are; They claim no common kin: Some are Aesir-Kin, Some are Elf-Kind, some are Dvalinn's daughters.

Dvalinn's daughters are dwarfs. So we basically have a passage saying that fates or "Norns" are extremely diverse, and may not always be Goddesses (Aesir-Kin). For me, this goes some way to explain the transformation of Latin "fata" into "fairy."

Another term closely associated with fates in Norse paganism is "Dis" or "Disir." This one is harder to explain. It can seemingly be translated simply as "Lady." However, the religious overtones of the word are also evident, and there were likely multiple times of year designated for "Disablot" which was essentially worship of the Disir. Sources refer to Disablot ceremonies in Spring, Autumn, and Winter. Disir were associated with fertility and death. They could assist at childbirth, and every family had a protective Dis of its own.[42] The Disir not only acted as midwives, but when present at the birth of a child, they could determine its destiny. If you think back to "Sleeping Beauty" the three fairies at the beginning actually play this role by assigning "gifts" like beauty to the princess when she is born.

In Slavic paganism, the exact counterparts of the Disir are the Rozhanitsy. More specifically, Rozhanitsy in Russian means "ones who give birth." Church chronicles chastise people in Russia for continuing to honor the Rozhanitsy, but are, of course, vague on the details. They are generally connected with the cult of ancestors, and are often considered analogous to the Roman penates who governed individual or domestic destiny.[43] This is supported by equivalent figures in other Slavic countries, such as the Slovene "Rojenice." A paragraph in a Slovene journal from 1844 briefly describes the Rojenice as fates who are associated with childbirth, as well as fertility and the fortune of the household.[44]

Suffice to say, the bewildering array of traits that we see associated with Frau Holle, Frau Perchta, and Baba Yaga strongly parallels the collection of traits associated with the Disir. It can also explain why they may sometimes appear as Goddesses, and other times as something humbler, like a fairy or a house spirit.

Moving to Southern Europe, we see a very similar tendency in Albanian folklore, where fates are known as the "Ora." There are said to be as many Ora as there are people, and each person is thought to be assigned an Ora as a guardian at birth. However, a chief "Ora" reigns over all others. To quote Albert Doja's article "Mythology and Destiny."[45]

> *The principal ora, who is beautiful,*
> *with eyes that shine like precious stones, presides*
> *from atop a big rock over the meeting of the three*
> *hundred ora. Their faces change according to the*
> *degree of happiness they mete out to the new baby.*

In some parts of Albania, however, the role of the Ora is replaced by another type of fate called a "Vitore." This has been interpreted as meaning "A spinster, a woman who spins" based on the word "vek / vegj" meaning "loom." The Vitore and the

Ora both function as fates, and as house spirits. As house spirits, they regularly take the forms of snakes: The Vitore can appear as a serpent with golden horns who brings gold; in other regions, she appears as a snake that protects the house and brings the family luck. The Albanians are not Slavs - rather their language belongs to its own branch of the Indo-European language family. However, if we look at their Slavic neighbors like the Slovenes, we can see that they too have a kind of household serpent in their folklore, which is said to dwell by the fireplace and bring luck. Similarly, the Vitore has a cognate in Baltic mythology, namely the Dalia or Dalis. The Baltic Dalia is not the Fate Goddess proper (that's Laima) but rather, the Dalia personifies the individual portion of luck distributed by Laima.[46] The association of the house spirit with the fireplace is not arbitrary. There are other examples of the link between the house spirit and a domestic fire.

This notion of a fate as a household spirit is fairly widespread in Eastern Europe. The Russian fate known as "Dolya" (lot or portion) is said to live behind the stove. When happy, she brings good luck. When unhappy, she becomes a hag and brings misfortune.[47]

By analogy with the Baltic "Dalia" we might presume that the Slavic "Dolya" was given to the household by Mokosh. This explains why the "Mokusha" of Russian folklore, recorded after Christianization, seems to have qualities of the female domestic spirit. In particular, she resembles the kikimora, a feminine household spirit who would tangle thread if spinning and needlework were not put away at night, and not protected by the sign of the cross. She was said to dwell around the oven or stove, like the Dolya, and was described as having chicken legs.[48] There is ambiguity, but the Kikimora and Dolya probably both refer to a type of Rozhanitsa, and Mokosh is (according to my interpretation) the Queen of the Rozhanitsy.

Another Baltic parallel can be found in the Baltic fairies known as the Laumes. The violation of spinning taboos is punished by fairies known as Laumes in a number of Lithuanian tales - very much like the Mokusha of the Russian North. However, Laumes are distinguished from the related Baltic fate Goddess known as Laima.[49] Based on this, the application of a fate Goddess's name (i.e. Mokosh) to a lesser fairy or spirit might not be a modern development, but rather something that dates back to ancient Balto-Slavic paganism.

While on the subject of Dolya, it should be noted that the dwelling place behind the stove is attributed to numerous other beings in East European folklore. Each of the following is said to live behind the stove:

- Aitvaras, a Lithuanian domestic spirit resembling a fiery snake.
- Asplenie / Zaltys, a literal grass snake kept beside the stove in Lithuania.
- The Kikimora, a female house spirit associated with spinning.
- Jezibaba - The Slovak version of Baba Yaga.
- Dolya, a household luck / fortune spirit of Russia and Ukraine

The case of Jezibaba is particularly intriguing. The link with the stove ties in with a number of spinster spirits mentioned in the previous section. The name "Jezi" in Slovak is directly related to the Russian "Yaga" and therefore Jezibaba (or Jenzibaba) can be literally translated as "Baba Yaga" in Russian. Both are thought to take their name from a common medieval (Old Slavic) character name.

In Slovakia, Jenzibaba was said to live behind the stove, and in one charm she is addressed much like Baba Torka; Slovak children would place their newly lost baby teeth behind the stove and say "Jenzibaba, here is a bone tooth for you, give me an iron one for it!"[50] This is nearly identical to the requests made of Baba Torka in Slovenia. Additionally, one Russian love charm begins with the surreal proclamation:

> *In the open field there are 77 copper bright red-hot stoves, and on each of those 77 copper bright red-hot stoves there are 77 Egi-Babas.*[51]

There are some fairy tales which strengthen Baba Yaga's connection to the domestic fire. In "Vasilissa the Fair", the heroine is sent to obtain fire from Baba Yaga's hut. She later returns with fire in a skull that has glowing eyes. Her family, which initially put out the fire as an excuse to send her to her death, reveals that they were unable to strike a spark while she was gone. The skull later burns the stepmother and her daughter to death.[52] This tale is probably best understood as a variation on AT 480, except with the unkind girl (the heroine's step-sister) having Baba Yaga's punishment brought back to her in the form of a fiery skull (rather than the step-sister being sent to Baba Yaga after the heroine returns with a reward). This fascinating tale is listed at the end of the chapter as a "Sample Tale."

The fact that people offered a tooth to Jezibaba in Slovakia is also extremely telling. Tooth offerings have a wide array of parallels throughout European and modern American folklore. Obviously, a lot of us know of the tooth fairy. In a lot of countries, including Germany and most Romance language speaking countries, a newly lost tooth is given to a mouse. In parts of Germany, children would throw their first lost tooth upon the stove, saying, "Little mouse, little mouse, my dear little brother, take my bone tooth and give me an iron one." Alternatively, in the southern German region of Swabia, the tooth was dropped directly into a mouse hole.

The Swedes of Finland addressed the Tomte or Locke (the hearth spirit) when offering a tooth. It is noteworthy that the name of the "Tomtorma" or Swedish house snake literally means "Tomte Snake." In Estonia, teeth that fell out were offered to the Stove Spirit.[53]

Triple Goddesses and the Mor Rigan

In one Russian tale, Baba Yaga responds to the hero's inquiry as follows: "Well, go then; my sister lives closer to there. Here's a ball of thread for you. Wherever the ball of thread rolls, follow it, and you'll come to my sister." Unsurprisingly, her sister is also a Baba Yaga. As is the third one after that. It is the third one who provides what the hero needs.[54]

Triads are as common in Slavic folklore as they are in Celtic folklore, not to mention many other Indo-European cultures as well. One of the most fascinating triads depicted in Slavic folklore comes from Slovenia. A summary from Slovenian folklore is quoted directly below:[55]

> *According to the tradition of Lokev, the female mythical being called Baba is connected on one side to the cave and on the other to the hill called Selezna Babica (Iron Baba, Granny, Midwife.) One of the legends says that one of the three fates called Rojenica, Sojenica, and Babica from the Vilenica Cave fled into the cave on the hill and was transformed from a midwife (In Slovenian, babica) to the evil Baba. The villagers wanted to regain assistance from Babica for their birthing mothers. To achieve this, they had to bury iron pokers from the oven at Zelezna Babica during a thunderstorm when three ninth children were born. The pokers attracted lightning, which caused Babica to run away and return to Vilenica Cave, to help birthing mothers again…*
>
> *…The connection between births and Babas from caves can also be noted in other traditions. In the region of Soca valley, the women who gave birth were told that "Wild Babas" brought new-borns from caves. In contrast, there are traditions that connect Babas from caves to death. In Skocjan, Baba Ancka from the cave cooked broad beans and took dead children with her.*

This one narrative combines nearly everything I have discussed in this chapter, from the Iron Woman to the Rojenice. It appears to depict a triad of Rojenice - a group of Goddesses associated with childbirth. Only one is named "Rojenica" but the meaning of all three names is fairly similar. While a single Fate might be an isolated house spirit, three together starts to look very mythological. This obviously parallels the three Fates or "Moirae" of Greek mythology.

In the Greek mythology of Homeric times, it's thought that there was one fate named "Moira." Later, evidence arises of a triad of "Moirae" or Fates. The Moirae were powerful Greek Goddesses whom even Zeus could not countermand. Superstitions about them survived up to modern times, including the tradition of leaving offerings of cake at caves where the Moirae were supposed to live.[56]

Some researchers have actually linked the three "Moirae" with the "Morrigan" (the triple Goddess of Irish mythology) as well as the three chief Norns of Norse mythology.[57]

There is some data to support this. In particular, the Morrigan of Irish mythology resembles the Germanic Disir / Idisi, which have been discussed previously. Some scholars like John Lindow have noted that the Disir can be indistinguishable from Valkyries - the battle maidens who would choose the fates of warriors on the field. Similarly, one of the Old High German "Merseburg Charms" mentions the *idisi* as maidens who give aid to warriors in battle.[58] The Valkyries choose those who will be slain in battle, which is reminiscent of the role played by a number of forms taken by the Morrigan. Among them, already mentioned (at the beginning), is the washer at the ford, who appears as an omen - a woman washing the clothes of the doomed before they are even dead. This is often specifically before battle.[59]

Among the supernatural women of Slavic folklore, those who govern the fate of men in battle do not seem to be typical. However, the element of the washer of the ford does track all the way across Europe with remarkable regularity. In Scotland she is called the Bean Nighe or fairy woman. She is said to sling her long breasts behind her back while washing the clothes of the doomed. It is advised that a man who sees her should sneak up behind her and drink milk from her breasts, so as to become her milk-kin. After this is done, she will reveal any secrets of the future that the man desires.[60]

This has strong parallels as far east as the Caucasus region of Russia. In the Circassian Nart Sagas, we see this same episode of "nursing at the hag's back" except it's with Kuldabagus, the Bitch of the Flying Wagon, who is basically playing the role of the Russian Baba Yaga, the keeper of the magic horses in many fairy tales.[61] Hags or ogresses who sling their breasts over their shoulders are actually bizarrely common. In some Russian fairy tales, Baba Yaga does have this strange talent for slinging back her breasts.[62] However, the episode that shows up in Scotland and the Caucasus of sneaking up behind her to become "milk kin" to her is pretty specific and striking.

Another interesting figure in Eastern Europe who slings breasts over her shoulders is the Hutsul Bohynia, also called the Diva-Baba. Hutsul (Carpatho-Ukrainian) folklore has remembered her as a vicious child-stealing she-devil, who is the mother of changelings. Her name "Bohynia" literally translates to "Goddess."[63]

The Polish counterpart of the Carpatho-Ukrainian "Diva-Baba" or "Bohynia" is the Dziwozona / Boginka, who goes by many names such as "klepaczki" but has many of the same functions as the Bohynia in Ukraine. She too has a penchant for replacing human children with changelings. In Polish folklore, she very clearly plays the part of a washerwoman with large breasts, similar to the Scottish Bean Nighe. Sometimes this is portrayed almost comically, for instance, she may use one of her large breasts as a laundry paddle.[64] In Białystok (Northeastern Poland) another name for this being was the "Mara."[65]

In Northern Russia, especially around Karelia, the spinning female house spirit discussed previously may actually be referred to as a "Mara" instead of a Kikimora.[66] In fact,

the "-mora" in Kikimora probably comes from the same root. This seems puzzling at first, because the Kikimora is a domestic spirit. However, some Russian sources say the Kikimora originated from the swamp. Thus, she could have enjoyed a previous existence as a swamp hag like the Bohynia.

Interestingly, in Latvian folklore, there is also a folk-Goddess named "Mara" who appears almost as a synonym for the fate Goddess "Laima." However, some researchers believe that this is a conflation with the Christian "Maria."[67] Fairy washerwomen are also fairly common in Romance language speaking countries.

In Spain, the fairy washerwoman appears as the Moura Lavadeira. The term "Moura" typically glossed as fairy, is thought to come from Celtic "MRVOS" meaning a dead or supernatural spirit.[68] It is extremely tempting to connect this figure with the Irish Goddess triad known as the "Morrigan." For one, obviously, the Morrigan is closely associated with the fairy washerwoman. Additionally, the name "Morrigan" is typically interpreted as meaning "Phantom Queen" with the "Mor-" root meaning "phantom" or "mora" specifically a nocturnal spirit.[69]

Certainly in Germanic languages like English, the term "Mare" or "Maere" is typically associated with nightmares (hence the name), and the spirits that were thought to cause them. The Russian Mara or Kikimora has the exact same association with nightmares as her Germanic counterpart. Thus, her name probably references the exact same Proto-Indo-European root as the Spanish "Mouro."

Moura's have a dazzling array of other functions in Iberian folklore. In some tales, they have the form of a snake or dragon who must be kissed in order to transform into a fairy woman, much like the xana (one of the other terms for a Spanish fairy).

As mentioned previously, this seems to connect her with the sovereignty Goddess. Some tales speak of pedra-mouras, which are mouras who inhabit a stone. For the purposes of this chapter, probably the most interesting are the moura-fiandeira (the spinning mouras). These fairies spin thread, and are often said to have created giant stone megaliths overnight. One large, wheel-like stone called Pedra Formosa at Citania de Briterios is said to have been carried on the head of a moura fiandeira while she was spinning thread with it as a spindle.[70]

It seems that to our ancestors, fate was closely associated with birth (specifically, being assigned at birth). Consequently, deities visiting children at birth were seen as merging fate with fertility. We see this tendency with the Rozhanitsas, as well as the Disir. On the other hand, death (Mora / Mara in many IE languages) was likely also associated with fate, and it was the flip side of fertility. This cycle also applied to the seasons, with the hag being destroyed each year to give rise to a younger Goddess. The renewal or destruction of an old "hag" obviously lends itself to a seasonal interpretation. This raises the question of the exact seasonal cycles that are embodied in the mythology of Mokosh. There are a number of sources that hint at this.

The Goddess and Seasonal Change

In Poland, some people still celebrate the spring equinox by constructing an effigy called *Marzanna.* The meaning of this name should be no mystery after reading the previous section. Traditionally, they made the effigy of straw or hemp, and dressed it up before parading it around. They then cast it into a body of water. On the way back, it was customary to bring back a "gaik." The gaik was a green branch or small tree adorned with ribbons. At the end of this ritual, they sang;

We have taken death from the village
And brought the green branch to the village.[71]

The practice has analogues across Eastern Europe. The same effigy is known as "Mara" or "Marena" among other Slavic peoples. In all cases, the figure(s) referred to as "Mara" are clearly a personification of winter.[72]

While the mythology is unclear, it does seem from a ritual standpoint that "Mara", "Marena", or 'Marzanna" was an aspect of Mokosh, at least originally. It is not clear if the Marzanna effigy should be identified with the last sheaf, which was often called "Baba" (The Old Lady). However, based on analogues to the Cailleach, it seems doubtful that they can be entirely separated.

The Celtic Cailleach was clearly the personification of winter. A Scottish term for her was the "Carlin." The Carlin / Cailleach was believed to be embodied in the last sheaf harvested. Yet she was also associated with winter storms.[73] In addition to the last sheaf, however, the Cailleach could be embodied by a log called "Cailleach Nollaigh" (Christmas Old Wife). This log was dragged through the village and beaten. It was eventually burned to banish death from the household and mark an end to winter.[74]

A closer analogue to the Polish Marzanna ritual is probably the Semik ritual in Ukraine and Russia. In East Slavic countries "Semik" was the 7th or 8th week after Easter, and it had a number of names, including Rusal'naia Week (Rusalka Week). This holiday seems to have fallen mostly in late May or early June - much later than the Spring Equinox tradition surrounding Marzanna in Poland. However, Marzanna effigies could also make an appearance as late as June. More specifically, on Ivan Kupala (Summer Solstice) the name "Marena" or "Morynka" was given to a tree branch decorated with flowers and ribbons. Essentially, this was the spitting image of the Polish "gaik." This Marena tree was then dismantled or even burned. Clearly, the Marzanna ritual has some connection to the effigy destruction that took place on Kupala Night and Semik.[75]

On Semik, it was believed that Rusalki were water nymphs who left the waters for a week to bring fertility to the land. The grass was believed to turn green beneath their feet. Grain also grew thicker in the fields where they frolicked. Birch trees were especially venerated at this time in Russia, due to their association with Spring and Summer. Sometimes a particular birch tree was cut down and brought to the village, where it was decorated and songs were sung.[76]

Most tellingly, however, the grand celebrations of Rusalka week often ended with a "farewell" or even a funeral for the Rusalka, which was intended to send it back to the waters. Sometimes a girl assumed the role of the "Rusalka" and sometimes an effigy was carried by a procession to the nearest river. In short, the female effigy rituals taking place in Spring and Summer are largely similar. However, these rituals are typically restricted to the first half of the year. They do not make an appearance in Autumn or Winter. One of the most interesting tales about the Rusalki showcases them as dangerous beings who attempt to drown men in the water. The story ends with the Rusalki stopping in the middle of drowning a man, and saying that their "elder" is calling them back home, thus ending Rusalka Week. There is no clarification on who this mysterious 'elder" Rusalka is.[77]

In Romanian folklore, Baba Dochia is clearly the equivalent of the Celtic Cailleach. To recap; In Romania, it is Baba Dochia who directs the poor girl to wash wool until it is white, which she accomplishes only with outside help. A nearly identical motif is found in Ireland, where the Cailleach forces the young Goddess Bride to wash dark fleece until it is white. The name "Baba Dochia" and "Cailleach" (Irish for hag) both appear in stories of Aarne Thompson type 480: The Spinner By the Well aka "The Kind Girl and the Unkind Girl." Baba Dochia also shows up as the winter hag in Hutsul lore from the Ukrainian Carpathians. One Hutsul legend tells how the Spring Wind appears in the form of a gallant youth on a horse. The horse kicks the ice woman Eudochia, bringing winter to an end.[78]

On the other hand, it would be wrong to see this Goddess as a simple villain. Romania also has a holy figure associated with the story type AT 480; St. Vineri, or Saint Friday, who is sometimes portrayed as governing taboos on spinning, and also has a chicken foot. This St. Vineri is the exact counterpart of the Russian St. Paraskevi - also meaning "Friday" in Greek. Her enforcement of spinning taboos is one reason that the Russian scholar Rybakov believed she was a disguise of the Slavic Goddess Mokosh.

Interestingly, however, the feast day of St. Paraskevi is October 28th. If you adjust for the Julian calendar, this actually means that Eastern Orthodox churches still using the old calendar would celebrate this feast on our (Gregorian calendar) November 10th. This corresponds very well to the transition date between Autumn and Winter. The date of November 10th is also very close to the Celtic Samhain, which could indeed be associated with the Cailleach. In Scottish folklore, it was said that Cailleach rises on Samhain to bring the ice and snow.[79] Oddly enough, the Irish and the Slavs both loved early November festivals, whereas the Germanic peoples tended to elevate December / Midwinter as their chief festival during the cold season. That's not to say Germans did nothing in November, or Slavs nothing in December - but there is a pattern in the relative prominence of November vs December festivals. This makes sense even from a resource standpoint; Few agrarian societies could have an enormous feast both in November and December.

The legends in Central Europe largely track with the Germanic tendency of celebrating around midwinter. Here, we see Frau Holle and Perchta assume the mantle. She is clearly associated with a holiday in December or even early January (in association with The Epiphany) much later than the Irish Samhain or the day of St. Paraskevi in Russia.

A final major piece of insight on this Goddess comes from a source that may seem unlikely; The Mordvins. The Mordvins are a Finno-Ugric language speaking minority in modern day Russia. However, like all Finno-Ugric people they have a long history of interaction with Indo-European language speakers. These ancient contacts with the Mordvins include the Old East Slavs, as well as Baltic and Indo-Iranian speakers, as evidenced by loanwords. Why the sudden pivot to the subject of the Mordvins? Because it turns out they have a fabulously well-preserved tradition which includes a Spinning Goddess named Ange Patyai. This Goddess is obviously a very close relative of the Slavic Mokosh.

Ange Patyai is the highest Goddess of the Mordvin pantheon. She is the mother of all of the other main deities worshipped by the Mordvins, except for the Heavenly Father deity, Cham-Pas. One of her sons is the solar deity, Nishke-Pas, arguably the most important Mordvin deity in terms of overall worship. She is also the mother of Purgine-Pas (The Thunder Child God).

This word "Purgine" in Purgine-Pas translates to "Thunder." The word is obviously an Indo-European loan related to the name of the Lithuanian Thunder God "Perkunas" and Slavic "Perun." Therefore, we have good reason to believe there are correspondences between the Mordvinic and Balto-Slavic mythologies.

One of the most fascinating things about Ange Patyai is that she has a number of festivals throughout the year. One of her main festivals is on Winter Solstice, but the other is the week of Semik. During her week from Christmas-eve to the new year in winter, and from the beginning of Semik to the following Thursday, traditional Mordvin women did not spin. To do so on either of these periods was considered a great sin.[80]

This is obviously similar to the spinning-related taboos associated with Mokosh and St. Paraskevi among ethnic Russians. The Goddess Ange Patyai has a number of illuminating characteristics in common with the figures described in this chapter; Ange Patyai lives both in heaven, and on earth. Her heavenly house is filled with unborn human souls, and with growing corn. She can take a very beautiful form in the sky, but when she descends to earth, she may change into an old woman. In this form, she is said to be "like iron" and the earth bends beneath her as she walks. She can also take the form of a great white and gold bird showering seeds from its beak. Sometimes in the summer at mid-day, one can see a thin shadowy veil moving over the corn fields; The Mordvins say this is the shadow of Ange Patyai. Like the Russians, the Mordvins celebrate Semik by setting up a decorated birch tree near a watercourse. This is one of two major festivals dedicated to Ange Patyai. The other one in Winter has a much more domestic character. Here too, however, the birch tree makes an appearance as kindling for the stove.

The Goddess also assigns an Ange Ozais or good guardian spirit to each babe. Mordvin legends talk about her creating good spirits by striking sparks that fell from heaven (Much like "God" creating angels in the legends of ethnic Russians). However, she often goes to visit children herself and does acts of kindness for them.

While Ange Patyai looms large over most other female deities, the Mordvins of Simbursk venerated at least one other figure as a prominent goddess; "Sorya" (a loan from Slavic "Zorya" meaning dawn) was said to be Ange Patyai's dearest granddaughter. John Abercromby's work on the beliefs of the Mordvins (already cited below) says little about her, but the name alone speaks volumes.

This strengthens the ties to the Slavic pantheon, and also suggests that there were in fact other important Goddesses within both pantheons. The Mordvinic material on this Goddess speaks for itself and requires very little analysis that hasn't been done already. Ange Patyai completes and reinforces this chapter's topics perfectly. The Slavic Mokosh / Paraskevi can be inferred to be a close relative of the Mordvin Ange Patyai, and perhaps more distantly to Frau Holle and the Cailleach. She was a Goddess of fertility, birth, and of the guardian spirits assigned at birth (which could share many qualities with her).

She had a major winter festival in November or December, but was probably celebrated prominently during the warm half of the year as well - thus casting doubt on any simplistic generalizations about her seasonal nature. The Eastern European effigy / tree rituals hint at a very complex and cyclic seasonal myth. This is also illustrated by folktales claiming Mokosh and Ange Patyai could take different female forms, including a young beauty or an old hag. This is consistent with the Celtic mythology around the Cailleach. Both can be linked to the magical transformation in stories about the "Loathly Lady." The land / fate Goddesses of ancient Europe were clearly dynamic figures that were not easy to categorize, but this chapter presents what I believe is a good outline.

Sample Tale: Baba Yaga and Vasilissa the Fair[81]

In a certain kingdom there lived a merchant. Twelve years did he live as a married man, but he had only one child, Vasilissa the Fair. When her mother died, the girl was eight years old. And on her deathbed the merchant's wife called her little daughter to her, took out from under the bed-clothes a doll, gave it to her, and said, "Listen, Vasilissa, dear; remember and obey these last words of mine. I am going to die. And now, together with my parental blessing, I bequeath to you this doll. Keep it always by you, and never show it to anybody; and whenever any misfortune comes upon you, give the doll food, and ask its advice. When it has fed, it will tell you a cure for your troubles." Then the mother kissed her child and died.

After his wife's death, the merchant mourned for her a befitting time, and then began to consider about marrying again. He was a man of means. It wasn't a question with him of girls (with dowries);

more than all others, a certain widow took his fancy. She was middle-aged, and had a couple of daughters of her own just about the same age as Vasilissa. She must needs be both a good housekeeper and an experienced mother.

Well, the merchant married the widow, but he had deceived himself, for he did not find in her a kind mother for his Vasilissa. Vasilissa was the prettiest girl in all the village; but her stepmother and stepsisters were jealous of her beauty, and tormented her with every possible sort of toil, in order that she might grow thin from over-work, and be tanned by the sun and the wind. Her life was made a burden to her! Vasilissa bore everything with resignation, and every day grew plumper and prettier, while the stepmother and her daughters lost flesh and fell off in appearance from the effects of their own spite, notwithstanding that they always sat with folded hands like fine ladies.

But how did that come about? Why, it was her doll that helped Vasilissa. If it hadn't been for it, however could the girl have got through all her work? And therefore it was that Vasilissa would never eat all her share of a meal, but always kept the most delicate morsel for her doll; and at night, when all were at rest, she would shut herself up in the narrow chamber in which she slept, and feast her doll, saying all the while:

"There, dolly, feed; help me in my need! I live in my father's house, but never know what pleasure is; my evil stepmother tries to drive me out of the white world; teach me how to keep alive, and what I ought to do."

Then the doll would eat, and afterwards give her advice, and comfort her in her sorrow, and next day it would do all Vasilissa's work for her. She had only to take her ease in a shady place and pluck flowers, and yet all her work was done in good time; the beds were weeded, and the pails were filled, and the cabbages were watered, and the stove was heated. Moreover, the doll showed Vasilissa herbs which prevented her from getting sunburnt. Happily did she and her doll live together.

Several years went by. Vasilissa grew up and became old enough to be married. All the marriageable young men in the town sent to make an offer to Vasilissa; at her stepmother's daughters not a soul would so much as look. Her stepmother grew even more savage than before, and replied to every suitor—

"We won't let the younger marry before her elders."

And after the suitors had been packed off, she used to beat Vasilissa by way of wreaking her spite.

Well, it happened one day that the merchant had to go away from home on business for a long time. Thereupon the stepmother went to live in another house; and near that house was a dense forest, and in a clearing in that forest there stood a hut, and in the hut there lived a Baba Yaga. She never let anyone come near her dwelling, and she ate up people like so many chickens.

Having moved into the new abode, the merchant's wife kept sending her hated Vasilissa into the forest on one pretence or another. But the girl always got home safe and sound; the doll used to show her the way, and never let her go near the Baba Yaga's dwelling.

The autumn season arrived. One evening the stepmother gave out their work to the three girls; one she set to lace-making, another to knitting socks, and the third, Vasilissa, to weaving; and each of them had her allotted amount to do. By-and-by she put out the lights in the house, leaving only one candle alight where the girls were working, and then she went to bed. The girls worked and worked. Presently the candle wanted snuffing; one of the stepdaughters took the snuffers, as if she were going to clear the wick, but instead of doing so, in obedience to her mother's orders, she snuffed the candle out, pretending to do so by accident.

"What shall we do now?" said the girls. "There isn't a spark of fire in the house, and our tasks are not yet done. We must go to the Baba Yaga's for a light!"

"My pins give me light enough," said the one who was making lace. "I shan't go."

"And I shan't go, either," said the one who was knitting socks. "My knitting-needles give me light enough."

"Vasilissa, you must go for the light," they both cried out together; "be off to the Baba Yaga's!"

And they pushed Vasilissa out of the room.

Vasilissa went into her little closet, set before the doll a supper which she had provided beforehand, and said:

"Now, dolly, feed, and listen to my need! I'm sent to the Baba Yaga's for a light. The Baba Yaga will eat me!"

The doll fed, and its eyes began to glow just like a couple of candles.

"Never fear, Vasilissa dear!" it said. "Go where you're sent. Only take care to keep me always by you. As long as I'm with you, no harm will come to you at the Baba Yaga's."

So Vasilissa got ready, put her doll in her pocket, crossed herself, and went out into the thick forest.

As she walks, she trembles. Suddenly a horseman gallops by. He is white, and he is dressed in white, under him is a white horse, and the trappings of the horse are white—and the day begins to break.

She goes a little further, and a second rider gallops by. He is red, dressed in red, and sitting on a red horse—and the sun rises.

Vasilissa went on walking all night and all next day. It was only towards the evening that she reached the clearing on which stood the dwelling of the Baba Yaga. The fence around it was made of dead men's bones; on the top of the fence were stuck human skulls with eyes in them; instead of uprights at the gates were men's legs; instead of bolts were arms; instead of a lock was a mouth with sharp teeth.

Vasilissa was frightened out of her wits, and stood still as if rooted to the ground.

Suddenly there rode past another horseman. He was black, dressed all in black, and on a black horse. He galloped up to the Baba Yaga's gate and disappeared, just as if he had sunk through the ground—and night fell. But the darkness did not last long. The eyes of all the skulls on the fence began to shine and the whole clearing became as bright as if it had been midday. Vasilissa shuddered with fear, but stopped where she was, not knowing which way to run.

Soon there was heard in the forest a terrible roar. The trees cracked, the dry leaves rustled; out of the forest came the Baba Yaga, riding in a mortar, urging it on with a pestle, sweeping away her traces with a broom. Up she drove to the gate, stopped short, and, snuffing the air around her, cried:—

"Faugh! Faugh! I smell Russian flesh! Who's there?"

Vasilissa went up to the hag in a terrible fright, bowed low before her, and said:—

"It's me, granny. My stepsisters have sent me to you for a light."

"Very good," said the Baba Yaga; "I know them. If you'll stop awhile with me first, and do some work for me, I'll give you a light. But if you won't, I'll eat you!"

Then she turned to the gates, and cried:—

"Ho, thou firm fence of mine, be thou divided! And ye, wide gates of mine, do ye fly open!"

The gates opened, and the Baba Yaga drove in, whistling as she went, and after her followed Vasilissa; and then everything shut too again. When they entered the sitting-room, the Baba Yaga stretched herself out at full length, and said to Vasilissa:

"Fetch out what there is in the oven; I'm hungry."

Vasilissa lighted a splinter on one of the skulls which were on the fence, and began fetching meat from the oven and setting it before the Baba Yaga; and meat enough had been provided for a dozen people. Then she fetched from the cellar kvass, mead, beer, and wine. The hag ate up everything, drank up everything. All she left for Vasilissa was a few scraps—a crust of bread and a morsel of sucking-pig. Then the Baba Yaga lay down to sleep, saying:—

"When I go out to-morrow morning, mind you cleanse the courtyard, sweep the room, cook the dinner, and get the linen ready. Then go to the corn-bin, take out four quarters of wheat, and clear it of other seed. And mind you have it all done—if you don't, I shall eat you!"

After giving these orders the Baba Yaga began to snore. But Vasilissa set the remnants of the hag's supper before her doll, burst into tears, and said:—

"Now, dolly, feed, listen to my need! The Baba Yaga has set me a heavy task, and threatens to eat me if I don't do it all. Do help me!"

The doll replied:

"Never fear, Vasilissa the Fair! Sup, say your prayers, and go to bed. The morning is wiser than the evening!"

Vasilissa awoke very early, but the Baba Yaga was already up. She looked out of the window. The light in the skull's eyes was going out. All of a sudden there appeared the white horseman, and all was light. The Baba Yaga went out into the courtyard and whistled—before her appeared a mortar with a pestle and a broom. The red horseman appeared—the sun rose. The Baba Yaga seated herself in the mortar, and drove out of the courtyard, shooting herself along with the pestle, sweeping away her traces with the broom.

Vasilissa was left alone, so she examined the Baba Yaga's house, wondered at the abundance there was in everything, and remained lost in thought as to which work she ought to take to first. She looked up; all her work was done already. The doll had cleared the wheat to the very last grain.

"Ah, my preserver!" cried Vasilissa, "you've saved me from danger!"

"All you've got to do now is to cook the dinner," answered the doll, slipping into Vasilissa's pocket. "Cook away, in God's name, and then take some rest for your health's sake!"

Towards evening Vasilissa got the table ready, and awaited the Baba Yaga. It began to grow dusky; the black rider appeared for a moment at the gate, and all grew dark. Only the eyes of the skulls sent forth their light. The trees began to crack, the leaves began to rustle, up drove the Baba Yaga. Vasilissa went out to meet her.

"Is everything done?" asks the Yaga.

"Please to look for yourself, granny!" says Vasilissa.

The Baba Yaga examined everything, was vexed that there was nothing to be angry about, and said:

"Well, well! very good!"

Afterwards she cried:

"My trusty servants, zealous friends, grind this my wheat!"

There appeared three pairs of hands, which gathered up the wheat, and carried it out of sight. The Baba Yaga supped, went to bed, and again gave her orders to Vasilissa:

"Do just the same to-morrow as to-day; only besides that take out of the bin the poppy seed that is there, and clean the earth off it grain by grain. Someone or other, you see, has mixed a lot of earth with it out of spite." Having said this, the hag turned to the wall and began to snore, and Vasilissa took to feeding her doll. The doll fed, and then said to her what it had said the day before:

"Pray to God, and go to sleep. The morning is wiser than the evening. All shall be done, Vasilissa dear!"

The next morning the Baba Yaga again drove out of the courtyard in her mortar, and Vasilissa and her doll immediately did all the work. The hag returned, looked at everything, and cried, "My trusty servants, zealous friends, press forth oil from the poppy seed!"

Three pairs of hands appeared, gathered up the poppy seed, and bore it out of sight. The Baba Yaga sat down to dinner. She ate, but Vasilissa stood silently by.

"Why don't you speak to me?" said the Baba Yaga; "there you stand like a dumb creature!"

"I didn't dare," answered Vasilissa; "but if you give me leave, I should like to ask you about something."

"Ask away; only it isn't every question that brings good. 'Get much to know, and old soon you'll grow.'"

"I only want to ask you, granny, about something I saw. As I was coming here, I was passed by one riding on a white horse; he was white himself, and dressed in white. Who was he?"

"That was my bright Day!" answered the Baba Yaga.

"Afterwards there passed me another rider, on a red horse; red himself, and all in red clothes. Who was he?"

"That was my red Sun!" answered the Baba Yaga.

"And who may be the black rider, granny, who passed by me just at your gate?"

"That was my dark Night; they are all trusty servants of mine."

Vasilissa thought of the three pairs of hands, but held her peace.

"Why don't you go on asking?" said the Baba Yaga.

"That's enough for me, granny. You said yourself, 'Get too much to know, old you'll grow!'"

"It's just as well," said the Baba Yaga, "that you've only asked about what you saw out of doors, not indoors! In my house I hate having dirt carried out of doors; and as to over-inquisitive people—well, I eat them. Now I'll ask you something. How is it you manage to do the work I set you to do?"

"My mother's blessing assists me," replied Vasilissa.

"Eh! eh! what's that? Get along out of my house, you bless'd daughter. I don't want bless'd people."

She dragged Vasilissa out of the room, pushed her outside the gates, took one of the skulls with blazing eyes from the fence, stuck it on a stick, gave it to her and said:

"Lay hold of that. It's a light you can take to your stepsisters. That's what they sent you here for, I believe."

Home went Vasilissa at a run, lit by the skull, which went out only at the approach of the dawn; and at last, on the evening of the second day, she reached home. When she came to the gate, she was going to throw away the skull.

"Surely," thinks she, "they can't be still in want of a light at home." But suddenly a hollow voice issued from the skull, saying:

"Throw me not away. Carry me to your stepmother!"

She looked at her stepmother's house, and not seeing a light in a single window, she determined to take the skull in there with her. For the first time in her life she was cordially received by her stepmother and stepsisters, who told her that from the moment she went away they hadn't had a spark of fire in the house. They couldn't strike a light themselves anyhow, and whenever they brought one in from a neighbor's, it went out as soon as it came into the room.

"Perhaps your light will keep in!" said the stepmother. So they carried the skull into the sitting-room. But the eyes of the skull so glared at the stepmother and her daughters—shot forth such flames! They would fain have hidden themselves, but run where they would, everywhere did the eyes follow after them. By the morning they were utterly burnt to cinders. Only Vasilissa was none the worse.

Next morning Vasilissa buried the skull, locked up the house and took up her quarters in a neighboring town. After a time she began to work. Her doll made her a glorious loom, and by the end of the winter she had weaved a quantity of linen so fine that it might be passed like thread through the eye of a needle. In the spring, after it had been bleached, Vasilissa made a present of it to the old woman with whom she lodged. The crone presented it to the king, who ordered it to be made into shirts. But no seamstress could be found to make them up, until the linen was entrusted to Vasilissa. When a dozen shirts were ready, Vasilissa sent them to the king, and as soon as her carrier had started, "she washed herself, and combed her hair, and dressed herself, and sat down at the window." Before long there arrived a messenger demanding her instant appearance at court. And "when she appeared before the royal eyes," the king fell desperately in love with her.

"No; my beauty!" said he, "never will I part with thee; thou shalt be my wife." So he married her; and by-and-by her father returned, and took up his abode with her. "And Vasilissa took the old woman into her service, and as for the doll—to the end of her life she always carried it in her pocket."

Endnotes

1. Johns, Andreas. Baba Yaga: The Ambiguous Mother and Witch of the Russian Folktale. NY etc.: Peter Lang, 2010. Page 75
2. The Field Day Anthology of Irish Writing, Volume 4, Ireland, New York University Press, 2002. Page 261
3. Marshall, Ruth. Limerick Folk Tales, 2016.
4. Corkery, Kate. Cork Folk Tales, 2017.

5. MacLeod, Sharon P. Celtic Myth and Religion: A Study of Traditional Belief, with Newly Translated Prayers, Poems and Songs. Jefferson, N.C: McFarland, 2012. Page 57
6. Eastwood, L. The Druid's Primer. Lanham: John Hunt Publishing, 2012. Pages 52, 59
7. Rolleston, Thomas William. Myths & Legends of the Celtic Race. United Kingdom, Constable, 1987. Page 132
8. Wacks, David A. Medieval Iberian Crusade Fiction and the Mediterranean World. 2019. Page 209
9. Wheeler, James T. The Life and Travels of Herodotus. London, 1855, Page 24
10. CARTER, MARTHA L. "A Scythian Royal Legend from Ancient Uḍḍiyāna." Bulletin of the Asia Institute, vol. 6, 1992, pp. 67–78.
11. Wilson, Constance M. The Middle Mekong River Basin: Studies in Tai History and Culture. DeKalb, Ill: Center for Southeast Asian Studies, Northern Illinois University, 2009. Pages 68-69
12. Morgan, Lee. Sounds of Infinity. Newburyport: Witches Almanac Limited, The, 2019
13. Sax, Boria. The Serpent and the Swan: The Animal Bride in Folklore and Literature. Blacksburg, Va: McDonald & Woodward Pub. Co, 1998. Page 240
14. Bain, R.N. and Noel L. Nisbet. Cossack Fairy Tales and Folk Tales, Project Gutenberg, 2009. Internet Resource. Pages 105-110
15. Monaghan, Patricia. The Encyclopedia of Celtic Mythology and Folklore. New York: Facts on File, 2008. Page 69
16. Gomme, George L. The Handbook of Folklore. Nendeln, Liechtenstein: Kraus Reprint, 1967. Page 97
17. Cleene, M, and Marie C. Lejeune. Compendium of Symbolic and Ritual Plants in Europe. Ghent: Man & Culture,2002. Page 156
18. Grimm, Jacob. Deutsche Mythologie. Wiesbaden: Marixverl, Page 370, 2014.
19. Knab, Sophie H. Polish Customs, Traditions and Folklore. New York: Hippocrene Books, 2017. Page 149

20. Johns, Andreas. Baba Yaga: The Ambiguous Mother and Witch of the Russian Folktale. New York [etc.: Peter Lang, 2010. Page 57
21. Kuret, Niko. "Babji Mlin: Prispevek K Motiviki Slovenskih Panjskih Končnic." Slovenski Etnograf. 8 (1955): 171-206.
22. Macmanus, Seumas. Donegal Fairy Stories: The classics Us, 2013. Page 245
23. Laurinkienė, Nijolė. "Stones-goddesses in Granaries =: Akmenys-deivės Svirnuose." Archaeologia Baltica. 15 (2011): 56-60.
24. Corkery, Kate. Cork Folk Tales, 2017.
25. Ugresic, Dubravka, and Ellen Elias-Bursac. Baba Yaga Laid an Egg. Page 316, 2011. Internet resource.
26. Johns, Andreas. Baba Yaga: The Ambiguous Mother and Witch of the Russian Folktale. New York [etc.: Peter Lang, 2010. Pages 77-78
27. Brezianu, Andrei, and Vlad Spânu. Historical Dictionary of Moldova. Page 121, 2007
28. Vaitkevičius, Vykintas, and Vykintas Vaitkevičius. Studies into the Balts' Sacred Places. Oxford, England: British Archaeological Reports, 2004. Page 35-36
29. Patterson, Rachel. Pagan Portals: The Cailleach. 2016.
30. Ivanits, Linda J. Russian Folk Belief. Armonk, N.Y: M.E. Sharpe, 1989. Pages 14, 35
31. Kropej, Monika, and Monika Kropej. Supernatural Beings from Slovenian Myth and Folktales. 2012. Page 49
32. Johns, Andreas. Baba Yaga: The Ambiguous Mother and Witch of the Russian Folktale. New York [etc.: Peter Lang, 2010. Pages 73-74
33. Johns, Andreas. Baba Yaga: The Ambiguous Mother and Witch of the Russian Folktale. New York [etc.: Peter Lang, Pages 75-76, 2010. 110-131
34. Grimm, Jacob, Wilhelm Grimm, Jack Zipes, and Johnny Gruelle. The Complete Fairy Tales of the Brothers Grimm. New York: Bantam Books, 2003. Internet resource. Pages 96-99
35. Patterson, Rachel. Pagan Portals: The Cailleach. 2016.
36. Ivanits, Linda J. Russian Folk Belief. Armonk, N.Y: M.E. Sharpe, 1989. Pages 14-16

37. Johns, Andreas. Baba Yaga: The Ambiguous Mother and Witch of the Russian Folktale. New York [etc.: Peter Lang, 2010. Page 60
38. Ivanits, Linda J. Russian Folk Belief. Armonk, N.Y: M.E. Sharpe, 1989. Pages 33-35
39. Johns, Andreas. Baba Yaga: The Ambiguous Mother and Witch of the Russian Folktale. New York [etc.: Peter Lang, 2010. Page 82
40. Olga Gorshunova, Svetlana Peshkova, Fertility and the Sacred Feminine in Central Asian Healing and Ritual Practices, Medical Anthropology and Bioethics E-journal, Issue 5. January, 2014.
41. Snorri, Sturluson. The Prose Edda: Tales from Norse Mythology. 2006. Internet resource. Page 29
42. Haywood, John. Northmen: The Viking Saga, 793-1241 AD. 2020. Page 6
43. Ivanits, Linda J. Russian Folk Belief. Armonk, N.Y: M.E. Sharpe, 1989. Pages 14-15
44. Kropej, Monika, and Monika Kropej. Supernatural Beings from Slovenian Myth and Folktales. 2012. Page 146
45. Doja, Albert. "Mythology and Destiny." Anthropos. 100 (2005): 449-462.
46. Doja, Albert. "Mythology and Destiny." Anthropos. 100 (2005): Page 457.
47. Coulter, Charles R, Patricia Turner. Encyclopedia of Ancient Deities. Hoboken: Taylor and Francis, 2013. Page 155
48. Coulter, Charles R, Patricia Turner. Encyclopedia of Ancient Deities. Hoboken: Taylor and Francis, 2013. Page 271
49. Monaghan, Patricia. Encyclopedia of Goddesses and Heroines [2 Volumes]. United States, ABC-CLIO, 2009. Page 287
50. Johns, Andreas. Baba Yaga: The Ambiguous Mother and Witch of the Russian Folktale. New York [etc.: Peter Lang, 2010. Page 61
51. Johns, Andreas. Baba Yaga: The Ambiguous Mother and Witch of the Russian Folktale. New York [etc.: Peter Lang, 2010. Page 59
52. Afanas'ev, A N, Norbert Guterman, Alexandre Alexeieff, and Roman Jakobson. Russian Fairy Tales. 2017. Page 439-447
53. Lecouteux, Claude. The Tradition of Household Spirits: Ancestral Lore and Practices, 2013. Page 131

54. Zipes, Jack, Martin Skoro, Helena Goscilo, and Sibelan E. S. Forrester. Baba Yaga: The Wild Witch of the East in Russian Fairy Tales. 2013. Internet resource. Page 62
55. Virloget, Katja Hrobat. "Caves as Entrances to the World Beyond, from Where Fertility Is Derived. The Case of SW Slovenia // Jame kot vhod v onstranstvo, od koder izvira plodnost. Primer JZ Slovenije." (2015).
56. PhD, Patricia M. Encyclopedia of Goddesses and Heroines. New World Library, 2014. Internet resource. Page 254
57. Shamas, Laura A. The Weird Sisters. Alexandria, VA: Alexander Street Press, 2008. Internet resource.
58. Lindow, John. Norse Mythology: A Guide to the Gods, Heroes, Rituals, and Beliefs. Oxford: Oxford University Press, 2002. Internet resource. Pages 227-228
59. Aldhouse-Green, Miranda J. Celtic Myths. London: British Museum Press, Page 28,1994.
60. Campell, John G. Superstitions of the Highlands and Islands of Scotland: Collected Entirely from Oral Sources. Glasgow: MacLehose, 1900. Pages 42-43
61. Colarusso, John. Nart Sagas.: Princeton University Pres, 2016. Pages 28-33
62. Warner, Elizabeth. Russian Myths. London: British Museum Press, Page 73, 2002.
63. Kot͡si͡ubyns'kyĭ, Mykhaĭlo, et al. Shadows of Forgotten Ancestors. United States, Canadian Institute of Ukrainian Studies, 1981. Page 44
64. Malinowski, Michał, and Anne Pellowski. Polish Folktales and Folklore. Westport, Conn: Libraries Unlimited, 2009. Page 191
65. Санникова О. В, Усачёва В. В. // Славянские древности: Этнолингвистический словарь: в 5 т. / под общ. ред. Н. И. Толстого; Институт славяноведения
66. Frog, Anna-Leena Siikala, and Eila Stepanova. Mythic Discourses: Studies in Uralic Traditions. Helsinki: Finnish Literature Society, 2012. Page 344
67. Kapalo, James A, Pocs Eva, and Ryan William. The Power of Words: Studies on Charms and Charming in Europe.

Budapest, Hungary: Central European University Press, 2013. Page 218

68. Lavandaie notturne nel folklore europeo: per una stratigrafia preistorica, in S.M. Barillari (ed.), Dark Tales. Fiabe di paura e racconti del terrore. Atti del Convegno di Studi sul Folklore e il Fantastico (Genova, 21-22 novembre 2009), Alessandria, Edizioni dell'Orso"
69. Transactions of the Yorkshire Dialect Society. United Kingdom, n.p, 1998. Page 19
70. Kachuba, John B. Shapeshifters: A History. London: Reaktion Books, Limited, 2019. Internet resource.
71. Knab, Sophie H. Polish Customs, Traditions and Folklore. New York: Hippocrene Books, 2017. Pages 86-87
72. Kotš̆i̮ūb̆yns'kyĭ, Mykhaĭlo, and Bohdan Rubchak. Shadows of Forgotten Ancestors. Littleton, Colo: Published for the Canadian Institute of Ukrainian Studies by Ukrainian Academic Press, 1981. Internet resource. Page 69
73. Monaghan, Patricia. The Encyclopedia of Celtic Mythology and Folklore. NY: Facts on File, 2008.Page 69
74. Patterson, Rachel. Pagan Portals: The Cailleach. 2016.
75. Warner, Elizabeth A. The Russian Folk Theatre, 2011. Internet resource. Page 30
76. Ivanits, Linda J. Russian Folk Belief. N.p., M. E. Sharpe Incorporated, 1989., Pages 9-10
77. Ivanits, Linda J. Russian Folk Belief. N.p., M. E. Sharpe Incorporated, 1989., Pages 80, 187
78. Vincenz, Stanislaw, Zdzisaw Czermanski, and H C. Stevens. On the High Uplands: Sagas, Songs, Tales and Legends of the Carpathians. 1955. Page 61
79. Patterson, Rachel. Pagan Portals: The Cailleach. 2016.
80. Abercromby, John. "The Beliefs and Religious Ceremonies of the Mordvins." The Folk-Lore Journal. 7.2 (1889): Pages 102-104
81. Ralston, William Ralston Shedden. Russian Fairy Tales: A Choice Collection of Muscovite Folk-lore. United States, Hurst, 1889. Pages 158-170

Chapter 3

Perun and the Drakenkampf

Exploring Elijah

In her book on Russian myths, the scholar Elizabeth Warner displays the fashionable dismissiveness towards Slavic mythology so prevalent in the scholarship of the current era. She writes:[1]

> *On the flimsiest of evidence, Afanasyev and his followers reconstructed a myth about Perun as a God of war, thunder, and fertility in nature. Lightning was interpreted by them as his weapon to dispel the demons of darkness and renew the power of the sun. In the twentieth century, this somewhat fanciful theory was expanded by scholars such as V.V. Ivanov and V.N. Toporov, who have postulated the existence of a foundation or primary myth concerning a duel between the Thunder God representing military interests and his opponent, Volos, representing nature and agriculture...*
>
> *... However, although the link between Ilya (St. Elijah) is clear, any direct connection between Ilya and Perun remains speculative. The profile of Ilya as the Thunderer, as he was known, probably owes more to the Old Testament account of the ascent to heaven of Elijah in a chariot of fire, and to early Christian moralistic writings in which fiery bolts of lightning are presented as God's weapons against Satan and his minions, than some atavistic memory of a pagan deity.*

To be sure, the mythological school of folklore research to which Afanasev belonged could be overly speculative and saturated with 19th-century romanticism. Much in the same way that Warner's radical skepticism of any Slavic paganism will probably be regarded as typical for the late 20th-century scholarship one day. Even Ivanov and Toporov are not above critique.

However - this stance that the folklore around St. Elijah springs purely from the Old Testament is at least as extreme as any mythological school stance from the 19th century. (Albeit in the opposite direction.)

First off, the notion of a Saint being perpetually responsible for thunder is obviously extra-Biblical. The Old Testament does claim Elijah ascended to heaven. In the Old Testament, he was even granted control over rain and fire (though interestingly, never explicitly the lightning bolt).

However, there is a difference between being associated with atmospheric phenomena in one instance, and being regarded as the actual cause of all thunderstorms. This distinction seems to be completely ignored by Elizabeth Warner, however. Furthermore, this interpretation of Elijah is totally unique to the Orthodox Christian sphere of influence in Eastern Europe. We see it in the Balkans and in East Slavic territories that were historically affiliated with Kievan Rus.

We see it in Finland, where the thunder deity Ukko is conflated with Elias.[2] Finland is not a particularly Orthodox country today, but Russian Orthodox influence was significant among the first missionaries there during the Middle Ages. In fact, the Finnish words for "Bible" and "Cross" are both borrowings from East Slavic missionaries, clearly attesting to the early influence of the Orthodox church there.[3] Therefore, this presence of a "Thundering Elijah" synonymous with Ukko in Finland can probably be explained as Russian Orthodox influence.

Likewise for the Caucasus. The Ossetians or "Alans", as they were known, came under heavy Eastern Orthodox influence from Byzantium[4] as well as influence from Russia from an early date.[5] Clearly, the concept of St. Elijah as a thundering Saint is prevalent in the Orthodox Christian world. It's clear that this interpretation is far from universal across Christian countries, however. It's not a typical feature in the folk traditions of Central or Western Europe.

In parts of Latin America, interestingly, we do see a "thundering Saint" in the form of Santiago [Saint James]. In these cases, a very similar argument has been made regarding continuity with the Incan thunder deity.[6] However, to say that traditions like this are a "natural" or logical outgrowth of Abrahamic scripture seems like a stretch. Clearly, there is something regional at play in cases like these. This picture of St. Elijah grows more complex once we look at the creation stories and dragon-slaying stories that are clearly associated with St. Elijah in the Orthodox world. Some of which are incredibly heretical from an Orthodox standpoint.

One creation narrative from the Carpatho-Rusyn Hutsuls claims that in the beginning, there were only three beings: God, the Aridnyk (Devil), and Alej (Elijah) the Spirit of God. God and the Aridnyk created the world together. God made the Aridnyk dive down to the bottom of the sea, and retrieve sand, which he then used to create land. After some time, Alej awoke and shook the earth with such force that it bent, causing mountains and valleys to form. As a result, God chained one of his hands to a rock but left his other hand free to shake the clouds (thunder). Another Hutsul narrative claims that, originally, God handed over the thunderbolt to the devil, but he abused it. So God gave it instead to Alej, who battled the devil and brought lighting back to heaven. Now when it thunders, Alej rides in a carriage and carries thunderbolts with him. Another tale claims that the Aridnyk will break free of his prison one day and do battle with Alej. In this fight, Alej's blood will fall upon the earth and cause it to be consumed by fire.[7]

There is a lot to unpack in the Hutusl traditions around Elijah. For one, his inclusion in an earth-diver creation story invites parallels to Finno-Ugric and Altaian mythologies, which also frequently have a creation story in which a cosmogonic diver retrieves sand from the bottom of the sea in order to create land. As we will see, many of these stories also have a conflict between brothers, or between a creator and a destructive or malevolent figure.

In Altaic mythologies, the exact counterpart of the Aridnyk is the malevolent Erlik. The Altaians have the same basic type of creation story in which Erlik is forced by the creator to dive down and retrieve sand to create the earth with. This story later has the creator bestow a spear upon his servant "Mandyshire" who uses it to overthrow Erlik and cast him down from heaven.[8] In some East Slavic creation narratives, we have the exact same earth-diving episode, followed by an episode in which St. Elijah uses thunder to "cast down" the devil and the evil forces.[9]

It's not clear where the Hutsul concept of Alej / Elijah as the spirit of God comes from, much less why he would be present at the beginning of the Earth's creation. In order to understand Elijah's presence at the creation of the world, we must clearly step outside of traditional Christian interpretations. Finally, these tales also make his control over thunder and lightning directly relevant to his role in the legend; i.e. Ilya's control over thunder is not just incidental in the Little Russian tale where he assists God in casting down the devil. His purpose in the narrative is *to thunder*. It is therefore his defining characteristic. The parallels to Altaian mythology also raise serious questions about how the entire range of these narratives could be explained as arising exclusively through the medium of Abrahamic religion.

The only thing which seems to be attached to a broader Christian tradition is the idea that Elijah will engage in a final battle, and that his blood will burn the world. This belief is apparently apocryphal but is nevertheless attested in some early Christian sources. For instance, the Old High German poem Muspilli includes the motif of Elijah's blood burning the world after an apocalyptic battle.

Some believe this tale also may have pagan origins - specifically due to parallels with Norse mythology, but this is controversial.[10] Nevertheless, the idea of a thunder deity battling a foe at the end of the world does have parallels to Norse mythology, specifically the battle between Thor and his foe Jormungandr during Ragnarok - the end of the world.[11]

In any case, this is the only aspect of the folklore around St. Elijah that seems traceable to a broader (non-Slavic) tradition in Christian Europe. It is noteworthy that this parallel also tracks all the way to Altaian mythology. According to Altaian mythology, Erlik and the spirits of darkness will rise up for a final battle at the end of the world. In this struggle, Maitere and Mandyshire will fight as the champions of the heavenly God Ulgen. When Maitere is slain, his blood will burn the earth with fire.[12]

The parallels between Slavic and Altaic mythologies are striking, but also frequently difficult to explain. In general, Russian orthodox influence on the Altaians has not been very strong. It is sometimes thought that the early Slavs fought alongside the Huns in the 5th century CE, in part because historical sources tell us that Atilla's funeral feast was called a "Strava." Even today, this term can be used for a meal in Slavic languages, and P.M. Barford acknowledges in his book on the Early Slavs that the word "may well have been" Slavic.[13] However, it could also be that Altaic mythology, like Slavic mythology, came under heavy Scythian influence. Whatever the reason, however, the long distance between the Hutsuls and the Altaians (geographically and culturally) probably translates into a Pre-Christian explanation for both narratives.

Another fascinating category of narratives about St. Elijah are the dragon-slaying narratives, predominantly found in the Balkans and in the Caucasus region. Again, a common element of both of these regions is that they are historically in the Orthodox Christian sphere of influence.

In Ossetian mythology, the identification of deities with saints is remarkably transparent, almost deliberately sacrilegious. The

Ossetian sea deity for instance is called "Donbettyr" (literally "Water Peter").[14] Despite his name, he has little if any connection to the canonical Saint Peter adopted from Orthodox tradition. The same holds true for Wacilla, the Ossetian Thunder God who borrows his name from Saint Elijah. It's noteworthy that the "Illa" ending in Wacilla is cognate to Russian and Bulgarian "Illya" possibly implying a direct borrowing from a Slavic (not Greek) form of the prophet's name. In Ossetian lore, the thunder wielding Wacilla is engaged in a perpetual battle with the serpent of chaos and destruction, Ruimon. He is constantly fighting to keep the serpent chained up, but sometimes the serpent succeeds in pulling him down to earth by its chain.[15]

Another Ossetian legend says that Wacilla chained up a similar monster called Artauz. When Artauz breaks free of Wacilla's chain, however, the world will end.[16] Here the parallels to Thor's apocalyptic battle with the sea-serpent Jormungandr are obvious.

In fact. Norse mythology is not the only well-attested Indo-European mythology that hints at a doomsday dragon motif in Proto-Indo-European mythology. Something similar happens with the three-headed dragon of Persian mythology, called Azi-Dahaka. According to Persian mythology, this dragon was imprisoned underneath Mt. Damavand after being defeated by the hero Thraetona. When Azi Dahaka breaks free, it is prophesied that he will bring about the end of the current world or epoch. In his book *"Heaven, Heroes, and Happiness"* Shann M.M. West argues that the apocalyptic many-headed monster foretold in the Book of Revelation is partly inspired by the Persian Azi Dahaka.[17] It is noteworthy that the name of the dragon-slayer in this narrative (Thraetona, later rendered "Fereydun") simply means "Third." This designation has great significance in Indo-European mythology, as we will see.

In any case, we can say that the apocalyptic narratives with the Slavic and Ossetian Elijah probably do hearken back to an earlier Proto-Indo-European myth about the end of the world or epoch. The Elijah / dragon-slaying myths are not all apocalyptic, however - in the Balkans, they are more typically associated with weather events like rain, thunder, and hail.

In Bulgarian folk tradition, it was believed that St. Ilya herded the clouds, which went to the sea to drink and then returned to scatter rain on the earth. Drought was thought to occur when the Saint was ill, and could not unlock the clouds, or when a mythological beast called a lamia stopped the water. A lamia was an odd beast, often possessed of three or nine heads. It was sometimes considered synonymous with a dragon but sometimes described as more of a chimera with the heads of a dog and the body of a lizard. In any case, St. Elijah was believed to cause thunderstorms while battling these drought-causing lamia, and lightning bolts were thought to be the arrows fired by St. Elijah during these struggles. When a lamia was decapitated, it was believed that fertile rivers sprang up from its body.[18]

Some Notes on the "Drakenkampf" Myths

In order to understand the significance of St. Elijah slaying a drought-bringing dragon, we must understand the drakenkampf motif more generally across Eurasia. Not only that, but there is a distinctively Indo-European variant of this myth, in which the slaying of the dragon results in the release of water.

We have already discussed the battle between Thor and his adversary, the sea-serpent Jormungandr.[19] Another excellent example of this Indo-European mythic struggle is found in the Vedic tradition of ancient India. In the Vedas, the thunder God Indra is the most highly praised of deities. Using Vajra (the thunderbolt) he conquers his chief opponent, Vritra, the first-born of dragons. For the benefit of mankind, he releases the waters hoarded by the dragon back upon the world. The Vedas declare "You won cows, O brave one. You won Soma (the divine food) You released the seven rivers so that they could flow."[20]

Dragon slaying episodes show up in many cultures. But they hold a special prominence in the mythological traditions associated with the Indo-European language family. This includes the Vedas, which were composed in Sanskrit - one of the most archaic Indo-European languages ever recorded. In fact, during the 2nd millennium BCE we have only three branches of the Indo-European language family attested at such an early date: Indic, Greek, and Anatolian. The Mycenaean Greek writing from this time period is extremely fragmentary, however, and doesn't provide us with a true glimpse of Greek mythology during the 2nd millennium BCE. On the other hand, we do have detailed Hittite myths from Anatolia during this time - and Hittite mythology provides another early example of an Indo-European dragon slayer myth.

In Anatolia, the Hittite storm God, Tarhunna, was believed to have defeated the sea-serpent, Illuyanka. This narrative seems to have been syncretized almost entirely with the neighboring mythological tradition of the Hurrians, a non-Indo-European people. Nevertheless, the Hurrian thunder God, Teshub, adopted a nearly identical battle against the sea-serpent, Hedammu.[21] The Anatolian languages formed a very distinctive clade of Indo-European languages that are widely believed to have separated from the "main" group at an early date. Nevertheless, the relationship to the broader Indo-European language family is not disputed for Hittite, Palaic, or Luwian - all of which seem to have been descended from the same basic "Proto-Anatolian" ancestor language.

By the Classical period, Greek writing obviously becomes far more prevalent. During this time, we do finally see some Greek dragon-slaying tales - and at least one of these involves Zeus himself. Another two preserve the motif of water being released when the dragon is slain.

The "dragon" slain by Zeus may seem dubious at first glance. He is in fact a humanoid giant with a multitude of dragon heads growing out of his body. I am talking about Typhon. Typhon may be an atypical dragon, but the final episode of his defeat by Zeus is interesting; Zeus hurls a massive mountain onto him, imprisoning him under Mt. Aetna. (Very reminiscent of Azi Dahaka's imprisonment under Mt. Damavand.) Furthermore, Typhon was the father of most dragons in Greek mythology, including the Hydra, and the dragon defeated by Hercules in the Garden of Hesperides.[22]

The battle between Hercules and the sons of Typhon is no coincidence. The dragon slaying narratives involving Hercules can be read as a continuation of the original fight between their fathers (Zeus, and Typhon). In particular, the defeat of the dragon of Hesperides has a fascinating example of water being released after a dragon's defeat. The day after Hercules defeated Ladon, the hundred-headed dragon guarding the golden apples of Hesperides, the Argonauts are said to have visited the same land by boat. The Argonautica describes how the heroes chance upon the nymphs of Hesperides, who are grieving for the dragon, and describe Hercules as follows;[23]

> *... for a man came yesterday, utterly destructive in his violence in bodily strength, and his eyes flared from under his fearsome brow - a man with no pity! Around his body, he wore the raw, untanned skin of an enormous lion, and he carried a stout olive branch and bow, with which he shot arrows and killed this beast. At all events, he too came here, like anyone traversing this land on foot, with savage thirst, and rushed throughout this area in search of water, which indeed he was not likely to see anywhere. But here near lake Triton is a certain rock, which - by his own devising, or else through a God's prompting - he kicked at the base with his foot and the water came gushing out in a flood. Leaning both of his hands and chest on the ground, he drank a huge quantity from the cleft rock...*

Another major example of this motif from Greek mythology can be found in the myth of Sybaris. Sybaris was a drakaina, or female dragon who was said to dwell in a cave near Mt. Parnassus in Greece. After she was defeated by the hero, Eurybatus, a spring emerged from a rock, and the locals referred to this spring as "Sybaris."[24]

The term "Drakenkampf" or "Dragon Struggle" is sometimes used as a synonym for "Chaoskampf." It was a term coined by the German scholar Gunkel to describe the motif of a primordial battle between Yahweh and chaos in Genesis 1:2, which he saw as derived from Marduk's battle against the Babylonian Dragon Goddess Tiamat.[25] For historical reasons, the study of Near Eastern mythology has often garnered more attention than Indo-European studies. Partially simply due to the abundance of written records from Near-Eastern societies. As such, the Indo-European dragon-slaying narratives have often been in the shadow of supposedly similar "Chaoskampf" myths from the Near East.

However, the topic of Indo-European dragon-slaying narratives has been studied on linguistic grounds, as illustrated by Calvert Watkins book, *"How to Kill a Dragon: Aspects of Indo-European Poetics."* In this book, Calvert Watkins strengthens the linguistic case for a relationship between dragon-slaying epics in Indo-European languages, in particular by highlighting similar language and terminology used across the entire language family.[26] However, it is not only on the grounds of linguistics that the Indo-European myths should be considered a distinctive group.

The Tiamat myth is often taken as the prototype of all Eurasian dragon-slaying narratives, and in some cases I would argue this has confused a great number of people about the actual origin of many dragon-slaying narratives. For one thing, it's not entirely clear what form Tiamat took in the earliest Mesopotamian myths that she featured in. This "dragon-slaying" myth is often projected back to the 4th millennium BCE on the grounds of cultural continuity between the Babylonians and earlier Mesopotamian societies. However, the earliest actual creation story from Mesopotamia is the Enuma Elish, which is thought to have been composed sometime between 1600 BCE and 1200 BCE, at least in the form that we know.[27] Therefore, the Babylonian Enuma Elish is of approximately the same date as the Hittite-Hurrian dragon-slaying myth involving the storm God, Teshub, from approximately 1250 BCE.[28]

Indeed, the worship of the Hurrian storm God Teshub is attested among the Hurrians from an early date, and the Hurrians had a presence in northern Mesopotamia as early as the 2nd millennium BCE.[29] Because the Hurrian religion seems to have been heavily syncretized with the Anatolian (Indo-European) mythology immediately to their west, we cannot rule out an Indo-European style dragon-slaying narrative about Teshub reaching Mesopotamia via the Hurrians as early as the 2nd millennium BCE. This is not to say that all Middle Eastern dragon-slaying narratives are of Indo-European origin. That is incredibly unlikely. However, the idea that we have early enough records from the Near-East to rule out Anatolian-Hurrian influences is probably false. The Anatolian languages Hittite, Luwian, and Palaic are generally believed to have descended from an Indo-European ancestor language that existed (presumably) within Anatolia by around 3,400 BCE. We cannot rule out a Hurrian dragon-slaying myth about the thunder God, Teshub, at any time later than about 3,000 BCE. Furthermore, the Indo-European influence on Middle Eastern mythology would probably increase throughout the 2nd millennium BCE - not just because of the expansion of the Hittite empire, but also the Indic elites of the Mitanni kingdom starting around 1500 BCE.[30]

It is well known that there were Indic elites with characteristically Indian names like "Tusratta" and "Artatama" ruling over the Hurrian speaking majority in the Mitanni kingdom in northern Syria by about 1500 BCE. More recently, a letter from Leilan Tel has been discovered which describes Indic soldiers (Maryannu) in the northern Levant as early as the 18th century BCE.[31]

The connection of the Thunder God, Tarhun to "Teshub" in the mythology of the non-Indo-European language-speaking Hurrians is interesting. We have no way of knowing how early the intermingling of Anatolian and Hurrian mythology took place. According to a model put forward by Yakubovich, the presence of a mixed Luwian-Hurrian culture at Kizzuwatna probably dates at least as early as the 17th century BCE, but possibly earlier.[32] Thus, from the 17th century BCE onward, the Hurrians in northern Mesopotamia, northern Syria, and eastern Anatolia were increasingly caught between two waves of Indo-European influence; one from the Anatolians in the west, and one from the Indic Maryannu in the east.

Any attempt to isolate Indo-European mythology from Hurrian mythology by the early 2nd millennium BCE is probably futile, and by the mid-2nd millennium BCE the joint interactions with Anatolian and Indic arrivals renders the entire Middle East a zone heavily influenced by Indo-European cultures.

Despite that, there probably are a couple of dragon-slaying narratives in the Middle East that can be dismissed as having no probable Indo-European origins. The Egyptian Apep, for instance, has legitimate similarities to Indo-European mythology, but no plausible source of transmission.

Additionally, the original form of the Enuma Elish does not explicitly identify Tiamat as a dragon. Indeed, it claims that Tiamat has "udders" and generally leaves her monstrous shape open to interpretation. It seems likely that Tiamat was sometimes, though not always conceived of as a dragoness.[33] While serpentine or dragon-like depictions of Tiamat are attested, they are inconsistent and may post-date an earlier period in which Tiamat simply personified the chaotic sea. Many depictions of Tiamat are from well after 2,000 BCE, which makes it difficult to truly separate them from a partially Anatolian-Hurrian syncretic culture that expands quite early throughout the Near East.

Certainly, by the time of the Baal Cycle in Canaan, which is another Near-Eastern myth about a serpent-slaying storm God, the Anatolian-Hurrian influences in the Levant were already significant - and had been for some time. Moor dates the Baal Cycle tablets to the 14th century BCE. This is actually one of the more convincing Near-Eastern parallels to the Indo-European dragon-slaying myths. Not the least because it involves an actual thunder God fighting an actual (clearly identified) serpent in the form of Lotan. The serpent Lotan even has multiple heads[34] which is typical for Indo-European mythology. However, the dating of this text to the 14th century BCE means it happened well after the Indo-European language-speaking Hittites established themselves as a major power in the Near East. Simultaneously, during the composition of the Baal Cycle, the Indic elites of the Mitanni kingdom still reigned.

It's important to note that the original myth about Tiamat being slain by Marduk has little in common with many Indo-European dragon-slaying narratives. In particular, there is no explicit usage of a thunderbolt, which appears as a remarkably consistent weapon across Indo-European mythologies. More importantly, the Enuma Elish is not a myth about the release of water. It is fascinating that Tiamat is associated with water, which could have facilitated syncretism with mythologies that did conceive of a mythic sea-serpent. Nevertheless, the Enuma Elish is a creation story. The mythological significance of Tiamat being slain is that her body is used to create the world.

In no Indo-European mythology does the dragon-slaying narrative have this association with world-creation. The closest we come to that is perhaps narratives about the end of the world, which could be interpreted as heralding a new epoch.

But this is generally framed as a future event in Indo-European mythology, not a past one. In Slavic mythology specifically, we can probably conclude that the dragon was a world-ending monster who was chained up somewhere. In addition to the legends involving a final battle with St. Elijah, there is also a curious Ukrainian legend about Easter Eggs. According to Ukrainian folklore, if the custom of making pysanky (Easter Eggs) ever dies out, then evil in the form of a terrible serpent will be unchained from a rock cliff, and will be free to overrun the world.[35]

Another key difference lies in the level of prominence given to the myth. In many Indo-European mythologies, the struggle between the Thunder God and dragon is incredibly prominent, and in fact there may be multiple prominent myths about dragon-slaying within a single Indo-European mythology (e.g. Typhon, Sybaris, and Ladon in Greek mythology). Yet in the Middle East, where we have countless competing cults and myths recorded in writing, we tend not to see a clear example of a dragon-slaying myth elevated to the level of supreme importance until relatively "late" (i.e. well into the 2nd millennium BCE) which raises many questions about isolation. In fact, the tendency for such myths to become significantly more prominent in the Middle East over the course of the 2nd Millenium largely coincides with the gradual influx of Indo-European influences, so that by the time the Baal Cycle emerges there is no longer any real argument for cultural isolation in the region.

In many ways, the Chaoskampf classification may be too general to be useful here. It glosses over some significant differences. While the similarities may not exactly be coincidental, there are still distinctive attributes of Indo-European mythologies (and some closely related mythologies like Hurrian) that can be identified. In order to speak of a truly "Indo-European" dragon slaying myth, it's clear that the thunderbolt and the release of water are key elements.

Other Evidence for Perun

It should be noted here that not all memories of Perun necessarily survived under the guise of a Christian saint. First of all, the deity's name "Perun" is clearly attested in the Russian Primary Chronicle.[36] The name itself offers little in the way of mystery. In many Slavic languages, the name refers to thunderbolts. Thus, in Old Russian we have "Perunu", in Belarusian "Piarun", and in Slovak "Parom." Expressions in Slavic languages about Perun resemble those about the Lithuanian thunder God, Perkunas (e.g. "May Perun's bolt strike you!") The etymology of the names "Perun" and "Perkunas" has a couple of interpretations. They could be derived from Proto-Indo-European *Per - meaning "strike" which would make Perun simply "The Striker." Alternatively, the names could come from *Perkwe meaning "oak." But to make matters more complicated, the name of the oak could come from the word for "strike" due to its tendency to be struck by lightning.[37]

In any case, the veneration of oaks dedicated to Perkunas (Lithuanian: Perkuno Azuolas) is well-attested in Baltic mythology. The Baltic Perkunas is depicted as an angry-looking man who spits fire and hurls an axe or hammer while pursuing devils or dragons called Aitvaras.[38]

It is noteworthy that the Lithuanian word for "devil" is Velinas, which is also the name for the God of the underworld. However, the struggle between Perkunas and Velinas, so meticulously reconstructed by Ivanov and Toporov, could simply stem from a Christianized legend about "the Devil." The Russian legend about the devil fleeing thunder may well have been borrowed into Lithuanian folklore, and if it was, then the Russian word for devil would simply be translated into "Velinas." In actuality, the dragon Aitvaras seems to be the most archaic mythological foe of Perkunas. It should be noted that while dragon slaying narratives are well attested in Indo-European mythologies, the dragon is almost never identified with the God of the Underworld. Thus in the Vedas, Vritra is not identified with Yama. In Greek mythology

Typhon is distinct from Hades. The Hittites also worshipped underworld deities, but there is no evidence that Illuyanka was honored among them.

Though not called "Perun" by name there is also a blatantly mythological "Thunder Emperor" mentioned by the folklorist Stanislaw Vincenz in his Sagas and Tales from the Carpathians. The description quoted below helps support many of the concepts reviewed so far:[39]

> *Arrogantly, contemptuously, and with his glittering scepter, the emperor points to the households and fields. And at once the black iron troops begin to strike with thunders... - Seize, emperor-fiend, thy fiery sword, and escape!... - Armed with the sacred word, I give thee road into the chasm, into the unknown; to the boundless ices, to the bottomless seas. There, go seek glory for thyself; fight the dragons, conquer the dragon palaces.*

Dumezil and the Second Function

You're just about ready to read the Chapter 3: Sample Tale. It features much of what we have discussed. Obviously, there is dragon-slaying. Recall also that the Iranian dragon slayer Thraetona (slayer of Azi Dahaka) has a name that means "third." As we will see in the next tale, Burya Bogatyr is also one of three brothers.

Furthermore, the name "Buria Bogatyr" translates roughly from Russian into "Storm Hero" or "Storm Champion." Which has obvious implications here. But the most complex aspect of this tale may be the birth of the three brothers. It contains many disorienting and fantastic details - yet fundamentally we have three brothers representing three functions:

1. Prince Ivan
2. The Storm Hero
3. Ivan the Maidservant's Son

These correspond to three social classes; The Prince, the Warrior, and the Peasant. To explain the significance of this, we need to touch upon Dumezil's Three Functions. Dumezil made a big splash in Indo-European studies, particularly in the 1950's. At the core of his thesis was the idea that the Proto-Indo-Europeans divided themselves into these three castes or social groups. According to Dumezil, these classes also tended to be reflected in the triplism of Indo-European mythology. Thus, there was a deity (or perhaps two deities) of the first function, representing sovereignty, law, and the priestly class. There was also a deity of the second function representing the warrior class - often a thunder God. Finally, there was a deity of the third function representing the producers, herdsmen, and / or farmers.[40] Dumezil's work is far too extensive to summarize here. But the basic concept of Dumezil's Tripartite Hypothesis is important for understanding this chapter's sample tale, which is titled "Ivan the Cow's Son."

Sample Tale: Ivan the Cow's Son[41]

(*author's translation*)

Once upon a time, there reigned the King and Queen of a certain kingdom. They were childless, and after ten years they called on all kings, cities, and commoners to see if anyone could cure the Queen of her barrenness. Princes and boyars gathered in the palace, where the Tsar lavished them with food and drink. He questioned them all, but none knew how to make the Queen fertile.

Then one day a peasant said he knew, and the king gave him a pile of gold coins. The peasant was told, however, that he would be expected to deliver the answer to the King's question in three days. As it turns out, the peasant had no idea how to cure the Queen of her barrenness!

He met an old woman who said: "Tell me, peasant, what are you thinking about?" He answered her: "Be quiet, old hag, don't pester me!" But she ran after him and said: "Tell me your thoughts; I am old, I know about everything." And the peasant thought to himself - perhaps she knows something.

"Old mother, I told the king I knew how the Queen could become pregnant, but I have no idea how."

"Oh, but I know that. Go to the King and tell him to have three silken nets prepared. In the sea outside the King's window, there always swims a golden-winged pike. When the King catches it and cooks it, and the Queen eats it, she will become pregnant.

The peasant boy went fishing in the sea on his own then. When he cast a silken net in the sea, the pike leaped out and tore one. Then the same thing happened to the next one and the next. Finally, the peasant used his own silken kerchief and belt, and in this manner, he finally caught the golden-winged pike. He was elated and brought it straight to the King. The King ordered it cleaned, cooked, and served to the Queen.

The cook cleaned the fish and tossed the entrails out the window. A cow found them and ate them. When the cooks placed the fried pike on its dish, the maidservant tore off a wing and tasted it. Thus all three of them - the cow, the maidservant, and the Queen all became pregnant at once.

After a while, the milkmaid came out of the cowshed and told the King that a cow had given birth to a human baby. The King was very surprised, and shortly thereafter heard that the maidservant had given birth to an identical boy. All three boys were magnificent! They grew by the hour like other boys would grow by the year. They quickly matured and sensed great power in themselves.

They came to their father, the King, and asked permission to see the town and its people. He acquiesced but warned them to behave responsibly and peacefully. He bid them farewell and gave them all the money they could carry.

And so the three fine young men set out. One was called Prince Ivan. One was called Ivan the Maidservant's son. The third was called Ivan the Cow's Son and nicknamed Buria Bogatyr (literally "Storm Hero). For a time, they walked but did not buy anything. Then Prince

Ivan saw some glass balls, and said to his brothers "Let us each buy a ball and throw it upward; whoever throws it highest will be the eldest brother." The brothers agreed and cast lots to see who should go first. Prince Ivan drew the lot to go first. He threw it high, but Ivan the Maidservant's son threw even higher. Buria Bogatyr threw so high that it disappeared from sight, and he said "From now on, I am your elder brother!"

Prince Ivan became angry. "How can that be? You are the cow's son. How can you be our eldest?!"

"It must be God's will for you to be obedient to me." Cow's Son replied.

They continued on the path until they reached the Black Sea. Deep beneath it, the great sea-serpent lurked. Prince Ivan said "Brothers, let whoever subdues this sea-serpent be called our elder." And the three brothers agreed.

"Well, then, Prince Ivan, subdue him! If you can do that, we shall call you our eldest." Said Buria Bogatyr.

To that end, Prince Ivan began to shout at the serpent. The serpent was not subdued and only grew wilder in response. Then Ivan the Maidservant's son tried to subdue him as well, to no avail. Then Buria Bogatyr gave a roar and hurled a piece of wood into the water. The serpent disappeared at once. Buria Bogatyr spoke once again "I am your eldest brother."

Prince Ivan grew angry. "We have no desire to be subordinate to you!"

"Then I will bid you farewell," replied Buria Bogatyr, and turned back towards his home. The two other brothers continued without him.

But when the King saw Ivan the Cow's Son returning without his brothers, he had him thrown in prison. For three days he was not given any food or water. The mighty champion banged his fist on the wall and shouted loudly. "Ask my foster father why he does not feed me! Know that your walls and bars are nothing to me. If I wish, I can smash them all with my bare hands."

This was all related to the King. The King finally came to him and said "What are you bragging about, Buria Bogatyr?"

"Foster father, why don't you feed me? I have done nothing wrong."

"Well, then what has happened to my sons? Where are your brothers?"

Ivan the Cow's Son told him everything.

"Very well then." Said the King. "I shall send orders for them to return."

Ivan the Cow's Son said: "No one except me can catch up with them, for they went to the land of the dragons, where dragons with six, nine, and twelve heads come up from the Black Sea." The King begged him to go after them. Ivan the Cow's Son made ready for his journey, took his mace and his steel sword, and left.

Ivan the Cow's Son walked and walked, and finally caught up with his brothers near the Black Sea, near the white hazelwood bridge. Alongside that bridge there stood a post, and on it was written that this was the place where the three dragons always came out of the sea.

"Hello, brothers!" He said when he found them. They were elated to see him, and replied: "Hello, Ivan the Cow's Son, elder brother."

"I see that what is written on this sign has perturbed you." Ivan the Cow's Son observed. He peered around the bridge and saw a hut on chicken legs with a cock's head. It had its front turned to the woods, and its back to them.

"Little hut, little hut" Ivan the Cow's Son cried out. "Stand with your back to the woods; Turn your front to us!" The hut turned around. The three brothers stepped inside and found a table set with meat and drink. In the corner, they found a wood-framed bed with a mattress of feather down. Buria Bogatyr said, "You see brothers, without me, you would not do so well as this!"

They sat down and ate, then went to sleep. When they arose, Ivan the Cow's Son said: "Brothers, tonight the six-headed dragon will come out of the sea; let us cast lots to see who will stand guard." They cast lots and the guard duty fell to Ivan the Maidservant's son. The Cow's Son said to him: "I must warn you; A little pitcher will jump out of the sea and begin to dance in front of you; do not look at it, just spit at it and smash it."

When Ivan the Maidservant's son stood guard, he quickly fell asleep. Buria Bogatyr knew very well how unreliable his brother was, and stood guard as well. He walked around, tapping the ground with his stick. Suddenly a pitcher jumped out of the sea and started to dance around. Buria Bogatyr spat on it and smashed it. Then a duck quacked, the ground opened, the sea surged, and out of the waters rose the great sea-serpent. It was a six-headed dragon. He hissed in a mighty voice "Come here, my steed, stand before me like a leaf before grass!"

The earth shook as the horse ran out. The dragon mounted his horse and rode toward the white hazelwood bridge. But the steed unexpectedly stumbled as he ran. "Why do you stumble, dead meat?" The dragon asked. "Your foe, Ivan the Cow's Son is nearby," replied the horse. "Liar!" Replied the dragon. "My enemy is not here. Ivan is not here - even his bones have not been brought here by the raven."

The Buria Bogatyr spoke up. "No raven has brought my bones. I walked here myself."

The dragon asked him if he was here to court his sisters or his daughters.

"No, dragon, I came to do battle. Not to become your brother." Replied Buria Bogatyr.

Buria Bogatyr swung his mace and cut off three of the dragon's heads. Then he swung again and cut off the other three. He cut the dragon's body into many pieces and tossed them into the sea. He tossed the heads under the white hazelwood bridge, and tied the reins of the horse to the legs of Ivan the Maidservant's son. The Bogatyr himself went back to sleep. The next morning, Ivan the Maidservant's son woke up to see a new horse. He was overjoyed and he cried to his brother. "You told me not to look at the pitcher but I did. And look what happened! I have a new horse."

Buria Bogatyr spoke; "The Lord has blessed you with a horse, but to me, he has promised something greater."

The next night guard duty fell to Prince Ivan. Buria Bogatyr told him the same thing about the pitcher. But the same thing happened, and Buria was forced to defeat a nine-headed dragon this time. When this battle was done, he chopped the dragon into pieces and cast them into the Black Sea. He hid the heads beneath the white hazelwood bridge and tied the reins of the dragon's horse to Prince Ivan's legs. Then he went back to sleep.

The next morning, Prince Ivan was overjoyed to see his new horse. "You told me not to look at the pitcher but I did. And look what happened! I have a new horse!" He exclaimed.

Buria Bogatyr spoke; "The lord has blessed you with a horse, but to me, he has promised something greater."

The third night was fast approaching when Buria Bogatyr, Champion of Champions, officially assumed guard duty. He set up a table and lit a candle before plunging a knife into the wall. He hung a towel on it, gave his brothers a pack of cards, and said: "Play cards, boys, and do not forget me; when the candle is about to run out, and when blood drips from this towel into the dish, come to the bridge to aid me."

Buria Bogatyr walked around, tapping the ground with his stick. Suddenly a pitcher jumped out of the sea and started to dance around. Buria Bogatyr spat on it and smashed it. Then a duck quacked, the ground opened, the sea surged, and out of the waters rose the great sea-serpent. It was a twelve-headed dragon. He hissed in a mighty voice "Come here, my steed, stand before me like a leaf before grass!"

The earth shook as the horse ran out. The dragon mounted his horse and rode toward the white hazelwood bridge. But the steed unexpectedly stumbled as he ran. "Why do you stumble, dead meat?" The dragon asked. "Your foe, Ivan the Cow's Son is nearby," replied the horse. "Liar!" Replied the dragon. "My enemy is not here. Ivan is not here - even his bones have not been brought here by the raven."

The Buria Bogatyr spoke up. "No raven has brought my bones. I walked here myself."

The dragon asked him if he was here to court his sisters or his daughters.

"No, dragon, I came to do battle. Not to become your brother," replied Buria Bogatyr. "Ah, you killed my two brothers, so you think you can defeat me too! We shall see about that. Let's agree, however, that if either of us falls to the ground, the other must not strike him."

Buria Bogatyr swung his mace and cut off three of the dragon's heads with his first strike. When he swung again, the dragon knocked him down. Ivan the Cow's Son called out: "Stop, dragon! Our agreement was not to strike a man while he lay on the ground." The dragon let him get up. Buria Bogatyr struck again, and three more dragon heads flew like cabbage heads.

The struggle grew fierce and bloody. They fought until both were exhausted. Buria Bogatyr knocked off three more heads, but his mace broke from the impact. In desperation, he removed a boot and hurled it at the hut where his brothers slept. Boards broke and flew, but still his brothers slept. He threw another boot to no avail. Finally, he hurled a piece of his mace at the stables, and broke the stable door. His brother's two horses galloped out and unsaddled the dragon. Elated, Buria Bogatyr rushed at the dragon and knocked off his remaining heads. He chopped the beast into pieces and threw them into the sea. He hid the heads underneath the white hazelwood bridge.

Buria Bogatyr took the horses and hid under the bridge with them, not bothering to wipe up the bloody mess. In the morning his brothers awoke to find the dish full of blood. They found the stables empty and their brother missing. They pondered and searched, but in the end, decided Buria and the dragons must have killed each other. "Their bodies must have vanished." They said with a shrug. "Let's go back home."

As they were preparing to leave, Buria Bogatyr popped out from under the bridge. "Deserting me, are you, my brothers?!" He cried. His brothers fell to their knees and begged for his forgiveness. In response, he only told them "God will forgive you. Now stop it, and sit down to eat. For without me, you would be without this food and drink."

They ate and continued on their path. When they had gone only two versts, Buria Bogatyr spoke. "My brothers, I forgot my riding crop. I need to go back to the hut, but you can go on without me." He rode to the hut and climbed down from his horse. He set the steed free in the sacred fields, and told him "Go, my good steed, listen for my call." Then he changed into a fly and flew into the little hut. There he waited on the stove.

After a while, Baba Yaga came in and sat down in the corner. One of her daughters-in-law came in and told her "Ah, mother, Buria Bogatyr has killed your son and my husband. I will get my vengeance on him, however; I shall transform into a green meadow. In the meadow, there will be a well. In the well, a silver cup. And I will also turn into a soft bed. The brothers will want to feed themselves and their horses and rest. When they indulge themselves in these comforts, they will be blown to smithereens." Her mother replied "A good revenge. That is what they deserve."

Then her second daughter-in-law came and said: "Ah, mother, Buria Bogatyr - Ivan the Cow's Son - has killed your son, my husband. But I will get my revenge by turning into a lovely garden. Fruits of every kind will hang above the fence, juicy and fragrant! They will want to pick them, and then they will be blown to smithereens!" Her mother said: "You also have thought up a good revenge!"

Then her third daughter-in-law came and said: "Ah, mother, Buria Bogatyr - Ivan the Cow's Son - has killed your son, my husband. But I will revenge myself for this insult: I will turn into a little hut. They will want to sleep overnight in it, but as soon as they set foot inside, they will be blown to smithereens." "Well, my good daughters-in-law, if you fail to kill them, I will run on ahead of them tomorrow, turn into a sow, and swallow them."

Buria Bogatyr heard everything while sitting on the stove and flew outside. He struck the earth and turned into a young man again. He whistled and shouted powerfully. "Great horse, stand before me as a leaf before grass!" The horse ran out; The earth shook. Buria Bogatyr sat upon him and rode on. When he caught up with his brothers, he said to them: "You see, I cannot live without such a riding crop!" And they replied. "Oh, brother, was it worth it to go back for this junk? We could have bought a new one."

The brothers proceeded through the steppes and valleys, and the day grew unbearably hot. They came upon a green meadow. And in the lush grass, they saw a wood-framed bed and a well. "Brother Buria Bogatyr." The younger of the two said. "Allow us to water our horses here."

But Buria Bogatyr said "This well is of the steppe. We shall not drink from it or take water from it."

He dismounted and started slashing at the well with his sword. Blood ran from the well, and suddenly the day became cool and pleasant. The heat faded away at once. "You see?" Spoke Buria Bogatyr. "This well water is foul, like blood."

They rode on farther. After a while, they came to a beautiful garden. Prince Ivan said to the eldest brother: "Allow us to pick an apple." "Oh, brothers, this garden is of the steppe. Perhaps the apples are old and rotten, and if you eat them, you may fall ill. First, let me see." He went into the garden and began to cut. He cut down all the trees, until nothing remained. His brothers became angry at him.

They rode on farther and soon came to a hut. The rain was coming down hard, and Buria Bogatyr's brothers implored him to stop for the night and rest inside the hut. "No, brothers." Said Buria. "Let's pitch our tents here and rest in the field tonight. The hut is old, and it could very well collapse on us."

He entered the hut and began to cut and slash at it. Blood ran from the walls of the hut as he struck it. "Do you see how rotten this hut is? Look at that!" He exclaimed. So the brothers rode farther on ahead, although Ivan the Maidservant's son and Prince Ivan grumbled in private about their brother. Finally, they came to a fork in the road, and Buria Bogatyr declared that they should take the path on the left. But his brothers replied: "You can do what you want. We won't go with you." So they went right, and Buria Bogatyr went left.

Buria Bogatyr came to a village next and saw that twelve blacksmiths were working. And he whistled with a mighty whistle, and called out loudly: "Blacksmiths, blacksmiths, come gather around here!" The blacksmiths heard him and all twelve of them came: "What do you want?" They asked.

"Stretch an iron sheet around the smithy." Without delay, they did it. "Forge twelve iron rods, blacksmiths, and heat the tongs red-hot. A sow will come to you and say: "Blacksmiths, blacksmiths, surrender my enemy; if you do not surrender him, I will swallow you and your smithy." Then you must say: "Oh, mother sow, take this fool from us, he has been a constant annoyance. Simply stick your tongue into the smithy, and we will put him on your tongue."

Not a moment later, a giant sow came to the smithy and called out loudly: "Blacksmiths, blacksmiths, surrender my enemy!" The blacksmiths answered all together; "Oh, mother sow, take this fool from us, he has been a constant annoyance. Simply stick your tongue into the smithy, and we will put him on your tongue." The sow was gullible and stuck a full cubit's length of her tongue inside the smithy. Buria Bogatyr grabbed it with red-hot tongs, and called out; "Take the iron rods, and beat her to a pulp!" They battered her hard until her ribs were showing.

"Now hold her tight boys." Said Buria Bogatyr, and he struck her with an iron rod mightily, snapping her ribs. The sow begged him "Buria Bogatyr, have mercy on my soul." To which he replied simply "Why have you swallowed my brothers?"

"I will spit them up immediately." She replied. He grabbed her ears and swung her body into the damp earth. The sow shattered into a swarm of evil spirits, and Buria Bogatyr addressed his brothers as they emerged. "Do you see what happened, you fools?" His brothers fell on their knees, begging once again for his forgiveness.

After a long journey eastward, the three brothers found their way to the distant land of India. They pitched their tents in the field, near the palace of the Indian King. The king looked out his window and saw the tents. He immediately summoned his prime minister, saying "Go, take a horse from our stable, and ride out to see why they have come here without permission."

The prime minister rode out, and he asked the brothers what kind of people they were. "Are you kings or princes, or great champions?" He asked. To this Buria replied "We are Great Champions. We have come to seek the hand of the king's daughter. Report back to your king that he must give her in marriage to Prince Ivan. On the other hand, let him send an army if he wishes to refuse."

The king heard this and asked his daughter whether she would marry Prince Ivan. She replied "No, father. I don't want to marry Prince Ivan. Send an army." Without delay, horns trumpeted and cymbals rang out. The troops were dispatched to the fields, and the massive horde frightened Prince Ivan and Ivan the Maidservant's son greatly.

Buria Bogatyr, on the other hand, was busy cooking his porridge. He stirred it once with a ladle, then went outside of the tent. With a single swing of the ladle, he knocked down half of the army. Next, he went back, stirred the porridge, and went out again. With his second swing, he knocked down the other half of the army. Only a one-eyed man and a blind man survived. "Go tell the king that he must give Princess Maria to Prince Ivan in marriage. Or if he wishes to send another army, let him come himself next time!"

The two survivors went to the king and told him what happened. Upon hearing the message from Buria Bogatyr, the king begged his daughter to reconsider. "My dear daughter, please marry Prince Ivan." The daughter replied. "Very well. We have no choice. Send for a carriage."

The carriage was sent, and before long it stood waiting at the gate. Prince Ivan arrived with his two brothers, and the king graciously received them as his guests. Music, drink, and delicious foods greeted them, and they were seated at oaken tables with decorated tablecloths. Buria Bogatyr whispered to Prince Ivan "Now listen, Prince Ivan. When the princess asks your permission to leave for an hour, tell her that she may go for two hours."

At length, the princess came to Prince Ivan and said: "Prince Ivan, let me to go to another room to change my dress." Prince Ivan let her go; she went out of the chambers. Buria Bogatyr followed behind her in silence. The princess struck herself against the porch, turned into a gull, and flew towards the sea. Buria Bogatyr struck the ground, turned into a falcon, and flew after her. The princess came to the seashore, struck the ground, and at once became a beautiful maiden. Facing the sea, she called out:

"Grandfather, grandfather, golden head, silver beard, I must speak with you!" Her grandfather emerged from the blue sea and said: "My dear granddaughter, what do you want?" "Prince Ivan is courting me; I do not want to marry him, but our army has been defeated. Grandfather, give me three hairs from your head; I will show them to Prince Ivan and ask him to guess what root this grass comes from." Her grandfather gave her three hairs from his head.

A moment later, she struck the ground, turned into a gull, and flew back to the palace. Buria Bogatyr struck the ground, transformed himself into an identical maiden, and said: "Grandfather, grandfather, come out again. I want to speak to you, I forgot to tell you something." The grandfather stuck his head out of the water, and Buria Bogatyr immediately grabbed it and tore it off. Holding the head, he struck the ground, turned into an eagle, and flew back to the palace before the princess arrived.

He met with Prince Ivan in a hallway, and said: "Prince Ivan, take this head from me. The princess will show you three hairs and ask you to guess from what root the "grass" came from. Just show her this head." A little later the princess came to Prince Ivan, showed him the three hairs, and said: "Prince Ivan, guess from what root this grass comes from; if you guess right, I will marry you. But if you cannot guess correctly, don't be surprised if I refuse." Prince Ivan took the head from under his coat and slammed it down on the table. "Here is your root." He replied calmly.

The princess thought to herself; "They are fierce knights!" Then she said: "Please, Prince Ivan, allow me to go to another room and change my dress." Prince Ivan let her go, and she went on the porch. She struck the ground, turned into a gull, and flew towards the sea.

Buria Bogatyr took the head from the prince, brought it out into the yard, and struck the head against the porch. As he did so, he said: "As you were before, head." The head flew forth, came to the sea ahead of the princess, and grew together with the body of her grandfather.

The princess arrived at the shore and struck the ground. Once again, she became a beautiful maiden. To the roaring sea, she said: "Grandfather, grandfather, come out and speak with me!" Her grandfather popped his head out and said: "My dear granddaughter, what do you want?" His granddaughter replied. "Did I not just see your head in our palace?!"

"I do not know, granddaughter, I have been sound asleep." He responded. To which she simply said; "No, grandfather, I saw your head there."

"Then indeed… it must have been torn off the last time we spoke." He concluded.

She struck the earth again, turned into a gull, and went back home. She changed her dress, came back to the banquet hall, and sat next to Prince Ivan.

The following day they got married in the church. After they returned to the palace, Buria Bogatyr confided with Prince Ivan in his bedroom. He showed his brother three rods; An iron one, a copper one, and a pewter one. "If you want to survive the night, let me lie with her in your place," he advised. Knowing his brother, Prince Ivan agreed. The princess was led to her marital bed that night, and she entered, completely unaware that Buria Bogatyr was pretending to be Prince Ivan beneath the covers. She heard him snoring and began to smother him with a pillow.

Buria Bogatyr jumped out from underneath her, took the iron rod, and beat her with it until it broke. Then he broke the copper rod and the pewter rod, beating her just as hard with these. Finally, the princess begged him to stop. She swore fervently that she would never try to kill Prince Ivan again. In the morning, Buria Bogatyr went to Prince Ivan and spoke with him. "Now brother, go and see how I have tamed your wife. All three rods have been broken. Now live happily together in love, and do not forget me."

Endnotes

1. Warner, Elizabeth. Russian Myths. Austin: Publ. in co-operation with British Museum Press [by] University of Texas Press, 2002. Page 20
2. Egeler, Matthias, and Wilhelm Heizmann. Between the Worlds: Contexts, Sources, and Analogues of Scandinavian Otherworld Journeys, 2020. Page 678-679
3. Helle, Knut. The Cambridge History of Scandinavia, 2016. Page 425
4. Whittow, Mark. The Making of Byzantium, 600-1025. Berkeley: University of California Press, 1996. Internet resource. Page 241
5. Vernadsky, George. Kievan Russia. New Haven [Conn.: Yale University Press, 1976. Pages 357-358
6. Steele, Paul R, and Catherine J. Allen. Handbook of Inca Mythology. Santa Barbara, Calif: ABC-CLIO, 2011. Internet resource. Page 199
7. Koenig, Samuel. "Cosmogonic Beliefs of the Hutsuls." Folklore, vol. 47, no. 4, [Folklore Enterprises, Ltd, Taylor & Francis, Ltd.], 1936, pp. 368–373
8. Abercromby, John. "The Beliefs and Religious Ceremonies of the Mordvins." The Folk-Lore Journal. 7.2 (1889): Page 133
9. WRATISLAW, Albert H. Sixty Folk-Tales from Exclusively Slavonic Sources. Translated, with Brief Introductions and Notes, by A.H.W. London: E. Stock, 1889. Page 155
10. Murdoch, Brian. Old High German Literature. Boston: Twayne Publishers,1983. Page 69-71
11. Archer, Peter. The Book of Viking Myths.2017. Page 119
12. Chadwick, Nora K, and Viktor M. Zirmunskij. Oral Epics of Central Asia. Cambridge: Cambridge University Press, 2010.
13. Barford, Paul M. The Early Slavs: Culture and Society in Early Medieval Eastern Europe. Ithaca, N.Y: Cornell University Press, 2001. Page 43

14. West, Morris. Indo-European Poetry and Myth. Oxford: Oxford University Press, 2007. Page 285
15. Aldhouse-Green, Miranda J. An Archaeology of Images: Iconology and Cosmology in Iron Age and Roman Europe. London: Routledge, 2012. Internet Resource. Page 231
16. ФГБУНСеверо-Осетинский институт гуманитарных и социальных исследований им. В.И. Абаева ВНЦ РАН и Правительства РСО-Алания, Таказов Федар Магометович, МИФОЛОГИЧЕСКИЕ АРХЕТИПЫ МОДЕЛИ МИРА В ОСЕТИНСКОЙ КОСМОГОНИИ, Владикавказ 2014. Pages 151-152
17. Winn, Shan M. M. Heaven, Heroes, and Happiness: The Indo-European Roots of Western Ideology. Lanham: University Press of America, 1995. Pages 217, 232
18. MacDermott, Mercia. Bulgarian Folk Customs. Philadelphia: Jessica Kingsley, 2010. Page 64
19. Archer, Peter. The Book of Viking Myths. 2017. Page 119
20. De, Bary W. T. Sources of Indian Tradition. Delhi [u.a.: Motilal Banarsidass, 1972. Pages 14-15
21. Ogden, Daniel. Dragons, Serpents and Slayers in the Classical and Early Christian Worlds: A Sourcebook. 2013. Page 260
22. Syropulos, Spyridon. A Bestiary of Monsters in Greek Mythology. 2018. Pages 47-48
23. Ogden, Daniel. The Oxford Handbook of Heracles. 2021. Internet resource. Page 154
24. Ogden, Daniel. Dragon in the West: From Ancient Myth to Modern Legend. 2021. Page 77
25. Steinmann, Andrew. Genesis: An Introduction and Commentary. 2019. Internet resource. Page 25
26. Watkins, Calvert. How to Kill a Dragon: Aspects of Indo-European Poetics. Oxford: Oxford University Press, 2001.
27. Smith, Jonathan Z. Map Is Not Territory: Studies in the History of Religions. Chicago: Univ. of Chicago Press, 1993. Page 72

28. Ogden, Daniel. The Legend of Seleucus: Kingship, Narrative and Mythmaking in the Ancient World. Cambridge: Cambridge University Press, 2020. Page 121
29. Hamblin, William J. Warfare in the Ancient Near East to C. 1600 BC. London: Routledge, 2007.
30. Anthony, David. The Horse, the Wheel, and Language, 2010. Internet Resource. Pages 46-49
31. Eidem, Jesper. "The Kingdom of Samsi-Adad and Its Legacies."2014. Pages 141-142
32. Bauer, Anna H. Morphosyntax of the Noun Phrase in Hieroglyphic Luwian. Leiden: Koninklijke Brill NV, 2015. Page 11
33. Fontenrose, Joseph E. Python: A Study of Delphic Myth and Its Origins. Berkeley: University of California Press, 1980. Page 153
34. Anderson, James S. Monotheism and Yahweh's Appropriation of Baal, 2015. Internet resource. Pages 53-55
35. Crump, Marty. Eye of Newt and Toe of Frog, Adder's Fork and Lizard's Leg: The Lore and Mythology of Amphibians and Reptiles. 2021. Internet resource. Page 179
36. Ivanits, Linda J. Russian Folk Belief. Taylor and Francis, 2015. Internet resource. Page 13
37. West, Morris. Indo-European Poetry and Myth. Oxford: Oxford University Press, 2007. Page 242
38. West, Morris. Indo-European Poetry and Myth. Oxford: Oxford University Press, 2007. Page 240
39. Vincenz, Stanislaw, Zdzislaw Czermanski, and H C. Stevens. On the High Uplands: Sagas, Songs, Tales and Legends of the Carpathians, 1955. Pages 63-64
40. Mallory, J P. In Search of the Indo-Europeans: Language, Archaeology, and Myth. New York, N.Y: Thames and Hudson, 2003. Pages 130-132
41. Narodnyia͡russkīia͡skazki, A.N. Afanas'eva. Russia, Tip. Gracheva, 1863. Pages 9-24

Chapter 4

Untangling the Beard of Volos

Background on Veles, Volos, and Velinas

As mentioned in my Chapter on Perun, the scholars Ivanov and Toporov famously constructed what they saw as a "Central Slavic Myth." Specifically, a myth in which the Thunderer Perun battles Veles, the God of the Underworld, who takes the form of a serpent.[1] As we have seen in Chapter 3, the argument for a struggle between Perun the Thunderer and a serpent or dragon is actually well-substantiated from Slavic folklore. The previous tale, involving the "Storm Bogatyr" and the dragons he battles, is an excellent illustration of this.

It's on the topic of Volos and Veles that the reconstruction by Ivanov and Toporov seems somewhat questionable. One of the most noteworthy pieces of evidence is in the 911 Rus treaty with Byzantium, in which the warriors swear by Perun, and "the rest of Rus" by Volos. In this treaty, Volos is called "Skoti Bog" (Cattle God).

Scholars have long tried to wrestle this description of Volos as a "Cattle God" into some framework that allows Volos to also be the "Lord of the Underworld" and the results have not always been convincing. It's difficult to understand why the God of the Underworld would be referred to simply as a "cattle god" even if he did happen to protect cows. Granted, it's not hard to imagine that a chthonic deity could have many functions - what's more puzzling is why an East Slavic pagan would describe them simply as a "cattle god." Surely, this would be a secondary or even third-tier function of an underworld deity? Attempts have been made to link the Baltic Velinas to cows, by showing that he had cows.[2]

The fact of the matter is, "Volos" is obviously (at least in part) a cognate to the Slavic word for "Ox." In Proto-Slavic, the word for "Ox" was "Vol."[3] This could be what's known as a folk etymology, where people forget the original meaning of a word and assign it to a more obvious meaning. Perhaps by the time of the Rus-Byzantine treaty of 911 CE, "Veles" no longer meant anything to many Old East Slavic language speakers - particularly peasantry. So perhaps they assimilated it with their word for "Ox." Still, it makes it less easy to shrug off or dismiss his function as a cattle God. Clearly, there was no mistake in assigning this role to Volos by the 911 treaty. It strains credibility to call the homophone with "Vol" a mere coincidence.

On the other hand, a deity called "Veles" is attested in East Slavic sources slightly less frequently. For instance, the bard and seer Boian is said to be the "Grandson of Veles."[4] This appears to link "Veles" with music and with prophetic ability. Farther west, there are a fascinating series of Czech references to Veles. A Czech translation of a German story from the 16th century similarly states of a malicious wife; "She should fly somewhere beyond the sea to Veles."

The earliest reference from this region seems to be a sermon from 1472, which tells the parishioners to leave their sins with Veles. A Czech novel of the 15th century has the protagonist say "What devil, or what dragon, or what Veles has incited you against me?"[5] Unlike the references to the East Slavic "Volos" these references from Czech manuscripts do seem to fit remarkably well with what we know about the Baltic deity, Velinas.

In some scholarly reconstructions, the Baltic divinity Velinas has ended up being the primary basis for reconstructing the Slavic Veles. This is partly understandable because Baltic mythology is better recorded. Yet the Slavic source material is not always cooperative in this endeavor. Even the Czech manuscripts, which place Veles "across the sea" differ from many Baltic-influenced reconstructions placing him underground. Even if placing the "otherworld" in various different locations is not contradictory in a mythological or cosmological sense, it is nevertheless atypical of Baltic mythology.

A search for an "Island of Velinas" in Baltic mythology appears to be fruitless. However, it is possible that we have a number of Slavic references to such an island. Perhaps the most noteworthy example is the Island of the Rachmani in Carpathian lore, which is described as a place where the virtuous dead live in a kind of paradisiacal existence. Legend has it that the Rachmani even send souls back to earth to be reborn.[6] Therefore, even the Slavic material that supports Veles as a God of the dead nevertheless portrays him quite differently from Baltic mythology.

For the purposes of this analysis, it's possible that one of the most valuable references to Volos comes from relatively recent Russian folk tradition. In Russia, a custom was long observed in which the last sheaf of grain was left standing in the corner of a field at harvest time. This is a widespread European custom and requires some analysis to put into context. We discussed some elements of this tradition in Chapter 2, in relation to Mokosh.

In some parts of Russia, however, the last sheaf of grain was called "The Beard of Volos."[7] As we will see, this connection between Volos and the last sheaf presents an excellent opportunity to analyze the deity known as "Volos" through the lens of an extremely widespread European Folk Tradition. At the same time, however, this connection also presents challenges for the current understanding of Volos among most scholars.

Ivan the Cow's Son and the Three Functions

One noteworthy illustration of Volos and his relationship to other deities is the example tale from Chapter 3 (Ivan the Cow's Son). In this story, we see representations of the three functions in the form of three brothers. However, none of these three figures is conflated with the dragons who do battle with the Storm Bogatyr.

Just to give a refresher, the scholar Dumezil and his students believed that Indo-European society was divided into three classes or "functions." Furthermore, they believed that these three functions were represented in Indo-European mythology.[8] This will be discussed some more in Chapter 6: Advanced Concepts in Indo-European Mythology.

For now, however, hearken back to the example tale from Chapter 3. The tale has the Storm Bogatyr slaying dragons.[9] Ivanov and Toporov would say that this represents Perun slaying Veles / Volos. Never mind that the story has three dragons - but that is how Ivanov and Toporov have reconstructed the dragon slaying myth of Slavic lore.

However, most scholars of comparative mythology who write about the Slavic pantheon also attempt to reconstruct a triad of deities representing the different Dumezilian functions. For instance, in "*Heaven Heroes and Happiness*" by M.M. Winn, we see that he assigns the Slavic Veles and the Baltic Velinas to the First Function based on their association with a presumptive "priestly class", even going so far as to link the name "Velinas" with the Vedic "Varuna."[10] And this interpretation is not unusual today among scholars. The scholar Michael Shapiro actually argues that Veles and Volos are different deities, and that they belong to the First and Third functions respectively.[11]

This can all sound like idle speculation. But the three functions proposed by Dumezil were real enough. We can see convincing examples of this across numerous Indo-European cultures. For instance, in the Nart Sagas of the Northern Caucasus, we see that the Narts are divided into three clans based on three attributes; Wealth, Wisdom, and Valor.[12] The tripartite model is generally valid for Indo-European studies, but even so, many attempts to reconstruct the Slavic Volos using comparative analysis can feel incredibly shaky.

In the story of Ivan the Cow's Son, it seems fairly clear that we have the three Dumezilian functions represented in Ivan the Storm Bogatyr (the warrior), Prince Ivan (embodying sovereignty) and Ivan the Maidservant's Son (the commoner - who, interestingly, is the second strongest of the three!). However, one thing that all three brothers have in common is that they all endeavor to "subdue" or slay dragons together. Furthermore, the dragons and their wives are equally eager to kill Prince Ivan and Ivan the Maidservant's Son as they are to kill Buria Bogatyr.[13] And this is all fairly typical across Indo-European mythologies. Certainly, Indo-European thunder Gods slay dragons. But very rarely, if ever, does the dragon adversary constitute a deity himself - at least not one with a formal cult. Therefore, if we do identify Volos with any Dumezilian function (which many scholars have done) then it seems unlikely that he could also be identified as one of the dragons who oppose the three functions in Ivan the Cow's Son. (Again, refer to the Sample Tale in Chapter 3.)

It must be admitted that the three brothers in this narrative do get into conflict. There is evidence in the tale of a struggle for sovereignty between the representatives of the three classes. If that's the case, then perhaps the struggle between Perun and Volos can be understood in these terms. However, even this struggle must be distinguished from the dragon-slaying episode.

The Baltic Velinas / Velnias

The Baltic image of Velinas is partly confounded by the fact that it has become a synonym for "Devil" in Lithuanian. Consequently, with later sources, we can never be quite sure what kind of "Velinas" we are talking about. Or even if they refer to the same figure.

A classic example is the earth-diver myth that "Velnias" supposedly features in from Lithuanian mythology. In these stories, Velinas helps God create the earth by diving down to the bottom of the sea and retrieving sand, which is used to make land.[14]

This is probably a pre-Christian narrative... but one that appears first in Slavonic Apocrypha. In Slavonic apocryphal tradition, it is common to see tales like this about "God" and the "Devil." As we will see in a later chapter, the Slavs may have picked up this narrative from the Avars, Bulgars, and Khazars. One of the most noteworthy discussions on the topic shows up in Frog / Siikala's book on Uralic mythology. They are very supportive of the idea that the Slavs borrowed it from groups like the Huns and Avars.[15]

The dualist earth-diver myth shows up as far east as Mongolia, so it is most definitely Pre-Christian. However, the form of it that shows up in Lithuanian folklore appears to be an exact replica of the variant that was borrowed into Russian folklore from even farther east. In short, there is probably no connection with Lithuanian mythology proper, despite the appearance of a "Velnias" in this story. A similar dilemma exists for reconstructions of Velinas and his battle against Perkunas. Is this the archaic Velinas of Lithuanian paganism, fleeing from thunder? Or just the Russian folk devil by another name?

Some of the more trustworthy material on Velinas can be found in an article by Marija Gimbutas. Her article[16] deserves a brief summary;

In early Lithuanian sources, Vels or Veliona is called "the God of the dead" and the "Velli" are called "days of the god of the dead." In Baltic toponymy, the root of his name shows up in names for bogs, swamps, lakes, and rivers. In fact, to avoid saying his name, he could be called Raistinis (He of the swamp) or Balinas (He of the bog). Dictionaries from as early as the 16th century are clear that "Piktis" is also a name for Velinas. All together, these names enable us to connect a network of similar figures associated with the dead and the underworld.

Another name for Velinas was Ragius, meaning "seer." The association with prophetic ability is pretty well substantiated. This could be a parallel with the Slavic Veles, whose grandson Boian was said to be a seer in his own right. Legends of the 20th century say that one can become clairvoyant if they rinse one eye in "Velinas Water." From a much earlier description of Lithuanian paganism, in 1595 by Henneberger, we hear that there was a holy spring in Lithuania where men went "to become one eyed." This obviously parallels the Germanic Odin who sacrificed one eye for a drink from a holy spring.

This is not the only indication of a possible parallel between Velinas and Odin. The Old Norse term "Valr" for the slain of the battlefield may be related. In a number of Lithuanian legends, the dead (referred to as Veles) could be seen marching through the sky in formation to do battle.

It is very interesting that Gimbutas calls him "Gabikis" that is - he of the threshing barn. As we will see, this barn held a special significance for harvest traditions in the Baltic region. She also calls the Aitvaras - a fiery snake - a demonic relative of Velinas. This creature is a kind of house spirit who steals grain and money for its owner.

As Gimbutas notes, there is one reference from a song that implies "Velli" owns cows. Though this hardly seems to make him a cattle God. Furthermore, it's not always clear whether a "Velli" refers to a deity.

The "Velli" in Lithuanian tradition were often simply the dead. Much as in Slavic countries, the Lithuanians practiced two major days of the dead - one around Easter, and one around All-Souls Day. The one around Easter was called "Veliu Velykos" and it was characterized by families visiting cemeteries for outdoor veneration of the dead. They often left eggs as offerings during this time.[17]

The late autumnal day of the dead was called "Velines." It often involved inviting the dead to a family feast at home. In fact, a cup full of offerings to the dead was poured into the hearth fire. The combination of harvest, hearth, and the dead seems to have been central to Velines. Straw was spread out over the table, along with bread and beer, and prayers to the dead were whispered over candlelight with the entire household present. Often taking place in late October, it was a feast following immediately after the harvest[18] very much like Halloween or Samhain in the west.

The Last Sheaf and the Old Man: An Overview

There is precious little to go off of with the Slavic deity Veles / Volos. However, perhaps the one real gem out of all of the rubble is "The Beard of Volos." Evidently, this was the term used by some Russians to describe a sheaf that was left unharvested in the field and "curled" to welcome fertility back to the field.

Last sheaf traditions form a major group of folk traditions in Europe. Sometimes they take slight variations - for instance, there are places where peasants bundle up the first sheaf and treat it ceremoniously as a sacred object. But in general, it usually tends to be the last sheaf or last patch of grain that is considered to have power. We've already discussed this in part in Chapter 2: Baba Yaga and Mokosh the Great Mother. As I discussed there, there are many traditions that involve personifying the last sheaf of grain as "The Old Woman." We see this not only with the Celtic winter hag Cailleach / Carlin, but also with Baba Yaga in Russia. In Russia, for instance, a patch of grain might be left in the corner of the field, and people would implore her by saying "Baba Yaga, you harvested our grain for us, and this is all that we've left for you."[19]

What we did not discuss in Chapter 2 was the Old Man, which is the masculine counterpart of the grain woman. This tradition has many similarities, but in the context of Volos it must be explored separately. Thus, for instance, in Germany, we sometimes see references to the last sheaf as the "Old Man" as well the "Old Woman." In Silesia, the Old Man or Old Woman is a sheaf that is made unusually large. Sometimes it is weighted with a stone. The puppet is hung up in the farmhouse, and remains there until a new Old Man is made next year. In Germany, the explanation offered for the large, heavy sheaf is that it expresses the wish for a good crop next year. This is what Sir James Frazer called "sympathetic magic," basically conjuring up "like with like." The idea was that a large, heavy sheaf would ensure a large, heavy crop next year.[20]

This association of a ceremonial sheaf of grain with sympathetic magic is known from Slavic countries as well. For instance, in Bulgaria, it was common to bundle up the first sheaf with red thread, and to lift it up while proclaiming "This year I can lift you, but next year may I not be able to do so!" Sometimes the last patch of grain was left in the field and braided, in which case it was called "The beard of the field" by some Bulgarians.[21] This parallels the "Beard of Volos" mentioned previously. In fact, we can say there was a general Slavic tendency to describe a ceremonially uncut patch of grain as a "beard."

A number of scholars have puzzled over why Volos would be associated with the last sheaf of grain during harvest. If he's an underworld deity, then why should he be associated with grain? This seems to be one of the reasons why Shapiro proposed "Volos" as a second deity, one associated with fertility, unlike the underworld deity Veles.[22] However, to say that deities of the last sheaf are purely "fertility" figures is to fundamentally misunderstand the ritual.

Recall that Baba Yaga is offered the last patch of rye in Russia, almost as an attempt to placate the fearsome hag of Russian folklore.[23] On the one hand, this does show that frightening chthonic figures like Baba Yaga could be associated with fertility. But it also tells us a lot about the perceived connection between harvest time and death. However, arguably the best illustration of the connection between the last sheaf and death is found in the Ukrainian Didukh.

The Ukrainian word "Didukh" can be derived from "Did" (meaning grandfather) and "Dukh" (meaning breath or spirit). It is a ceremonial sheaf made from grains harvested from the field. It was believed to house the spirits of dead family members, and through it, the dead were literally brought into the household for the winter cycle of celebration. The Didukh was given a place of honor during Christmas in many Ukrainian households. Finally, in early January, it was taken to the field and burned to free the spirits.[24, 25]

It seems that the Ukrainians have preserved the connection between the Didukh and the cult of ancestors better than most in Europe. Other Slavic countries do not necessarily preserve such an elaborate tradition, but the term "Dziad / Ded / Did" meaning "grandfather" is regularly used for the last sheaf in most Slavic languages. In Poland, for instance, it was customary during Christmas time to hang a sheaf of grain upside down on the ceiling. It was often called the Baba (Grandmother) or Dziad (Grandfather).[26]

Perhaps it would be good to circle back to the harvest traditions of the British Isles, however. We've seen how consistently the terms "Grandmother", "Grandfather", "Old Woman", and "Old Man" are used across many European folk traditions. We can now better understand the Scottish and Irish traditions of constructing a harvest effigy called "The Carlin" or "The Cailleach." These are both terms that can be translated as "hag" or "old woman." And these have been partially explored in Chapter 2: Baba Yaga and Mokosh the Great Mother. What remains to be explored is the husband of the Goddess known as Cailleach in Celtic lore.

The husband of the Cailleach is sometimes simply identified as "The Bodach." Which means essentially "Old Man." We know very little about him, except that the two are worshipped together in some cases. In Scotland, for instance, they are honored as two large stones at Tigh na Calliche, along with a third stone representing their daughter Nighean.[27] The other major role given to the figure "Bodach" involves Magh Mell, the Celtic otherworld. According to Irish lore, Boadach the Eternal is the King of Magh Mell, a land without sorrow or old age.[28] In short, we are beginning to see how the association between Volos and a patch of grain actually strengthens the case for identifying him as a God of the dead.

There is some evidence for a connection between the Baltic Velinas and harvest traditions. The Lithuanian All Saints Day, also known as Velines, clearly stresses harvest imagery. As mentioned previously, it followed the Fall Equinox. This tradition clearly involved the worship of ancestral spirits at the hearth.[29]

Recall that Czech sources place Veles "across the sea." This does not necessarily conflict with the role of an otherworld deity, because similar ambiguities are known from other mythologies. Similarly, the abode of Boadach the Eternal, Magh Mell, could be reached by many routes. In some Irish legends, a cave can be a gateway to the Otherworld. However, the most popular path to the Otherworld was by voyaging across the sea.[30] While this is not necessarily a contradiction, it is a significant difference from Baltic mythology, which generally does not emphasize a blessed island. In fact, it almost appears that the Slavic conception of the Otherworld may be closer to the archaic Indo-European one here. This could be one aspect of Baltic mythology that has been lost. Or alternatively, it may be that the Slavs were influenced by another Indo-European culture like the Scythians.

Whatever the case, the view of Volos existing on a blessed island is probably emphasized more in Slavic tradition than the view of him being underground. This is something that is not always stressed, in part because of the work by scholars like Ivanov and Toporov in equating Veles with the Baltic Velinas. In some respects, the connection between the two is substantiated by their mutual association with the dead - but in some ways, it may lead to some distortion as well.

One thing that adds further context to this tradition is the importance of the double-ear, or double-stalk of grain. These anomalous stalks of grain are difficult to find, but not impossible. In many European cultures, it was considered lucky to find them. In Bulgaria, for instance, the double-eared stalk of grain was called "The Tsar of the Field" and a reward could be offered to field hands who found one.[31]

In some Slavic countries, the double-ear was venerated as a kind of fertility deity. In the Mogilev province of northern Russia, the stalks with double ears were called "sporysh" and were gathered up in large numbers to be bundled with the last harvested sheaf, which was woven into a decorative wreath. The term "sporysh" or "sporysz" also shows up in Ukraine and Poland respectively, where it is typically considered to be a kind of spirit. In Ukraine, the sporysh was believed to bring wealth to its owner, much like a house spirit.[32]

In Baltic tradition, the term for a double-ear of grain was "Jumis."[33] This relates to an archaic Indo-European term for "twin." However, the term "Jumis" or "Jumi" is widely distributed across various communities of Baltic and Finnic language speakers, and it requires its own analysis in order for us to truly understand the ancient significance of the name.

Balto-Finnic Jumi and the Vedic Yama

In some Baltic traditions, as mentioned previously, the meaning of "Jumis" is simply a double-eared sheaf of grain. However, the deeper meaning is far more extensive. In Finnish, Estonian, and Latvian, the term Jumi or Jumis can refer to any two things growing together as one. This applies to double ears, double fruits, double potatoes, even eggs with two yokes. Being "in Jumi" can refer to two individuals who form a pair, possibly even in coitus.[34]

Why does this name matter? We get a good summary of the significance in "*Indo-European and the Indo-Europeans*" by Thomas Gamkrelidze and Vjaceslav Ivanov.[35]

> *Incest between the twins occurs in different variants of the myth: the twins are brother and sister who found the human race. This is the clearest in the Indo-Iranian myth of Yama, a late echo of which is preserved in dialogue between Yama, the first human, and his sister Yami, who tries to persuade him to commit incest. The Indic name "Yama" goes back to the Proto-Indo-European word for "twin", archaic PIE *Q'emo-: Sanskrit "Yama" (twin), Avestan "Yema" (twin), Latin "geminus" (twin), Middle Irish "emain" (twin), Latvian "jumis" (double fruit, double head of grain.)*

If you know anything about Hinduism, or even Buddhism, then you know what happened to the Vedic Yama after he died. As the first man to die, he became the lord of the underworld. Despite his mortal origins, he was fully deified in Indian tradition, and in the Vedas, we are told that his kingdom is reserved for good souls.[36]

Thus, it seems we have linked the Slavic God of the dead, Volos, with the Vedic God of the dead, Yama. Through "The Beard of Volos", a seemingly agrarian tradition, we have illuminated a connection between the two. With significant help from the Balto-Finnic Jumi, the connection becomes a lot more obvious. And the link helps explain some other things as well. Recall that at the beginning of this chapter, I questioned why a God of the Dead would be referred to simply as "Cattle God" which is what the Russian treaty with Byzantium calls Volos. To the modern mindset, the connection seems nonsensical. However, from a Proto-Indo-European standpoint, it makes a shocking amount of sense.

The Proto-Indo-Europeans were herdsmen. And we have significant evidence that they believed that the afterlife (at least one of them) was a blissful pasture full of cattle. In Hittite to "go to the meadow" was an expression that meant "to die." In the Rig-Veda, the land to which Yama has shown us the way is called a cattle-pasture (gavyuti). Similarly, one title of the Iranian Yima was "He who has good herds."[37]

There seems to be little doubt that the Balto-Finnic Jumi is related to the Vedic Yama. Not only is this supported by Indo-European comparative linguistics, but there is a reference from a "Johannes Tornaeus" penned in 1672, which notes that the Lapps and Finns considered Jumi their forefather or patriarch, and that the Finns honored him highly.[38] This matches the Vedic description of Yama almost perfectly. What's more, the reference is so early that it could not possibly be influenced by any western knowledge of the Vedas.

Furthermore, there are even references to incest between the Baltic Jumis and his sister Jumalina. For instance, one Latvian folksong says the following:[39]

Jumis looks for Jumalina,
Walking in the field
The brother is seeking a bride
Asking his sister

As noted in the source above, the Latvian material clearly parallels Indo-Iranian myths about Yama and his sister Yami, or the Iranian Yima and Yimak. Undoubtedly, like them, Jumis and Jumalina were considered to be the progenitors of humanity. Their connection to the cult of ancestors was therefore the primary grounds for their deification.

In the Vedas, the portrayal of Yama is unquestionably positive. There are some indications in Balto-Finnic lore of a dark side to his western counterpart Jumi. According to the Finns, Jumi can take the form of a blind archer whose arrows cause sickness. For instance, a boil or rash is sometimes referred to as "Jumi's Shot." The name Jumi is also associated with various "death omens" which are referred to in Finnish as "kuolemanjumi." For instance, a large crack or bang, or a cross randomly forming from two stray splinters was sometimes considered a "kuolemanjumi" - an omen predicting someone's death. The Finns also knew of the international folk-belief that the death-tick predicts death with its ticking, especially if heard through a door wall. Consequently, the death tick was called "jumin koi." Consequently, we can see that Jumi was sometimes feared for his association with death.[40]

However, there is no doubt about his association with the last sheaf. Latvian songs tell how Jumis sleeps in the summer, but in the fall, he flees from the reapers approaching him in the field. Finally, Jumis is caught, either in the last sheaf or the last handful of flax. In many cases, the "Jumis" wreath is woven from double-eared grain stalks. Once it is brought indoors, it is hung on the wall or the ceiling or placed on the floor of the granary. There is also a custom in Latvia of leaving the last few stalks of grain or a handful of flax in the field, tying the ears or flax capsules at the top in a knot: This shock-shaped sheaf is also called "Jumis."[41]

There is a similar figure in the folklore of the Komi-Zyrians, who are a Finno-Ugric ethnic group native to the lands just northeast of historically "Russian" territory. In their folklore, there is a mistress of grain and cereals called "Joma" who in modern folklore tends to be nearly indistinguishable from Baba Yaga. In Komi mythology, she and her twin brother Vojpel were both children of the Sky Father God "Jen." However, the wicked underworld God Omel tricked their mother into opening the gates of heaven, causing Joma and her twin brother to fall to earth. A number of scholars have interpreted "Joma" as an Indo-Iranian loan, cognate to Yami / Yimak, the twin sister of Yama / Yima. That's in part because Komi mythology identifies Joma and her twin brother Vojpel as the progenitors of humanity.[42]

We know very little about Vojpel, other than the fact that his idol had four faces - not unlike the Zbruch idol and the Slavic deity Sventovit (discussed later in this chapter). It has also been noted that the "Pel" in Vojpel can probably be translated roughly as "Grandfather."[43]

One final note about the Balto-Finnic Jumi relates to his association with mock weddings around late autumn. Playful performances imitating marriages of young girls seem to have been one of the longest-surviving elements of the Jumi festival among Finnic peoples.[44]

This provides an odd parallel to mock weddings that traditionally happened in Russia during the feast day of the twin brother Saints Cosmas and Damian. Specifically, during their feast day in November, girls would dress up a "Kuzka" scarecrow made from straw, supposedly representing Saint Cosmas, and perform a mock wedding.[45] The Saints Cosmas and Damian will be one of the primary topics in Chapter 8: Svarozhichi - Sons of Svarog. For now, however, it is enough to note that the traditions of Jumi apparently attached themselves to the cult of two twin brother Saints. This is unlikely to be a coincidence, considering that the name "Jumi" comes from the Proto-Indo-European word for "twin." As we will see, there seems to have been a substantial survival of Pre-Christian traditions associated with these two brother Saints. In particular, the veneration of both saints was closely associated with the threshing barn.

Curcho, Kursis, Keyri, and Khors

Interestingly, neither "Veles" nor "Volos" are listed in Vladimir's Kievan pantheon. For over a century, it has puzzled scholars that an idol of Volos stood in the merchant's quarter of Kiev, but there is no mention of him among the idols erected by Prince Vladimir.[46]

However, there is a "Khors" listed among Vladimir's idols, which is strikingly close to the names of some Baltic deities of the harvest. In most Old Russian chronicles, "Khors" is actually spelled more like "Hr'suh." Or as Borissoff renders it "xursu." This is very close to Baltic counterparts "Curcho" and "Kursis." Borisoff has a compelling study which links the Slavic Khors with these Baltic harvest deities. He quotes the following description of Curcho from France Mone:[47]

> *The image of the Curcho was destroyed after the harvest and re-done annually, he was the protector of all field fruits, food and drink was in his care, he was a cheerful table God.*

Borisoff also notes that one well-attested symbol associated with Curcho was the bull. This provides another possible parallel with Volos, whose name is related to Proto-Slavic "Vol" meaning "Ox." We are reliant on a limited collection of manuscripts for our view of Curcho, and there's not much more that we do know. However, Borisoff does not omit the Lithuanian Kursis from his analysis either. He rightly links it with the Old Prussian Curcho.

The "Kursis" of Lithuanian folk tradition is easily recognizable as a relative of the Balto-Finnic Jumis. The Kursis was a straw effigy constructed during harvest. It was given to harvest workers who lagged behind in their work.[48]

Recall that in Scotland, the old hag or "Cailleach" was a sheaf that was created by the man who got his harvest done first. It was then passed on, until the sheaf finally landed with the last man to finish harvesting.[49] Thus, the Kursis directly parallels traditions of the last sheaf found as far west as the British Isles.

In parts of Lithuania, the Kursis was especially associated with flax and with the threshing barn. The Kursis was an effigy said to represent the spirits who dried the grain after harvest. During flax-breaking, men would engage in an elaborate game to try and fob off the Kursis on another group, encouraging others to "take the Kursis" from them.[50]

The old canard about Khors as a "Sun God" seems to be a relic of 19th century scholarship. As Borisoff notes, the Iranian word for sun "Khor" does not explain the "s" ending in Khors. Furthermore, Khors was not called "Khors" in many sources, but rather "Hrsuh." The evidence for the solar etymology is therefore extremely weak.

On top of that, the sounds "Kh" and "R" are extremely common in the Iranian lexicon. Far from narrowing the options down, the consideration of Iranian loan-words actually brings dozens of candidates to the fore. These include the Ossetian word "Khorz" meaning "good."[51] This is actually a more plausible Iranian etymology, not just because it sounds closer to "Khors" than Ossetian "Khor" but also because a similar word for "good" (khorosho) has been borrowed into East Slavic languages. If there is an Iranian etymology, this one is more likely. However, as Borisoff notes, an Iranian etymology is by no means needed.

A very similar tradition to the Baltic Kursis and Curcho is known in Finland. On All-Saint's day, they would construct a straw effigy called "Keyri Old Man." The Swedes in Finland had a similar tradition on Christmas but they would call him "Jul-Gubbe" (Yule Old Man). They would place the effigy at the table as a guest of honor, and treat him to a drink.[52] It is interesting that the Swedes in Finland linked Keyri with the Germanic tradition of Yule - normally a holiday associated with Odin. Once again, we can see a connection with the Norse All-Father.

It's plausible, then, that Khors and Volos could both be names for a similar type of harvest deity. It's unclear why he would be called "Khors" in Vladimir's pantheon but "Volos" in the merchant's quarter of Kiev. However, the evidence suggests that Volos was a name associated with the commoner class. In the treaty with Byzantium, Volos is said to be the God that "All of Rus" swears by, as opposed to Perun who received the oaths of the warriors. Perhaps the two names had slightly different connotations. For instance, perhaps the name "Volos" had vulgar associations that were eschewed in favor of the more dignified name 'Khors" under Vladimir's official pantheon.

Sventovit as a Hybrid Last-Sheaf Deity

The temple of Arkona was secluded on the island of Rugen, just off the coast of northeastern Germany. At 926.4 km2 (357.7 sq mi) it is the largest island in modern day Germany. For comparison, this makes it only slightly larger than the Isle of Mull in Scotland (second largest of the Hebrides).

The early inhabitants of the region occupied by the Wends were probably Germanic peoples. Rugen seems to have been no exception, with the "Slavic" tribal identity emerging relatively "late." The entire Polabian Slavic region is best understood as the result of the Sukow-Dziedice culture, which expanded in the 6th century, presumably absorbing many Germanic groups left over from the migration period.[53]

Medieval sources portray the Slavic tribe on Rugen, the Rani, as an influential and warlike people. The other Slavic tribes apparently held the temple on Rugen in high regard, and in the 12th century CE after the destruction of Radogosc a century earlier, the temple of Arkona off the coast of Rugen largely assumed its place as the chief pagan temple. In the 11th century, the chronicler Thietmar wrote that Radogosc held primacy among the pagan temples. By the 12th century, following the destruction of the temple of Radogosc, Helmold writes of the Rani "They are a cruel people living at the heart of the sea. They are above all devoted to idolatry; they are superior to other Slavonic peoples. They have a King and a very famous temple. Because of the special service in the temple they are most respected."[54]

The Rani were adversaries of the Danes for centuries, and in many ways, they seem to have functioned almost as Slavic "Vikings" who periodically raided the Danish coast.

Scholars seem to agree that the island of Rugen became the last major center of Slavic paganism after the destruction of the temple of Radogosc. Partly for this reason, the rites of Rugen may offer the most detailed description of medieval Slavic paganism.

The statue of Sventovit at Arkona had four faces. Saxo writes that he had two faces facing forward and two backward. He had a sacred horse, much like the one at Radogosc. He also had a sword and a drinking horn. One ritual that took place was the ceremonial divination by drinking horn. The priest would take the horn of Sventovit's idol, and foretell the bounty of the coming year based on how full it was.[55]

A very similar ritual is described by William of Malmesbury, regarding the pagan Wends;[56]

> *But the Vindelici (Wends) worship Fortune, and putting her idol in the most eminent situation, they place a horn in her right hand, filled with the beverage, made of honey and water, which by a Greek term we call 'hydromel'. St. Jerome proves, in his eighteenth book on Isaiah, that the Egyptians and almost all the eastern nations do the same. Wherefore on the last day of November, sitting round in a circle, they all taste it; and if they find the horn full, they applaud with loud clamours: because in the ensuing year, plenty with her brimming horn will fulfill their wishes in everything: but if it be otherwise, they lament.*

It's not clear whether or not there might have been a Goddess with similar functions to Sventovit. Just as the last sheaf in harvest rituals can be called an "Old Man" or an "Old Woman" it's possible that a Mokosh-like Goddess could be referenced here. The classical reference to "Fortuna" aside, this is still a solid independent corroboration of the ritual described at the temple of Sventovit in Arkona. It also places the ritual in late November, which is more specific than the designation used by Saxo "after harvest."

Another telling ritual performed at Arkona was the cake ritual. The priest stood behind a large cake and asked "Can you see me?" When the people said that they could not, he replied "May you not see me next year either." In other words, may the cake be just as large next year.[57] This has parallels to the various European harvest traditions already discussed. This also resembles the practice of making the last sheaf large and heavy to ensure a large and heavy crop.[58]

There is also an especially strong parallel to the Russian autumnal veneration of the dead ancestors (Dedy / Dziady). After serving a ceremonial meal and inviting the dead to dine with them, the man of the house would hide behind a pile of cakes and perform the exact same ritual, asking "Can you see me?" The date of this ritual coincided with the day of St. Demetrios.[59]

The feast of St. Demetrios could look a lot like All Saint's Day in Russian Orthodox tradition. It often coincided with rites to honor the dead, and it was on October 26th. For those of us who use the Gregorian calendar, that would be equivalent to our November 8th. Therefore, the connection of these November rituals with harvest and the cult of ancestors is probably quite old. Recall that the Lithuanian holiday of Velines occurred at approximately the same time of year.[60]

However, this far west, we must also look to Germanic parallels. And this yields some interesting connections as well. In parts of Germany, it was customary to leave a patch of grain in the corner of the field unharvested for "Woden's horse."[61] As we have seen, this type of tradition suggests a connection to the Indo-European Lord of the Dead. And it seems doubtful that such correspondences would be lost on the migration period Slavic or Germanic tribes.

This obviously provides a link to the last sheaf tradition in Russia, the so-called "Beard of Volos." This appearance of a connection between Volos and Woden is no coincidence. There was also a folkloric Russian spirit known as the "Volosen", who would punish those who spun thread on New Year's Eve.[62] This is very reminiscent of the taboos on spinning overseen by the "Mokusha" elsewhere in Northern Russia, or by Frau Holle in Germany. However, in Germany, Woden's horse was also believed to trample a distaff that had flax left on it during the twelve nights of Christmas.[63] What does this mean?

It means that the connection between Volos, Woden, and the last sheaf is not just a coincidental similarity. It is evidently part of a larger web of relationships, which also includes Goddesses of spinning like Holle and Mokosh. It's possible that the Slavic "Fortuna" with her horn, mentioned by William of Malmesbury, represents a similar connection between Sventovit and a counterpart Goddess (Mokosh?)

One final piece of evidence for a connection between Sventovit and the cult of ancestors is the horse. According to Saxo, the Rani believed that Sventovit rode the horse at night against his enemies. This stresses how clearly Sventovit is not a Sun God, at least in the traditional sense of being a lord of light and warmth only. Rosik's excellent book on the Slavic religion according to German chronicles makes a rare slip in trying to portray Sventovit as a solar deity.[64] The Liutician deity Svarozic may have been. But the source material is quite clear that Sventovit of Rugen was a nocturnal rider. Additionally, Saxo says that the proof of his riding was seen in the fact that the horse was found steaming with sweat in the morning, as though freshly ridden.[65]

In German folklore, there was a class of spirit who was believed to ride horses at night until they were found covered in sweat the next morning. These spirits were generally feminine and were called "Maras" or nightmare hags.[66] In some scholarship of the 19th century, these fearsome nocturnal riders were connected with Woden and the einherjar.[67] Some of the scholarship from this period deserves scrutiny. Still, at a minimum, the connection between Sventovit and the Germanic Mara seems to confirm his chthonic attributes. The Germanic "Mara" is a distant cognate of Irish "Morrigan" meaning "Phantom Queen."[68]

There are some specific reasons to believe Sventovit's cult - and the religion of the Polabian Slavs more generally - had Germanic influences. The cult of Sventovit involved divination using the sacred white horse of his temple. This demonstrates some surprising continuity with Iron Age Germanic traditions; According to Tacitus, the Iron Age Germans practiced divination with white horses.[69] In fact, it looks like there was an unbroken tradition of horse divination in northeast Germany from the era of Tacitus up to the fall of Rugen in 1168. All the more reason to view Sventovit as a syncretic deity, not entirely Slavic or Germanic.

It's also an open question whether "Khors" may have been a synonym for the same type of Slavic deity (as discussed in the previous section). If so, then syncretism between a Proto-Slavic "Khors" and Woden would be likely, if they were at all related, because a few major epithets of Odin could have produced a homophone. These include a few of Odin's names, including Har and Herjan.[70]

Indeed, this coincidental homophone may have played a significant role in the development of the deity, and it may be one reason why the Varangian influenced elites of Prince Vladimir preferred to have an idol to "Khors" over "Volos" in their pantheon. This is unlikely to be the origin of the deity's name, however. The one proposed by Borisoff (linking it with the Old Prussian Curcho) is probably more convincing. It also happens to indicate very similar associations with harvest, and with the latter half of the year.

The one line of argument against this interpretation of Sventovit as a chthonic deity is potentially the Zbruch idol, which has been likened to Sventovit. Indeed, the parallels are significant. They include four faces, and a drinking horn. Still, we are talking about an idol from western Ukraine - far from Rugen, which is now part of Germany. The distance has led many scholars like Stanislaw Rosik to stress caution in explicitly equating the two. However, it is worth noting that the Zbruch idol shows a four faced God in heaven, above a middle panel showing humans, and an even lower panel depicting the underworld.

Still, the distance between the Zbruch river and Rugen is significant enough to warrant caution. The links may be real - but even so, they could be incredibly nuanced. Furthermore, as I have stressed, the Otherworld was not a physical "place" in ancient European cosmology. And indeed, it's not clear that the abode of Volos was ever thought of as being underground. There is stronger evidence of it being envisioned as a pasture or island. Finally, syncretism with Wodan could account for much of this nuance.

The Zbruch idol does not lend itself only to one line of argument, however. It also can be connected with the sphere of the afterlife. Many scholars have noted that it resembles the stelae of the Pontic steppe nomads (Scythian and Turkic peoples). In fact, some go so far as to attribute it to nomad invaders rather than Slavs. This seems like an extreme position. But the influence of the steppe is evident in the Zbruch idol. The primary function of such stelae among steppe nomads was funerary.[71, 72, 73, 74]

Because we know that Woden was associated with the last sheaf tradition in Germany, we cannot rule out syncretism. Particularly among the Polabian Slavs, who lived in what is today Northeastern Germany. The Germanic influence on these groups was probably significant. Consequently, it may be best to treat Sventovit as a syncretic figure, not entirely identical to, or unrelated to the East Slavic Volos. On the other hand, the last sheaf tradition connecting Woden and Volos was probably a legitimate one going back to Proto-Indo-European commonalities. Therefore, one could argue that Sventovit was a uniquely Rugian but totally legitimate form of Volos.

Indo-European and Slavic Afterlife Beliefs

In the writings of Ibn Fadlan, there is a tantalizing reference to Slavic afterlife beliefs. One inhabitant of Rus told him Arabs were fools, because they put their loved ones into the ground for worms, whereas "we burn them in an instant, so that at once and without delay they enter Paradise."[75]

The people referred to as "Rus" by Ibn Fadlan were descended from a Varangian ruling elite who originated from Sweden. It's likely their culture was already quite syncretic. However, the strict stance on cremation is more characteristic of early Slavic practices than Viking age Scandinavian practices. Unlike the early Slavs, the Viking Period Scandinavians had fairly diverse burial practices.[76]

It seems likely that fire was connected to the cult of the dead in Balto-Slavic culture, in part because of its involvement in funerary practices. Recall that on Velines day, in Lithuania, offerings to the dead were made directly to the hearth fire.[77] In Ukraine, we have seen that the sheaf known as the Didukh was burned in the field in January. Also, in many Baltic and Slavic countries, rooster sacrifices to the fire in the grain drying barn were commonly held in November. The patron of the grain drying fire was often a hearth deity called Dimstapatis (literally "Master of the House") by the pagan Lithuanians.[78] His counterparts in Russia were the Ovinnik of the grain drying barn, and the house spirit known as the Domovoi, who was also called the "Master of the House" (Gospodar) in some East Slavic territories. Scholars are agreed that the Domovoi was connected with the cult of ancestors, and when Russians moved to a new residence, they believed that they needed to bring coals from the hearth with them so that their Domovoi could follow them.[79]

As we will see in later chapters, the cult of ancestors is inseparable from the cult of fire in Slavic tradition. (Reference Chapter 8: Svarozhichi - Sons of Svarog.) Another important concept revealed in this passage from Ibn Fadlan is the idea of "Paradise." This implies a view of the afterlife that was (in some cases at least) bright and cheerful, not gloomy or frightening.

The emphasis on cremation seen in the passage recorded by Ibn Fadlan illustrates that the Scandinavian-descended elites of Kievan Rus were already adopting some Slavic cultural attitudes. However, there is also evidence that the Slavs were influenced by Germanic peoples - including the Norse - in their funerary customs. An interesting example of this is the adoption of the obol - a coin used to pay the ferryman to cross over the river of Styx. We naturally think of this as a Greek custom, and so it was originally. But by the early Middle Ages, it was actually fairly widespread among various Germanic peoples, as well as former Roman provinces. For this reason, the East Slavs seem to have adopted the practice gradually due to Scandinavian influence. Initially it was limited to the far north - precisely in those regions were Norse travelers penetrated. Gradually, however, it became fairly widespread among the East Slavs. It was also adopted by the Moravians, around the modern-day Czechia, at an early date. Even among some Christian Russians and Ukrainians, we can still see that the concept of the obol has survived. In East Slavic folk tradition, the ferryman of the dead is often called "St. Nicholas" but the custom has persisted.[80] Interestingly, there is a widely circulated argument from the scholar, Upenskij, that St. Nicholas absorbed many of the traits of Volos. This is based on, among other things, the apparent identification of the Beard of Volos as "Nicholas' Beard" in some Russian folk traditions.[81]

While the adoption of the obol tradition could indeed coincide with Christianity, it seems that the introduction of this concept to the East Slavs and Moravians predates systematic Christianization. Therefore, it's plausible that this tells us something about Slavic paganism. Perhaps they did adopt some notion of a ferryman who guides souls across the water to the afterlife. Perhaps this view resonated with the early Slavs because they already had similar notions about the afterlife. Perhaps by adopting the obol, and invoking the reassurance of a "ferryman" psychopomp, the Slavic aversion to inhumation (versus cremation) was partially reconciled.

At the beginning of this chapter, I mentioned the Carpathian traditions surrounding the mythical "Island of the Rachmani." This deserves some context. In Carpathian Galicia and Ukraine, it was commonly believed that the virtuous Rachmani lived on a paradisiacal island in the east, where the sun rises. It was believed that the people of the Carpathians were related to them, and that the Rachmani somehow had powers to preserve and sustain those living on earth. A widespread tradition held that Easter eggs (Pysanky) should be floated across the sea during Rachman Easter, so that the Rachmani could eat once a year. If this tradition ever died, it was thought that the world would end.[82]

This has a number of parallels, not just to mythical islands, but also the use of eggs as an offering. Recall that eggs were often left at graves by the Lithuanians around Easter, for the celebration of Veliu Veliken.[83] Another mythical island in Slavic tradition was the isle of Buyan, which seems to have been a very similar sort of blessed realm without death. According to folk tradition, the waters of life flow from the white rock Alatyr on the island of Buyan.[84]

In folktales, we know that this "water of life" has the power to restore the dead to life. We also hear that the personified Dawn "Zarya" resides on Buyan. This is consistent with its identification with the island of Rachman, which also lies in the East. Interestingly, one Russian charm to transform into a werewolf may give us an anthropomorphic glimpse at Volos, depicted as a wolf residing on the blessed isle:[85]

In the ocean, on the island of Buyan in the open plain,
Shines the moon upon an aspen stump,
Into the green wood, into the spreading vale.
Around the stump goes a shaggy wolf;
Under his teeth are all the horned cattle;
But into the wood the wolf goes not,
In the vale the wolf does not roam.
Moon, moon! golden horns!
Melt the bullet, blunt the knife, rot the cudgel,
Strike fear into man, beast, and reptile,
So that they may not seize the grey wolf,
Nor tear from him his warm hide.
My word is firm, firmer than sleep, or the strength of heroes.

A blessed island is fairly widespread in various Indo-European myths. The Greeks, of course, knew of the Elysian Island. The Irish talked of a western island without death, known as Tir An Og, or Magh Mell. It seems the Slavs also conceived of the otherworld in this manner.

Yet we should avoid simplistic generalizations about the otherworld or land of the dead in ancient cosmology. Modern day Hinduism identifies Yama as the God of the Southern direction. In many parts of the world, he essentially functions as an underworld deity. Yet one ancient passage of the Vedas claims that Yama dwells in heaven.[86] And there are similar dilemmas with the Celtic Otherworld, which can be stumbled upon in a cave as well as across the sea.

A connection between Volos and the wilderness is evident from the folkloric survival of his name under the form "Volosatik" which denoted a kind of goblin, generally a wood goblin.[87] This appears to connect Volos with the Leshi - the Master of the Forest in Russian folklore. This may seem odd based on the chthonic and agricultural associations that have been reviewed so far. However, there is some striking parallelism with Mokosh, who also seems to have been associated with the last sheaf, and with the wild spirits of nature. (See Chapter 2: Baba Yaga and Mokosh The Great Mother.) According to some north Russian harvest traditions, the "Old Woman" of the corn field did indeed flee back into the forest after harvest.[88]

More commonly, however, it was the Rusalki or water nymphs who fertilized the grain field. Indeed, the name "Mókuš" survived as a synonym for a water nymph. This provides a striking parallel for the survival of the term "Volosatik" for forest spirit. The connection between Mokosh and Volos seems quite strong, and they seem to have shared many of the same fundamental roles. We have already spoken about the spirit "Volosen" and his association with New Year's eve spinning taboos. We discussed a very similar association with Mokosh in Chapter 2: Baba Yaga and Mokosh The Great Mother. The connection between the spirits of nature and the spirits of the dead was well known in early Slavic culture, which is evident in the use of the term "Mavka" or "Niavki" (Undead) to denote a water nymph or forest nymph in some Slavic folk traditions (See Chapter 9: Death and the Soul in Slavic Paganism). In all likelihood, the association of Mokosh and Volos with nature spirits is a part of the same "chthonic" portfolio that we would expect for any Slavic deity associated with the dead or the cult of ancestors.

In Russian folk belief, the Rusalki were believed to transfer fertility from the waters to the grain field when they walked on land during the Summer.[89] Perhaps we can infer a similar connection between the "Volosatik" of the forest and the "Old Man" of the grain field. It's almost as if the Slavs believed that spirits of the wilderness needed to transfer fertility to the "domesticated" field of the farmer. Still more bizarre, the nature spirits who brought life to the soil were often conceived of as spirits of the dead themselves. It's as though the forests and streams were gateways, or portals through which fertility could flow into our world from the otherworld. We will see a fascinating illustration of this concept in the Sample Tale at the end of this chapter, titled "The Youthful Hermit of the Isle of Rachmans."

The blending of agricultural and forest attributes may be a uniquely Slavic concept, even though the core elements of Volos can be traced back to Proto-Indo-European mythology. It should be noted that most cultures would divide agriculture and the forest into separate domains. Perhaps the Proto-Slavs saw a connection between the two because they came from the border of the forest-steppe zone, in modern day western Ukraine. The "true" steppe zone was an arid grassland dominated by nomadic pastoralists. However, the cooler and less arid lands directly north of these nomads were a mixture of forest and steppe. The wetter climate that facilitated the growth of trees also made this land less ideal for nomadic pastoralism, and more conducive towards agriculture. It may be that the cult of Volos emerged from this region. This would explain the uniquely Slavic attempt at merging the two domains- one "wild" and one cultivated by man. We will further discuss the role of ecology around the forest-steppe borderland in Chapter 8.

Unchaining Volos and the Dragon

In Chapter 3, we talked about a world-ending serpent chained up until doomsday. It seems highly unlikely that Volos, Lord of the Blessed Isle was consistently identified with this entity. Perhaps he could be associated with serpents as a chthonic deity, but he was not a true adversary of the Gods.

An adversarial relationship with Perun is plausible, but probably not of the cosmic significance portrayed by Ivanov and Toporov. In Lithuanian mythology, Perkunas does sometimes strike the household serpent known as the Aitvaras with lightning.[90] This figure could be connected with the last sheaf (The beard of Volos) which is often associated with a wealth-stealing house dragon. Certainly, we see some dragon associations with the Ukrainian Sporys and Balto-Finnic Jumis.[91] However, it's not clear if these should be considered manifestations of Volos himself, or rather one of his minions. Neither should we assume that the Aitvaras is simply a typical domestic ancestor spirit. As Greimas notes, the Aitvaras often appears as an "Anti-Kaukas" (Anti-House Spirit) who steals prosperity (skalsa) from the household, and who provides false "returning" coins. Indeed, Greimas notes that unlike with a typical house spirit, people are often eager to get rid of an Aitvaras.[92]

Here we see the hazards of simply equating all "dragons" or "serpents" with each other in Indo-European mythology. In Lithuanian mythology, house spirits bring prosperity (skalsa) and can indeed take the form of a serpent. But the Aitvaras can also represent a skalsa-stealing serpent - essentially the mirror image of a house spirit. In the context of Indo-European mythology, however, the adversary of the thunder God is without exception a resource-stealing serpent. To identify the last sheaf (Jumis / Didukh) entirely with the Aitvaras is somewhat nonsensical from a practical standpoint. According to Lithuanian folklore, the Aitvaras tends to attract lighting from Perkunas, and may consequently set the house on fire. It's not clear why the last sheaf would be carried inside if it was expected to set the house on fire.

It should be stressed that the household snake of the ancient Greek domestic cult was never conflated with Typhon, the cosmic adversary of Zeus. Neither was Hades, the Greek deity of the underworld, ever conflated with Typhon. Though Hades could indeed take the form of a snake in some traditions, not all snakes were identical in Greek mythology. Greek culture had an abundance of serpents; Hades could be associated with the serpent.[93] The Genius of the household could also be a serpent in Greek tradition.[94]

Typhon was a serpentine monster. These figures were not interchangeable in Greek mythology. We should not assume that all serpentine imagery in Slavic mythology constituted a single mythological figure either.

On the one hand, folklore could easily blur these ancient divisions, and lead to consolidation of all chthonic entities under the identity of the "Devil." Since "Velnias" means devil in modern-day Lithuanian, it seems likely that all chthonic figures from Lithuanian mythology were intermingled under this name. However, this should not be taken as evidence for a single cohesive mythological figure.

In Balto-Slavic lore, it's clear that the God of the dead (Volos, Velinas, or Jumis) is closely associated with these household serpents. However, even this probably doesn't rise to the level of identification. For one thing, the house spirit is a local spirit, distinct from the Lord of the Dead - but probably subservient to him. In Baltic mythology, we can see that a chthonic deity like "Puskaitis" could be petitioned in order to receive a house spirit from him.[95] The term Puskaitis means "He of the Elder Bush" and is probably an archaic Balto-Slavic term for a chthonic deity. A similar term of the same meaning - Buznyshni - shows up in Ukrainian as a synonym for "Devil."[96] Secondly, it can be argued that the "Aitvaras" pursued by Perkunas in Baltic mythology is not a house spirit proper, but rather an "Anti-House Spirit" as noted by Greimas. This interpretation is more in line with other Indo-European mythologies.

While the equating of Volos with the dragon adversary of Perun has become popular, it was never universally accepted among scholars. B.A. Rybakov objected strongly to the identification of Volos with the dragon and believed there were issues with seeing them as adversaries.[97] This position by Rybakov is rarely talked about in the same breath as Toporov, despite the fact that he was an equally prominent and dedicated scholar of Slavic mythology.

In Chapter 3, I discussed the dragon as an apocalyptic monster who was prophesied to bring about the end of the world. It seems likely that there was such a doomsday dragon in Slavic mythology - a Russian charm preserves a memory of a fiery serpent chained up in a house of bronze at the bottom of the sea.[98]

This is strikingly similar to the Aitvaras, which is also a kind of fiery serpent. The main difference being that this serpent is clearly of cosmological significance, probably relating to the prophesied doomsday monster. Volos probably would not have been this doomsday figure in most Slavic mythological systems. While they may have been related, it's clear that most Indo-European mythologies divided these roles at an early date.

Even Norse mythology seems to have taken pains to separate the world-ending trickster Loki from the "proper" deities. In the case of Loki, he is clearly related to the Balto-Finnic Jumis just as Odin is. In one Finnish narrative, the trickster "Lukka" or "Luho" steals the sun and brings it to his cavern so that his two farmhands (both called Jumi) can see.[99] "Louhi" is normally understood to be the Finnish Goddess of the underworld. Undoubtedly, this figure "Luho" is a relative of Louhi. That's clear from the name, and also from the theft of the sun. One passage of the Kalevala refers to Louhi as "Wicked Louhi, Toothless witch of Sariola, Stealer of the silver sunshine."[100] However, the appearance of a male "Lukka" or "Luho" in Finnish lore invites comparisons to Loki - who was imprisoned in the underworld until Ragnarok. On the other hand, Loki had no cult in Norse society. To the extent that the "deity" functions of Jumis existed, they seem to have been off-loaded to a second figure who was distinct from Louhi / Loki. For the Germanic peoples, this figure was "Odin."

It's worth noting that these malevolent associations with Jumis seem to be more characteristic of Finnish folklore than Baltic folklore. It is in the Finnish and Estonian traditions that we see the greatest emphasis between Jumi and disease, and the least on agriculture. By contrast, it is in the Baltic country of Latvia that the associations with agriculture come to the fore.[101] This tendency can be explained as contamination with the "Wicked Louhi" of Finnish mythology, who was far more denigrated than most Indo-European underworld deities. Such contamination would likely be greatest among Finnic language speakers, and less intense among Baltic peoples. Presumably, the early Slavs would have been even less impacted by Finnic influences than the Balts.

The Norse "Loki" may also reflect an attempt to process the characteristic disdain for the underworld that permeated Finnish mythology. However, the Slavic Volos may not have received such heavy Finnic influence, which may have translated into less villainization of the underworld deity than in the Baltic region.

As mentioned at the beginning of this chapter, the dragon who battles a storm God is hardly ever deified or worshipped in Indo-European culture. It is curious that Ivanov and Toporov have drawn upon such a prevalent Indo-European myth while interpreting it in a way that is contradictory to most of these mythologies. In the case of the Vedic Yama, there is no doubt whatsoever that he is distinct from Vritra - the dragon slain by Indra's thunderbolt. The two figures are totally separate from one another. Yama had a cult. The dragon Vritra presumably did not.

In Chapter 3: Perun and the Drakenkampf, I discussed the possibility of a malevolent "Erlik" figure borrowed from Altaic mythology. It is indeed possible that syncretism with Erlik could produce a villainized "Volos" similar to that implied by Ivanov and Toporov's reconstruction. However, this syncretism with Altaic mythology is unlikely to have been implemented uniformly or consistently among the Slavic tribes. Furthermore, even some Altaic peoples divided the Indo-Iranian ancestor figure Yima (cognate to Vedic Yama) from the malevolent Erlik. In Altaian mythology, the ancestor hero Shal-Jime is the counterpart of the Iranian Yima, and he is given a more prestigious position than Erlik.[102]

Furthermore, Volos may indeed have been a deity of the First Function in Dumezil's tripartite model of early Proto-Indo-European society. He may well have been related to a priestly, legalistic, and / or magical social class, such as the one posited by Dumezil. Such a class is attested in Kievan Rus in the form of pagan priests called "Volkhvy." The etymology of "Volkhv" is unknown, but a connection to Volos has been suggested.[103]

As the narrative at the end of Chapter 3 shows (see Ivan the Cow's Son) the mythical representatives of these three functions could come into a sort of "internal" conflict for divine sovereignty. However, "Ivan the Cow's Son" also clearly demonstrates that the classical Indo-European dragon-slaying episode could be external to (and separate from) the conflict between the three functions.

Sample Tale: The Youthful Hermit of the Isle of Rachmans[104]

Such, for instance, is one story of the trees which has been handed down for many ages. There was in the land of the Rachmans a great old cembra-pine. Its name is secret. Its name has been passed down from its arboreal foremother. While it was still in the youth of its years it asked the Rachman fathers to give it this name, that it might be written down for remembrance, in the monasteries and on the cliffs. So it related to the Rachman elders at Eastertide. So it whispered; "My fathers and this Rachman earth have poured juices into me, the juices of salvation. These juices gave me knowledge of that which my ancient fathers knew, and also what has been passed down from the Rachman fathers in the wilderness; what the tree souls and the Rachman souls have whispered to each other.

"This knowledge was entrusted only to one tree, though a certain being, through a youthful hermit who had entered into an everlasting betrothal with this tree; and so the trees cannot yet rustle together with this knowledge. They do not proclaim it in chorus. I alone preserve it in my resinous blood; it grows in my veins, in my pitch; it extends, it grows strong, and from me it passes into the souls of the Rachmans.

That hermit was a child of God's youth, of the line of stars, of the heavenly luminaries. He descended from the starry worlds by the steps. Like a mountain spring he revived the world. He reconciled with the world, he soaked himself in the sap of the tree, with its branches he extended thousands of arms to the world, he sent his gaze through the needles and the leaves of the trees. With thousands of green eyes, he looked out on the world, where the sources of youth were hidden. With his gaze he opened them, with his nod he concentrated them. He poured youth all through the world in waterfalls. The stars welcomed him, welcomed him as their own. The heavenly choirs exulted in him from the starry cathedrals and altars.

Thus he came to the greatest of happiness, and then, to his eyes, the green leaves mournful pictures floated, from the most distant of worlds, where they do harm to one another and live in despair, where they are tormented and wandering in darkness. Weeping choruses rang to him with their groans. Once more in spirit the seer floated out from the tree, and thought, "This holiness is not complete, it is not like that of the stars, so long as creatures akin to us are buried in those great darknesses, in that chaos of groans. There is no greater salvation, no greater happiness, than to flame and shine in the darkness."

"Of all the trees who have become my friends and brothers - the trees of mystery, the trees of wisdom, the trees of fondness - one will be famed most of all: the tree of my cross." And a cembra-pine began to murmur to him - a pine as lofty as the brow of God, an ancient mother-pine, whose name is secret: "I guess thy desire. I will float with thee across the sea, teacher. Take me as the mast of the vessel. Adopt me as thy tree of living, thy tree of dying. The same irons shall pierce my body and thine. Thy blood will mingle with my resin."

"Then the cembra-pine asked the fathers, the oldest of the Rachmans, to cut her down, to send her by the great river, and by the lakes, down to the sea. The young hermit floated with her. The Uplands said farewell to them. They were tumultuous with their blessing. On the shore of the sea was a ship; it had a lofty mast. As a mast like a cross the pine rose above the waves, as once it had risen above the slope of the upland. It listened to the farewell of the bells, it looked out to the waves. And they sailed by the sun over the great seas, towards Jerusalem, towards Mount Zion. And as they floated, the hermit said to the mast: "Sister of secret name, from thee nothing in this world is a secret!"

That is the story told in the Rachman land about the youthful hermit, the unique seer. And so the Rachman hermits pay heed to the stories told by the trees. And they hear the groans from the distant abysses, and wait for the suffering souls to invite them to their festivals, to their sacrificial festivals. But when they know everything from the root to the little leaves rustling highest in the sun, when they have heard the ancient things from before the centuries, that which passes in whispers down the generations of the trees, these old men disappear, they depart. No one knows where. No one has come upon their traces. But has anyone sought them? Perhaps in that land they know something, only they do not talk of it: that having overheard the rustle of the sacred cembra-pine - her name is secret - these old men follow in her tracks; that they themselves sail to other lands in order to renounce happiness, to win new happiness, to be born anew, to become related to many other families, to pour the Rachman wine into their blood.

Until the tree shall give birth to great and numerous stars, until it shall rustle over all the world; it will sing, and it will whisper, and it will gaze down at the world in the great firmament. That is what the ancient past has handed down, brother, and so the future will show. Such are the sacred festivals, and such are ours, of today.

Endnotes

1. Warner, Elizabeth. Russian Myths. Austin: Published in co-operation with the British Museum Press [by the] University of Texas Press, 2002. Page 20

2. Myth in Indo-European Antiquity. S.l.: UNIV OF CALIFORNIA PRESS, 2021. Page 90
3. Hrusevsky, Mychajlo S, and Andrzej Poppe. History of Ukraine-Rus': 1. Edmonton: Canadian Inst. of Ukrainian Studies Press, 1997. Page 194
4. Myth in Indo-European Antiquity. S.l.: UNIV OF CALIFORNIA PRESS, 2021. Page 89
5. Jakobson, Roman, Linda R. Waugh, and Stephen Rudy. Contributions to Comparative Mythology: Studies in Linguistics and Philology, 1972-1982. Berlin: De Gruyter Mouton, 2010. Internet resource. Page 36
6. Vincenz, Stanislaw, Zdzisław Czermanski, and H C. Stevens. On the High Uplands: Sagas, Songs, Tales and Legends of the Carpathians, 1955. Pages 336-339
7. Ivanits, Linda J. Russian Folk Belief. M E Sharpe Incorporated, 1989. Internet resource. Page 12
8. Mallory, J P. In Search of the Indo-Europeans: Language, Archaeology, and Myth. New York, N.Y: Thames and Hudson, 2003. Pages 130-132
9. Russian Fairy Tales. New York: Pantheon, 1973. Pages 234-249
10. Winn, Shan M. M. Heaven, Heroes, and Happiness: The Indo-European Roots of Western Ideology. Lanham, Md: University Press of America, 1995. Pages 96-98
11. Michael Shapiro, Neglected evidence of Dioscurism (Divine Twinning) in the Old Slavic pantheon" Journal of Indo - European Studies 10(1-2), 1982:137-166
12. Winn, Shan M. M. Heaven, Heroes, and Happiness: The Indo-European Roots of Western Ideology. Lanham, Md: University Press of America, 1995. Page 72
13. Russian Fairy Tales. New York: Pantheon, 1973. Pages 234-249
14. Tautosakos Darbai. Vilnius: Lietuviu Literaturos ir Tautosakos Institutas, 2007. Page 56
15. Frog, Anna-Leena Siikala, and Eila Stepanova. Mythic Discourses: Studies in Uralic Traditions. Helsinki: Finnish Literature Society, 2013. Page 135

16. Myth in Indo-European Antiquity. S.l.: UNIV OF CALIFORNIA PRESS, 2021. Pages 87-92
17. Trinkunas, Jonas. Of Gods & Holidays: The Baltic Heritage. Vilnius: Tverme, 1999. Page 119
18. Trinkunas, Jonas. Of Gods & Holidays: The Baltic Heritage. Vilnius: Tverme, 1999. Pages 128-129
19. Johns, Andreas. Baba Yaga: The Ambiguous Mother and Witch of the Russian Folktale. New York [etc.: Peter Lang, 2010. Page 57
20. Frazer, James G. The Golden Bough: A Study in Magic and Religion. London: Macmillan, 1922. Internet resource. Pages 402-403
21. MacDermott, Mercia. Bulgarian Folk Customs. Philadelphia: Jessica Kingsley, 2010. Page 247
22. Michael Shapiro, Neglected evidence of Dioscurism (Divine Twinning) in the Old Slavic pantheon" Journal of Indo - European Studies 10(1-2), 1982:137-166
23. Johns, Andreas. Baba Yaga: The Ambiguous Mother and Witch of the Russian Folktale. New York [etc.: Peter Lang, 2010. Page 57
24. Christmas in Ukraine. Chicago, IL: World Book, 1998. Page 34
25. Katchanovski, Historical Dictionary of Ukraine. Lanham, MD: Scarecrow Press, 2013. Page 181
26. Knab, Sophie H. Polish Customs, Traditions and Folklore. New York: Hippocrene Books, 2017. Page 33
27. Kingshill, Sophia, and Jennifer B. Westwood. The Lore of Scotland: A Guide to Scottish Legends, 2012. Page 353
28. Wall, Richard. Medieval and Modern Ireland. Gerrards Cross: Colin Smythe, 1988. Page 64
29. Trinkunas, Jonas. Of Gods & Holidays: The Baltic Heritage. Vilnius: Tverme, 1999. Page 128-129
30. Ellis, Peter B. The Ancient World of the Celts. New York: Barnes & Noble, 1999. Internet resource. Page 181
31. MacDermott, Mercia. Bulgarian Folk Customs. Philadelphia: Jessica Kingsley, 2010. Page 247
32. Oinas, Felix J. "Jumi: A Fertility Divinity." Journal of the Folklore Institute, vol. 18, no. 1, Indiana University Press, 1981, Page 84

33. Eliade, Mircea. The Encyclopedia of Religion: Volume 2: Auth to Butl. New York: Macmillan, 1987. Page 55
34. Oinas, Felix J. "Jumi: A Fertility Divinity." Journal of the Folklore Institute, vol. 18, no. 1, Indiana University Press, 1981, Page 84
35. Gamkrelidze, Thomas V, Vjaceslav V. Ivanov, Roman Jakobson, and Nichols Johanna. Indo-European and the Indo-Europeans: A Reconstruction and Historical Analysis of a Proto-Language and Proto-Culture. Part I: the Text. Part Ii: Bibliography, Indexes. 2010. Internet resource. Page 680
36. Coulter, Charles R, and Patricia Turner. Encyclopedia of Ancient Deities. Jefferson, N.C: McFarland, 2012. Page 512
37. West, Morris. Indo-European Poetry and Myth. Oxford: Oxford University Press, 2007. Page 393
38. Oinas, Felix J. "Jumi: A Fertility Divinity. Journal of the Folklore Institute, vol. 18, no. 1, Indiana University Press, 1981, Page 71
39. Jones, Lindsay. Encyclopedia of Religion: Volume 14. Detroit: Macmillan Reference USA, 2005. Page 9420
40. Oinas, Felix J. "Jumi: A Fertility Divinity." Journal of the Folklore Institute, vol. 18, no. 1, Indiana University Press, 1981, Page 74
41. Oinas, Felix J. "Jumi: A Fertility Divinity." Journal of the Folklore Institute, vol. 18, no. 1, Indiana University Press, 1981, Page 80
42. Blazek, Vaclav. (2005). Indo-Iranian elements in Fenno-Ugric mythological lexicon. Indogermanische Forschungen. 110. Pages 163-164.
43. Konakov, N D, Vladimir Napolskikh, Anna-Leena Siikala, and Mihaly Hoppal. Komi Mythology. Budapest: Akademiai, 2003. Pages 141, 351-352, 373
44. Oinas, Felix J. "Jumi: A Fertility Divinity." Journal of the Folklore Institute, vol. 18, no. 1, Indiana University Press, 1981, Pages 69-70
45. Русский традиционный календарь: на каждый день и для каждого дома /Некрылова, А. РИПОЛ классик, 2017. Page 554
46. Warner, Elizabeth. Russian Myths. London: The British Museum Press, 2002. Page 15

47. Borissoff, Constantine L. "Non-Iranian Origin of the Eastern-Slavonic God Xursu/xors." Studia Mythologica Slavica. 17 (2014): 9-36.
48. Greimas, Algirdas J. Of Gods and Men: Studies in Lithuanian Mythology. Bloomington: Indiana University Press, 1992. Page 187
49. Frazer, James G. The Golden Bough: A Study in Magic and Religion. London: Macmillan, 1922. Internet resource. Page 116
50. Muir, Alister D. Flax: The Genus Linum. London: Routledge, 2003. Page 264
51. Филологические науки. Вопросы теории и практики Philology. Theory & Practice 2021. Том 14. Выпуск 5. С. 1524-1528 | 2021. Volume 14. Issue 5. P. 1524-1528
52. Gray, Louis H. The Mythology of All Races: In Thirteen Volumes. New York: Cooper, 1964. Page 248
53. Barford, P M. The Early Slavs: Culture and Society in Early Medieval Eastern Europe. London: British Museum, 2001. Pages 63-66.
54. Słupecki, Leszek P. Slavonic Pagan Sanctuaries. Warsaw: Institute of Archaeology and Ethnology, Polish Academy of Sciences, 1994. Page 24
55. Słupecki, Leszek P. Slavonic Pagan Sanctuaries. Warsaw: Institute of Archaeology and Ethnology, Polish Academy of Sciences, 1994. Page 28
56. Słupecki, Leszek P, Roman Zaroff, and Andrej Pleterski. "William of Malmesbury on Pagan Slavic Oracles: New Sources for Slavic Paganism and Its Two Interpretations." Studia Mythologica Slavica. (1999): 9-20.
57. Słupecki, Leszek P. Slavonic Pagan Sanctuaries. Warsaw: Institute of Archaeology and Ethnology, Polish Academy of Sciences, 1994. Pages 28-29
58. Frazer, James G. The Golden Bough: A Study in Magic and Religion. London: Macmillan, 1922. Internet resource. Pages 402-403

59. MacCulloch, John A, Jan Máchal, and Louis H. Gray. The Mythology of All Races: In Thirteen Volumes. New York: Cooper Square Publ, 1964. Page 282
60. Trinkunas, Jonas. Of Gods & Holidays: The Baltic Heritage. Vilnius: Tverme, 1999. Pages 128-129
61. Northern Mythology, Comprising the Principal Popular Traditions and Superstitions of Scandinavia, Northern Germany, and the Netherlands. London, 1851. Page 164
62. Michael Shapiro, Neglected evidence of Dioscurism (Divine Twinning) in the Old Slavic pantheon" Journal of Indo - European Studies 10(1-2), 1982:137-166
63. Northern Mythology, Comprising the Principal Popular Traditions and Superstitions of Scandinavia, Northern Germany, and the Netherlands. London, 1851. Page 164
64. Rosik, Stanislaw, and Anna Tyszkiewicz. The Slavic Religion in the Light of 11th and 12th-Century German Chronicles (Thietmar of Merseburg, Adam of Bremen, Helmold of Bosau): Studies on the Christian Interpretation of Pre-Christian Cults and Beliefs in the Middle Ages. 2020. Page 123
65. Jensen, Kurt Villads. Crusading at the Edges of Europe: Denmark and Portugal C.1000 C.1250. S.l.: ROUTLEDGE, 2019. Page 173
66. Raudvere, Catharina. Narratives and Rituals of the Nightmare Hag in Scandinavian Folk Belief. 2020. Internet resource. Page 65
67. The Nineteenth Century: A Monthly Review. London: Sampson Low, Marston & Co, 1879. Vol.5, Page 1109
68. Transactions of the Yorkshire Dialect Society. Bradford: Byles, 1902. Page 19
69. Rosik, Stanislaw, and Anna Tyszkiewicz. The Slavic Religion in the Light of 11th and 12th-Century German Chronicles; Thietmar of Merseburg, Adam of Bremen, Helmold of Bosau): Studies on the Christian Interpretation of Pre-Christian Cults and Beliefs in the Middle Ages. 2020. Page 130
70. Snorri, Sturluson, and Rasmus B. Anderson. The Younger Edda, Also Called, Snorre's Edda, or the Prose Edda: An English

Version of the Foreword, the Fooling of Gylfe, the Afterword, Brage's Talk, the Afterword to Brage's Talk, and the Important Passages in the Poetical Diction (skaldskaparmal). Chicago: Scott, Foresman, 1901.

71. Leach, Stephen D. A Russian Perspective on Theoretical Archaeology: The Life and Work of Leo S. Klejn. London: Routledge, 2016. Internet resource.
72. Rosik, Stanislaw, and Anna Tyszkiewicz. The Slavic Religion in the Light of 11th and 12th-Century German Chronicles (Thietmar of Merseburg, Adam of Bremen, Helmold of Bosau): Studies on the Christian Interpretation of Pre-Christian Cults and Beliefs in the Middle Ages. 2020. Page 365
73. Telegin, Dmitriy Y, and James P. Mallory. The Anthropomorphic Stelae of the Ukraine: The Early Iconography of the Indo-Europeans. Washington: Institute for the study of man, 1994.
74. Cunliffe, Barry W. The Scythians: Nomad Warriors of the Steppe. 2021. Internet resource. Page 309
75. Classen, Albrecht. Rural Space in the Middle Ages and Early Modern Age: The Spatial Turn in Premodern Studies 2012. Internet resource. Page 183
76. Barford, P M. The Early Slavs: Culture and Society in Early Medieval Eastern Europe. London: British Museum, 2001. Page 201) (DuBois, Thomas A. Nordic Religions in Teh Viking Age. Philadelphia: University of Pennsylvania Press, 1999. Pages 70-71
77. Trinkunas, Jonas. Of Gods & Holidays: The Baltic Heritage. Vilnius: Tverme, 1999. Page 128-129
78. West, Morris. Indo-European Poetry and Myth. Oxford: Oxford University Press, 2007. Page 270
79. Ivanits, Linda J. Materials for the Study of Russian Folklore. University Park, Pa.: Pennsylvania State University, 1978. Internet resource. Page 18
80. Łukasz Miechowicz, Coins in the Western and Eastern Slavs burial practices in the Middle Ages –relicts of pagan beliefs or a sign of Christian traditions? Rome, Constantinople and Newly-

Converted Europe. Archaeological and Historical Evidence. Kraków – Leipzig – Rzeszów – Warszawa 2012, Pages 613-624

81. Michael Shapiro, Neglected evidence of Dioscurism (Divine Twinning) in the Old Slavic pantheon" Journal of Indo - European Studies 10(1-2), 1982:151-152
82. Vincenz, Stanislaw, Zdzisław Czermanski, and H C. Stevens. On the High Uplands: Sagas, Songs, Tales and Legends of the Carpathians, 1955. Pages 336-339
83. Trinkunas, Jonas. Of Gods & Holidays: The Baltic Heritage. Vilnius: Tverme, 1999. Page 119
84. Phillips, Charles, and Michael Kerrigan. Forests of the Vampire: Slavic Myth. New York: Barnes & Noble Books, 2003. Page 89
85. Ralston, William R. S. The Songs of the Russian People: As Illustrative of Slavonic Mythology and Russian Social Life. London: Ellis & Green, 1872. Page 406
86. MacDonnell, A A. Vedic Mythology. Strassburg: Trubner, 1897. Page 171
87. Rzhevsky, Nicholas. The Cambridge Companion to Modern Russian Culture. Cambridge: Cambridge University Press, 2015. Page 181
88. Johns, Andreas. Baba Yaga: The Ambiguous Mother and Witch of the Russian Folktale. 2004. Page 57
89. Ivanits, Linda J. Russian Folk Belief. M E Sharpe Incorporated, 1989. Internet resource. Pages 77,81
90. Greimas, Algirdas J. Of Gods and Men: Studies in Lithuanian Mythology. Bloomington: Indiana University Press, 1992. Page 47
91. Oinas, Felix J. "Jumi: A Fertility Divinity." Journal of the Folklore Institute, vol. 18, no. 1, Indiana University Press, 1981, Pages 82, 84
92. Greimas, Algirdas J. Of Gods and Men: Studies in Lithuanian Mythology. Bloomington: Indiana University Press, 1992. Pages 43–50
93. Bell, Malcolm. Morgantina Studies, Volume I: The Terracottas. 2014. Internet resource. Pages 89-90, 106
94. Nilsson, Martin P. The Minoan-Mycenaean Religion and Its Survival in Greek Religion. Lund: Gleerup, 2013. Page 328

95. Greimas, Algirdas J. Of Gods and Men: Studies in Lithuanian Mythology. Bloomington: Indiana University Press, 1992. Pages 20-23
96. Kotsiubynskyi, Mykhailo, and Bohdan Rubchak. Shadows of Forgotten Ancestors. Littleton, Colo: Published for the Canadian Institute of Ukrainian Studies by Ukrainian Academic Press, 1981. Internet resource. Page 47
97. Ivanits, Linda J. Russian Folk Belief. M E Sharpe Incorporated, 1989. Internet resource. Page 31
98. Afanasev, A N, and Leonard A. Magnus. Russian Folk-Tales (translated from the Russian). London, Kegan Paul, Trench, Trubner, New York, E. P. Dutton [1916: Detroit Gale Research Co, 1974. Page 340
99. Oinas, Felix J. "Jumi: A Fertility Divinity." Journal of the Folklore Institute, vol. 18, no. 1, Indiana University Press, 1981, Page 73
100. LONNROT. Kalevala. DEVOTED Publishing, 2017. Page 399
101. Oinas, Felix J. "Jumi: A Fertility Divinity." Journal of the Folklore Institute, vol. 18, no. 1, Indiana University Press, 1981, Page 72,75,76,80
102. Drahomanov, Mychajlo. Notes on the Slavic Religio-Ethical Legends: The Dualistic Creation of the World. Bloomington, 1961. Pages 46-47
103. Perkowski, Jan L. Vampire Lore: From the Writings of Jan Louis Perkowski. Bloomington, Ind: Slavica Publishers, 2006. Internet resource. Page 563
104. Vincenz, Stanislaw, Zdzislaw Czermanski, and H C. Stevens. On the High Uplands: Sagas, Songs, Tales and Legends of the Carpathians. 1955. Page 342-343

Chapter 5

The Zoryas as Sea Maidens

Neil Gaiman has probably done more to popularize the Zoryas in the English-speaking world than anyone else. In his book, *"American Gods"* (and in the show) the Zoryas feature as three sisters who govern the different phases of the day. They are presented as follows:

- Zorya Utrennyaya (the Zorya of the morning)
- Zorya Vechernyaya (the Zorya of the evening)
- Zorya Polunochnaya (the Zorya of midnight)

Gaiman's portrayal of these three Goddesses has had such an impact on popular perception that some people actually think he invented the concept of three Zoryas. I think some of the suspicion comes from the similarity to the triple Goddess in Wicca (the mother, the maiden, and the crone).

While the similarity is striking, it is clear that this is not the inspiration for the three Zoryas (literally, the three "dawns") of Slavic mythology. More likely, the triple Goddesses of Celtic mythology helped inspire the triad in Wicca, and triple Goddesses throughout Eastern Europe are related to their Celtic counterparts.

We can find evidence of the triad from Polish songs. One reads as follows:[1]

Zarze, zarzyca, three sisters,
Our Lady went on the sea collecting golden foam;
Saint John met her; And where are you going, mother?"

The image of a Zorya collecting foam on the sea is noteworthy. As I have often tried to emphasize, the dawn maidens are also sea maidens in Slavic folklore. We see another example in a Ukrainian tale:[2]

> *Well, I can tell thee all about the ways of the sun, for I am the sun's own daughter. So now I'll tell thee the whole matter. Go back to this nobleman and say to him that the reason why the sun turns so red as he sets is this: Just as the sun is going down into the sea, three fair ladies rise out of it, and it is the sight of them which makes him turn so red all over!*

It is interesting that the three dawns attend the amorous sun in this tale, whereas one of them encounters "Saint John" in Poland. As we'll see, the dawn maidens are probably connected with Summer Solstice, which is the night of St. John.

A third story in Lithuania helps strengthen the case for three lovely sea maidens associated with different times of day, as well as with St. John. The story is titled "Jonas, the Godson of John the Baptist."[3] To quote the tale:

> *Presently, in the evening, a lass came out of the sea and wanted to go up to the horse and stroke him, but he kicked out and galloped away. She went away. Around midnight, another lass came - she also wanted to come up very close, but he ran away from her too, and she went away. Just before dawn, the third one came out. As she kept approaching the horse, he kept going further and further and lured her away from the sea.*

I should stress that Lithuanian mythology proper is distinct from that of neighboring Slavic peoples. The Lithuanian language belongs to the Baltic branch of the broader Balto-Slavic language family, not the Slavic branch like Russian or Polish. Lithuanian mythology sometimes has Ausrine in a triad of Goddesses, along with Zleja (midday) and Breksta (night.)[4]

More typically in Lithuanian mythology, the dawn Goddess Ausrine is contrasted with the dusk Goddess Vakarine. Typically, there is no third sister.

In fact, the concept of three goddesses governing the daily cycle is so rare in Baltic lore that the few references in Lithuanian folklore might reflect recent "spill-over" of the concept from Belarus or Poland. It's plausible that Baltic mythology had just two goddesses of the daily cycle originally (Ausrine and Vakarine) which is what we see in most sources from Lithuania and Latvia. By contrast, the triad of "Zoryas" may be a concept that was unique to Slavic culture originally. Folklore is always complicated, but in general, the Slavic countries place more emphasis on the triad rather than the dyad. These Goddesses sometimes appear in the form of stars. This is seen in Slavic and Baltic sources as well. In one Lithuanian narrative, the sun (Saule) appears as the mother of Ausrine (the morning star) and Vakarine (evening star).[5] There are Russian charms which invoke "Maria the Morning Star" and "Marem'iana the Evening Star."[6]

It is interesting that names like "Maria" are associated with the morning star or dawn. This likely goes back to the designation of the dawn or morning star as a sea maiden. Thus, in Lithuanian, Ausrine is called "Mariu Pana" (Sea Maiden)[7] or Mariu Zvaigzde (Sea Star).[8] The Russian and Ukrainian cognate of Lithuanian "Mariu" (of the sea) would be "Morya." Very similar in sound.

The Zoryas as Fairytale Maidens

I would strongly argue that the Russian folktale heroine Maria Morevna (literally "Maria Sea-Daughter") is a dawn Goddess. The tale, titled simply "Maria Morevna" is a well-known one.[9] She and her Serbian counterpart from the tale of "The Golden Apple Tree and the Nine Peahens" both have significant connections to Zerasha, a mythological woman from the

Ossetian Nart Sagas. In the Nart Sagas, we catch a glimpse of Sarmatian mythology; the Ossetians speak a language which is directly descended from that of the ancient steppe nomads, the Scythians and Sarmatians.

In the Ossetian myth, the dove maiden Zerasha is the daughter of the Sea God Donbettyr. As a dove, she takes flight with her sisters and steals golden apples from the clan of the Narts. The twin brothers Akshar and Akshartag pursue her after Akshar strikes her wing with an arrow. Later she marries Akshar, but the two brothers quarrel and kill each other, to be rapidly usurped by St. George (Uastyrdzhi). Zerasha herself gives birth to twins, then dies. George resurrects Zerasha in her tomb with his magical whip and gets her pregnant with Satanaya, who is literally born from her mother's tomb.[10]

The Golden Apple theft episode has many parallels to Indo-European mythologies. However, variants in which the apple-thief is a maiden who marries the hero are a minority. More typically, the hero pursues the bird and eventually obtains a damsel who is distinct from the initial quarry. In many tales, the apple stealing bird is actually a shapeshifting monster (giant, witch, dragon, etc.), and the damsel is only won when the monster is tracked to its lair and slain.

Even in Eastern Europe, this version is common. In one Polish tale, it's a nocturnal bird of prey who turns out to be an evil witch.[11] In this one, she is actually the ferocious mother of the three fairytale maidens, who could represent the Zoryas.

Speaking more broadly though, this basic story type in which a hero pursues a magical bird is classified as Aarne-Thompson folktale type 550 "The Golden Bird." It's found across Europe, and even as far abroad as Quebec. However, some narratives are more "magical" than others. Versions in which the Golden apple-thief and damsel are combined into one character appear to be limited mainly to three regions:

- The Northern Caucasus (Nart Sagas)[12]
- The Balkans and the Carpathians.[13, 14]
- Some East Slavic territories.[15,16]

In most other regions, it is rare to find stories of AT 550: The Golden Bird in which the fruit-stealing bird shapeshifts into a beautiful maiden. With a few exceptions, the regions listed above seem to represent the primary distribution range of this tale type. There are some caveats to this generalization. There is a very similar tale in Poland called "Argelus and the Swans." However, the name of this hero (Argelus) is taken directly from the Hungarian version, making its "Polish" provenance unclear.

Suffice to say, the distribution of this tale type is consistent with steppe nomad origins, particularly in association with the last Sarmatian nomads of the migration period. Some Slavic groups in the Balkans and Carpathians such as the Croats may have originated from Slavicized Sarmatian tribes. Almost simultaneously, Scytho-Sarmatian elements among the Huns, Avars, and Magyars could also have been transmitted into the same regions.

Interestingly, in the Nart Sagas of the Ossetians, both Zerasha and Satanaya have many parallels with Slavic fairy tale heroines. Zerasha is a dove maiden and a daughter of the Sea God Donbettyr.[17] Similarly, the "surname" given to Maria Morevna in the eponymous Russian tale (Morevna) simply means "Sea-Daughter." The Golden Apple theft episode associated with Zerasha in the Nart Sagas, as we have seen, also parallels those of Slavic folktale heroines. Perhaps the most famous is the fabulous maiden who shapeshifts into a peahen in the Serbian tale "The Nine Peahens and the Golden Apples."

The tale of Maria Morevna in Russia is nearly identical to the Serbian one involving golden apples, even if the bird maiden / apple theft episode at the beginning is missing from it. Since writing this, I've actually come across a Russian tale called "The Witch and

Her Servants" from Andrew Lang's *"Yellow Fairy Book"* (cited on the previous page, when discussing the regional distribution of these tale types.) This tale is basically Maria Morevna combined with AT 550: The Golden Bird. In it, a character appears who is Maria Morevna in all but name. She is a swan-maiden who steals magical fruit and is later abducted by a Koschei-like villain. Thus, there is both a Serbian tale and a Russian tale proving that the character "Maria Morevna" (Maria Sea-Daughter) is linked to a Slavic variant of AT 550. It is difficult to explain this unless both Slavic tales are related to those of the Nart Sagas, where the golden apple stealing bird is also a Sea-Daughter.

Even in stories where the warrior woman / sea-daughter does not steal golden apples, there are Russian tales in which the warrior maiden (also called Seenyglazka) has the apples of youth stolen from her, along with the water of life. Actually, Aarne-Thompson Type 551 "Water of Life" is closely associated with AT 550, which is reflected in their numbering. Both tale types often involve a king who dreams of a magical item (bird, water) that will make him young or cure him. Obviously, the golden apples of youth are related as well.

Frequently, the quest which begins with the fabulous bird (AT 550) ends with the hero being resurrected with the water of life (AT 551). It is noteworthy that the earliest written example of AT 550 is from a 13th century Middle Dutch source (discussed later in this chapter). This story already combines these two motifs of the golden bird and the water of life. In oral tales collected several centuries later (e.g. by Grimm), the association is still evident.

The connection between Zarya (dawn) and the water of life is also clear in some Russian charms. One spell against illness places a maiden named "Zarya" (dawn) on the mythical island of Buyan. She sits there upon the white stone "Alatyr", from which flow rivers of healing water. Interestingly, this figure is replaced with the Virgin Mary in some spells.[18]

Even when the sea-maiden or dawn-maiden is not explicitly identified with the apple-stealing bird, she still nevertheless appears in many Slavic variants of Aarne-Thompson Folktale Type 550 - the Golden Bird. We see this in the Ukrainian tale "Anastasia the Lovely Maid of the Sea." In this tale, the hero first pursues the firebird, but later stumbles onto Anastasia the Lovely Maid of the Sea. The two simply aren't identified with one another.[19]

Here, I should cite *"Gods and Men: Studies in Lithuanian Mythology"* by Algirdas Greimas. I read this book after formulating many of the ideas in this chapter. However, I was pleasantly surprised to find that he discusses many similar Lithuanian folktale motifs in connection with Ausrine, the Morningstar / Dawn Goddess of Lithuanian mythology.[20] The Lithuanian narrative he recounts is especially close to the Ukrainian version of AT 550, Anastasia the Lovely Maid of the Sea. The fact that he independently linked this story type with the Baltic dawn / morning star Goddess helped give me the confidence to continue doing the same for Slavic folklore.

In another tale of AT 550, the Czech tale "Zlatovlaska" (Goldenhair), the hero finds a golden feather and is sent after the golden bird. Then he finds a luminous golden hair, and is sent after the maiden it came from (Princess Zlatovlaska). When he finally tracks her down, we are told the following about her:

> *She's the golden-haired daughter of the King of the Crystal Palace. Do you see the faint outlines of an island over yonder? That's where she lives. The king has twelve daughters but Zlatovlaska alone has golden hair. Each morning at dawn a wonderful glow spreads over land and sea. That's Zlatovlaska (Goldenhair) combing her golden hair.*[21]

Later, Zlatovlaska will resurrect the hero with the water of life (an element of Aarne-Thompson Type 551). There's also a lengthy Romanian wonder tale called "The Dawn Fairy" which follows the same pattern, with the Dawn Fairy herself reviving the hero at the end.[22, 23] Suffice to say, the Slovak Zlatovlaska and Romanian Dawn Fairy have numerous similarities to one another. In "Anastasia, the Lovely Maid of the Sea", the water of life is replaced with magical milk, but the idea is the same.

There is also an English tale very similar to the Czech story "Zlatovlaska." Both are Aarne-Thompson Type 550 - the golden bird. However, the English story substitutes "the sister of the sun" for Zlatovlaska. The title of the story is actually "Sister of the Sun.[24] I cannot completely speak for English folklore, but in Slavic folklore this tale would clearly be linked with the dawn Goddess.

Returning to the subject of Zlatovlaska's golden hair, however, it should be noted that in the Nart Sagas, the sea maiden "Zerasha" is literally named "Golden Hair." (Zer - means gold in Ossetian.) The Proto-Slavic word for dawn "zorja" is thought by linguists to be related to the Proto-Baltic-Slavic word for "glow." However, I suspect it is an Iranian loan that comes from the exact same root.

On one final note on the Nart Sagas of the northern Caucasus, I should talk about Zerasha's daughter. As I mentioned, after being impregnated by St. George in her own tomb, Zerasha's body gives birth to Satanaya.[25]

This can be interpreted as a myth of rebirth. However, it also reads like a Christian attempt to kill off and then "recreate" her as the daughter of a saint. Perhaps it is for this reason that Satanaya also has much in common with the Slavic fairy tale maidens mentioned previously. It is interesting that the Russian Seenyglazka is a guardian of the apples of youth, rather than a Golden apple-thief. In this respect, Seenyglazka actually resembles Zerasha's daughter Satanaya, who plays the role of golden apple keeper[26] rather than the apple-thief. On the other hand, the Peahen maiden of Serbian poetry is clearly related to Maria Morevna, as well as the Ossetian Satanaya and Zerasha. She appears to blend characteristics of all three seamlessly.

Another interesting trait of Satanaya is her appearance as a warrior maiden, under the title "Sana Satanaya." In one Nart tale, she slays her lover then kills herself. Where she falls, a spring of healing water bubbles up. This is oddly similar to the Russian tale "Water of Life, Water of Youth, Water of Death." Both stories feature a warrior maiden who strikes down a man then suffers regret. Both warrior maidens magically produce healing waters. In the case of "Sana" Satanaya, she is clearly equated with Sana, the food of the Gods.[27] An obvious cognate to the Vedic Soma. In fact, the Nart Sagas of the Northern Caucasus may be the only corpus of Indo-European mythology which links golden apples (the food of the Gods in Norse mythology) with the food of the Gods in Vedic tradition (Soma).

Another interesting aspect of Satanaya is that she is associated with Aarne-Thompson type 302 - The Giant With No Heart In His Body. In one story, she must trick an ogre into revealing his hidden weakness, the magical secret to his invincibility.[28] In many Slavic stories, this role is given to the heroine who is abducted by Koschei the deathless.[29] In Russian tales, the villain Koschei is the abductor of many different fairytale maidens with similar attributes - among them Maria Morevna.

In a Pashtun tale from the Afghan-Pakistan region, a similar villain abducts a damsel with a luminous face. This light is not figurative - when she is abducted, the hero tracks her by talking to witnesses who saw "a strange light" flying across the sky as she was carried off by a Deo (Daeva). This brief description suggests celestial characteristics. This tale also features AT 551 "the water of life."[30] Overall, it seems clearly connected with the same themes as in Eastern Europe.

The Dawn Goddess in Indo-European Mythology

I will need to speak briefly about the divine twins in Proto-Indo-European mythology. In short, these are recurring twin Gods that show up in many Indo-European cultures. They are typically depicted as youthful sons of the Sky Father, associated with horses, who attend a consort Goddess with solar characteristics. Their sun Goddess consort is typically rescued from the sea, or some other "watery peril."[31]

The mythology is mainly reconstructed using Greek, Vedic, and Lithuanian culture. The Greek Dioscuri correspond clearly to the Vedic Aswins, and the Baltic Dieva Deli. This is pertinent to the episode of the Nart Sagas explained above, because Zerasha is retrieved from the sea and marries the hero, Akshar. Later, Akshar and his twin brother Akshartag quarrel over her and both of them die.

Interestingly, Zerasha's daughter Satanaya (born from her tomb) also marries one of two twin brothers. (one of her two half-brothers). This strengthens the idea that Satanaya is, in some sense, Zerasha reborn.

Most of all, it helps confirm the solar aspects of Zerasha, because she is clearly the consort of divine twins. In Baltic mythology, a similar role is occupied by Saules Meitas (interpreted as the young or "maiden" sun or as the sun Goddess's daughter). She has a relationship with the two Dieva Deli, and they greet her on summer solstice.[32] This background is discussed further by me in Chapter 6: Advanced Concepts in Indo-European Mythology.

Reflexes of the divine twins have also been noted among pairs of saints in Slavic folk tradition. In Belarusian songs, St. George and Nicholas have a number of traits reminiscent of the Asvins, and they attend a female "Zaranica" (Aurora or dawn). Another interesting trait of Zaranica is her association with dew. According to a folk riddle, the dawn dropped a key, and the sun picked it up again. The answer is "dew."[33]

In Komi-Permyak mythology, we actually catch a glimpse of Zaran as a mythical Goddess ancestor of the Permyak people. She marries an earthly man named Perm, but must return to heaven after bearing him children. This places her in a role similar to other sovereignty Goddess ancestor tales like those of Aine. (See Chapter 2 for a review of the sovereignty Goddess concept.)

In Komi-Permyak mythology, we also see that the tears of Zaran become summer dew.[34] While the Komi-Permyaks are a Finno-Ugric ethnic minority in northwest Russia, Zaran's mythology is almost certainly of Indo-European origins. Not only is the name "Zaran" a probable loan from East Slavic or Iranian, but the concept of dew as tears of the dawn Goddess also shows up in Classical mythology. Specifically with the death of Memnon, son of Eos / Aurora, we see that the tears of Eos become dew.[35] Summer dew is considered magical or sacred in a number of European folklore traditions. Oftentimes it is gathered on the summer solstice. This tradition is attested across Europe.[36]

The Vedic dawn Goddess Ushas deserves some special attention. Most scholars believe that the Proto-Indo-European religion had a dawn Goddess, cognate to Greek Eos, Vedic Ushas, and Baltic Ausrine. However, her prominence in the Vedic religion means that some of the most detailed descriptions of the dawn goddess are found in Indian culture.

In the Vedas, Ushas appears as the most lauded of Goddesses, the vivifier and renewer of life itself. She is to be distinguished from the daughter of the Sun (Suryah, daughter of the male sun God Surya) Rather, she is the consort of the male Surya, not his daughter who marries the divine twins. However, Baltic mythology blurs the line between the dawn and the sun's daughter.[37]

We have already seen that there are signs that the Slavic "Zorya" assimilated aspects of both the sun and dawn goddess. For instance, the Belarusian tendency to group Zaranica with two "twinned" saints.[38] This suggests a union with the divine twins, which would be associated - not with the Vedic dawn Goddess - but with the Vedic sun goddess "Suryah", who has the divine twins as groomsmen or suitors.[39] This is despite the obvious fact that "Zorya / Zarya" means "dawn" in virtually all Slavic languages.

It is noteworthy that Ushas has a sister named Ratri - the night Goddess. While she is typically viewed favorably, she is sometimes associated with barrenness and gloom. She may be confronted or chased off by her more luminous kin, such as Agni and Ushas.[40]

The Dark Sister, Serpent Infestation, and Whipping

A Russian proverb says this about day and night: "A sister (night) goes to pay a brother (day) a visit, but he hides from his sister."[41] The notion that day and night are created by an endless chase around the world can be found from Norse to Egyptian mythology.

In the Russian tale "The Witch and the Sun's Sister" the hero is pursued by his iron-toothed sister, who seeks to devour him just as she devoured the rest of their family. Ultimately, the hero is rescued by the majestic "Sister of the Sun" who uses deception to get the witch to catapult the hero into the sky, and safely through her window.[42]

The sister of the sun is not described in as much detail as I'd like. She does, however, give the hero the apples of youth earlier in the tale. Recall that "Sister of the Sun" is the same term used to describe the maiden associated with an English variant of AT 550: The Golden Bird.

The Russian tale "The Witch and the Sister of the Sun" has been compared to mythological episodes from the northern Caucasus. For instance, in Ossetian mythology, there is a malevolent figure who pursues her brother (the moon) and tries to devour him.

The Abkhazian variant of this myth is strikingly similar to the Russian fairy tale, even down to the detail of a mouse warning the hero (The moon) that his sister has eaten her family and is coming to devour him. In this Abkhazian narrative, the figure who saves the protagonist is the sun herself, rather than "the sister of the sun" as in the Russian tale. Unlike in Ossetian mythology where the sun can be conceived of as a brother of the moon, the Abkhazians make the sun his wife. Still, the narrative is remarkably similar. It's quite likely that the protagonist in the Russian tale should also be understood as the personified sun or moon. As Magometovich himself notes in his guide to Ossetian mythology, such narratives are typically associated with the "Sister of the sun" or "Dennitsa the Morning Star" in Slavic folktales.[43]

In the Vainakh variant of this myth, the ravenous sister Mozh actually pursues both of her brothers - the sun and the moon.[44] Therefore, this narrative could be told about either of the two luminaries.

The dark, treacherous, or threatening sister is a staple of Slavic folk tradition. Examples of this can be found in Ukrainian tales, such as Little Tsar Novishnyi and the False Sister.[45] In this tale, the sister is seduced by a dragon, and sends her brother off on dangerous quests in the hopes that he will die.

This motif of the treacherous sister feigning illness and sending her brother off on dangerous quests also has some parallels farther East. We see it among the Selkups of Siberia, where it is associated with Icheche, a son of the sky god who hunted a great elk in the sky and subsequently became a star in the sky.[46] The core of this narrative about a cosmic elk hunter seems to be Uralic, but nevertheless, it hints at the mythological origin of the treacherous sister myth in Russian folktales.

In one story, the treacherous sister is juxtaposed with the attractive warrior maiden, who resembles Maria Morevna. In "The Milk of the Wild Beasts" a sister and brother escape from an iron-furred bear. The sister is seduced and feigns illness. She sends her brother to retrieve the milk of wild animals on the pretext of "curing" her, but actually to get rid of him. Ultimately, she tries to kill him. When the hero exposes and overcomes her, he leaves her tied to a tree. Later he comes across a warrior maiden who agrees to marry him if he beats her in combat. When he does, she agrees to marry him.[47]

So the treacherous sister appears to be juxtaposed with the attractive dawn Goddess, who can be identified as the warrior-maiden Maria Morevna or "the sister of the Sun." We can perhaps also identify her with midnight - or Zorya Polunochnaya.

However, we sometimes see the exact opposite, where the evil supernatural female figure is contrasted with the benevolent sister. In the song of Marinka, Marinka the witch transforms Dobrynya into a golden horned auroch. In some versions, it is Dobrynya's benevolent sister who threatens Marinka with magic of her own and rescues him. Ultimately both archetypes appear interchangeably in the roles of lovers and sisters of the protagonist in many stories.

There is one other fascinating detail about this arrangement; the scary sister and dawn sister are connected by a bizarre cycle of transformation and rebirth. The key to this transformation is... whipping. Or at least beating.

It may be in "Ivan Goroh" that we get the clearest explanation. The treacherous wife in this tale sides against the two brothers, and goes over to the side of the serpents. This parallels the "wicked sister" seduced by dragons in other folk narratives. Later, Ivan Goroh "whips the serpent blood out of her" so that she can walk in human guise again.[48]

The notion of treachery associated with serpent blood or a serpent infestation appears in a number of Slavic folktales. In some variants of the bylina of Mikhailo Potyk, we see the beautiful swan maiden Marya become corrupted by serpents from within, and morph into a dragon of the underworld. The hero must beat her with metal rods, and remove the snakes from within the body of the swan maiden before restoring her with the water of life.[49] Serpent infestation also shows up in the song about the witch Marinka. It is fascinating that the serpents within Marinka are discovered after her body is burned.[50] This is reminiscent of Slavic spring traditions, which often involved the destruction and / or disposal of a "Marena" effigy representing winter (see Chapter 2).

Additional stories with the serpent infestation motif can be found in Serbia[51] and Hungary.[52] In general, they confirm the links laid out here between serpent infestation, the treacherous female, and a juxtaposition between lover and sister.

Another consistent pattern with these tales is that they are often associated with two mythological brothers or twins. The Serbian tale cited here opens with two brothers - Paul and Radool, who are likened to two tall Larch trees. They love their sister Yelitza, which enrages Paul's wife with jealousy, and causes her to commit murder. Here it is the wife, not the sister, whose bones become infested with serpents. As mentioned, the tale of Ivan Goroh ends with the titular character taming his brother's wife by "whipping the serpent's blood out of her."

In Mansi mythology, from western Siberia, we have a similar myth involving two brothers who are sons of the Mansi Sky Father God, Num-Torem. These are the two brother deities Tagt-kotil-Torem and Aj'as Torem. According to legend, Aj'as Torem's intended bride ran away from her wedding. Tagt-kotil-Torem beat her until all of the unclean and evil creatures came out of her. Afterwards, she became obedient, and quit her habit of turning into a magpie.[53]

As we will see in later chapters, there are a significant number of parallels between Slavic mythology and Uralic mythologies. It's not entirely clear why. It could represent some direct interaction between the two groups, but parallel borrowings (e.g. from Indo-Iranian peoples) should not be ruled out either. This will be discussed further later. However, I do also discuss some of the rationale for seeking out these correspondences in Chapter 1, particularly so as to outline why they are not unexpected. In Chapter 8: Svarozhichi - Sons of Svarog, however, we will discuss why the seven sons of Num-Torem (The Ob-Ugrian Sky Father) seem to be particularly rich in parallels to Slavic folklore figures.

For now, however, it seems reasonable to conclude that there was a Slavic myth about a "dark" serpent-infested sister (Marena) who sought to devour her brothers who almost certainly represented heavenly luminaries. One or both of these twins were consorts of the Dawn Goddess (Zaranica / Zorya Utrennyaya) who often appears to have rescued her brother(s). However, in some cases the dawn goddess seems to have "transformed" into Marena by serpent infestation or to have otherwise been replaced by her.

It is noteworthy that Marya the white swan gets a beating in her own grave, because her lover is buried with her at her request. Also, before she is a serpent woman, she is initially a lovely swan maiden. In all, she is buried for three months (a quarter year) before rising. It is difficult not to see a seasonal significance in this.[54]

Of course, there is a heavy dash of sexism in these narratives about snake women getting beatings. However, the many versions tend to shuffle around the blame. In Ivan the Cow's Son, the beating at the end is horrific by modern standards. In Mikailo Potyk, the transformation of Marya into a dragon in her own grave is arguably the most horrific aspect, not the means of curing her.

It's worth noting that the idea of lightning "enlivening" the land before spring is a plausible symbolic source for this myth. There is also a long tradition of flagellation as an act of purification in some religious traditions, so some of the inspiration could be ritualistic. Indeed, there is a springtime ritual of playfully whacking girls with a small branch in many Slavic countries. Finally, I should note that even in a modern context, whipping can have some ambiguous connotations.

Katicic and Belaj, Jarilo and Marena

In "*A Review of Contemporary Research On Croatian Mythology In Relation to Natko Nodilo*" Suzana Marjanac says the following:[55]

> *Contemporary research on Croatian mythology is marked by Katičić and Belaj who reconstructed the Croatian pantheon with Perun the Thunderer as the supreme deity by reconstructing the Ancient Slavic belief system and incorporating it into a wider Indo - European framework (Indo-European comparative mythology). Using the holy rhyme "hoditi – roditi" ("to walk – to give birth") during the period between 1984 and 1987, Katičić began reconstructing the fragments of ancient Slavic mythical tales of the divine hero of fertility and vegetation.*

In this reconstruction, the fertility hero Jarilo marries Mara, his sister, who is identical to the winter effigy (Marena) that is cast into the water each spring. Both are children of Perun. They commit incest with one another through ignorance, and engage in a divine marriage on Summer Solstice. There are some additional details of interest in this reconstruction. The Goddess Mara engages in a courtship ritual whereby she presents a red or golden apple to the handsome young fertility hero (St. George / Jarilo). Later, however, she kills him and turns into an evil hag.[56]

On the surface, the idea of reconstructing "Croatian mythology" seems bizarre and nationalistic. To the extent that Croatian mythology is reconstructable, it should be virtually identical to most South Slavic mythology. If not most Slavic mythology in general. It seems unlikely that any reconstruction focusing on just one of the thirteen Slavic countries would be fruitful. Furthermore, any sample of folklore limited to only one Balkan country is invariably going to be a statistically "small" and localized sample of Balkan folklore. Not only that, but the identification of truly archaic elements from Slavic folklore is dependent on recognizing widespread patterns across distant and isolated communities. Without a broad comparative analysis from numerous Slavic countries, there is no objective means of identifying the folk traditions that are most likely to be ancient.

Moving back to Katicic and Belaj, some aspects of their reconstruction appear compelling at first glance. Katicic and Belaj were very much correct about the association of Summer Solstice with an incestuous divine union. In Russia, poetic ballads sung on Kupala (summer solstice) tell of how a brother and sister met and married without recognizing each other and were turned into flowers as punishment.[57]

Additionally, there was a tradition of pairing the male "Kupalo" effigy on Summer Solstice with a tree called the "Morynka."[58] This is an obvious cognate to the female Marena effigy disposed of each spring, personifying death and winter. However, its presence during Summer Solstice is puzzling if we equate the name "Marena" exclusively with winter. If we compare this to Polish tradition, however, it becomes much clearer. In Polish tradition, "death" is cast into the river in spring in the form of the effigy of Marzanna. Subsequently, a decorated tree is brought back to the village symbolizing new life.[59] The Russian "Morynka" tree of summer solstice is therefore not the winter effigy, but its exact opposite.

Another thing which may have confused Katicic and Belaj is the obvious similarities of the words for "death" and "sea" in many Indo-European languages. Thus in Russian, "Mor" means pestilence, but "Morje" means "sea." This goes all the way back to Proto-Indo-European *mer - (die) and *mori (sea or wetland).[60]

As we have seen, Marzanna in Poland is explicitly identified as an effigy representing death and winter. In South Slavic lore, the equivalent figure is "Mara." Conversely, the terms "Mariu" (Lithuanian) and "Morevna" (Russian) and even Welsh "Morgen" are related to the sea, and not necessarily to death. As mentioned previously, the Slavic Sea-Daughter has a number of characteristics in common with the dawn or the morning star. Recall that "Mariu Zvaigzde" (Sea Star) is an epithet for the Morningstar / Dawn Goddess Ausrine in Lithuanian lore.[61] In Russian charms, this is paralleled by "Maria Morningstar and

Marem'iana Evening Star" which are invoked together against the midnight demon.[62]

So, we should ask ourselves, is there any chance that the morning star could substitute for "Mara" in Katicic and Belaj's reconstructions? The answer is yes - absolutely. And it's obvious. As mentioned earlier, the morning star is the sister of the sun in Bulgarian folklore.

Not only that, but a Bulgarian legend says that on Enyovden (St. John's Night) around Summer Solstice, the sun forgot which way to go. The morning star, his sister, pointed the way. On his return journey, the sun took a bath. Because of this, people were urged to bathe on St. John's Night.[63] This not only connects a brother and sister with summer solstice, but also with bathing. In Russia, the name for summer solstice is "Kupala" which is derived from the verb "kupat" (to bathe). The term for the male effigy, "Kupalo" is from the same root.[64] Therefore, the Bulgarian legend about the sun taking a bath provides a compelling explanation for the name of Summer Solstice (Kupala / Kupalo) across multiple Slavic languages.

This may also explain why people bathed themselves on Kupala night. Because the waters of the earth were thought to have been "touched" by the sun, all natural water and dew may have been regarded as holy at this time.

Regarding the courtship of Jarilo and Marena (according to adherents of the Katicic and Belaj school) it is believed that a divine proposal involving the gift of a golden apple is involved. This is very reminiscent of the Nart Sagas, where the sea-maiden Zerasha steals a golden apple and is soon married to the man who pursues her. More to the point, however, in Serbia we see the same concept associated with "the sister of the sun." To quote Ralston:[65]

The Sun's Sister is a mythical being who is often mentioned in the popular poetry of the South-Slavonians. A Servian song represents

a beautiful maiden, with "arms of silver up to the elbows," sitting on a silver throne which floats on water. A suitor comes to woo her. She waxes wroth and cries,
"Whom wishes he to woo?
The sister of the Sun,
The cousin of the Moon,
The adopted-sister of the Dawn."
Then she flings down three golden apples, which the "marriage-proposers" attempt to catch, but "three lightnings flash from the sky" and kill the suitor and his friends.
In another Servian song a girl cries to the Sun—
"O brilliant Sun! I am fairer than thou,
Than thy brother, the bright Moon,
Than thy sister, the moving star [Venus?]."

Similarly in Romanian folklore, the sister of the Sun is called Sanziene, which is also the term for Summer Solstice (a holiday closely associated with her). Folk songs in Romania tell how the Sun sought to wed his sister Sanziene.[66] Granted, the Romanian language is not Slavic, (Romanian comes from Latin) but Slavic influences are significant. Also, Sanziene is a moon Goddess, but this is likely an inheritance from Roman mythology. Her name likely comes from "Sancta Diana." The similarities are more striking than the differences, however. In particular, the rituals of making flower crowns and bathing in dew are very reminiscent of those found among Slavic peoples. Claudia Costin notes that flowers were an important part of the Summer Solstice holiday, and that Sanziene was "The Lady of Flowers" in Romanian folklore.[67] This is interesting, and it recalls the Russian Summer Solstice ballads that sing about a brother and sister who were turned into flowers after marrying.

The "Sister of the Sun" may actually be a recurring title for a Goddess in Indo-European cultures. Recall that the same term shows up for the heroine in an English variant of AT 550, The

Golden Bird. It's also fairly common in Russian tales. In one Russian tale that has already been discussed, the sister of the sun is actually the benevolent female character, and the "bad" one is the hero's monstrous sister whom she tricks to get the protagonist to safety. In this tale, the sister of the sun also gives the hero the apples of youth.

No matter how you slice it, the attempt to link "Mara" the winter Goddess to golden apples is a serious misstep on the part of Katicic and Belaj. They have clearly confused the Sea-Daughter (Morevna) with her sister, Death (Marena). That this reflects deliberate wordplay is obvious, and should be expected for anyone who studies Slavic folklore. The pagan intent was obviously to link the two etymologies in order to highlight the duality and relatedness of the two sisters. In a sense, Katicic and Belaj are half correct, because Mara / Marena is a part of that duality. However, by failing to link her with the morning star or the sea-maiden, they leave a large chunk of the equation out. And it's the part of the equation that was actually most celebrated, based on summer solstice traditions.

References to the incestuous marriage are found in Slovene summer solstice songs as well: In Slovenia, on the eastern flank of the alps, the study of midsummer pagan folklore often revolves around the stories about Kresnik. Zmago Smitek has an excellent paper on the subject of the Slovene Kresnik. He summarizes the Slovene narratives related to him as follows:

> *It is therefore important that a mention of Kresnik's wife (Deva, Alencica, Vesina, Zora, Marjetica) is also present in his "mythological" tradition. One case clearly states that the maiden he saved became his sweetheart. Such notions about the original couple were also present in a part of the territory along the Slovene-Croatian border. Partly they are linked to the St. John's Day (Summer Solstice) celebration, but much more recognizable are elements of the Zeleni Jurij (Green George/Jarilo) ceremonies.*

> *Songs sung in Adlesici and Tribuce in Bela krajina describe a bride awaiting the arrival of a mythological hero from the afterworld; sometimes she sets out on a difficult journey to meet him on her own. Some Zeleni Jurij songs mention the bride as sister Mara whom Jurij marries on his journey from the land of the dead into the world of humans. It is possible to discover allusions to incest in Croatian songs in the "kaj" dialect.*[68]

The folklore of Kresnik is actually incredibly complicated. He sometimes appears to have solar attributes. Sometimes he appears as a thunder God. Sometimes he appears to be one of two divine twins. There is also a tradition in which a Kresnik is a type of local spirit or even a person with special powers. This is why Zmago Smitek distinguishes Kresnik's "mythological" tradition from less mythic variants of the Kresnik folklore. Nevertheless, Smitek correctly identifies that many of the Slovene traditions around Kresnik are extremely similar to the Croatian narratives used by Katicic and Belaj to reconstruct the myth of Jarilo and his sister / wife Mara - including associations with St. John's night, fertility, a heroic rescue, and incest.[69]

It is worth noting the names Zmago Smitek lists as synonyms for Kresnik's wife / sister. "Zora" leaps out as the most striking, as it clearly means "dawn." The story involving the name "Vesina" is described by the scholar Monica Kropej in detail. In this version,[70] Kresnik escapes from the otherworld with the daughter of the Snake Queen. Later, another maiden named Vesina is trapped in a tower by a dragon, and Kresnik must defeat it in order to free her. Later, Kresnik's wife Vesina notices he disappears every night to commit infidelity, and startles him one night causing him to fall to his death. This is seemingly a narrative about the sun's daily journey to the otherworld.

It is fascinating that the name "Vesina" is Slovene for "Spring". Thus, the Goddess he rescues is once again the opposite of the winter effigy, far from being synonymous with her. Yet Katicic would certainly link the other name "Marjetica" with "Marena" the name of the winter effigy that was cast out in spring. How can we resolve this list of names? The three can only be reconciled if we treat "Marjetica" as being derived from the word for "sea" rather than "death." Alternatively (or perhaps simultaneously) Marjetica literally translates to "Daisy" in Slovene which could be another reference to the association between Summer Solstice / St. John's Night and flowers. One thing is for sure though - it does not relate directly to the name "Marena." It is tempting to conclude that Marena is a daughter of the "snake queen" mentioned in Kresnik's lore, but not the Goddess of renewal "Zora / Vesina." We catch a hint of this juxtaposition in one Serbian song referring to the morning star and her sister.[71]

Lo! The maiden greets the day-star! "Sister!
Sister star of morning! Well I greet thee;
Thou dost watch the world from thine uprising
To thy sinking hour. In Herzgovina,
Tell me didst thou see the princely Stephan?"
... - (Abridged)
"Gently the morning star responded:
"Lovely sister! Beautiful young maid,
True, I watch the world from my uprising
To my setting; - and in Herzgovina
Saw the palace of Princely Stepan;
And that snowy palace wide open,
And his horse was saddled, and was ready;
And he was equipped his bride to visit:
But not thee - not thee - another maiden;
False tongues three have whispered evil of thee;
One said - thine origin is lowly;
One, that thou art as treacherous as a serpent
And a third - that thou art dull and dreamy.

The line about being "treacherous as a serpent" might be dismissed by someone who has not studied the folklore of the morning star in Slavic culture. However, for me, and hopefully for any reader who has followed thus far, this looks like something that is not at all coincidental. As I have noted, the "treacherous sister" is consistently associated with serpents, and is often contrasted with the heavenly sister of the sun. The treacherous sister could be Marena, but also Zorya Polunochnaya. (The midnight sister in the Zorya triad.) This is perhaps hinted at in the Russian charm where Maria Morningstar and Mar'iama Evening Star are invoked against the midnight demon (their third sister?). The evening star and morning star are therefore not always assigned different roles, and may sometimes be impossible to distinguish. The "dark" member of the triad is quite distinct, however, and this may give the impression of a dyad within the triad.

A Genealogy of the Zoryas

I have strayed quite a bit from the initial proposition of a triad of Zoryas, and there is a reason for that; A trio is not always evident in the folklore. Oftentimes, a single personified "Zarya", "Zorya", "Zaranica", or "Zora" appears. This typically seems to be Zorya Utrennyaya - the dawn of the morning or morning star. In many cases, she may seem to have a dark counterpart. However, the references to three sisters who emerge from the sea is also widespread. This raises the question of their genealogy.

Genealogy is one of the hardest parts of mythology to reconstruct. This is probably in part because even pagans often had confused or conflicting genealogies for their mythological figures. We can see examples of this confusion even in Greece, where we have an excellent record of mythological beliefs.

Obviously, at least one Sea-Daughter is the sister of the Sun. Yet she is also called a daughter of the Sea King. In the Malalas Chronicle, however, we see the Sun Tsar referred to as the son of Svarog. Furthermore, a critical reading of Wendish sources suggests that all major deities are children of Svarog, the God of Gods. She could be the Sun God's half-sister, through the maternal line only. However, there are some tales which seem to suggest that brother and sister were both abducted together. We see this confusion in the Polish tale of the Waterman's Daughter[72] versus the Czech tale of the Waternick.[73] Both also resemble the Russian "The Sea King and Vasilissa the Wise"[74] The three stories are almost the same, and the Waterman / Waternick / Sea King are all very consistent characters across narratives. However, they disagree about whether the hero escapes with his sister or with the daughter of his aquatic captor

In Maria Morevna, the hero gives away a sister called "Maria" in marriage to another, but later he marries a stranger named "Maria Morevna."[75] In this Russian tale, there is no obvious confusion - it appears that the hero's sister Maria is distinct from Maria Morevna, and is given to someone other than the hero. However, in the analogous tale from the Abkhazian Nart Sagas, there is extreme confusion over this part of the story - a detail that clearly puzzles Colarusso based on his footnotes.[76]

Even in the Kresnik cycle, we can see that the hero's sister / wife claims to be an "orphan" who does not know who her true parents are. She is one of three maidens, and the only one who seems to have a different heritage from the other two.[77] Based on this, we can perhaps reconstruct the Zoryas as three sisters, but with Zorya Utrennyaya (the morning star) as a half-sister and foster child of the Sea King. We see precisely this type of arrangement in the Romanian tale of Harap Alb, which features an AT 550 bird maiden; towards the end, the hero must distinguish "The Red King's" real daughter from his adopted one who looks exactly the same.[78]

The theme of incest between the Sun and his sister (the Dawn Goddess, Morning Star, or Moon) is remarkably consistent throughout Eastern Europe. It is reminiscent of a Russian tale where a brother hunts for a woman who fits his wedding ring, only to discover that his sister does. He pursues his sister with amorous intent, only to end up marrying Baba Yaga's daughter who looks exactly like her.[79] Also, there is a lengthy tale from the Karelian storyteller Korguev that opens exactly the same way - with a brother pursuing his sister because his wedding ring only fits her. Later, the intended bride of the brother turns out to be a serpent-infested swan maiden.[80] We've discussed enough in previous sections to guess at the significance of this.

So we may say that the Zoryas can all appear identical, but one has a malicious streak, and another is not a "biological" daughter of the Sea King at all, but a sister of the Sun. This contradicts the Nart Sagas, which portray Zerasha as a daughter of Dobettyr the Sea God. This could be an attempt to reconcile a celestial Balto-Slavic genealogy with an Iranian one, where the maiden was said to be the daughter of the Sea God.

If she is a half-sister of the other Zoryas, then who is her mother?

It's probably in Romania where the parentage is most clear: The mother of the Woods is the mother of Zorila (Dawn), Murgila (Dusk), and Miazanoapte (Midnight).[81] This "Mother of the Woods" or Mamapadurei is a figure of Romanian folklore who lives in a forest, in a hut that revolves on fowl's legs, and a fence stuck full of skulls. She kidnaps children, and generally corresponds to Baba Yaga.[82] Thus, all three dawn Goddesses can probably be considered daughters of the hag figure (Mokosh, or a member of another triad to which Mokosh belongs)

There is some confusion surrounding the midnight Zorya, however, who seems to quite literally "become her mother" in many narratives. When she transforms into her most monstrous form, she is difficult to distinguish from the "hag" or Baba Yaga symbolic archetype. For example, in "The Witch and the Sun's Sister" the evil sister engages in the very "Baba Yaga-like" task of sharpening her teeth before pursuing the hero in a dramatic chase, and gnawing through many obstacles thrown in her way. Thus Zorya Polunochnaya / Marena can also sometimes become indistinguishable from Mokosh.

Sample Tale: The Golden Apple Tree and the Nine Peahens[83]

Once there was a king who had three sons. In the garden of the palace grew a golden apple-tree, which, in one and the same night would blossom and bear ripe fruit. But during the night a thief would come and pluck the golden apples, and none could detect him. One day the king deliberating with his sons, said: "I would give much to know what happens to the fruit of our apple-tree!" Thereupon the eldest son answered: "I will mount guard to-night under the apple-tree, and we will see who gathers the fruit."

When evening came, the prince laid himself under the apple-tree to watch; but as the apples ripened, he fell asleep and did not wake until next morning, when the apples had vanished. He told his father what had happened, and his brother, the second son, then offered to keep guard that night. But he had no more success than his elder brother.

It was now the turn of the youngest son to try his luck, and, when night came on, he placed a bed under the tree, and lay down and went to sleep. About midnight he awoke and glanced at the apple-tree. And lo! the apples were just ripening and the whole castle was lit up with their shining. At that moment nine peahens flew to the tree and settled on its branches, where eight remained to pluck the fruit. The ninth, however, flew to the ground and was instantly transformed into a maiden so beautiful that one might in vain search for her equal throughout the kingdom.

The prince immediately fell madly in love with his visitor and the fair maiden was not at all unwilling to stay and converse with the young man. An hour or two soon passed but at last the maiden said that she might stay no longer. She thanked the prince for the apples which her sisters had plucked, but he asked that they would give him at least one to carry home. The maiden smiled sweetly and handed the young man two apples, one for himself, the other for his father, the king. She then turned again into a peahen, joined her sisters and all flew away.

Next morning the prince carried the two apples to his father. The king, very pleased, praised his son, and on the following night, the happy prince placed himself under the tree, as before, next morning again bringing two apples to his father. After this had happened for several nights, his two brothers grew envious, because they had not been able to do what he had done. Then a wicked old woman offered her services to the malcontent princes, promising that she would reveal the secret to them. So on the next evening the old woman stole softly under the bed of the young prince and hid herself there. Soon afterward the prince came and at once went to sleep just as before. When midnight came, lo! the peahens flew down as usual; eight of them settling on the branches of the apple-tree, but the ninth, descending on the bed of the prince, instantly turned into a maiden. The old woman, seeing this strange metamorphosis, crept softly near and cut off a lock of the maiden's hair, whereupon the girl immediately arose, changed again into a peahen, and disappeared together with her sisters. Then the young prince jumped up and wondering what had been the reason for the sudden departure of his beloved began to look around. He then saw the old woman, dragged her from under his bed, and ordered his servants to fasten her to the tails of four horses and so to destroy her. But the peahens never came again, to the great sorrow of the prince, and for all that he mourned and wept.

Weeping will not move any mountain, and at length the prince resolved to go through the wide world in search of his sweetheart and not return home until he had found her. As a good son, he asked leave of his father who tried hard to make him give up such a hazardous scheme and promised him a much more beautiful bride in his own vast kingdom—for he was very sure that any maiden would be glad to marry such a valiant prince.

But all his fatherly advice was vain, so the king finally allowed his son to do what his heart bade, and the sorrowful prince departed with only one servant to seek his love. Journeying on for a long time, he came at length to the shore of a large lake, near which was a magnificent castle in which there lived a very old woman, a queen, with her only daughter. The prince implored the aged queen, "I pray thee, grandmother, tell me what you can about the nine golden peahens?" The queen answered: "O, my son, I know those peahens well, for they come every day at noon to this lake and bathe. But had you not better forget the peahens, and rather consider this beautiful girl, she is my daughter and will inherit my wealth and treasures, and you can share all with her." But the prince, impatient to find the peahens, did not even listen to what the queen was saying. Seeing his indifference, the old lady bribed his servant and gave him a pair of bellows, saying: "Do you see this? When you go to-morrow to the lake, blow secretly behind your master's neck, and he will fall asleep and will not be able to speak to the peahens."

The faithless servant agreed to do exactly as the queen bade, and when they went to the lake, he used the first favourable occasion and blew with the bellows behind his poor master's neck, whereupon the prince fell so soundly asleep that he resembled a dead man. Soon after, the eight peahens flew to the lake, and the ninth alighted on the prince's horse and began to embrace him, saying: "Arise, sweetheart! Arise, beloved one! Ah, do!" Alas! the poor prince remained as if dead. Then after the peahens had bathed, all disappeared

Shortly after their departure the prince woke up and asked his servant: "What has happened? Have they been here?" The servant answered that they had indeed been there; that eight of them bathed in the lake, while the ninth caressed and kissed him, trying to arouse him from slumber. Hearing this, the poor prince was so angry that he was almost ready to kill himself.

Next morning the same thing happened. But on this occasion the peahen bade the servant tell the prince that she would come again the following day for the last time. When the third day dawned the prince went again to the lake, and fearing to fall asleep he decided to gallop along the marge instead of pacing slowly as before. His deceitful servant, however, pursuing him closely, again found an opportunity for using the bellows, and yet again the prince fell asleep.

Shortly afterward the peahens came; eight of them went as usual to bathe, and the ninth alighted on the prince's horse and tried to awaken him. She embraced him and spoke thus: "Awake, my darling! Sweetheart, arise! Ah, my soul!" But her efforts were futile; the prince was sleeping as if he were dead. Then she said to the servant: "When thy master awakes tell him to cut off the head of the nail; then only he may be able to find me again."

Saying this the peahen disappeared with her sisters, and they had hardly disappeared when the prince awoke and asked his servant: "Have they been here?" And the malicious fellow answered: "Yes; the one who alighted on your horse ordered me to tell you that, if you wish to find her again, you must first cut off the head of the nail." Hearing this the prince unsheathed his sword and struck off his faithless servant's head.

The prince now resumed his pilgrimage alone, and after long journeying he came to a mountain where he met a hermit, who offered hospitality to him. In the course of conversation the prince asked his host whether he knew anything about the nine peahens; the hermit replied: "O my son, you are really fortunate! God himself has shown you the right way. From here to their dwelling is but half a day's walk; to-morrow I will point you the way."

The prince rose very early the next morning, prepared himself for the journey, thanked the hermit for giving him shelter, and went on as he was directed. He came to a large gate, and, passing through it, he turned to the right; toward noon he observed some white walls, the sight of which rejoiced him very much. Arriving at this castle he asked the way to the palace of the nine peahens, and proceeding he soon came to it. He was, of course, challenged by the guards, who asked his name and whence he came. When the queen heard that he had arrived, she was overwhelmed with joy, and turning into a maiden she ran swiftly to the gate and led the prince into the palace. There was great feasting and rejoicing when, later, their nuptials were solemnized, and after the wedding the prince remained within the palace and lived in peace.

Now one day the queen went for a walk in the palace grounds accompanied by an attendant, the prince remaining in the palace. Before starting the queen gave her spouse the keys of twelve cellars, saying: "You may go into the cellars, all but one; do not on any account go into the twelfth; you must not even open the door!"

The prince soon began to speculate upon what there could possibly be in the twelfth cellar; and having opened one cellar after the other, he stood hesitatingly at the door of the twelfth. He who hesitates is lost, and so the prince finally inserted the key in the lock and the next moment had passed into the forbidden place. In the middle of the floor was a huge cask bound tightly round with three strong iron hoops. The bung-hole was open and from within the cask came a muffled voice which said: "I pray thee, brother, give me a drink of water, else I shall die of thirst!" The prince took a glass of water and poured it through the bung-hole; immediately one hoop burst. Then the voice spake again: "O brother give me more water lest I should die of thirst!" The good-hearted prince emptied a second glass into the cask, and a second hoop instantly came asunder. Again the voice implored: "O brother, give me yet a third glass! I am still consumed by thirst!" The prince made haste to gratify the unseen speaker, and as he poured in the water the third hoop burst, the cask fell in pieces, and a great dragon struggled out from the wreck, rushed through the door and flew into the open. Very soon he fell in with the queen, who was on her way back to the palace, and carried her off. Her attendant, affrighted, rushed to the prince with the intelligence, and the news came as a thunderbolt.

For a time the prince was as one distraught, but then he became calmer and he resolved to set out again in search of his beloved queen. In his wanderings he came to a river, and, walking along its bank, he noticed in a little hole a small fish leaping and struggling. When the fish saw the prince, it began to beseech him piteously: "Be my brother-in-God! Throw me back into the stream; someday I may, perhaps, be useful to you! But be sure to take a scale from me, and when you are in need of help rub it gently." The prince picked up the fish, took a scale from it, and threw the poor creature into the water; then he carefully wrapped the scale in his handkerchief.

Continuing his wanderings, he came to a place where he saw a fox caught in an iron trap, and the animal addressed him, saying: "Be my brother-in-God! Release me, I pray, from this cruel trap; and someday, perhaps, I may be helpful to you. Only take a hair from my brush, and, if you are in need, rub it gently!" The prince took a hair from the fox's tail and set him free. Journeying on, he came upon a wolf caught in a trap. And the wolf besought him in these words: "Be my brother-in-God, and release me! One day you may need my help, therefore, take just one hair from my coat, and if you should ever need my assistance, you will have but to rub it a little!" This likewise the prince did.

Some days elapsed and then, as the prince went wearily on his way, he met a man in the mountains, to whom he said: "O my brother-in-God! Can you direct me to the castle of the king of the dragons?" Luckily the man knew of this castle and was able to tell the way to it; he also informed the prince exactly how long the journey would take

The prince thanked the stranger and continued his journey with fresh vigour until he came to where the king of the dragons lived. He entered the castle boldly and found his wife there; after their first joy of meeting, they began to consider how they could escape. Finally, they took swift horses from the stables, but they had hardly set out before the dragon came back. When he found that the queen had escaped, he took counsel with his courser: "What do you advise? Shall we first eat and drink, or shall we pursue at once!" The horse answered: "Let us first refresh ourselves, for we shall surely catch them." After the meal, the dragon mounted his horse and in a very few minutes they reached the fugitives. Then he seized the queen and said to the prince: "Go in peace! I pardon you this time, because you released me from that cellar: but do not venture to cross my path again, for you will not be forgiven a second time."

The poor prince started sadly on his way, but he soon found that he could not abandon his wife. Whatever the cost he must make another attempt to rescue her, and so he retraced his steps, and on the following day entered the castle again and found his wife in tears. It was evident that they must use guile if they were to elude the magical powers of the dragon-king, and after they had thought upon the matter, the prince said: "When the dragon comes home to-night, ask where he got his horse; perchance I may be able to procure a steed that is equally swift: only then could we hopefully make another attempt to escape." Saying this he left his wife for a time. When the dragon-king returned, the queen began to caress him and to pleasantly converse; at length she said: "How I admire your fine horse! Certainly he is of no ordinary breed! Where did you find such a swift courser?" And the dragon-king replied: "Ah! his like is not to be got by every one! In a certain mountain lives an old woman, who has in her stables twelve wondrous horses; none could easily tell which is the finest! But in a corner stands one that is apparently leprous; he is, in fact, the best of the stable, and whoever becomes his master, may ride even higher than the clouds. My steed is a brother of those horses, and if anyone would get a horse from that old woman, he must serve her for three days. She has a mare and a foal, and he who is her servant must tend them for three days and three nights; if he succeeds in guarding them and returns them to the old woman, he is entitled to choose a horse from her stable. But, if the servant does not watch well over the mare and its foal, he will indeed lose his life."

Next morning, when the dragon had left the castle, the prince came and the queen told him what she had heard. Hastily bidding his wife farewell, he went with all speed to the mountain, and finding the old woman, he said to her: "God help you, grandmother!" And she returned the greeting: "May God help you also, my son! What good wind brought you here, and what do you wish?" He answered: "I should like to serve you." Thereupon the old woman said: "Very well, my son! If you successfully watch my mare and its foal for three days, I shall reward you with a horse which you yourself are at liberty to choose from my stable; but if you do not keep them safe, you must die."

Then she led the prince into her courtyard, where he saw stakes all around placed close together, and on each save one was stuck a human head. The one stake kept shouting out to the old woman: "Give me a head, O grandmother! Give me a head!" The old woman said: "All these are heads of those who once served me; they did not succeed in keeping my mare and its foal safe, so they had to pay with their heads!" But the prince was not to be frightened at what he saw, and he readily accepted the old woman's conditions.

When evening came, he mounted the mare and rode it to pasture, the foal following. He remained seated on the mare, but, toward midnight, he dozed a little and finally fell fast asleep. When he awoke, he saw, to his great consternation, that he was sitting upon the trunk of a tree holding the mare's bridle in his hand. He sprang down and went immediately in search of the tricky animal. Soon he came to a river, the sight of which reminded him of the little fish, and taking the scale from his handkerchief, he rubbed it gently between his fingers, when lo! the fish instantly appeared and asked: "What is the matter, my brother-in-God?" The prince answered: "My mare has fled, and I do not know where to look for her!" And the fish answered: "Here she is with us, turned into a fish, and her foal into a small one! Strike once upon the water with the bridle and shout: 'Doora! Mare of the old woman!'"

The prince did as the fish told him; at once the mare and her foal came out of the water; he bridled the mare, mounted and rode home; the young foal trotting after. The old woman brought the prince some food without a word; then she took the mare into the stable, beat her with a poker, and said: "Did I not tell you to go down among the fish?" The mare answered: "I have been down to the fish, but the fish are his friends and they betrayed me to him." Thereupon the old woman said: "To-night you go among the foxes!"

When evening came, the prince mounted the mare again and rode to the field, the foal following its mother. He determined again to remain in the saddle and to keep watch, but, toward midnight, he was again overcome by drowsiness and became unconscious. When he awoke next morning, lo! he was seated on a tree-trunk holding fast the bridle. This alarmed him greatly, and he looked here and he looked there. But search as he would, he could find no trace of the mare and her foal. Then he remembered his friend the fox, and taking the hair from the fox's tail out of his handkerchief, he rubbed it gently between his fingers, and the fox instantly stood before him. "What is the matter, my brother-in-God?" said he. The prince complained of his misfortune, saying that he had hopelessly lost his mare. The fox soon reassured him: "The mare is with us, changed to a fox, and her foal into a cub; just strike once with the bridle on the earth, and shout out 'Doora, the old woman's mare!'" He did so, and sure enough the mare at once appeared before him with the foal. So he bridled her and mounted, and when he reached home the old woman gave him food, and took the mare to the stable and beat her with a poker, saying: "Why did you not turn into a fox, you disobedient creature?" And the mare protested: "I did turn into a fox; but the foxes are his friends, so they betrayed me!" At this the old woman commanded: "Next time you go to the wolves!"

When evening came the prince set out on the mare and the same things befell as before. He found himself, the next morning, sitting on a tree-trunk, and this time he called the wolf, who said: "The mare of the old woman is with us in the likeness of a she-wolf, and the foal of a wolf's cub; strike the ground once with the bridle and exclaim: 'Doora! the mare of the old woman!'" The prince did as the wolf counselled, and the mare reappeared with her foal standing behind her.

He mounted once again and proceeded to the old woman's house, where, on his arrival, he found her preparing a meal. Having set food before him, she took the mare to the stable and beat her with a poker. "Did I not tell you to go to the wolves, you wretched creature?" she scolded. But the mare protested again, saying: "I did go to the wolves, but they are also his friends and they betrayed me!" Then the old woman went back to the house and the prince said to her: "Well, grandmother, I think I have served you honestly; now I hope you will give me what you promised me!" The old woman replied: "O my son, verily a promise must be fulfilled! Come to the stable; there are twelve horses; you are at liberty to choose whichever you like best!"

Thereupon the prince said firmly: "Well, why should I be particular? Give me the leprous horse, standing in that corner." The old woman tried by all means in her power to deter him from taking that ugly horse, saying: "Why be so foolish as to take that leprous jade when you can have a fine horse?" But the prince kept to his choice, and said: "Give me rather the one I selected, as it was agreed between us!"

The old woman, seeing that he would not yield, gave way, and the prince took leave of her and led away his choice. When they came to a forest he curried and groomed the horse, and it shone as if its skin were of pure gold. Then he mounted, and, the horse flying like a bird, they reached the dragon-king's castle in a few seconds.

The prince immediately entered and greeted the queen with: "Hasten, all is ready for our flight!" The queen was ready, and in a few seconds, they were speeding away, swift as the wind, on the back of the wonderful horse.

Shortly after they had gone, the dragon-king came home, and finding that the queen had again disappeared, he addressed the following words to his horse: "What shall we do now? Shall we refresh ourselves, or shall we go after the fugitives at once?" And his horse replied: "We may do as you will, but we shall never reach them!"

Upon hearing this the dragon-king at once flung himself upon his horse and they were gone in a flash. After a time the prince looked behind him and saw the dragon-king in the distance. He urged his horse, but it said: "Be not afraid! There is no need to run quicker." But the dragon-king drew nearer, so close that his horse was able to speak thus to its brother: "O brother dear, tarry, I beseech you! else I shall perish in running at this speed!" But the prince's horse answered: "Nay, why be so foolish as to carry that monster? Fling up your hoofs and throw him against a rock, then come with me!" At these words the dragon-king's horse shook its head, curved its back, and kicked up its hoofs so furiously that its rider was flung on to a rock and killed. Seeing this, the prince's horse stood still, its brother trotted up, and the queen mounted on it. So they arrived happily in her own land, where they lived and ruled in great prosperity ever after.

Endnotes

1. Czernik, Stanisław. Stare Złoto: O Polskiej Pieśni Ludowej. Warszawa: Państwowy Instytut Wydawniczy, 1962. Page 238
2. Bain, R N. Cossack Fairy Tales. London: A.H. Bullen, 1902, Pages 178-184
3. Slančiauskas, Matas, Robert Staneslow, Ieva Skaržinskaitė, and Ona Pelickiene. Folk Tales of Northern Lithuania: Šiaures Lietuvos Pasakos. 2015.
4. Monaghan, Patricia. Encyclopedia of Goddesses and Heroines. United States: New World Library, 2014. Internet resource. Page 168
5. Harrison, E J. Lithuania: Past Present. Forgotten Books, 1901. Internet resource. Page 167
6. Ryan, W.F. The Bathhouse at Midnight: An Historical Survey of Magic and Divination in Russia. Stroud: Sutton, 1999. Pages 169, 178
7. Monaghan, Patricia. Encyclopedia of Goddesses and Heroines. [2 Volumes]. United States, ABC-CLIO, 2009. Page 285
8. Archaeoastronomy. Chalfont St. Giles, Eng.: Science History Publications, 1979, Volumes 22-23, Page 73
9. William, Ralston S. R. Russian Fairy Tales: A Choice Collection of Muscovite Folk-Lore. 2019. Internet resource. Pages 97-108
10. Tales of the Narts: Ancient Myths and Legends of the Ossetians. S.l.: PRINCETON UNIVERSITY PRES, 2020. Pages 3-7
11. Kuniczak, W S, and Pat Bargielski. The Glass Mountain: Twenty-eight Ancient Polish Folktales and Fables. New York: Hippocrene Books, 1997. Internet resource. Page 59
12. Tales of the Narts: Ancient Myths and Legends of the Ossetians. S.l.: PRINCETON UNIVERSITY PRES, 2020. Page 3-7
13. Mijatovicka, Elodie L, and William DENTON. Serbian Folk-Lore: Popular Tales Selected and Translated by Madam Cs. Mijatovics. Edited, with an Introduction, by W. Denton, 1874. Page 43-44

14. Zalka, Csenge V. Dancing on Blades: Rare and Exquisite Folktales from the Carpathian Mountains. 2018. Internet resource. Page 40-41
15. Zalka, Csenge V. Dancing on Blades: Rare and Exquisite Folktales from the Carpathian Mountains. 2018. Internet resource. Page 41
16. Lang, Andrew. The Yellow Fairy Book. London: Abela Pub, 2010. Pages 209-233
17. Tales of the Narts: Ancient Myths and Legends of the Ossetians. S.l.: PRINCETON UNIVERSITY PRES, 2020. Pages 3-7
18. Ziolkowski, Eric. A Handbook of Biblical Reception in Jewish, European Christian, and Islamic Folklores, De Gruyter 2017
19. Bain, R N. Cossack Fairy Tales. London: A.H. Bullen, 1902, Pages 92-102
20. Greimas, Algirdas J. Of Gods and Men: Studies in Lithuanian Mythology. Bloomington: Indiana University Press, 1992. Pages 64-111,
21. Mouse, Anon E, and Illustrated J. A. N. MATULKA. The Shoemakers Apron-20 Czech and Slovak Childrens Stories: Twenty Illustrated Slavic Children's Stories. 2017. Internet resource.
22. KREMNITZ, Mite, and J M. PERCIVAL. Roumanian Fairy Tales, Collected by M. Kremnitz. Adapted and Arranged by J.M. Percival. 1885. Pages 191-241
23. Lang, Andrew. The Violet Fairy Book, 2014. Pages 157-177
24. Lang, Andrew, and Henry J. FORD. The Brown Fairy Book. Edited by Andrew Lang. with Eight Illustrations by H. I. Ford. London: Longmans & Co, 1904. Pages 215-232
25. Tales of the Narts: Ancient Myths and Legends of the Ossetians. S.l.: PRINCETON UNIVERSITY PRES, 2020. Page 21
26. Colarusso, John, and Adrienne Mayor. Nart Sagas from the Caucasus: Ancient Myths and Legends of the Circassians and Abkhazians. 2016. Pages 50-51
27. Colarusso, John, and Adrienne Mayor. Nart Sagas from the Caucasus: Ancient Myths and Legends of the Circassians and Abkhazians. 2016. Pages 129-131, 184, 216

28. Tales of the Narts: Ancient Myths and Legends of the Ossetians. S.l.: PRINCETON UNIVERSITY PRES, 2020. Page 108
29. The Russian story book, containing tales from the song-cycles of Kiev and Novgorod and other early sources. London, Macmillan and Company, Limited, 1916. Pages 302-304
30. Ahmad, Aisha, and Roger Boase. Pashtun Tales: From the Pakistan-Afghan Frontier. London: Saqi, 2008. Pages 208-215
31. Vajda, Edward J. James P. Mallory and Douglas Q. Adams, Eds. Encyclopedia of Indo-European Culture. London: Fitzroy Dearborn, 1997. Page 161
32. West, Morris. Indo-European Poetry and Myth. Oxford: Oxford University Press, 2007. Page 228
33. Sanko, Siarhei. (2018). Reflexes of Ancient Ideas about Divine Twins in the Images of Saints George and Nicholas in Belarusian Folklore. Folklore: Electronic Journal of Folklore. 72. 15-40.
34. Konakov, N D, Vladimir Napolskikh, Anna-Leena Siikala, and Mihaly Hoppal. Komi Mythology. Budapest: Akademiai, 2003. Page 386
35. Hard, Robin, and H J. Rose. The Routledge Handbook of Greek Mythology: Partially Based on H. I. Rose's a Handbook of Greek Mythology. 2020. Internet resource. Page 468
36. Frazer, James G. Adonis, Attis, Osiris, Studies in the History of Oriental Religion, by J. G. Frazer. London: Macmillan, 1907. Page 204
37. West, Morris. Indo-European Poetry and Myth. Oxford: Oxford University Press, 2007. Page 228
38. Sanko, Siarhei. (2018). Reflexes of Ancient Ideas about Divine Twins in the Images of Saints George and Nicholas in Belarusian Folklore. Folklore: Electronic Journal of Folklore. 72. 15-40.
39. West, Morris. Indo-European Poetry and Myth. Oxford: Oxford University Press, 2007. Page 227
40. Kinsley, David R. Hindu Goddesses: Visions of the Divine Feminine in the Hindu Religious Tradition; with New Preface. Berkeley: University of California Press, 1997. Page 14

41. Ralston, William R. S. The Songs of the Russian People: As Illustrative of Slavonic Mythology and Russian Social Life. London: Ellis & Green, 1872. Page 350
42. William, Ralston S. R. Russian Fairy Tales: A Choice Collection of Muscovite Folk-Lore. Australia, Floating Press, 2014. Pages 200-209
43. ФГБУНСеверо-Осетинский институт гуманитарных и социальных исследований им. В.И. Абаева ВНЦ РАН и Правительства РСО-Алания, Таказов Федар Магометович, МИФОЛОГИЧЕСКИЕ АРХЕТИПЫ МОДЕЛИ МИРА В ОСЕТИНСКОЙ КОСМОГОНИИ, Владикавказ 2014. Pages 148-149
44. советская этнография 1990, академия наук ссср, 1990. Page 106
45. Bain, R N. Cossack Fairy Tales and Folk-Tales. London: A.H. Bullen, 1902. Internet resource. Pages 47-78
46. Napolskikh, Vladimir V, and Natalja A. Tuckova. Selkup Mythology. Budapest: Akad. K, 2010. Pages 76-77, 156
47. Afanasev, A N, Norbert Guterman, Alexandre Alexeieff, and Roman Jakobson. Russian Fairy Tales, 2017. Pages 304-307
48. Bain, R N. Cossack Fairy Tales. London: A.H. Bullen, 1902, Page 290
49. Hapgood, Isabel F, and Francis J. Child. The Epic Songs of Russia. with an Introductory Note by Professor Francis J. Child. Pp. xiii. 358. C. Scribner's Sons: New York: Boston, Mass. Printed, 1886. Pages 214-222, 353
50. Bailey, James, and T G. Ivanova. An Anthology of Russian Folk Epics. 2015. Internet resource. Page 105
51. Hero Tales and Legends of the Serbians. London, 1914. Pages 206-207
52. Ortutay, Gyula. Hungarian Folk Tales, 1962. Pages 120-140
53. Gemuev, Izmail N, and Anna-Leena Siikala. Mansi Mythology. Budapest: Akad. K, 2008. Page 44
54. Hapgood, Isabel F, and Francis J. Child. The Epic Songs of Russia. with an Introductory Note by Professor Francis J. Child. Pp. xiii.

358. C. Scribner's Sons: New York: Boston, Mass. printed, 1886. Pages 214-222

55. Marjanić, Suzana. "A Review of Contemporary Research on Croatian Mythology in Relation to Natko Nodilo." Traditiones. 47.2 (2018): 15-31.
56. Marjanić, Suzana. "The Dyadic Goddess and Doutheism in Nodilo's the Ancient Faith of the Serbs and the Croats." Studia Mythologica Slavica. 6 (2003): 181-203. Print
57. Reeder, Roberta F. Russian Folk Lyrics. Bloomington u.a: Indiana Univ. Press, 1993. Page 65
58. Warner, Elizabeth A. The Russian Folk Theatre. 2011. Internet resource. Page 30
59. Knab, Sophie H. Polish Customs, Traditions and Folklore. New York: Hippocrene Books, 2017. Pages 86-87
60. Mallory, James P, and Douglas Q. Adams. Encyclopedia of Indo-European Culture. London: Fitzroy Dearborn, 1997. Pages 150, 503
61. Archaeoastronomy. Chalfont St. Giles, Eng.: Science History Publications, 1979. Volumes 22-23, Page 73
62. Ryan, W.F. The Bathhouse at Midnight: An Historical Survey of Magic and Divination in Russia. Stroud: Sutton, 1999. Page 169
63. Nicoloff, Assen. Bulgarian Folklore: Folk Beliefs, Customs, Folk-Songs, Personal Names. Cleveland: Author, 1990. Page 29
64. Kivelson, Valerie A, and Christine D. Worobec. Witchcraft in Russia and Ukraine, 1000-1900: A Sourcebook, 2021. Internet resource. Page 146
65. William, Ralston S. R. Russian Fairy Tales: A Choice Collection of Muscovite Folk-Lore. 2019. Internet resource. Pages 183-184
66. Bartók, Béla. Rumanian Folk Music: Carols and Christmas Songs (Colinde). Netherlands, Springer Netherlands, 2012. Page 253
67. Costin, Claudia. Folkloric Aspects of the Romanian Imaginary and Myth. 2018. Internet resource. Pages 21-24
68. Smitek, Zmago. "Kresnik: an Attempt at a Mythological Reconstruction." Studia Mythologica Slavica. 1 (1998): 93-118.

69. Smitek, Zmago. "Kresnik: an Attempt at a Mythological Reconstruction." Studia Mythologica Slavica. 1 (1998): 93-118.
70. Kropej, Monika. Supernatural Beings from Slovenian Myth and Folktales. Ljubljana: ZRC Publishing, 2012. Pages 36-37
71. Bowring, John, and Vuk Karadžić. Servian Popular Poetry =: Narodne Srpske Pjesme. London: printed for the author, 1827. Internet resource. Page 123,
72. Sienkiewicz, Henryk, Reymont W. St, Boleslaw Prus, Adam Szymanski, Stefan Zeromski, Juliusz Kaden-Bandrowski, Zofia Nakowska, Wacaw Sieroszewski, Sergiej Nowikow, Else C. M. Benecke, and Marie Busch. 67 Tales from Poland, 2017.
73. Baudis, Joseph. Czech Folk Tales. N.Y: Kraus Reprint, 1971.
74. Afanasev, A N, Norbert Guterman, Alexandre Alexeieff, and Roman Jakobson. Russian Fairy Tales, 2017. Pages 427-438
75. William, Ralston S. R. Russian Fairy Tales: A Choice Collection of Muscovite Folk-Lore. 2019. Internet resource.
76. Colarusso, John. Nart Sagas from the Caucasus: Myths and Legends from the Circassians, Abazas, Abkhaz, and Ubykhs, 2016. Internet resource. Page 32
77. Kropej, Monika. Supernatural Beings from Slovenian Myth and Folktales. Ljubljana: ZRC Publishing, 2012. Page 41
78. Roznoveanu, Mirela. Old Romanian Fairy Tales: 2nd Edition, XLIBRIS, 2013. Page 76
79. Russian Fairy Tales. New York: Pantheon, 1973. Pages 351-356
80. Haney, Jack V. Long, Long Tales from the Russian North. Jackson: University Press of Mississippi, 2013. Pages 73-90
81. Costin, Claudia. Folkloric Aspects of the Romanian Imaginary and Myth. 2018. Internet resource. Page 69
82. Johns, Andreas. Baba Yaga: The Ambiguous Mother and Witch of the Russian Folktale. 2004. Page 75
83. Mijatovicka, Elodie L, and William DENTON. Serbian Folk-Lore: Popular Tales Selected and Translated by Madam Cs. Mijatovics. Edited, with an Introduction, by W. Denton. 1874.

Chapter 6

Advanced Concepts in Indo-European Mythology

This book has already delved into Indo-European comparative mythology a lot. So much so that a crash course on the topic may seem silly at this point. And there is some material like the dragon-slaying motif involving a thunder God that won't be reviewed in depth here. But this chapter is intended to ensure readers have a basic understanding of the topic, and its history. Since almost the beginning of its discovery, the Indo-European language family has been repeatedly tied to the study of comparative mythology.

The first scholars of the 19th century, though often overzealously romantic, did make some valid observations. For instance, it did not take long for people to link the Vedic Sky Father deity "Dyaus Pitar" (literally meaning Sky Father) with Jupiter and Zeus. Sure enough, linguistics has shown that Greek "Zeus", Latin "Ju", and Sanskrit "Dyaus" all come from the Proto-Indo-European word for "Sky."[1]

Many scholars were also quick to draw parallels between European dragon-slaying tales, and the dragon-slaying narrative of the Vedas involving Indra (see Chapter 3: Perun and the Drakenkampf). They also betrayed a lot of their preconceptions while interpreting this material, however. For instance, George W. Cox wrote of the Vedic and Greek dragon-slaying myths that the only difference between them was that the Greeks who recounted the story:

> *...Recount without understanding it. They are no longer conscientious that Geryon, Typhon, Echidna, and Orthros, Python,*

> *and Kerberos are names for the same thing, and that the combats of Herakles, Perseus, Theseus, and Kadmos with these monsters denote simply the changes of the visible heavens.*[2]

Thus, while 19th-century scholars drew some meaningful connections between Vedic and European mythology, they had a tendency to reduce every myth to a metaphor for a specific natural phenomenon. To be sure, the Vedic tale in which the thunder God Indra slays a dragon to release water (rain) does lend itself to that interpretation. However, the absolute reduction of myths to nothing more than a representation of physical phenomena was very characteristic of the 19th-century mythological school. The scholars of the 19th century did have the bright idea of analyzing European folktales and folklore for traces of mythology, however. While the scholars of the 19th-century weren't always very adept at their analysis, it's worth noting that this area of research has been largely neglected since the Romantic period. Despite the near-certainty that some folktale elements are in fact derived from ancient tradition.

Much of what we associate with Proto-Indo-European culture today was reconstructed by the scholar Dumezil, who took a very different path focused on the social structure of early Indo-European society. It is widely recognized that Dumezil's work led to a revitalization of the field in the mid-20th century. Before we get much further, I want to make sure to provide some clarity on his work. It is critical for understanding many of the analyses in Chapters 3, 4, 5, 7, and 8.

This section is supposed to give a decent overview of the field of Indo-European studies, especially where mythology is concerned. However, I also want to provide some of my own insights in order to better clarify my positions on comparative mythology.

Indo-European Creation Stories

Creation stories are a logical enough starting point when researching a mythology. Or so we would think. In our modern understanding of religion and mythology, the creation of the world seems to take precedence over most other types of myth. However, it's worth noting that many Indo-European cultures have not provided us with an abundance of mythology on creation. The Vedas contain some references to creation, but this is clearly not their primary concern. Their primary concern is praising the Gods and recounting their feats. The Vedas are also very focused on ritual. And it's likely that many other Indo-European cultures did not consider creation to be the most important element of their mythology.

As we will see when we discuss Dumezil's tripartite system in the next section, the case could be made that the Proto-Indo-European mythology reflects a culture more concerned with the origins and internal workings of its own community than they were with the creation of the universe. However, in those few cases where we can obtain a kind of Proto-Indo-European creation story, they do seem to have one element in common - The element of a primordial sacrifice or victim who is dismembered. The Proto-Indo-European creation myth is typically reconstructed mainly from Norse and Vedic mythology. Norse mythology cites the dismemberment of the giant Ymir as an act of creation, and in the Vedas of India there is a similar myth about Purusha.

The Gylfaginning in Snorri's Prose Edda reads as follows:[3]

From Ymir's flesh was earth created, and from blood, sea; rock of bones, trees of hair, and from his skull the sky.

This has often been compared with the Vedic creation story involving Purusha. To paraphrase the Purusha hymns in the Vedas:[4]

> *The Man has a thousand heads; he has a thousand eyes, and a thousand feet. Completely covering the earth, he overflows it by ten fingers. The man is none other than the universe, that which is past and that which is to come. He is the master of the immortal domain, because he grows beyond food-…On the sacred palanquin they sprinkled Man (that is,) the sacrifice that was born in the beginning. Through him, the gods performed sacrifice along with the saints and the seers. From this sacrifice offered in its total form, the speckled fat was drawn off. From this we made the animals of the air, those of the desert, and those of clusters…-His mouth became the Brahman, the Warrior was the product of his arms, his thighs were the artisan, from his feet were born the servant. The moon was born from his consciousness, from his gaze was born the sun, from his mouth Indra and Agni, from his breath was born the wind.*

The mythology around Purusha is obviously the most detailed and well-developed. Indeed, this hymn laid the groundwork for much of the future development of Hinduism. The Ymir myth is the only other example which is easily placed into a mythological narrative about creation.

Some researchers have attempted to derive the name of the Norse giant "Ymir" from the Proto-Indo-European word for "twin" which is reconstructed as *yémHos, cognate to Latin "Gemini" and Sanskrit "Yama." As Mallory says in his "*Encyclopedia of Indo-European Culture*":

> *Clearly related in structure is the related Indo-European creation myth that comprises the sacrifice of "Twin" by his brother "Man."*[5]

It's worth noting that we have already discussed these figures "Yama" and *yémHos" in Chapter 4: Untangling the Beard of Volos. We will tie this all together in another chapter. However, while Ymir and Purusha are the most obvious examples, it could be argued that most branches of the Indo-European family have some variant of this myth hidden away.

When it comes to Russian culture, a lot of researchers of IE cultures have tended to focus on the Dove Book, or Golubnaya Kniga. This apocryphal Russian text combines a number of interesting motifs, some Christian, some not. One passage in the text appears to describe the universe as arising from God's body:

> *The wide world is from the Holy Spirit, Christ himself, the Heavenly Father; the Sun is from God's face, Christ himself, the Heavenly Father; the young bright moon is from God's breast Christ himself the Heavenly Father; the dark nights are from God's hair, Christ himself the Heavenly Father; the morning dawn is from God's garments, Christ himself the Heavenly Father; the stars are from God's eyes, Christ himself the Heavenly Father; the tempestuous wind is from God's breath, Christ himself the Heavenly Father; the fine rain is from God's tears, Christ himself the Heavenly Father.*

In addition to this passage from the Dove Book, there is also a fascinating Belarusian legend about a statue that was shattered long ago. Wherever a body part crashed, they founded a village. Thus Golovichi is where they found a head. Gornovschina was founded where they found the breast. Puzovo is where they found the belly. The scholar Boganeva explores the Indo-European elements in both of these East Slavic narratives.[6]

However, not all dismemberment myths emphasize the cosmogonic aspect of creation. In the Purusha hymn, we can see that the first sacrifice is also associated with the genesis of life, and of people (in that case, different castes of people).

This emphasis on the genesis of life also shows up with the primordial bull-cow Gavaevodata in Persian Zoroastrianism. When the cow was slain, according to Persian mythology, its marrow, organs, seed, and soul were used to populate the world with animal life.[7] At first glance, the association with a cow seems like an anomaly, but there's probably a link to the Norse myth of creation, which also features a cow.

In Norse mythology, the primordial cow Audhumla is not identical to the first sacrifice Ymir, but features right beside him in the creation story. The Gyfaginning describes how there came into being a cow called Audhumla, and how four rivers of milk flowed from its teats, and how it fed Ymir.[8]

Neither is this the only Scandinavian story featuring creation from a cow. A more recently recorded Icelandic folktale claims that Drangey Island (a small island off the coast of Iceland) was created when the sun came up and turned her troll owners to stone. The trolls became two stacks of rock, whereas the cow became Drangey island itself.[9]

Granted, this is a story about the creation of just one small island. However, as we have already seen in Belarus (with the story of the shattered statue) some of these narratives are of a local nature. This should not be seen as contradicting the more "cosmic" versions of the story, but rather mirroring them. The local creation stories reflect the cosmic ones, or vice-versa.

In Greek mythology, the initial search for a "first sacrifice" myth is disappointing at first glance. Much of the cosmogony in Greek myth can be considered analogous to Near-Eastern models, and Hesiod's Theogony has no clear-cut example of a "first sacrifice" myth.

It is in the Dionysian mysteries where I have noted the most tantalizing hints of a Proto-Indo-European creation story in Ancient Greece. Specifically, we see similar narratives in association with the Orphic mysteries, a secretive cult which was supposedly initiated by the poet Orpheus.

Orphic beliefs are difficult to pin down with specificity, but there is a widely attested Orphic belief that humans were created from the bodies of titans. Either their limbs, ashes, or blood. The specific variant quoted from Olympiodorus is one of the latest and best known. In his narrative, the Titans attack Dionysus, who turns into a bull to try to escape them. The titans then tear him (still in the form of a bull) limb from limb and devour him, thus symbolically performing the sacrificial Dionysian rite of Omophagia. Later, Zeus incinerates the titans and mankind is created from their ashes.[10] According to the late Roman writer Olympiodorus, the implication is that humans have some "titanic" essence in them, but also some Dionysian essence.[11] Thus, humans are the product of a sacrificial rite involving a divine bull-man.

Some scholars dispute the antiquity of this myth, but a thorough sweep of the evidence reveals too much early evidence. Plutarch, for example, offhandedly mentions that the dismemberment of Dionysus is an allegory for *diakosmesis* (essentially, the creation of the cosmos).[12] This brings us awfully close to the Vedic myth of Purusha, and probably places the narrative (or something similar) at least as early as the 1st century CE. In fact, there are a lot of parallels between the perverse skepticism towards Slavic paganism that many scholars seem to have contracted, and the perverse skepticism about the Orphic mysteries. It has become very fashionable to say that the anthropogony of humans from Zagreus was a "late" invention. However, Indo-European studies would suggest otherwise.

There is a complex but stunningly convincing case, made by Llewelyn Morgan at Cambridge, that the episode of *bugonia* (the genesis of bees from the body of a dead ox) in Virgil's Georgics is actually an Orphic allegory. This is difficult to fathom, until you realize that Greek philosophers like Porphyry frequently spoke of bees as a symbol for human souls. The narrative from Virgil's Georgics features the sacrifice of an ox (in honor of Orpheus) and the genesis of bees from its body. Morgan convincingly illustrates that the Greek legends of bugonia represent a widespread concept of human souls originating from a sacrificial ox, which was apparently present in the Eleusinian Mysteries as well as the Orphic Mysteries.[13]

The origins of this myth in Greece are hard to pin down, but Porphyry seems to have associated it with the Eleusinian mysteries, which were a close relative of the Dionysian mysteries. On the subject of bees and human souls, he writes the following:[14]

> *the moon... they called Melissa* ['bee'], *because... bees are begotten of bulls. And souls that pass to earth are bull-begotten*

Other "local" variants of the bull dismemberment myth show up in Ireland and perhaps Spain. In the Irish epic *Tain Bo' Cualnge* two mythical bulls fight each other. One tears the other apart, creating the Irish landscape out of his body. The one called "Donn" also dies shortly after the fight, and his body forms part of the island's landscape. This is after he dismembers his rival, Findbennach Ai and uses his body parts to create pieces of the Irish landscape as well. This is fascinating from the perspective of Indo-European studies, because "Donn" is generally considered to be the Lord of the Dead in Irish Mythology.

Thus, we have a parallel to the Vedic Yama, who became a Lord of the Dead by first "dying" himself. In fact, scholars have reconstructed a Proto-Indo-European myth in which his precursor, *yémHos is sacrificed in order to create the earth and cosmos. The death of Donn in Irish mythology appears to confirm this reconstruction.[15]

I actually had some misgivings about the *yémHos creation story reconstructed by scholars of Indo-European comparative mythology. The primary reason was that I simply didn't see a strong connection between the Vedic Yama and the Norse Ymir. The names do show a similarity, but in a mythological sense the connection between the two (analyzed individually) is not very compelling. Yama is the first man to die, and hence the

Lord of the Underworld. He does not play a central role in any Vedic creation narrative. Ymir is a giant who is dismembered by the Gods to create the world. Furthermore, the obvious Vedic analogue to Ymir is Purusha, who has already been discussed in this chapter.

In fact, it may be that the Indo-Iranian traditions tended to separate these roles - but there is compelling evidence that many European mythologies combined them. In Iranian mythology as well, we can see that the first human being Gayomart dies, and his blood falls to the Earth, thus causing the first mortal man and mortal woman to spring up from the soil. These are Mashya and Mashyana, and they appear to have a great deal more in common with Yama and his sister Yami than Gayomart himself does.[16] Thus, in Proto-Indo-Iranian mythology, it may be that a primordial sacrifice gave rise to Yama and his sister Yami, rather than being strictly identified with them. At the same time, however, the European evidence does seem to suggest that the division between the first sacrifice and *yémHos could be hazy at times - or even nonexistent.

Fernando Coimbra draws a connection between the Irish Tain Bo Cuailnge and a Spanish ritual recorded in Quinta do Recondo, in the municipality of Quiroga, Lugo, Galicia during the 16th century. In this ritual, Spanish peasants apparently drove a bull along the boundary lines of a new property, and erected stone markers where necessary. After they sacrificed the bull, they used its blood to mark the same route that it had walked, thus marking the boundaries with blood.[17]

With this example we can see that myths often reflect rituals, and vice versa. It can be impossible to say which came first: The ritual or the myth. The foundational rite of drawing the boundaries around a property and marking it with sacrificial blood is well attested in Indo-European tradition. In some sense, however, ancient people also thought that the land itself was "created" by a kind of foundational sacrifice.

I would draw a parallel between the "boundary marking" ritual in Spain and the foundation myth associated with the city of Rome. Many of us know that it ends in tragedy; With Romulus killing his brother Remus. According to one account, Romulus began building his town on the Palatine hill, and drew a furrow around it with a sacred plough. Along the furrow, he built a wall and a trench. When Remus saw this, however, he mocked Romulus and jumped over the wall and the trench to show him how easily the town could be taken.

Romulus grew angry and killed his brother Remus, saying "Thus perish everyone who may attempt to cross these walls."[18] It's possible that the tale was originally a depiction of a settlement-founding ritual, similar to the boundary-marking ritual recorded from Quiroga Lugo, except with a human sacrifice. There is also a hint of moralism in the tale, showing that Remus died because he broke a major taboo by interfering with the ceremonial marking of settlement boundaries - something that was probably sacrosanct in the ancient worldview.

The piece of evidence that finally convinced me of the *yémHos creation / foundation myth is the narrative of Romulus and Remus, which I presumed I knew fairly well, but which actually yielded many striking surprises. A number of scholars have derived Remus from *yémHos, arguing that the substitution of "Y" for "R" is purely for alliteration with the name Romulus. I agree that this is likely. As we all know, Remus was killed by his brother. However, there is a narrative about Romulus being dismembered as well. Dionysus of Halicarnassus wrote that the patricians killed Romulus because he was behaving like a tyrant. According to him, they dismembered his body, smuggled away the butchered parts hidden in their robes, and secretly buried those remains in the earth. The connection between the dismembered body of Romulus and various locations of the Roman landscape feels very mythical, and indeed, the fanciful episode makes very little sense if taken as a literal historical event.[19]

All of this material will be critical for understanding the reconstruction in Chapter 8: Svarozhichi - Sons of Svarog. In particular, we must discuss the Krakow foundation myth, which features two sons of Krak who slay a dragon together. After this dragon-slaying episode, however, an episode of fratricide arises; One brother slays the other, and subsequently assumes the throne of Krakow.[20]

This narrative has often been treated as an early episode of Polish history. However, there have been some scholars like Santos Marinas who have noted parallels between this legend and Proto-Indo-European mythology. As Marinas notes, "This legend appears to reflect an old Indo-European myth of foundation."[21] We will see in Chapter 8 that there are numerous reasons for regarding it as such. In fact, we will deal with the divine twins and dragon-slaying narratives towards the end of this chapter as well.

While the first sacrifice of a man and / or cow is undeniably the most pervasive motif associated with Indo-European creation stories, there is another concept which is less frequently explored, but perhaps just as significant. There is a recurring tendency for Indo-European creation narratives to speak of a clash between "hot" and "cold" forces, sometimes represented by fire and ice, and in other cases fire and water. The most striking example of this is definitely from Norse mythology. According to the Voluspa, creation arose from the combination of Muspell's fire in the south, and the freezing ice of Niflheim in the north. According to Norse tradition, it was these two forces which combined to create the world from the Ginnungagap which lay between them.[22]

However, Ossetian folklore has also preserved a tradition about the creation of the world from the mutual nullification of "hot" and "cold" elements. According to one Ossetian myth, God became angry with the sun and struck it with his dagger. A piece of the sun then fell through the sky. Later, God threw his dagger at the moon. The tail flew off of the moon, raising a strong wind. The moon shed tears that fell on the severed "tail" turning it into mist. This mist then fell upon the piece of the sun, which cooled it down. After it cooled, the earth formed from the piece of the sun.[23] This myth is fascinating, in part because it attributes the primordial clash of heat and cold to two celestial deities, or heavenly bodies (the sun and moon). It is obviously compatible with the Norse cosmology as well - so much so that it may qualify as a Proto-Indo-European creation concept.

In Vedic tradition, the fire God Agni is sometimes a creator deity. He is sometimes imagined as having been born out of the waters at the time of creation. Like the sun-god Savitr, the water-born Agni is also called Apám Nápat 'progeny of the waters."

Apám Nápat is described as the one who "created all things."[24] It's possible that we see a memory of the same tradition in this myth, though it is perhaps less obvious than in Ossetian lore.

Dumezil's Tripartite Theory

Roman historians recorded that when the 10th Roman legion of the 1st Century BCE found out that they were being sent to Africa, they mutinied. After a series of failures by officials who attempted to placate them, Historians claim that the General Julius Caesar was able to subdue them with a single word; *"Quirites."* If Roman historians are to be believed, this one word shamed the 10th legion into submission.[25]

The Roman legionnaires were clearly ashamed to be called "Quirites." But what was a Quirite, exactly? It essentially meant "civilian." That is, someone who was not from the aristocratic class, and also not a soldier. A commoner. In a literal sense, it came from the Latin roots "Co-" (together) and "Vir-" as in (Virile, Manly). Therefore, the Co-Viria was fellow men, or fellow male kinfolk who shared the community with you. In a sense, it meant "citizen." What does this have to do with the tripartite division of Indo-European societies postulated by Georges Dumezil?

One of the best illustrations of his thesis is the Archaic Capitoline Triad. That is, the triad of deities who were once worshiped as the primary deities at the old Capitol of Rome. In the original formula, these three deities included Jupiter, Mars and Quirinus. The name "Quirinus" here refers to an obscure Roman deity, one whose name is obviously cognate to Latin "Quirites" (civilian). Regarding the other two, Mars is obviously the God of War. And Jupiter is the King of the Gods. So in the archaic triad of Rome, we have the God of common citizens, the God of war, and the King of the Gods. This perfectly illustrates the tripartite division of society proposed in Dumezil's tripartite theory. In short, Dumezil proposed that the triplism found throughout Indo-European mythology reflected an archaic conception of the division of society among the Proto-Indo-Europeans.[26]

This triad can look slightly different across different Indo-European mythologies. The Roman pantheon placed Jupiter as the King of the Gods, but this role was not always given to the God of Thunder. In fact, the case can be made that the thunder deity most typically embodied the second function, which is to say the warriors. The Greeks and Romans elevated the cult of thunder to make it synonymous with the Proto-Indo-European *Dyēus Ph2ter ("Father Sky"). However, no other Indo-European culture seems to have done this.

Even with the Vedic material in India, Dumezil tended to place the thunderer, Indra, firmly into the second function. It is noteworthy that the Vedas retain a memory of an elder "Dyaus Pita" (Father Sky in Sanskrit) who is distinct from the main thunder-hero Indra. There is one big caveat with Dumezil's tripartite structure as applied to Vedic culture; Whereas in Europe we often have one deity for each rung of the triad, the

Vedas often have a "dvanda" or pair at each rung. Thus for the third function (commoner class) we have the Asvins (divine twin horsemen). In the martial role of the second function, Dumezil places Indra and Vayu. In the first function, the dvanda of Mitra-Varuna occupies the priestly / legalistic role.[27] And yes, if you're linking the Sanskrit term "dvanda" with "dyad" or "duo" you're right. As you can see, spotting Indo-European cognates is not always so hard.

In Germanic culture, we see a similar triad at the temple of Uppsala. There, scholars have identified the triad of Odin, Thor, and Freyr. Once again, we see the typical placement of Thor in the role of warrior deity. The magical or priestly first function is unambiguously identified with Odin. Freyr is well-established as a fertility deity.[28]

But it is not always just triads of deities. The origin stories of Indo-European states and clans often involve a narrative about it being founded by three brothers, or three paternal ancestors. These figures may or may not be deified - more typically the Gods representing three functions are more of an abstraction. But tripartition is also seen in narratives about ethnic / state origins.

The textbook example of this is probably the Scythian origin myth recounted by Greek sources - most notably Herodotus, who took a great interest in the Scythians. These narratives aren't always easy to interpret through Greek sources. For instance, many sources refer to the progenitor of the three Scythian paternal ancestors as "Hercules", which is obviously a Greek interpolation. More accurately, it was apparently a mythological figure known as "Targitaus" who coupled with a half-serpent maiden and sired three sons; Leipoxais, Arpoxais and Coloxais.

According to the Scythian legend, three sacred treasures descended from heaven - a golden bowl, a golden axe, and a golden plow with a yoke.[29] It's safe to say these represent the three functions, with the bowl presumably being ceremonial and sacred. Only Colaxaïs was able to touch the treasures without being burned, however.

Because of this sign, the other two brothers abdicated their claim to rule over the Scythians (so the legend goes). We clearly see how this narrative supported the divine right to rule for the descendants of Colaxaïs, who claimed to be masters of all three functions - thus reducing the descendants of the other two to little more than their servants.[30] This is an extreme propagandist take on the three functions - one that obviously supported the divine mandate of the so-called "Royal" Scythians. However, in most other respects, it is fairly true to the tripartite hypothesis of Dumezil.

Another meaningful element of the tripartite division in Scythian legend is probably the animal bride. In this case, it is a serpent woman. The case can be made that this is an archaic Indo-European sovereignty symbol, as explored in Chapter 2: Baba Yaga and Mokosh The Great Mother. As I mentioned in that chapter, a snake-woman ancestor was also claimed by some Spanish noble houses[31] which is strikingly similar to the legend used by the royal Scythians to justify their divine origins.

However, it is not only the snake woman who appears as the mother of the three functions. It appears that we have a very similar "Scythian" myth of tripartite origins preserved in some Mongolian myths. A number of Mongolian ethnic groups claim descent not from a snake woman, but from a swan maiden. However, the details are very clearly similar to that of the Classical Scythian origin story.

According to the legends of the Terte clan of the Sayan Mountains, a Mongol ancestor named Toorei migrated to the Tunkhen valley and one day saw several swans flying by a lake. When they landed, they took off their bird clothing and revealed themselves to be daughters of Han Hormusta Tenger. He stole the clothing of one of the women, preventing her from flying away. They fell in love and married. She had three sons who became the ancestors of three clans. The eldest son was a shaman, and his descendants became princes and political leaders among the Buryats. The middle son was called Terte, and he became the ancestor of many shamans. The youngest son, Bata, fathered a lineage that produced many Buddhist lamas.

According to the Buryat legend recounted by Sarangerel, the destiny of Toorei's three lineages was predicted by his swan-wife.[32] Interestingly, this appears to trace the divine mandate for social organization firmly back to the swan-maiden foremother. Once again, we can see that material from so-called "Uralic" and "Altaic" traditions can greatly enhance our understanding of Indo-European mythology. Clearly, the linguistic differences do not necessarily override the evidence for related traditions. In some cases, like with this narrative, the influence of the Scythians is extremely obvious. This narrative is an obvious Mongolian borrowing of a Scythian origin myth, although they trace their descent back to a swan maiden rather than a snake woman.

Neither is this the only hint of ancient Iranian influence on the Mongolian religion. The name "Han Hormusta" is used here as a synonym for "Tenger," which denotes the Sky Father deity of Mongolian mythology. However, the name "Hormusta" is not of Mongolian origins. Most scholars now agree that this name comes ultimately from Persian "Ahura Mazda" (the Zoroastrian chief deity).[33] As we will explore in Chapter 11: Chernobog and the Earth-diver Myth, there is some significant evidence for early Iranian influence on the nomads of the Mongolian Steppe, dating well before the time of Islam.

Clearly the prevalence of these animal maiden myths is noteworthy. They do not seem to have been a uniquely Scythian concept. As I mentioned earlier, even Spanish nobility preserved some elements of the "snake woman ancestor" legend to explain their aristocratic origins. The evidence suggests that the animal spouse narrative is an extremely archaic element of these Indo-European myths justifying the hierarchical social divisions in many ancient societies. Why is that?

Animal Spouses: A Tribe or Clan Origin Myth?

The people of the Pontic-Caspian Steppe region could not have always existed under a system of strict social stratification. In general, the origins of most Eurasian social stratification can be traced back to the agricultural revolution, which in West Eurasia originated from the Near East (modern day Iraq, Syria, Anatolia, etc).

Ancient DNA studies on the Yamnaya and others associated with the Proto-Indo-Europeans show that they were largely a mixture of two groups, or distinct source populations. About half of their ancestry appears to have come from the Caucasus, which may well have already begun the process of transferring "Near Eastern" cultural developments northward to the Pontic region. However, approximately half of their ancestry came from the so-called 'Eastern Hunter Gatherers." These "Eastern Hunter Gatherers" were largely related to the hunter-gatherer populations of Siberia, just to their east. The early hunter-gatherer populations who gave rise to the Indo-Europeans probably had no notion of a professional warrior class, much less a strict tripartite society.

Interestingly, however, if we look at other populations who were closely related to Eastern Hunter Gatherers, like the people of Siberia, we do see some signs of phratry or clan divisions based on animal ancestors. In particular, the eastern Khanty are known for having three exogamous clans of the Bear, Elk, and Beaver.[34] It is not hard to see how such a system could give rise to the Dumezilian tripartite society when mixed with increasing social stratification,

The Bear seems to have been a widespread cultic ancestor across North Eurasia. Among the Uralic peoples in particular, stories about clan origins involving a bear or bear spirit are common. A typical Uralic narrative about how the bear was lowered down to earth from heaven is preserved among the Khanty and Mansi. According to them, the bear was a son of the Sky God Num-Torem who descended to earth to become an ancestor of the Por Phratry. Similar narratives are found in the folklore of the Sami and Finns.[35]

There is evidence that even some Indo-European language speakers retained this archaic memory of a "Bear Clan" ancestor myth as well. A common element of this type of myth is that ancestral connections to an animal (e.g. a bear) is used to justify some sort of taboo. In the case of the bear, it is common for Siberian and Mongolian peoples to observe a taboo around the speaking of the name of the bear, precisely because it is associated with the cult of ancestors. Indeed, a common term used to avoid speaking the real word for bear in Mongolian is "baabgai" meaning "father."[36]

One interesting observation that has been made about the Germanic and Balto-Slavic languages is that they also seem to have inherited a taboo associated with the name of the bear, which in Proto-Indo-European was something like "*hrktos" (hence Greek Arctos and Latin Ursus). In Northern Europe, however, it seems that the Germanic and Balto-Slavic peoples used circumlocutions or "nicknames" for the bear. Thus, in Germanic languages, the old Indo-European word for bear has been replaced by a circumlocution meaning "The Brown One." In Slavic languages like Russian, they say "Medved" which means "Honey Eater." Very similarly, the original word for bear in Lithuanian has been replaced by "Lokys" which may mean "Breaker."[37]

Interestingly, Finnish has some very similar circumlocutions like "Honey Eater" and "Honey Paw" or "Forest Beauty" all with the express purpose of avoiding the "true" name of the bear.[38] We have no ancient Indo-European source that explicitly explains this taboo, but it can be inferred by the Balto-Slavic and Germanic tendency to "forget" the original name of the bear used by other Indo-European languages. Additionally, the belief in a taboo on the name of the bear is attested in relatively recent European folklore. For instance, the Slavic Hutsuls of western Ukraine avoided even referring to the bear as the "Medved" (honey-eater). Because this became the "true" name of the bear, they believed it was necessary to call him "The Little Uncle" or "The Big Hairy One."[39] In Finland, we know that this type of avoidance of the "true" word for bear was probably connected with the belief in a totemic bear ancestor, which was a widespread belief among Finno-Ugric and Siberian peoples.

The presence of such an idea among the Germanic and Balto-Slavic peoples could almost be explained by Finno-Ugric influence on Northern Europe, except that this would need to have taken place independently with Germanic as well as Balto-Slavic languages. It's almost certain that the Proto-Germanic and Proto-Balto-Slavic languages were fully separated from one another by the time that the Finno-Ugric languages spread to the Baltic. (Refer to Chapter 1, in which I discuss a likely 1st millennium BCE expansion of Proto-Finno-Ugric to the Baltic region.) Furthermore, as we will see, the evidence of this bear-ancestor hero tradition can be found well outside of Northern Europe.

One of the most famous examples of this is Jean de l'Ours (John the Bear) from French Folktales. Jean de l'Ours is a fairly typical "strong-man" hero, a familiar archetype in European folktales. However, it is noteworthy that the French folktales about him portray him as the offspring of a human woman who was kidnapped by a bear. Later he became a blacksmith.[40] It has been noted by Russian scholars that these narratives closely parallel Siberian totem-ancestor myths about the bear. For comparison, we can point to very similar heroes from Siberian and Finno-Ugric traditions.

One such figure is the Komi Kudim-Os, a culture hero of the Komi people whose mother also supposedly mated with a bear, and who was also famed for his skill in blacksmithing.[41]

Also in Greek mythology, we see a very similar sort of ancestral connection between the Bear and the Arcadians. Specifically, Callisto is turned into a bear. Callisto gives birth to Arcas (whose name is cognate to Arctos, meaning bear) thus tracing the lineage of the first Arcadian King back to a bear-mother. Interestingly, King Lycaon (cognate to Lykos meaning wolf) tried to sacrifice Arkas, causing Zeus to turn him into the first werewolf. As we will see, this appears to connect the bear and wolf to the ancient Koryos tradition of the Proto-Indo-Europeans. In summary, however, we have little reason to think that Indo-European cultures required contact with Finno-Ugric peoples in order to come up with a bear cult.

What seems more likely is that this is a general characteristic of Eastern Hunter-Gatherer traditions, as well as other groups who have significant North Eurasian heritage. Because we know that even the Yamnaya had significant Eastern Hunter-Gatherer ancestry we cannot rule out a bear cult of some kind persisting in Indo-European society since the Mesolithic. It may have been reformed under the social transformations of the bronze age, but this does not mean that it completely vanished. However, the Finno-Ugric narratives about totemic animal ancestors are still very useful for recognizing the evidence for such concepts in Indo-European cultures. In particular, the naming taboos and legends about the origins of a people or dynasty springing from an animal-spouse seem to be a defining characteristic of North-Eurasian totemic traditions. On top of that, however, the traditions of Finno-Ugric peoples are a hybrid of Indo-European and Paleosiberian influences anyway - possibly making it impossible to separate the bear cult traditions of either group.

Obviously, the snake woman and swan maiden myths from the previous section show that the animal ancestor is often the fore-mother of all three functions. That may not be a mistake. It may be that the three functions initially were intended to be divisions within the tribal unity, rather than a division between discrete tribes. As such, the tribal ancestor animal spirit could be regarded as the common ancestor of all three classes within the tribe. This is an element of the "three sons" myths that is often overlooked. Over time, of course, these narratives tended to become stories about three different communities of people. For instance, the Germanic people believed that the three sons of Mannus became the ancestors of the Herminiones, Istwaeones, and Ingvaeones[42] who all corresponded to real ethnic divisions among the Germanic tribes.

It is perhaps noteworthy that the divine twins also frequently seem to be associated with animal-totem traditions. That's not surprising, because many Indo-European cultures have a myth about the divine twins founding a city, tribe, or dynasty. Thus, for instance, the Saxons traced their descent back to the two brothers Hengist and Horsa (whose names literally mean "Horse and Stallion"). They also had a sister named "Swana" (Swan).[43] For the Romans, the mythic founders of Rome were Romulus and Remus. The Kings of Sparta traced their royal line directly back to the Dioscuri. In fact, the divine horseman twins of ancient Greece were the tutelary deities of the Spartan Kings.[44]

It seems that there was a very direct attempt to connect these divine twin traditions with an ancestor animal-spouse tradition. One of the Dioscouri (Polydeuces) was hatched from an egg that was laid by Leda in the form of a Swan, though interestingly, the other was born in the conventional way.[45] As we have seen, the Swan Maiden ancestor legend can also be found as far east as Mongolia. We can also connect this to some other Bird Maiden stories, for instance the Nart Sagas, in which Akshartag (himself a twin brother) sires the twin heroes Warzemaeg and Khamyts with the dove-maiden Zerasha.[46] The swan-maiden motif also shows up in India, particularly in the tale of her marriage to King Pururavas, the mythical founder of the so-called "Solar Dynasty" in Indian tradition.[47]

Another Greek tradition claims that the maiden Arne, also known as Melanippe (meaning Black Horse) was born as a foal initially before being turned into a woman. After being impregnated by Poseidon, she gave birth to the two twin brothers: Aeolus and Boeotus. Through Aeolus and Boeotus, Arne became the ancestor of the Boeotians, as well as the people of the Aeolian Islands.[48] This presents an odd parallel to the birth of the Asvins in Vedic tradition, which also involves their mother Saranyu taking the form of a mare. After Saranyu and Vivasvat couple in the form of a mare and horse, she gives birth to the divine twin horsemen.[49]

However, it is not only birds and mares that are inserted into this role. We also see a connection with wolves. Most of us already know the tale about the twins Romulus and Remus being nursed by a she-wolf. In Polish folktales, the two brothers Waligora and Wyrwidab are nursed by a she-bear and a she-wolf respectively.[50] Interestingly, these two brothers slay a dragon together in the most widely circulated Polish folktales where they feature.[51] This is a trait they share with the two legendary sons of Krak, the founder of Krakow, who similarly slew the Wawel dragon together.[52] It would probably not be a stretch to say that the sons of Krak are the "historicized" version of the Polish divine twins, and the folktale heroes Waligora and Wyrwidab are the folkloric memory of the same mythological archetype.

The divine genealogies of a family, clan, tribe, or dynasty obviously occupied a central role in many Indo-European cultures. The details could vary greatly from family to family, but in general they involved the formulaic combination of a few familiar elements. The divine twins were frequently involved. Similarly, a generation of three brothers (representing three functions) was often substituted for or added to the genealogy of the divine twins. Finally, a totemic animal-spouse ancestor was usually added to the narrative.

It is remarkable how consistently the animal-spouse ancestor is relegated to the maternal lineage of a king or hero. This may have been due to the Proto-Indo-European tendency for Kings to inherit their social status from the paternal line (i.e. you could only be a King if you were the son of a King). The same may have held true for elite warriors - to claim a non-human paternal ancestor was to essentially forfeit any inheritance, including social status if you lived in a patriarchal culture such as the Proto-Indo-European culture. However, the preservation of a very "primitive" looking memory of animal totemism is still evident in the maternal line, which demonstrates that these animal-spouse ancestors still served an important purpose for affirming the identity of the tribe or family. Furthermore, as symbols of the first men and / or founders of the society, the divine twins could easily become the inheritors of animal-totem symbolism from the earliest layer of tribal tradition, thus leading to myths in which the twins seem to embody the animal spirit on an abstract (rather than literal) level.

As we have seen, this animal ancestor may have been the most archaic element of these narratives, going back even to the Eastern Hunter-Gatherers of the Mesolithic Pontic-Caspian region. These Eastern Hunter-Gatherer traditions may have been very similar to those of the Finno-Ugric peoples, who showed up in most of Northern Europe much later. The animal selected for these ancestor legends could obviously vary from family to family, but the most prevalent among Indo-European cultures seem to be the Bear, Wolf, Snake, Mare, and Swan. Various other regional types obviously existed. For instance, Scottish Clans such as the MacCodrums often claimed descent from a Selkie - a Seal Maiden - and a mortal man.[53] However, the Seal would not have been familiar or relevant among many

Indo-European cultures, which explains the limited distribution of this motif. With all of that said, however, there are reasons to believe that the Wolf carried very special importance for the Indo-Europeans. So much so that it deserves its own section. We must have a discussion about the Koryos tradition.

Koryos: The Wolf Rites of the Mid-Winter

The associations surrounding wolves are an interesting rabbit-hole to go down in Indo-European studies. We see a hint of their significance in the Romulus and Remus myth, with the she-wolf suckling the two young heroes. The ritual significance of wolves goes well beyond that, however. In honor of Romulus and Remus, the Romans celebrated a wolf-holiday known as Lupercalia. This seems to have been in commemoration of the she-wolf who suckled them.

To start with, two groups of runners - young boys from the Quinctii and Fabii noble families were selected. This was intentional, because they were believed to be descended from Romulus and Remus respectively. They started at the Lupercal, the cave where the twins Romulus and Remus are said to have been suckled by a she-wolf.

The priests would sacrifice a goat and wipe the bloody knife upon their foreheads. The blood was then wiped off with milk-soaked wool. The boys would run, wearing only goatskin loincloths, and whipping people (especially women) with strips of goatskin. According to Plutarch, a dog was also sacrificed at Lupercalia.[54]

That is a good segue into a discussion on the Koryos. You might be saying "dog sacrifice?" In many cultures, this would be unusual. And the Classical world is no exception. However, there are reasons to believe that dog / wolf sacrifice marked a major Proto-Indo-European ritual in the distant past.

This was something that actually popped into the public eye recently with a major study by archaeologists David Anthony and Anne Pike-Tay. They were part of a team excavating a site of the Srubnaya culture, in Bronze Age Eastern Europe. The team began to find numerous dog sacrifices, and some wolf sacrifices as well. As the finds accumulated, they decided to consult ancient historical sources and comparative religious studies to see if anything paralleled what they were uncovering. An obscure element of the reconstructed Proto-Indo-European religion came to their attention; The Koryos. To quote David Anthony and Pike-Tay at length:[55]

> *The youthful war-bands referenced in Indo-European traditions shared several basic characteristics that were summarised by Meiser (2002), reiterated by Mallory (2007)*
>
> 1. *They were composed of adolescent (post-pubescent, pre-adult) males who were initiated together as an age-class cohort.*
> 2. *The boy/warriors came from prominent families.*
> 3. *They were sent away to live in the 'wild' outside their own society for a number of years...*
> 4. *They wore animal skins and appeared as if they were wolves or dogs.*
> 5. *Their raids could result in the founding of new settlements. It can be argued that the legends of Romulus and Remus, the first kings of Rome suggest that youthful war bands played a prominent role in the narrative tropes about the founding of that city.*

Vedic texts dated after 1000 BCE referred to a group of outsiders called Śvapaca. To paraphrase another source:[56]

> *This (Svapaca) roughly translates to 'dog-cooker' but it can also be understood as 'nourished by dogs'. Among the Śvapaca were the people called Vrātyas or 'dog-priests'. They were known for performing a midwinter ceremony called Ekāstakā at the winter solstice, when Indra, the god of war, was born along with his retinue.*

> *The young initiates were taken to an opening in the forest, south of the village, called the Sabha. It was a place where corpses were burned and buried, where Rudra, the god of death and uncultured wildness, was near. The newly initiated warriors lived as dogs in the wild, with no contact with their families, for four years. They remained together in the wild practicing warfare and storytelling until the next winter solstice when the raiding season would start again, and this would continue for four years. At the end of four years, there was a sacrifice to transform the dog-cookers into responsible adult men. They discarded and destroyed their old clothes, and were welcomed back into their settlements as adult members of the community.*

This had been inferred to have analogies as far west as Europe, among other cultures of the broader Indo-European language family. In the Bronze Age Srubnaya culture excavation at Krasnosamarskoe, Russia, however, the proof is in the pudding; 51 dogs and 7 wolves there were sacrificed and roasted in midwinter.

Aside from the Roman myth of Romulus and Remus, there are a few other traces of a connection between the Koryos tradition and the divine twins. In the Nart Sagas, there is a recurring name "Waerz-" or "Waerg-" which is ostensibly cognate to Old English Warg and Sanskrit Varka (as well as Slavic "Volkh"). This would translate to "wolf." In the Nart Sagas, we see this same root in the name of the divine twin's father; The father of Akshar and Akshartag is called "Warhag." Later, we see the more prominent twin Akshar father another pair of twins - and these are the two who feature in most of the actual Nart Saga adventures. Their names are "Warzamag" and "Khamyts." According to John Colarusso, "Warzamag" may translate to "Great Wolf."[57]

Archaeologists uncovering the 1st century CE Sarmatian tumulus at Kobyakovo found an interesting golden torc which depicts the same scene three times over: Two canine-headed warriors battling a dragon together, armed with clubs.[58]

It is interesting that this find casts the two wolf brothers in the role of dragon slayers - very similar to the Slavic foundation myths discussed previously. Also in Polish folklore, the two heroic brothers Waligora and Wyrwidab (Literally "Mountain-Leveler and "Oak-Twirler") are abandoned in the woods as babies. One is fed by a she-wolf, and the other is cared for by a bear. As mentioned, Polish tales have the two brothers work together to slay a dragon that is terrorizing a kingdom.

Also mentioned previously, the Greeks told tales of how King Lycaeon (from Greek "Lykos" meaning wolf) tried to sacrifice the son of Zeus and Callisto, who was named "Arcas" (from "Arctos" meaning bear). According to the myth, Zeus then cursed Lycaon, causing him to transform into a wolf.[59] The myth offers another tantalizing connection between the wolf and bear cults in Indo-European mythology. One that appears to be well-supported by the Polish folktale heroes Waligora and Wyrwidab. For the Greeks, however, the story of King Lycaeon was more than just a myth. It formed the basis for a living cult that persisted for centuries in Arcadia. Evidently Arcadians would make pilgrimages to Mount Lycaeon, where they would take part in ecstatic rites that are obviously connected with the Proto-Indo-European Koryos tradition. In fact, some Romans thought that Lupercalia was derived from the Arcadian wolf-cult.[60] However, this seems unlikely since Wolf-Cults were widespread among Indo-European cultures.

Undoubtedly, however, one of the clearest survivals of the Koryos tradition was through the Norse cult of Odin. In fact, one of Odin's main titles was "Herjan" which was directly derived from "Koryos." Or more directly, from Proto-Indo-European "Koryonos" (Meaning "Leader of the Koryos Band). We see the continuation of this tradition in the Wild Hunt, which Odin was believed to lead during Midwinter.[61]

With that said, however, the date of the wolf ritual could vary depending on culture. Lupercalia was in February, which makes it appear to almost mark the end of the ritual rather than the beginning. The opposite may have happened for the Iranians, who gave the name "Varkazana" (The month of wolf men) to the month corresponding to late October / early November.[62] Clearly, this was a ritual which could shift in either direction chronologically, although the associations with Midwinter are by far the most consistent across Indo-European cultures.

Odin did, of course, have a pair of wolves at his side. A number of scholars have connected this with the Koryos tradition. However, a common association with Odin was also the berserker rage. Medieval chronicles make it clear that the warriors of Odin were often considered to be "berserkers" (from the Norse term for "Bear Shirt"). These berserkers were so-named not just because they wore bear skins, but also because of the animalistic frenzy they worked themselves into. Historical sources attest that bear-skins and wolf-skins may have been the standard garb of Odin's fighters.[63] Under the title of "Herjan" Odin was perhaps the most recognizable successor of the older Indo-European *Koryonos* - the leader of the wolf-skinned (and perhaps sometimes bear-skinned) retinue of wild men.

As we will see, there are a couple of South Slavic divinities (covered in Chapter 8: Svarozhichi - Sons of Svarog) who seem to have inherited the role of wolf-shepherds. These two figures appear to inherit some of the mythological symbolism of the *Koryonos,* but they also transform it somewhat by creating a seasonal dyad - a pair of figures who govern two different halves of the year. Interestingly though, one of these two wolf shepherds claims the month of November, which would roughly correspond to the Iranian month of *Varkazana* (The month of Wolf-Men).

The Divine Twins: Mainstream Views

The divine twins of Indo-European mythology will be discussed a lot here, clearly. Some of the connections drawn here are fairly novel, even though the divine twins themselves have been discussed in academia for decades. There is some value in clarifying what is part of mainstream research and what is not. Most scholars agree that the Proto-Indo-European religion had a pair of divine twin horsemen. They are best attested via the Dioskouroi (Castor and Polydeuces) from Greek mythology and the Asvins in Vedic tradition. The Asvins are literally the plural of Sanskrit "Asva" (horse). Similarly, the Dioskouroi were called horsemen (leúkippoi, eúippoi, leukopoloi) or sometimes leukò póló Diós, meaning "the white colts of Zeus."[64] Both figures are also called progeny of the Sky Father (Dyeus). Dioskouroi literally means "The youths of Dios" - that is - the boys of Zeus.[65] The Vedas say that the Asvins are children of the sun God Vivasvat. However, an offhand reference to them as "Divo Napata" (Offspring of Dyaus) seems to confirm a similar genealogy was once known to the Vedic Indian tradition.[66]

Some portray the divine twins as relatively minor, quasi-mortal deities who are the defenders of mankind. That's the official interpretation by scholars like Shann Winn.[67] In reality, there are reasons to believe that the divine twins were significantly demoted to a quasi-mortal status in Greek mythology. Certainly, this was the case for their sister Helen, who appears to take her name from the Greek word for sun (Helios). This seems to reference the widespread Indo-European belief that the twins are brothers and / or consorts of the sun Goddess. We see this in the Vedas as well, where the Asvins are consorts of Surya, the sun maiden. In the Iliad, however, their sister Helen retains her solar attributes in name only. Her status as a sun Goddess has been stripped from her.[68]

In all likelihood, her brothers the Dioskouroi were "demoted" from cosmic status in Classical times as well. Their quasi-mortal status in Classical Greek mythology may therefore be a later development. Some scholars interpret the divine twins as being barely divine - but this is mainly extrapolated from Greek sources, and there are reasons to question the antiquity of this view. Their partnership with the Sun Goddess is perhaps the most compelling reason for assigning them "full" divine status - at least in their original form.

Likewise in Baltic mythology, we tend to see that the divine twins are consorts of the maiden sun. In Latvian mythology, she is called "Saules Meitas" and she has a close relationship with the Dieva Deli - the two youthful sons of Dievas, the Sky Father.[69] This may all sound familiar, as I have briefly discussed this partnership between the divine twins and the dawn Goddess in Slavic mythology (See Chapter 5: The Zoryas as Sea Maidens). In short, the divine twins are often reconstructed as important deities in the Proto-Indo-European religion who acted as twin horsemen, and who represented the two horses who pulled the solar chariot which carried their sister / consort. They are almost universally recognized as sons of Dyeus-the Heavenly Father deity.[70]

Researchers are divided on the relationship between the Vedic Asvins, and the twins Yama and Manu. As discussed at the beginning of the chapter, Yama was the first man to die, and thus the God of the underworld. His name is unambiguously from Proto-Indo-European *yémHos (twin). And indeed, Yama does have a twin brother in Manu. To make matters more complicated, the Vedas seem to simultaneously differentiate between Yama, Manu, and the Asvins, while also stressing their familial connections. According to the Vedas, the Asvins were born when Vivasvat took the form of a horse and coupled with Saranyu while she was in the form of a mare. However, Manu and Yama are also children of Saranyu, which hardly seems like a coincidence.

Perhaps the most that can be said is that the Vedas do distinguish these figures. (Albeit while stressing their relatedness.) In European traditions, however, divine twins can often appear to have qualities of both pairs. Thus, for example, the divine twins Hengist and Horsa in Saxon lore are clearly named "stallion" and "horse" thus associating them with the Asvins or horsemen. However, they have at least as much in common with Romulus and Remus - two brothers with alliterative names who also acted as legendary founders. Yet most Indo-European scholars connect Remus with Yama, rather than with the Asvins.[71]

As mentioned previously, Yama was the first man to die. He accepted mortality as his lot, and thus became a kind of deified dead man, associated with the afterlife. There are some significant parallels here to the Dioskouroi; Apparently one of the Dioskouroi was immortal, but the other was mortal. This is because they were (miraculously) half-brothers as well as twins, and only one was descended from Zeus. When one of them died, an agreement was made that they would split time in the underworld evenly, alternating each day.[72]

As the first man to die, it seems that the Vedic Yama may be related to the "mortal" half of the Dioscuric pair. The Vedas say that the Gods created night after Yama died, so that his sister's grief would fade with time.[73] In Greek mythology as well, the fate of the Dioskouroi relates to the diurnal cycle; Supposedly they trade places with each passing day, switching back and forth between Olympus and the underworld. It's not explicit, but the daily switching of the Dioskouroi could also have referenced a myth explaining the origin of night and day. Neither should this be surprising if, as scholars say, the Dioskouroi were the horses who pulled the solar chariot![74]

Of course, this is not to dismiss the distinctiveness of the Vedic Yama, or the Asvins. In the Vedic tradition, these figures are distinct. However, in Europe the distinction between these different "types" of twins is not always apparent. As we will discuss though, there are reasons to believe that more than one pair of divine twins once existed in Proto-Indo-European mythology - even if the exact delineation between them has been obscured with time.

The Divine Twins: Author's Observations

In his encyclopedia on Indo-European culture, Mallory discusses the idea of a Mare Goddess as the progenitor of the divine twins.[75] We have discussed this already somewhat, but there is a deeper network of connections involved. In particular, Mallory acknowledges that the mare Goddess mother is found in Vedic tradition, where the Goddess Saranyu takes the form of a mare, and conceives the Asvins. Mallory discusses a controversial parallel between Saranyu and "Erinys" which was a title used for a Goddess (identified with Demeter) who took the form of a mare before being impregnated by Poseidon (in the form of a horse, of course). Mallory acknowledges that linguistically, a connection between the name "Saranyu" and "Erinys" is plausible. (Greek often mangled words from Proto-Indo-European beyond recognition for non-linguists) Nevertheless, he expresses some skepticism about the mythological connection. Mallory's skepticism may be premature, however. He reaches his conclusion without reviewing the other obvious parallel in Greek mythology: Arne.

I would propose that Arne (pronounced Arni) seems to be nothing more than a deformation of Ancient Greek "Erinys." And her mythology bears this out. Her other common name was "Melanippe" (meaning Black Horse) and she was even born as a foal before she took human form. Furthermore, she was impregnated by Poseidon, eventually giving birth to the twins Aeolus and Boeotus. These brothers went on to become the progenitors of the Aeolian islanders and the Boeotians respectively.[76]

This almost perfectly parallels the narrative of Erinys and her impregnation by Poseidon - with one noteworthy addition; She gives birth to a pair of twins who go on to become progenitors of a people. This also almost perfectly parallels the conception of Manu, Yama, and the Asvins by the Mare Goddess Saranyu. In the Vedas, Saranyu's children Manu and Yama are the progenitors of humanity. In Greek mythology, the twin brothers of Arne are only the progenitors of the Boeotians and Aeolians. However, the mythological significance of these two narratives is still very similar.

The substitution of two completely different deities for the paternal line is noteworthy. The Vedic people placed the Sun God Vivasvat into this role, and the Boeotians chose Poseidon. In fact, neither of these Father figures are likely to be Proto-Indo-European. The male sun deity was a prominent feature of the early Indo-Iranian religion, but not necessarily in most other branches of the IE family tree. Similarly, the Myceneans of Crete venerated Poseidon above Zeus, which could indicate that Poseidon was the divine forefather in the original "Pre-Indo-European" culture of the Aegean.[77] Nevertheless, the concept of a Mare-Goddess mother of the divine twins appears to have been known to multiple branches of the Indo-European family tree.

There are also some other tantalizing examples of this motif in less well-preserved Indo-European mythologies. Another fascinating example of this may be the Irish land Goddess Macha, who does not turn into a literal horse, but is forced to compete in a horse race while pregnant. After winning the horse race, Macha delivered a pair of twins who lent their name to "Emain Macha" (Literally "twins of Macha") the historical royal seat of Ulster.[78] Similarly, there is one unusual Russian folktale titled "Ivan Bull's Son." This is very much like "Ivan the Cow's Son" at the end of Chapter 3. However, the defeat of Baba Yaga takes a bizarre turn in this variant; The hero turns Baba Yaga into a mare, which he then rides to exhaustion.[79] Some scholars have also interpreted a common Russian embroidery design as depicting the Goddess "Mokosh" flanked by two horsemen.[80]

It's unclear to me how accurate this interpretation is, but further studies could show this to be an archaic Indo-European motif.

Between Baba Yaga, Macha, and Demeter "Erinys", the evidence seems to suggest that the mother of the divine twins tended to be a land or earth Goddess of some sort in European tradition. It's not clear from the Vedic material if she had these associations outside of Europe however.

Regarding the father of the divine twins, you might think that this is an "open and shut" case. And many scholars would agree with you that the father of the divine twins (in the original Proto-Indo-European mythology) was always implicitly Dyeus, the Sky Father. This simple reconstruction has stood for decades. However, I must challenge it with another bold proposal; The Proto-Indo-European mythology probably had multiple generations of divine twins. We will need to change our focus slightly in order to see the proof of this idea.

The Welsh Mabinogion provides one of the most compelling examples in Celtic literature of an Indo-European divine twin tradition. And it all starts with the house of Don. We are told very little about the parent figure Don, except that Don has a daughter named Arianrhod, and two sons named Gwydion and Gilvaethwy.[81] Right away, the alliteration in the two names "Gwydion and Gilvaethwy" should put you on the alert for divine twin symbolism. The examples of alliteration among legendary twin brothers in Indo-European cultures form a long list; We have, of course, discussed the Anglo-Saxon Hengist and Horsa, and the Roman Romulus and Remus. There was also a Latvian "Turo and Tusco" legend.

The real similarity to other divine twin traditions comes in with the next generation of Welsh Gods. Their sister, Arianrhod is impregnated by Gwydion and gives birth to two twin brothers; One named Dylan is "baptised" and immediately jumps into the sea, where he swims like a fish. The other is *Lleu Gyffes* the Welsh counterpart of the Irish God Lugh.[82] There are some strong parallels here to the Nart Sagas. For one thing, we see a hint of at least two generations of divine twins in both stories:

1. Akshar and Akshartag followed by Warzemaeg and Khamyts (Sons of Akshartag) in the Nart Sagas.[83]
2. Gwydion and Gilvaethwy, followed by Dylan and Lleu Gyffes (Sons of Gwydion) in the Welsh Mabinogion.[84]

Another key piece of evidence lies in the genealogy of the mother who births the second generation of divine twins (Welsh Arianrhod / Ossetian Zerasha) Arianrhod is a daughter of the house of Don, and Zerasha is a daughter of Donbettyr.

A lot of ink has been spilled over whether the Welsh 'Don' is cognate to the Indo-Iranian word "Danu" meaning "water." With the additional correlations from the Nart Sagas though, this seems virtually indisputable. Just as Arianrhod is a daughter of the house of Don who births divine twins, so too is the Ossetian Zerasha a daughter of the sea-deity "Donbettyr" who gives birth to divine twins. Arianrhod has a close relationship with an older generation of twins (her brothers Gwydion and Gilvaethwy) and Zerasha is also accompanied by an older generation of divine twins. (her husband and brother-in-law, Akshar and Akshartag). The divine genealogy shown in these examples seems to be directly from the Proto-Indo-European religion itself.

Actually, in the Nart Sagas, and in Celtic lore, it can be argued that we have a third generation of heroes who are cut from the same cloth. In both traditions, one of the second-generation twins goes on to father a culture hero who can boil water with the heat of his body. In the Nart Sagas, the second generation twin Khamyts sires Batraz, who is molten hot at birth, and must jump into the sea (much like the Welsh Dylan). This causes the sea itself to boil from the heat of his body. According to the Nart Sagas, this "quenches" his steel skin - a trait he shares with his cousin Sosruko.[85] Sosruko is not Batraz's twin, but as his cousin, he perhaps symbolically completes the third generation of divine hero pairs.

In Welsh mythology, we are not told whether the second generation of twins (Dylan and Lleu Gyffes) have children. However, if we look at the Irish counterpart of Lleu - the deity Lugh - we see that he does have a son named Cu Chulainn who can boil water with his body heat. Specifically, when Lugh's son Cu Chulainn is enraged, he must be immersed in three barrels of water, two of which he boils off.[86]

The tempering of Batraz's cousin Sosruko is even more interesting. After Sosruko is born, Warzamag must help Satanaya temper the infant Sosruko's steel skin in wolf's milk.[87] This is very reminiscent of Roman mythology, in which the twins Romulus and Remus are suckled by a she-wolf.

Later a gap in the steel tempering of Sosruko's skin will spell his doom. The Welsh *Lleu Gyffes* has a similar "near-invulnerability" with a special weakness. He eventually reveals that he can be slain only by a javelin wrought on mass on Sunday, and while standing with one foot on a buck and the other in a bath by the bank of a river.[88]

The parallels with Cu Chulainn are even more significant - his big weakness is that he will be doomed the day that he eats dog meat.[89] This directly links him with the weakness of Sosruko, which is that he has a weak spot that was not tempered with wolf's milk. Both of these weaknesses are probably related to the *Koryos* tradition discussed earlier. That's on top of the motif of both figures being "quenched" or boiling water with their bodies.

Cu Chulainn almost appears to embody a generation of twin horsemen on his own. According to the legend of his birth, twin foals destined to become his war-horses were born on the day that he was born.[90] In fact, when we consider that the Ossetian Batraz also has a "cousin" (Sosruko) who completes the third pair of divine heroes, it seems likely that there were originally three generations of divine twins.

Lleu Gyffes is, of course, the Welsh counterpart of the Irish Lugh. With Lugh, the divine twin association is less obvious. He is actually said to be one of three triplets in one Irish legend.[91] Interestingly, however, one Irish folktale has Lugh's father Cian promise the sea God "half of what he gains" during his adventures in the abode of the wicked Balor. Later, he conceives a child with the Balor's daughter and must therefore give up his son (the equivalent of Lugh, as memorialized in Irish folklore).[92] The folktale says that there was only one son, and since he could not be divided in two, Manannan got him in whole. However, it's tempting to interpret Manannan's request for "half of what you gain" as a veiled reference to a forgotten twin - perhaps an Irish counterpart to the Welsh Dylan (the brother of *Lleu*) who jumped into the sea at birth.

This is actually a common folktale motif of "Invoking the law of surprise" (to quote the Witcher) and ultimately giving up a child to a water spirit or sea deity by accident. We see almost the same thing in a Russian tale; The Sea King and Vasilissa the Wise. In this tale, the hero must go to the sea king because his father made the mistake of promising "That which he did not know he had" in return for a favor. This, of course, means that he must give up his newborn son. Once he is grown, the boy arrives in the abode of the sea king and falls in love with his daughter. In some versions of this tale, the daughter of the Sea King is portrayed as a lovely bird maiden[93] very much like the Ossetian Zerasha. What can we reconstruct based on all of this? A Proto-Indo-European mythical genealogy, exquisitely preserved in Welsh and Ossetian mythology.

The first generation of divine twins were sired by Dyaus, the Heavenly Father. Later, however, they courted the daughter of the house of Don (Zerasha /Arianrhod), a beautiful sea maiden. With

her they sired a second generation of divine twins. (Warzamag + Khamyts / Lleu Gyffes + Dylan)
Many years later, one of these sons from the second generation descended to earth and sired a hero of our people; A warrior who raged so fiercely that he could boil water with the heat of his body. (Batraz / Cu Chulainn)

For simplicity, see also **Figure 3** below, which illustrates the basic reconstruction.

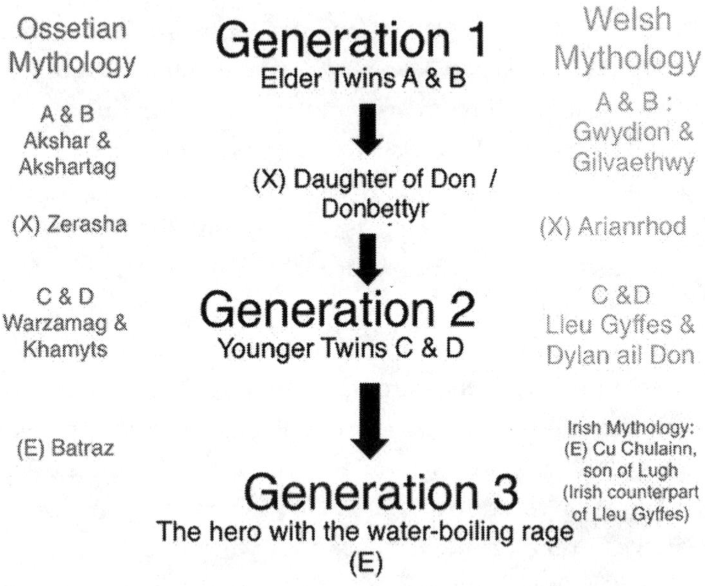

Figure 3: Proposed evidence for a multi-generational genealogy including more than one generation of divine twins in Indo-European mythology. Celtic mythological evidence is shown on the right, and Ossetian mythological evidence is shown on the left.

This also helps explain why we sometimes see divine twins who are not descended from the Sky Father Dyeus. In some cases, this might simply be the degradation of Indo-European mythology. However, even well-preserved Indo-European mythologies frequently show us a pair of divine twins who are not descended from Dyeus. Thus, for example, Romulus and Remus are not descended from Jupiter, but from his son Mars. Very similarly, the Vedic Asvins are more typically said to be children of Vivasvat. Despite being occasionally called "Divo Napata" (progeny of Dyaus) the official Vedic genealogy makes the Asvins children of the sun deity.[94] Much like Mars is a son of Jupiter, however, Vivasvat is a son of Dyaus Pitar. Possibly marking both deities (Mars and Vivasvat) as "first generation" divine twins.

Therefore, this genealogy is not just a bold claim - it has implications that could help us interpret dilemmas that have long plagued Indo-European comparative mythology. If we consider that the divine twins in many traditions could be "next generation" twins the dilemma disappears.

Of course, most Indo-European mythologies did not preserve this genealogy. The parallels are striking between Ossetian and Welsh mythology, but it seems likely that the various generations of divine twins became interchangeable in some cases. In the case of Romulus and Remus, for instance, we have what looks like a creation by dismemberment myth, derived from the archaic Proto-Indo-European *yémHos*, despite the fact that the twins in question are at least two generations removed from Dyeus the Sky Father. Therefore, while the three generations explored here may have been known in the Proto-Indo-European mythical genealogy, we cannot say that they remained neatly divided in all cultures.

In the Vedas, we see a very garbled variant of this genealogy in which Manu, Yama, and the Asvins all belong to the same generation. For reasons already explored at the beginning of this chapter (see Creation Myths) this seems unlikely to have been the case in Proto-Indo-European mythology. Yama would most likely need to belong to the most ancient generation of twins. However, in later Indian traditions, we do see some hint of multiple generations of twins. Specifically, Madri, the wife of King Pandu, is said to have conceived the twins Sahadeva and Nakula after lying with both of the Asvins.[95]

ATU 300 and 303: Blood Brothers and Dragon Slayer

No discussion about the divine twins of the Nart Sagas would be complete without also discussing folktales. In this case, the narratives surrounding Akshartag and his brother Akshar show a remarkable correspondence with European folktales of ATU (Aarne-Thompson-Uther) type 300 and 303. These correspond to the "Blood Brothers" and "Dragon-Slayer" folktale motifs, which frequently occur together. In fact, we have reviewed some of these tales, including the Polish tale of Waligora and Wyrwidab - the brothers nursed by a She-Wolf and She-Bear.[96] A Slovak tale combining the two is summarized below:[97]

Two identical twin brothers growing up with their poor mother decide one day to go out into the world. Their mother cries and worries over them at first, but finally asks that they go hunting and catch some meat to take with them before leaving. The brothers go out hunting for three days, and each day they come back with a new pair of "tamed" wild animals which apparently obey them. The first night they come home with two wolves, then two bears, then two lions.

Upon setting off, they come to a linden tree. One brother says to the other:

> *Hey, let's part ways here. But first, let's carve our names into this tree and stick our knives in. Whoever returns to this spot first should take out the knife near his brother's name, and if blood flows from it then he is alive. But if water flows from it, then he is surely dead!*

Here we have our first parallel to the Nart Sagas. In the latter, Akshartag tells his brother before going into the sea after the dove-maiden: "If the waves throw up bloody foam on the shore, that means I am no longer in the land of the living!"[98]

Going back to the story, the eldest son comes across a village that is all draped in black. The locals tell him that a twelve headed-dragon guards the local wellspring, and demands a sacrifice each year. If they do not provide a sacrifice to the dragon, he is told that the entire village would die of thirst. However, the King's daughter is apparently the newly selected sacrifice, and consequently, the King is offering his daughter to whoever slays the dragon. Sure enough, the elder brother and his three wild beasts slay the dragon. However, the coachman decapitates the eldest brother and claims that he slew the dragon (which is typical for this tale type).

After the wild beasts resurrect their master using a magical herb, the oldest brother returns and sets the record straight by revealing he knows where the dragon's tongues are hidden. The coachman is dealt with, and the oldest brother marries the princess. The end... but not actually.

Later, the oldest brother goes hunting and is turned to stone by a witch. (Actually Jezibaba in disguise.) The youngest brother happens upon the kingdom after discovering that his brother is dead from the water flowing from his name on the tree. The princess thinks he is her husband, and the two sleep together, but the youngest brother places his sword between them in order to ensure he does not get too close to his brother's wife. Later, he goes into the same forest as his brother in search of him, and kills the old hag (turning her to stone with her own wand.) He restores his brother and the petrified animals, and both twins return to the kingdom triumphant.

The tale has many components that point to its antiquity. The scenario with the "sword in the bed" as a separator between a man and a woman also shows up in Indo-European mythological epics. That includes not only the Norse Volsung Saga, but also the Nart Sagas, where the hero Akshar is mistaken for his twin brother Akshartag, and therefore must place a sword between him and his brother's wife, Zerasha.[99]

And this is not the only case in which the Akshar / Akshartag cycle of the Nart Sagas seems to link up with folktales of ATU 303. In the Nart Sagas, the two brothers must guard the golden apples of the Narts from the shapeshifting dove-maidens (Daughters of the sea-God Donbettyr) who have been stealing them. This narrative from the Nart Sagas can be summarized formulaically using the ATU folktale type index as ATU 550: The Golden Bird, followed by ATU 300/303 (twin brothers, dragon slayer). The motif of brothers defending a tree of golden apples from a thieving bird is obviously reminiscent of Norse mythology, and therefore its presence in the Nart Sagas of the Northern Caucasus is no coincidence. It also shows up in folktales of the ATU 550 "Golden Bird" variety, even as far west as Quebec.[100]

In one German folktale, "The Two Brothers" we see something very similar. This tale from the Grimm's collection opens with two brothers, and an episode of ATU: 550, The Golden Bird. What follows, however, is typical ATU 300 / 303, more or less in line with the Slovak version above. So, we have almost the exact same folktale type formula as in the Nart Sagas (ATU 550 + 303 - in roughly that sequence) except this one is from Germany, obviously.[101]

On top of that, the Slovak variant isn't the only one to mention a water-blocking dragon. This is fairly typical for tales of ATU 300 and 303. There is a very odd connection between these folktales of ATU 300 / 303 and the hagiographic legends surrounding St. George the dragon slayer. To explain why will require another brief discussion.

St. George also was traditionally said to have slain a dragon that was withholding or poisoning water that a kingdom depended upon for sustenance.[102] This has parallels to many figures of Indo-European mythology, such as the Vedic dragon Vritra[103] and Greek Drakaina Sybaris.[104] Any reader should know by now that there is an extensive association between dragon-slaying narratives and the release of water. For more on this, reference Chapter 3: Perun and the Drakenkampf. However, while Chapter 3 explores the dragon-slaying motif in connection with the Indo-European thunder God, there is something else going on with St. George and the folktales of ATU 303. As we will see, this is part of the less understood Proto-Indo-European narrative involving dragons and the divine twins.

Water-withholding dragons called "lamia" are also well known in the folklore of Bulgaria.[105] Bulgaria, or as it was known, "Thrace" was also the birthplace of the Pre-Christian deity known as the "Thracian horseman." This figure became popular in the Roman Empire, and a number of scholars have noted that the pagan iconography of the Thracian Horseman eventually blended into the iconography of St. George the Dragon Slayer.[106, 107]

The imagery of the Pre-Christian Thracian Rider in modern day Bulgaria deserves some description. Reliefs show the rider almost always galloping from left to right, towards a tree with a serpent entwined. His right hand is raised and holds a spear or other weapon as if about to strike the serpent.[108] Interestingly, there is sometimes a second horseman in the background who rides in the opposite direction.[109]

Neither is Bulgaria the only place where we see that St. George adopted attributes of the divine horsemen. In the Ossetian Nart Sagas, "St. George" (called Uastyrdzhi by the Ossetians) actually appears as the usurper of Akshar and Akshartag. Specifically, he helps bury the twin's corpses and eventually lies with the late Akshartag's wife - Zerasha, supposedly becoming the forefather of later Nart Generations through their daughter Satanaya.[110]

Thus in a very direct sense, the Nart Sagas push the idea of "St. George" acting as a replacement for Akshartag. This may have been part of an explicit policy on the part of the Orthodox Christian Church, similar to the one described in Chapter 3 with St. Elijah and the Thunder God. In much the same way that the Orthodox Christian world seems to have "converted" thunder deities into "St. Elijah", it seems that horseman deities tended to be deliberately merged with St. George.

The motif of dragon-slaying and water release in association with the Thracian horseman and St. George is complimented by European folktales of ATU 300 / 303, which often have two brother heroes slaying a dragon together. This appears to confirm that dragon-slaying was an attribute of the divine twin horsemen since ancient times.

It may seem tempting to reject the European Folktales of ATU 300 / 303 outright as "recent' folklore, unrelated to anything ancient. To be sure, folktales as we know them were largely recorded in just the past 200 years. However, we should bear in mind that this tale type is found well outside of Europe. Stories of ATU 300 and 303 featuring two brothers can be found at least as far east as India.[111] Unfortunately, a mapping of these narratives is beyond the scope of this chapter. Suffice to say, the pairing of two brothers in folktales about dragon-slaying cannot be dismissed as being purely a European motif.

I would also like to reference the Krakow foundation legend again, because it seems to involve a very early example of this narrative from Europe. The earliest reference to the two sons of Krak slaying the Wawel dragon comes from the Polish Chronicle of the 13th century.[112] This 13th century date for the Polish Chronicle is not incredibly ancient, but by no means recent either. We have also already discussed the Scythian torc from Kobyakovo which shows two canine-headed warriors battling a dragon together, armed with clubs.[113] This can also be interpreted as a representation of mythical twin heroes from an Indo-European mythology or epic.

As we can see, the St. George and the dragon motif can probably be traced back to European folktales of ATU 300 / 303, which are themselves an echo of narratives about divine twin horsemen slaying a dragon. We have reviewed enough evidence here to show that this was part of a standard Indo-European myth.

Interestingly, most of the motifs associated with ATU 550, 303, and 300 (all listed here) can also show up in folktales about three brothers! One such tale is "The Three Brothers and the Golden Apples" in Bulgaria.[114] We have already discussed the narrative from the Nart Sagas in which two brothers must seek out the thief of the golden apples. The antiquity of the "three brother" version is clearly established in Irish mythology by the Three Sons of Tuireann. In this tale, we see an odd variant in which the Celtic God Lugh sends three brothers to obtain the golden apples for him.[115] clearly, the heroic feats associated with the divine twins can easily be applied to a trio of brothers as well. This is worth discussing.

In Indo-Iranian mythologies, the dragon-slayer is typically one of three brothers. We see this with the Persian Dragon-Slayer Thraetona, as well as the Vedic deity Trita. The Vedic Trita appears to have devolved into a mere sidekick of the Thunderer Indra.[116] As I hope I have shown, however, the divine twins can (occasionally) fulfill the exact same role of dragon-slaying. However, the Thunderer and "third" brother seems to have more frequently assumed this role in Indo-Iranian cultures. One possibility is that we are dealing with more than one version of the same Proto-Indo-European hero narratives; Some talk about two brothers, and others champion a "third" who puts the first two to shame. Both of the variants appear quite ancient, and they could well have coexisted within a single Proto Indo-European culture. Indeed, one detail that is often overlooked in these reconstructions is that the Proto-Indo-Europeans themselves probably had many tribes with slightly different mythologies. We might not be able to reconstruct all of the diversity that existed among these tribes, but neither should we be baffled by the presence of more than one version of a particular myth.

In Chapter 3: Perun and the Drakenkampf, I introduced one tale of ATU 300 / 303 featuring the "Storm Bogatyr" as one of three brothers. This brother slays dragons, and generally embarrasses his brothers. It seems obvious that he represents the thunder deity Perun. However, it must be stressed that a "third brother" is sometimes absent from the exact same types of narratives. In many cases, it is not difficult to find similar tales of Aarne-Thompson Types 300 / 303 (Blood Brothers and Dragon Slayer) which appear to invoke the mythology of the divine twins rather than the Thunder God. When discussing St. George, the Dragon Slayer, it appears to be the divine twin horseman tradition, not the tradition of the Storm God, which is being invoked under Christian guise.

Endnotes

1. Knowles, James. The Nineteenth Century and After. Volume 6, London: Constable, 1877. Page 753
2. Cox, George W. The Mythology of the Aryan Nations: Vol. 2. Port Washington, NY: Kennikat Press, 1969. Page 327
3. Guerber, Helene A. Myths of the Norsemen: From the Eddas and Sagas. London: George G. Harrap, 1908. Page 3
4. Bonnefoy, Yves, Wendy Doniger, and Gerald Honigsblum. Asian Mythologies. Chicago, Ill: University of Chicago Press, 1993. Page 32
5. Mallory, J P. Encyclopedia of Indo-European Culture. London: Fitzroy Dearborn, 1997. Page 129
6. Boganeva, E. "Contemporary Recordings of Belarusian Folk Biblical and Non-Biblical Etiological Legends in the Comparative-Historical Aspect." Folklore (Estonia). 72 (2018): 59-88.

7. Bane, Theresa. Encyclopedia of Beasts and Monsters in Myth, Legend and Folklore. 2016. Internet resource. Page 13
8. Lindow, John. Norse Mythology: A Guide to the Gods, Heroes, Rituals, and Beliefs. Oxford: Oxford University Press, 2002. Page 324
9. Simpson, Jacqueline. Icelandic Folktales and Legends. Stroud: Tempus, 1972. Pages 83-84
10. Greek Drama. 2019. Page 185
11. Kinsey, Brian. Gods and Goddesses of Greece and Rome. Tarrytown: Marshall Cavendish, 2012. Internet resource. Page 274
12. Thum, Tobias. Plutarchs Dialog De E Apud Delphos: Eine Studie. 2013. Page 192
13. Morgan, Llewelyn. Patterns of Redemption in Virgil's Georgics (Cambridge Classical Studies). Cambridge University Press, 1999. Pages 144-146
14. Gimbutas, Marija. The Gods and Goddesses of Old Europe: 7000 to 3500 BC Myths, Legends and Cult Images. Berkeley: University of California Press, 1974. Page 182
15. Lincoln, Bruce (1991). Death, War, and Sacrifice: Studies in Ideology & Practice. Univ. of Chicago Press. Page 35
16. Dumezil, Georges. The Destiny of a King. Chicago: University of Chicago Press, 1988. Page 60)
17. Coimbra, Fernando. The Horse and the Bull in Prehistory and in History. 2016. Internet resource.
18. Ihne, Wilhelm. Early Rome. London: Longman, 1877. Page 32
19. Woodard, Roger D. Myth, Ritual, and the Warrior in Roman and Indo-European Antiquity. Cambridge: Cambridge University Press, 2013. Pages 50-51
20. Quaestiones Medii Aevi. Volume 10. Warszawa Ed. de l'Univ. de Varsovie. 2005. Page 386
21. Santos, Marinas E. "Reassessment, Unification, and Enlargement of the Sources of Slavic Pre-Christian Religion." Russian History. 40.1 (2013): 32.

22. Leeming, David A. From Olympus to Camelot: The World of European Mythology. Oxford [England: Oxford University Press, 2003. Internet resource. Page 152
23. ФГБУНСеверо-Осетинский институт гуманитарных и социальных исследований им. В.И. Абаева ВНЦ РАН и Правительства РСО-Алания, Таказов Федар Магометович, МИФОЛОГИЧЕСКИЕ АРХЕТИПЫ МОДЕЛИ МИРА В ОСЕТИНСКОЙ КОСМОГОНИИ, Page 47, Владикавказ 2014
24. Nagy, Gregory. Greek Mythology and Poetics. 2018. Internet resource. Page 100
25. Fantham, Elaine. Roman Readings: Roman Response to Greek Literature from Plautus to Statius and Quintilian. Berlin: De Gruyter, 2011. Page 511
26. Belier, Wouter W. Decayed Gods: Origin and Development of Georges Dumezil's "ideologie Tripartie. 2015. Internet resource. Pages 84-87
27. Belier, Wouter W. Decayed Gods: Origin and Development of Georges Dumezil's "ideologie Tripartie. 2015. Internet resource. Page 173
28. Belier, Wouter W. Decayed Gods: Origin and Development of Georges Dumezil's "ideologie Tripartie. 2015. Internet resource. Pages 103-106
29. Herodotus, and Isaac Littlebury. The History of Herodotus. London: Printed for D. Midwinter et al, 1787. Page 217
30. Claessen, H J. M, and Peter Skalnik. The Early State. 2011. Internet resource. Page 426
31. Wacks, David A. Medieval Iberian Crusade Fiction and the Mediterranean World. 2019. Page 209
32. Sarangerel, Chosen by the Spirits: Following Your Shamanic Calling. Rochester, Vt: Destiny Books, 2001. Pages 3-4
33. Balzer, Marjorie M. Religion and Politics in Russia: A Reader.2015. Internet resource. Page 249
34. Siikala, Anna-Leena, and Oleg Ulyashev. Hidden Rituals and Public Performances: Traditions and Belonging Among the Post-

Soviet Khanty, Komi and Udmurts. Helsinki: Finnish Literature Society, 2011. Page 69

35. Siikala, Anna-Leena, and Oleg Ulyashev. Hidden Rituals and Public Performances: Traditions and Belonging Among the Post-Soviet Khanty, Komi and Udmurts. Helsinki: Finnish Literature Society, 2011. Pages 92-93
36. Varner, Gary R. The History & Use of Amulets, Charms and Talismans. Raleigh, N.C.: Lulu Press, Inc, 2008. Page 53
37. Mallory, James P, and Douglas Q. Adams. Encyclopedia of Indo-European Culture. London: Fitzroy Dearborn, 1997. Page 55
38. Hallowell, A I. Bear Ceremonialism in the Northern Hemisphere. Philadelphia, 1926. Page 50-51
39. "Hallowell, A I. Bear Ceremonialism in the Northern Hemisphere. Philadelphia, 1926. Page 51
40. Chainey Dee Dee, Winsham Willow, Treasury of Folklore: Woodlands and Forests. S.l.: BATSFORD LTD, 2021.
41. Konakov, N D, Vladimir Napolskikh, Anna-Leena Siikala, and Mihaly Hoppal Komi Mythology. Budapest: Akademiai, 2003. Page 185
42. Rydberg, Viktor, and Rasmus B. Anderson. Teutonic Mythology. 1889. Page 104
43. Winn, Shan M. M. Heaven, Heroes, and Happiness: The Indo-European Roots of Western Ideology. Lanham, Md: University Press of America, 1995. Page 149
44. Malkin, Irad. Myth and Territory in the Spartan Mediterranean. Cambridge: Cambridge University Press, 2003. Page 25
45. Daly, Kathleen N, Marian Rengel. Greek and Roman Mythology a to Z. New York: Facts On File, 2004. Page 87
46. Tales of the Narts: Ancient Myths and Legends of the Ossetians. S.l.: Princeton University Press, 2020. Pages 3-7
47. Chidatman. The Sacred Scriptures of India. Volume 5, New Delhi, India: Anmol Publications, 2009. Internet resource. Page 105
48. Byghan, Yowann. Sacred and Mythological Animals: A Worldwide Taxonomy. 2020. Pages 109-110

49. Mallory, James P, and Douglas Q. Adams. Encyclopedia of Indo-European Culture. London: Fitzroy Dearborn, 1997. Page 232
50. Tylor, Edward B. Primitive Culture: Researches into the Development of Mythology, Philosophy, Religion, Language, Art and Custom. New York: H. Holt, 2018. Internet resource. Page 255
51. Kuniczak, W S, and Pat Bargielski. The Glass Mountain: Twenty-eight Ancient Polish Folktales and Fables. New York: Hippocrene Books, 1997. Internet resource. Pages 45-49
52. Quaestiones Medii Aevi. Volume 10. Warszawa Ed. de l'Univ. de Varsovie. 2005. Page 386
53. Silver, Carole G. Strange and Secret Peoples: Fairies and Victorian Consciousness. Oxford: Oxford University Press, 2009. Page 111
54. Roy, Christian. Traditional Festivals: A Multicultural Encyclopedia. Santa Barbara, Calif: ABC-CLIO, 2005. Internet resource. Page 255
55. Pike-Tay, Anne & Anthony, David. (2016). Dog Days of Winter: Seasonal Activities in a Srubnaya Landscape. 10.2307/j.ctvdjrq7b.20.
56. "6 Late Bronze Age Midwinter Dog Sacrifices and Warrior Initiations at Krasnosamarskoe, Russia." (2019): 97.
57. Colarusso, John. Nart Sagas from the Caucasus: Myths and Legends from the Circassians, Abazas, Abkhaz, and Ubykhs. 2016. Internet resource. Pages 16 - 17
58. Yulia, Ustinova. The Supreme Gods of the Bosporan Kingdom: Celestial Aphrodite and the Most Hight God. Leiden: Brill, 1999. Page 279
59. Littleton, C S. Gods, Goddesses, and Mythology: Volume 1, Achelous-Arachne. 2005. Page 824
60. A Commentary, Mythological, Historical, and Geographical on Pope's Homer, and Dryden's Aeneid of Virgil; with a Copious Index. London: J. Murray, 1829. Page 512
61. Dissertation Abstracts International: A, B. Ann Arbor, Mich: University Microfilms International, 1997. Page 1730

62. Kershaw, Kris. The One-Eyed God: Odin and the (indo)germanic Mannerbunde. Washington D.C: Institute for the study of man, 2000. Page 171
63. Willis, R. World Mythology. New York: Metro, 2012. Page 196
64. Puhvel, Jaan. Comparative Mythology. Baltimore: The Johns Hopkins University Press, 1993. Page 142
65. Burkert, Walter. Greek Religion. Cambridge, Mass: Harvard University Press, 1985. Page 212
66. Dini, Pietro U. Mitologia Baltica: Studi Sulla Mitologia Dei Popoli Baltici: Antologia. Genova: ECIG, 1995. Page 50
67. Winn, Shan M. M. Heaven, Heroes, and Happiness: The Indo-European Roots of Western Ideology. Lanham, Md: University Press of America, 1995. Page 138
68. Euripides, and Robert E. Meagher. The Essential Euripides: Dancing in Dark Times. Wauconda, Ill: Bolchazy-Carducci, 2002. Internet resource. Page 217
69. Mallory, James P, and Douglas Q. Adams. Encyclopedia of Indo-European Culture. London: Fitzroy Dearborn, 1997. Page 163
70. Mallory, James P, and Douglas Q. Adams. Encyclopedia of Indo-European Culture. London: Fitzroy Dearborn, 1997. Page 161
71. Puhvel, Jaan. Comparative Mythology. Baltimore: The Johns Hopkins University Press, 1993. Page 288
72. Matheson, Susan B. Polygnotos and Vase Painting in Classical Athens. Madison, Wis: University of Wisconsin Press, 1995. Page 228
73. Achuthananda, Swami. The Reign of the Vedic Gods. 2018. Page 547
74. Mallory, James P, and Douglas Q. Adams. Encyclopedia of Indo-European Culture. London: Fitzroy Dearborn, 1997. Page 161
75. Mallory, James P, and Douglas Q. Adams. Encyclopedia of Indo-European Culture. London: Fitzroy Dearborn, 1997. Page 280
76. Byghan, Yowann. Sacred and Mythological Animals: A Worldwide Taxonomy. 2020. Pages 109-110

77. Cahill, Michael A. Paradise Rediscovered. Carindale, Qld: IP (Interactive Publications, 2012. Page 498
78. Marsh, Richard, Elan Penn, and Frank McCourt. The Legends & Lands of Ireland. Sterling Pub Co Inc, 2006. Page 63
79. Haney, Jack V. The Complete Russian Folktale. Volume 3. United Kingdom, M.E. Sharpe, 1999. Page 18
80. Вологодчина: невостребованная древность. N.p, WP IPGEB. Page 389
81. Monaghan, Patricia. The Encyclopedia of Celtic Mythology and Folklore. New York, N.Y: Checkmark Books, 2008. Page 213
82. Squire, Charles. The Mythology of the British Islands. New Edition, Illustrated. Pp. x. 446. Blackie & Son: London, 1910. Pages 261-262.
83. Tales of the Narts: Ancient Myths and Legends of the Ossetians. S.l.: Princeton University Press 2020. Pages 3-18
84. Squire, Charles. The Mythology of the British Islands. New Edition, Illustrated. Pp. x. 446. Blackie & Son: London, 1910. Pages 261-262.
85. Higham, Nicholas J. King Arthur: The Making of the Legend. S.l.: Yale Univ Press, 2021. Page 85
86. Proceedings of the Harvard Celtic Colloquium, 29: 2009. United Kingdom, Harvard University Press, 2011. Page 94
87. Tales of the Narts: Ancient Myths and Legends of the Ossetians. S.l.: Princeton University Press, 2020. Pages 73-74
88. McCulloch, John A, and Jan Machal. The Mythology of All Races: 3. Boston, 1918. Page 97
89. O'Connor, Ralph. The Destruction of Da Derga's Hostel: Kingship and Narrative Artistry in a Mediaeval Irish Saga. 2013. Page 74-75
90. Aldhouse-Green, Miranda J. Animals in Celtic Life and Myth. London: Routledge, 2002. Page 190
91. Martin, J D. The Untold History of the Celts. Cavendish Square Publishing, 2017. Internet resource. Pages 110-111

92. Squire, Charles. The Mythology of the British Islands. New Edition, Illustrated. Pp. x. 446. Blackie & Son: London, 1910. Pages 236-237
93. Afanasyev, Alexander. Russian Folktales from the Collection of A. Afanasyev - a Dual-Language Book. 2014. Pages 87-110
94. Mallory, James P, and Douglas Q. Adams. Encyclopedia of Indo-European Culture. London: Fitzroy Dearborn, 1997. Pages 232, 331
95. Williams, George M. Handbook of Hindu Mythology. Santa Barbara, Calif: ABC-CLIO, 2011. Internet resource. Page 218
96. Kuniczak, W S, and Pat Bargielski. The Glass Mountain: Twenty-eight Ancient Polish Folktales and Fables. New York: Hippocrene Books, 1997. Internet resource. Pages 45-48
97. Cooper, David L, and Pavol Dobsinsky. Traditional Slovak Folktales. Armonk, N.Y: M.E. Sharpe, 2001. Internet resource. Pages 2-10
98. Tales of the Narts: Ancient Myths and Legends of the Ossetians. S.l.: Princeton University Press, 2020. Pages 3-7
99. West, Morris. Indo-European Poetry and Myth. Oxford: Oxford University Press, 2007. Pages 436-437
100. Barbeau, Marius. The Golden Phoenix: And Other French-Canadian Fairy Tales. Henry Z. Walck, 1970. Pages 7-25
101. Grimm, Jacob, Wilhelm Grimm, Jack Zipes, and Johnny Gruelle. The Complete Fairy Tales of the Brothers Grimm. New York, NY: Bantam, 1992. Pages 230-247
102. Ogden, Daniel. The Dragon in the West: From Ancient Myth to Modern Legend. 2021. Internet resource. Page 168
103. Achuthananda, Swami. The Reign of the Vedic Gods.2018. Page 29
104. Ogden, Daniel. The Dragon in the West: From Ancient Myth to Modern Legend. 2021. Internet resource. Pages 77-78
105. MacDermott, Mercia. Bulgarian Folk Customs. Philadelphia: Jessica Kingsley, 2010. Page 64
106. Ryan, W F. The Bathhouse at Midnight: An Historical Survey of Magic and Divination in Russia. Magic in history. Stroud: Sutton, 1999. Page 242

107. Fol, Aleksandur, and Steven Runciman. Thracian Legends. Sofia: Sofia-Press, 1976. Page 36
108. Hoddinott, Ralph F. Early Byzantine Churches in Macedonia and Southern Serbia: A Study of the Origins and the Initial Development of East Christian Art. London: Macmillan, 1963. Page 54
109. Fol, Aleksandur, and Steven Runciman. Thracian Legends. Sofia: Sofia-Press, 1976. Page 18
110. Tales of the Narts: Ancient Myths and Legends of the Ossetians. S.l.: Princeton University Press 2020. Pages 14-22
111. Steel, Flora-Annie. Tales of the Punjab, Told by the People (classic Reprint). Forgotten Books, 2015. Page 129-143
112. Quaestiones Medii Aevi. Volume 10. Warszawa Ed. de l'Univ. de Varsovie. 2005. Page 386
113. Yulia, Ustinova. The Supreme Gods of the Bosporan Kingdom: Celestial Aphrodite and the Most Hight God. Leiden: Brill, 1999. Page 279
114. The Three Brothers and the Golden Apples, Varna International Publications. Scott Cairns. 2016
115. O'Duffy, Richard J. Oidhe Chloinne Tuireann: The Fate of the Children of Tuireann. Dublin, M.H. Gill, 1901. Page 95
116. West, Morris. Indo-European Poetry and Myth. Oxford: Oxford University Press, 2007. Page 260

Chapter 7

Deus Otiosus

In the 12th century, the German missionary Helmold of Bosau recorded his surprise at encountering among the Slavs on the Baltic a belief in a single heavenly God, who ignored the affairs of this world, and who delegated the governance of it to certain spirits begotten by him.[1] Scholars often interpret this as a "Deus Otiosus" or idle God.[2] This term has a long history in religious studies, which I would like to review. I've noticed recently that this is a concept that is not always grasped when I discuss Slavic paganism.

If you search for the history of the term "Deus Otiosus" you are likely to encounter research on a number of indigenous cultures that were first encountered by the West during the colonial period. One of the major fields where the concept is discussed seems to be West African cultural studies. In particular, the Nuer and Bantu people are believed to have conceived of "God" as having retired into the sky, and as interacting with people through intermediary spirits.

However, this has been interpreted in a number of different ways by Western scholars. Some view this God as "retired", whereas others see him as too good for direct worship. Some scholars have claimed that all worship of lesser divinities is in fact an indirect veneration of the creator who governs through them. Yet clearly, the worship of the creator does take place in West African traditions, albeit less frequently than with the "lower" spirits that live closer to mankind. The general idea seems to be that the creator, like a West African King, should be seen by his subjects only infrequently.[3]

One example is provided by Yoruba mythology, in which the supreme God is called Olorun, or Olodumare. He is distinguished from his children, the Orisha, who form the Yoruba pantheon of about 400 divinities. There are major and minor Orishas, and some can also be designated as "primordial" Orishas - that is, Orishas which Olodumare himself sent down from heaven at the time of creation. Of these, the primordial Orisha "Obatala" can actually be considered the one who administered the act of creation directly, and who often serves as the acting leader of most other Orishas.[4] Olodumare is therefore very far removed from the center stage of Yoruba mythology.

Of course, the African religious traditions cannot have interacted significantly with those of the pagan Slavs in Eastern Europe. This is clearly part of a broader tendency among various cultures. However, the study of other traditions with the concept of a Deus Otiosis can help us to avoid applying modern or Christian biases to Helmold's description of the Slavic "God of Gods."

In the context of Eastern Europe, the next nearest well-attested examples are probably those of the Uralic peoples. The Uralic language family includes Finnish, Sami, Estonian, and Hungarian in Europe, but it extends as far east as Siberia where the Khanty, Mansi, and Samoyedic languages can be found. Among the Mansi of western Siberia, for example, we can see that there was a notion of three layers of heaven, with the God of the highest layer being remote and inaccessible to mankind.[5]

Or, very similarly in Komi mythology, the "Good" creator Jen is said to have retired to the heavens and interacts with the human world only rarely.[6] The Uralic peoples are very much distinct from the Slavs, and historically have tended to live east and / or directly north of the Balto-Slavic language speakers - but there are regions like modern day Belarus where they would have shared a border or contact zone of some sort with Balto-Slavic neighbors.

This is another of the many signs that I have noted indicating Slavic mythology is closely related to Uralic mythology. I discuss this in my later chapters on afterlife beliefs, and on dualism. It is not clear, however, whether this is due to direct influence. There are also possible indirect or intermediary cultures that could have produced this similarity between Uralic and Slavic cultures without the early Slavs necessarily coming into strong direct contact with Uralic cultures. (Which the West Slavs and South Slavs probably didn't.)

For instance, it is possible that the early Slavs absorbed large numbers of Baltic language speakers (themselves close linguistic relatives of the Slavs). Today, the Baltic language speakers are mostly limited to Latvia and Lithuania. But we know from hydronyms (river / lake names, among other things) that they lost a great deal of territory to the Slavs, and once occupied a much larger area.[7] The case for Uralic-Baltic contact is not a difficult one to make - so let's leave it at that.

Another possible source for the convergence is the influence of the Steppe nomads. Initially, Uralic and Slavic people are thought to have come under the influence of the nomadic Iranian peoples called the Scythians. Unfortunately, we know relatively little about the mythology of these earliest steppe nomads. Later, it would have been the Altaic nomads who arrived in Eastern Europe, as they began to replace the Iranian-language speaking nomads around the 4th century CE.[8]

A very similar conception of "God" does appear in the so-called "Tengrist" religion of Altaic peoples. This includes people like the Mongols, Tungus, and Turks of Central Asia - most likely the Huns as well. In Tengrism, the Sky Father Tengri is said to be extremely distant from humankind and can be contacted directly only by a shaman. As such, he is not truly "idle". Much as with African traditions, the degree of "idleness" is debatable, but once again the emphasis on special conditions for "God's" interaction with humans seems to confirm that this is the exception rather than the rule.

The exact relationship of Altaic and Uralic peoples is extremely complex. It was once thought that they might be genetically related - that is - descended from a single ancestor language. Today, it is more common to speak of a Ural-Altaic "area" or "belt." The languages may not have always been related, but due to ages of contact throughout North Eurasia, they can still be treated as belonging to an interrelated family of cultures that extends from Mongolia to Finland.[9]

Sure enough, there are a number of parallels that can be cited between Slavic, Uralic, and Altaic mythologies. I will discuss the Ural-Altaic connection further in chapter 11, where I review the earth-diver creation myth and North Eurasian Dualism. The same pattern can be seen with the concept of the "distant" creator of Altaic mythology. In the 19th century, the scholar John Abercromby drew a number of parallels between the (Uralic) Mordvin creation story, and another Turkic one recorded from the Altai region. It begins with a very familiar dualistic earth-diver creation story.

There are some hints in this story of a decentralized theology, where the lesser divinities have tasks delegated to them. Maitere appears as the loyal servant of God, and a culture hero who descends from heaven to teach mankind various arts such as the growing of barley and onions. There is also the figure known as "Mandyshire" who has an interesting role; at the behest of the creator, he drives Erlik (the evil God) down from heaven and causes him and his servants to hide beneath the earth. To do this, Mandyshire uses his own strength, but also relies upon the creator to create and bestow a divine spear upon him.[10] As noted in Chapter 3, this episode with Mandyshire is extremely similar to some Slavic creation story episodes involving Illya (St. Elijah).

Going back to the Altaic creation myth, however, it is the end of this story that drives home the creator's status of a Deus Otiosus, as quoted in part below;[11]

> *Then God spoke to mankind; "I have made for you cattle, I have made for you food, I have caused lovely, pure water to flow upon the surface of the earth that you may drink it; I have helped you, now do ye good also! Now will I go away, I will not return soon...--Now I go afar, when I return I will at that time see your good and your evil. In my place now there shall help you Yapkara, Mandyshire, (and) Shal-Jime. Yapkara, see well to it! If Erlik would take the dead of mankind, tell it to Mandyshire; Mandyshire is strong, he will conquer Erlik. Shal-Jime, see well to it that the evil spirits remain under the surface of the earth; if they come up onto the surface of the earth, tell it to Maitere. Maitere is strong, he will conquer them. Pondo-Sunku shall make fast the sun and the moon..."*

Thus, we can see that the Altaians had a full pantheon of deities, even within the framework of a creator and an evil "devil" figure in the form of Erlik. Mandyshire appears to be the equivalent of the thundering Illya / Perun in Slavic creation legends, whereas Maitere obviously is associated with fertility and civilization to some extent (he teaches man how to farm). Even the old Indo-Iranian underworld God "Yima / Yama" clearly is still deified and is not apparently conflated with the "devil" figure of Erlik. All of these beings, however, are clearly in a league beneath the creator himself.

Interestingly, the "Gods" that the creator assigns tasks to in the Altai legend all seem to correspond to figures from Indian and Iranian religious traditions. Maitere is apparently the Turkic word for the Boddhisattva known as "Maitreya" - a widely venerated figure in Buddhism. As for the name "Shal-Yime" it is thought to correspond to the Iranian "Yima" and more distantly - the Vedic "Yama" who is actually the keeper of the underworld. Fittingly, in the Altaian myth, Shal-Yime seems to be assigned the role of a psychopomp (a gatherer and transporter of human souls) as well as a custodian of the dangerous subterranean spirits, whom he is charged with keeping underground.

Of course, the hierarchy described here could also be linked with some traditions among the Indo-European language-speaking cultures (which is what the early Slavs were). However, there are also some key differences. These Indo-European equivalents seem to avoid the strong hierarchy of a Deus Otiosus tradition, where the primordial deity is worshipped less than his children precisely because he is seen as being much greater and "higher" than them. Rather, in Indo-European mythology, there is an impression that the younger Gods truly have conquered and bested their progenitors (often depicted as giants and titans) rather than simply having tasks delegated by the primordial God.

It is fascinating that in the Vedas, the primordial God is sometimes said to be Tvastr, the craftsman who forged Indra's thunderbolt.[12] This is reminiscent of some East European and Altaic creation stories, where the role of the thunder God seems to be bestowed by the creator in the form of a weapon. In the context of Slavic mythology, it is tempting to equate Svarog with the figure who bestows the thunderbolt upon Perun.

We know from the Russian chronicles that the Slavic God Svarog was associated with blacksmithing. Furthermore, he was considered to be the father of Dazhbog, who is referred to in one Russian chronicle as "the Sun Tsar."[13] In his book, Stanislaw Rosik reviews a remarkably copious amount of German writing attesting that the Polabian Slavs venerated a "Son of Svarog" (Svarozic) as their most prominent deity. We see references to "Svarozic" as the primary Polabian deity from multiple German clergymen writing decades apart from one another. Therefore, we can say that Svarozic's prominence is not in question. Additionally, Helmold is very clear that the importance of Polabian deities was directly determined by their degree of blood-relatedness to the supreme God. It would be somewhat surprising if the chief deity of the Polabians was not a direct offspring of the "God of Gods" who rules from afar. Therefore, based on this, it appears that Svarog is the "God of Gods" mentioned by Helmold, and Svarozic, his son, was the deity nearest to him in importance. There is a caveat, which Rosik also notes, namely that there may well have been multiple "sons" or emanations from Svarog, and hence more than one "Svarozic."[14] We will be discussing this in Chapter 8: Svarozhichi - Sons of Svarog. In any case, however, the role of Svarog seems clear.

The elevation of a heavenly blacksmith deity is reminiscent of some Slavic and Turkic creation legends with dualistic elements. In a number of these myths, the creator and his evil counterpart participate in the creation of spirits to fight on their behalf in the cosmic struggle. Sometimes they do this by striking sparks with stone, but in other legends, they hammer anvils to create their respective "armies" or supernatural progeny.[15] It is tempting to see Svarog in this role in the context of Slavic mythology.

Interestingly, in Finnish mythology, it is Ukko the thunder God who acts as the heavenly and aloof Deus Otiosus. However, there is also a heavenly smith deity named Ilmarinen who was said to have forged the vault of the sky, and who could be a close relative of the Slavic Svarog. According to "Mythic Discourses: Studies in Uralic Traditions" printed by the Finnish Literature Society in 2012: "Ukko appears to have displaced *Ilmari as both central sky-god and master of thunder at some point during the Iron Age."[16]

Among the Khanty and Mansi, who belong to a Finno-Ugric branch much farther east than the Finns, the equivalent figure appears to be the heavenly father Num-Torem. The sons of Num-Torem seem to correspond to the main nature Gods worshipped by other Uralic peoples.[17] According to some myths, the heavens have seven layers, with Num-Torem occupying the highest, and his sons occupying the lower levels.[18] As I will discuss later, we can make a compelling argument that at least some of the children of Num-Torem in Khanty mythology correspond to the children of Svarog in Slavic mythology. It is tempting therefore to link Num-Torem to Svarog. Certainly, both seem to have been relatively "distant" or inaccessible progenitor deities in their respective pantheons.

On the other hand, there is some confusion implicit in this reconstruction based on characteristics of Num-Torem in Khanty mythology. According to some lore, Num Torem and Kul themselves have a father figure who dwells above them. In fact, even Torem's father sometimes is said to have a father above him.[19] Thus, while Svarog may have been the progenitor of all or most deities worshipped by mankind, there are hints that he may not have been the first being in existence. For those of us who grew up in a Judeo-Christian culture, this is an important distinction. Likewise in Komi mythology, the "idle" sky God Jen and his evil brother Omol are both children of the primordial mother duck Chezh.[20]

Instead of speaking about a single Deus Otiosus, in North Eurasian traditions it might be more useful to speak of a hierarchy of accessibility, with the progenitor of the Gods being *nearly* inaccessible, with the exception of intermediaries who exist in the form of his children. However, there may also be additional "tiers" of divine beings above that entity - who are even further beyond human reach.

Endnotes

1. Rosik, Stanislaw, and Anna Tyszkiewicz. The Slavic Religion in the Light of 11th and 12th-Century German Chronicles (Thietmar of Merseburg, Adam of Bremen, Helmold of Bosau): Studies on the Christian Interpretation of Pre-Christian Cults and Beliefs in the Middle Ages. 2020. Page 379
2. Doninger, Wendy. Merriam-webster's Encyclopedia of World Religions. Springfield, Mass: Merriam-Webster, 2000. Page 288

3. Ukpong, Justin S. "The Problem of God and Sacrifice in African Traditional Religion." Journal of Religion in Africa. 1983.
4. Stokes, Jamie. Encyclopedia of the Peoples of Africa and the Middle East. New York: Facts On File, 2009. Page 750
5. Gemuev, Izmail N, Vladimir V. Napol'skih, Anna-Leena Siikala, and Mihaly Hoppal. Mansi Mythology. Budapest: Akademiai, 2008. Page 102
6. Siikala, Anna-Leena, Mihály Hoppál, Nikolaj D. Konakov, and Vladimir V. Napol'skih. Komi Mythology. Budapest: Akadémiai K, 2003. Page 134
7. Grünthal, R. (2012). Baltic loanwords in Mordvin. In R. Grünthal, & P. Kallio (Eds.), A Linguistic Map of Prehistoric Northern Europe (pp. 297-343). (Mémoires de la Société Finno-Ougrienne). Suomalais-Ugrilainen Seura
8. History of Humanity: 3. London: Routledge, 1996. Page 466
9. Robbeets, Martine, and Walter Bisang. Paradigm Change: In the Transeurasian Languages and Beyond, 2014. Page 312
10. Abercromby, John. "The Beliefs and Religious Ceremonies of the Mordvins." The Folk-Lore Journal. 7.2 (1889): 65-135.
11. Dragomanov, M P, and Earl W. Count. Notes on the Slavic Religio-Ethical Legends: The Dualistic Creation of the World. Bloomington, Ind: Indiana University, 1961. Pages 46-47
12. Parmeshwaranand, Encyclopaedic Dictionary of Vedic Terms. New Delhi: Sarup & Sons, 2000. Page 645-651
13. Warner, Elizabeth. Russian Myths. Austin: Publ. in co-operation with British Museum Press [by] University of Texas Press, 2002. Page 16
14. Rosik, Stanislaw, and Anna Tyszkiewicz. The Slavic Religion in the Light of 11th and 12th-Century German Chronicles (Thietmar of Merseburg, Adam of Bremen, Helmold of Bosau): Studies on the Christian Interpretation of Pre-Christian Cults and Beliefs in the Middle Ages. 124-125, 2020. Pages 101, 108, 124-125
15. Dragomanov, M P, and Earl W. Count. Notes on the Slavic Religio-Ethical Legends: The Dualistic Creation of the World. Bloomington, Ind: Indiana University, 1961. Pages 132-133

16. Frog, Anna-Leena Siikala, and Eila Stepanova. Mythic Discourses: Studies in Uralic Traditions. 2012. Page 218
17. Wiget, Andrew, and Olga Balalaeva. Khanty: People of the Taiga: Surviving the Twentieth Century. Fairbanks, Alaska: University of Alaska Press, 2011. Page 106
18. Harva, Uno, and Uno Harva. The Mythology of All Races. Volume 4, Finno-Ugric; Siberian. New York: Cooper Square Publishers, 1964. Page 404
19. Wiget, Andrew, and Olga Balalaeva. Khanty: People of the Taiga: Surviving the Twentieth Century. Fairbanks, Alaska: University of Alaska Press, 2011. Page 104
20. Siikala, Anna-Leena, Mihály Hoppál, Nikolaj D. Konakov, and Vladimir V. Napol'skih. Komi Mythology. Budapest: Akadémiai K, 2003. Page 371

Chapter 8

Svarozhichi - Sons of Svarog

Dazhbog the Svarozhich

The cult of Svarog and his son(s) is one of the few unifying concepts that can be demonstrated across all of Slavic territory. Among the East Slavs, there is a famous 10th-12th century interpolation inserted into the Malalas Chronicle which has some interesting things to say about Svarog, and one of his sons. It says that "Dazhbog" is the "Tsar Sun", and the son of Svarog. In the same chronicle, Svarog himself is identified with Hephaestus.[1, 2]

The name Dazhbog is independently attested in other East Slavic sources. We know that the idols erected by Vladimir in Kiev included a "Dazhbog."[3]

Regarding "Svarog" among the East Slavs, it should be noted that the only other reference we have to him is an indirect one; A Christian author remarks that people still pray to "Svarozhich" (literally "Svarog-son") under the grain drying barn, where the fire was kept.[4, 5] However, to even begin speaking about the significance of this, we need to understand the cultural significance of the grain drying barn throughout northeastern Europe. And it is extensive, as it includes not only Slavic but also Baltic practices.

In Lithuania, the Jauja or threshing barn was built much like its counterpart in Russia. It was a two-tiered structure with room for a fire to be lit at the bottom, and a place for harvested grain to be stored up top. The heat would rise to the top level and dry the grain so it would not molder. To ancient people, it must have seemed like living proof of the purifying, apotropaic power of fire. The Lithuanians would sacrifice a rooster to the hearth goddess Gabija here, or sometimes a male fire God called

Gabjaujis.[6] The Baltic material makes it clear that the grain-drying barn is a place for the cult of fire. It is noteworthy that Gabjauja, the festival of Gabjaujis, took place in late autumn.[7] This is quite typical of Baltic and Slavic paganism. In Russia as well, a grain-drying barn spirit known as the Ovinnik would be offered a rooster, customarily on September 4th and on November 1st. Interestingly, one source on the Baltic religion describes this grain-drying barn fire deity as "Dimstapatis" which literally means "Master of the House." This is an archaic Indo-European term which is also used for the Vedic Indian fire deity Agni (called "Dampati" in Sanskrit).[8]

Unsurprisingly, some scholars equate the "Svarozhich" of the grain drying barn with the "Tsar Sun" Dazhbog. After all, the connection between fire and the sun is a natural one. We see a very similar concept in the Vedas, where Apam Napat, the child of the waters, is an igneous primordial deity who emerges from the sea itself. He is equally identified with Agni (Fire) and with the sun deity Savitr.[9] Indeed, the prominence of a male solar deity is evident throughout the Vedas, very different from Baltic and Germanic mythologies which both have a Sun Goddess. Although connected with the Balto-Slavic fire cult, the solar attributes of the Slavic deity Dazhbog can likely be attributed to Indo-Iranian influence. More specifically, it would be the Iranian branch, represented by the Scythians, which brought Dazhbog west. Neither is this the only indication of an Indo-Iranian connection.

Among the Ossetians, the cult of the hearth fire is closely associated with Safa. Safa is an interesting figure, associated not only with the hearth-fire but also with the hearth chain on which the cauldron is suspended. Interestingly, Safa also features as a kind of blacksmith deity.[10] However, this would make him the "secondary" blacksmith deity in Ossetian mythology, after the heavenly smith Kurdalaegon. It's not hard to imagine that Dazhbog also was a kind of secondary smith God, deriving his metalworking attributes from his father Svarog, who was apparently equated with the Greek Hephaestus.

Safa also featured in marriage ceremonies, which is not unusual for Indo-European cultures. The practice of leading a new bride three times around the hearth of her new household is well-known among Indo-European cultures.[11] During an Ossetian marriage as well, the man would lead his bride around the hearth in order to entrust her to the protection of Safa.[12]

Another critical element of Safa's worship is the celebration of the New Year holiday "Artkhuron." During this time, people would traditionally pray to the Ossetian hearth deity. And prayers from this holiday have led researchers to conclude that "Artkhuron" was little more than one of Safa's names or epithets.[13] Interestingly, the name "Artkhuron" is a compound of the Ossetian words for "fire" (art) and "solar" (khuron). Therefore, the most straightforward interpretation is to simply translate the term as "Solar Fire."[14, 15] Based on this, we have reason to identify Safa as a solar deity as well as a hearth deity in Ossetian tradition.

The blacksmith functions of Safa are consistent with the Slavic fire deity "Svarozhich" who was called by this name, seemingly in an attempt to evoke the functions of his blacksmithing father, Svarog. Safa was also a deity of marriage and the hearth, which suggests that he could function as a patron deity of the household and of the family. This provides another possible connection to the Slavic Dazhbog; According to the Lay of Igor's Campaign, the Russian people are collectively called the "Grandchildren of Dazhbog."[16] This close familial relationship with the sun deity is very compatible with a cult combining both solar and hearth functions. And considering that we know Dazhbog was a son of Svarog (a Svarozhich) there is little real reason to deny his connection to the East Slavic "fire god" Svarozhich.

It's worth noting that among the Ossetians, the sun is referred to as "Khur", and is typically seen as male when personified.

This has led some scholars to claim that the East Slavic "Khors" was a solar deity. However, in Ossetian, "Khorz" can simply mean "good."[17] The word for "grain" in Ossetian is also "Khor." In Avestan Persian, "Har" can also mean to watch over, defend, or protect.[18] It is directly derived from Proto-Indo-European *Ser - (to protect).[19] Therefore, in an Iranian language, "Har" could simply mean "defender" or "watching one." It could also denote a "Good" deity, or a deity of the grain.

The sounds Kh/ H/ and R are incredibly common in Iranian languages. It's not clear if Khors is an Iranian loan. If it is, however - this does not narrow the etymology down. On the contrary, attributing Iranian origins to the name "Khors" multiplies the uncertainties tenfold. Additionally, because Dazhbog is described as the "Tsar Sun" in one of the few Russian sources that describes the attributes of a Slavic deity, there are some inherent problems with the notion that the Slavs had another deity whose name simply meant "Sun." Certainly, a mythology may have more than one solar deity. However, this requires a level of abstraction - and such abstraction would normally not permit one of the two deities to simply be named "Sun." One might have a name corresponding to darkness or winter, and the other might be associated with light and summer. However, under such a system, it would be very surprising if one of them was simply referred to as "sun." Even from a religious standpoint, this could be confusing for most people - and would probably have been avoided.

Actually, "Hrsuh" would be closer to most original spellings of the name than "Khors" despite modern conventions of writing it this way. And no Iranian etymology for this name need be assumed, as Constantine Borisoff rightly notes.[20]

Cosmas and Damian: Divine Twin Saints

We have mentioned the long-standing Balto-Slavic tradition of offering a rooster in the threshing barn or grain-drying barn (which tended to be the same structure). Recall that the Lithuanians would sacrifice a rooster to the hearth fire God called Gabjaujis during a festival called Gabjauja in late autumn.[21, 22]

We have also mentioned analogous traditions surrounding the Russian barn spirit or "Ovinnik." However, this brings us to one of the more puzzling traditions in Russian folk Christianity - namely the cult of the two brothers Cosmas and Damian. I will argue that the folk traditions surrounding these saints have preserved a rich pagan legacy. For one thing, the Saints Cosmas and Damian (sometimes called Kuz'ma Demyan in Russian) were sometimes the recipients of the grain-drying barn rooster offering in late autumn, typically on November 1st. This was rationalized by turning Cosmas and Damian into the patron saints of chickens. However, the site of these butcherings was still the threshing barn.[23] And scholars have long noted that these offerings are basically identical to those made for the grain-drying barn spirit in other Balto-Slavic traditions.

We know that the grain drying barn fire was sometimes worshipped under the name "Svarozhich." Obviously, this lends itself to the interpretation that "Kuz'ma Demyan" is simply Svarozhich. And this is not a new interpretation. The Russian scholar Rybakov also held the view that both saints simply absorbed the cult of Svarog.

On close analysis, it's clear that most of the attributes reviewed previously, with the Ossetian Safa, are also present in the cult of Kuz'ma Demyan. As Linda Ivanits notes, the Saints were associated with both blacksmithing and marriage. There are folksongs imploring the two saints to help "Forge a wedding."[24] This motif of a smith who forges a wedding appears to be very ancient. It also shows up in the Russian bylina (epic song) about Svyatogor. In this song, the protagonist is told by a giant plowman named Mikula (Nicholas) that there is a mysterious smith in the northern mountains who forges the destinies of those who will marry.[25]

The smith is not described in detail, but this reference to "forging the fates of those who will marry" signals how archaic the concept is. The oral epic songs known as byliny are some of the oldest elements of East Slavic culture - and the bylina of Svyatogor is probably among the oldest. Surely, it is no coincidence that this ancient concept has embedded itself in the folklore of the Saints Cosmas and Damian. The fact that a giant ploughman named "Mikula" tells us where the smith lives is also interesting. These two figures - the smith and the plowman - may be understood as a pair. In fact, they may be twin brothers.

One noteworthy aspect of the Saints Cosmas and Damian is that they were considered twin brothers in their canonical hagiography.[26] Furthermore, the brother saints Cosmas and Damian weren't just smiths in East Slavic folklore; They were also saintly ploughmen.

In East Slavic legends, the brothers Kuzma and Demyan are said to have forged the first plough for mankind. Shortly thereafter, they encountered a dragon who was terrorizing the land. After striking the dragon with hammers and harnessing it, they used it to plow out a massive furrow called the "dragon's banks" or "dragon's ramparts." Afterwards the dragon is said to have been so thirsty that it tried to drink the Dnieper dry and exploded. Sometimes the Saints Boris and Gleb (another pair of brother saints) are inserted into the exact same narrative.[27, 28, 29] The basic elements of the story vary somewhat, but these are all typical features found throughout Russia and Ukraine.

Some scholars like Ryabkov interpreted "Kuzma-Demyan" as a single Saint representing Svarog. However, the interchangeability of Cosmas and Damian with another pair of brother saints - Boris and Gleb - suggests that the element of two brothers is a non-arbitrary part of this narrative. And we see another big hint of this in Poland.

Recall that the tale of the Wawel Dragon involves the Krakow foundation story. In this tale from the 13th century, the two sons of Krak slay a dragon together.[30] They trick it into eating sulfur. According to some later versions, the Wawel dragon then drinks so much water from the Vistula that it bursts.[31] The ploughman motif is missing. But the elements of two brothers and a dragon drinking from a river until it bursts are all strikingly similar to the East Slavic dragon ploughmen narratives, and both appear to be archaic elements of the Wawel Dragon legend in Poland. Once again, we see strong evidence that the presence of two brothers is an ancient element of these narratives.

The two sons of Krak are obviously princes. The Krakow rulers claimed descent from them. In fact, the younger brother attempted to succeed as ruler of Krakow by killing his own brother. As princes involved in a fratricidal conflict for succession, there are some additional parallels to the East Slavic Orthodox Saints Boris and Gleb.

The Saints Boris and Gleb were the very first saints canonized under the impetus of the Russian Orthodox Church. Kievan Rus had just adopted Christianity, and what did they do? They canonized two dead Russian Princes. The narrative may not even be historical. According to the legend, however, they were killed by a brother during a war of succession. Therefore, they were two brother princes of the ruling dynasty in Russia who died from fratricide. (Though not at the hands of one another.) The parallels to the foundation legend of Krakow are obvious. What's more striking, however, is that the texts describing their martyrdom and canonization make it extremely clear that they are patrons of the ruling dynasty (the Rurikid dynasty). In a very real sense, they became divine twin ancestors of the ruling elite in Kievan Rus.

The scholar Stephen Maczko has already argued that this reflects a Pre-Christian ancestor cult of the Rurikid dynasty who ruled early Kievan Rus. He quotes the Russian Chronicle "The clan (rod) of the just is blessed, says the prophet, and their family will be blessed." To this he adds; "It is apparent that the author specifically wishes to emphasize the fact that the martyrdom (of the Princes Boris and Gleb) has meaning for the fate of the ruling house of Kievan Rus as a whole."[32] Therefore, it would appear that this pair of brother saints also acquired ancient East Slavic pagan elements. And in the case of Boris and Gleb, that may have been the initial intent of their canonization; The twin Saints were intended to legitimize and sanctify the royal line, just as an earlier mythological tradition about twins had in Pre-Christian Kievan Rus.

I have one final note that may not seem relevant just yet; It's worth noting that the autumnal sacrifice of the rooster to Cosmas and Damian took place around November 1st, during one of their two major feast days. Interestingly, for the Russian peasantry, the main feast day of Boris and Gleb was May 3rd. Therefore, these two pairs of brother saints have a lot in common, but it's important to note that their feast days are almost exactly 6-months apart (half a year).

Reviewing Jumis, *YemHos, and the Fratricide Motif

We've discussed how Polish chronicles depict the two sons of Krak (the founder of Krakow) as both slaying the Wawel dragon together. Later, one of the two brothers commits fratricide.[33] This has many parallels to folklore about Boris and Gleb, as well as Cosmas and Damian. (Both pairs of Orthodox Saints who are brothers.)

In Chapter 6: Advanced Concepts in Indo-European Mythology, we talked about how this parallels the foundation legend of Rome, with Romulus and Remus. In his paper calling for the expansion of research on Slavic paganism, Marinas notes, "This legend appears to reflect an old Indo-European myth of foundation."[34]

Also in Chapter 6: Advanced Concepts in Indo-European Mythology, we discussed the reconstructed Proto-Indo-European creation myth in which a being is dismembered to create the world. In particular, scholars have reconstructed a proto-myth in which this being was known as *yemHos, meaning "twin." As such, he was the precursor to the Vedic Yama, the first mortal, and first man to die. Yama also became the God of the underworld for this reason.

In Chapter 4: Untangling the Beard of Volos, we reviewed numerous connections between Volos, Yama, and the Balto-Finnic deity Jumis. Feel free to review these chapters if any of this information seems unfamiliar. In Chapter 4, I also noted that the mock weddings celebrated with Jumis are oddly similar to those involving the Saints Kuzma Demyan. Specifically, girls would dress up a straw effigy as Kuzma (Cosmas) and pretend to marry him. Similar joke marriages took place with Jumis among Finnic peoples[35] and it's extremely tempting to link these with the analogous rituals involving "Kuzma" in Russia.[36] These agrarian effigies of "Jumis" are, in turn, closely related to the Beard of Volos - the last sheaf of grain saved from the harvest.

And some of the European harvest effigies or fetishes are explicitly connected with the threshing barn. For instance, the Lithuanian Kursis - a straw effigy associated with the flax harvest - was typically placed in the threshing barn. This is the same structure that in Russian folk tradition came to be associated with the twin brother Saints Cosmas and Damien. In Ukraine, the last sheaf of grain bundled up was called the "Didukh" and it was brought indoors for the winter because it was believed the house the souls of the dead ancestors. A number of Slavic traditions stress the importance of the double-eared stalk of grain, which was often bundled up with a wreath or ceremonial sheaf. This double-eared stalk or bundle of stalks was called the "Sporysh" or the "Tsar of the Field" in Slavic countries. The Balto-Finnic "Jumis" (meaning double or twin) also referred to the double-eared sheaf. In Latvia, the Jumis was said to pursue his sister Jumalina in the field, seeking to marry his sister. This appears to be a direct parallel with the Indo-Iranian Yama and Yami (Vedic) or Yima and Yimak (Iranian) who became the progenitors of humanity through incest. This was discussed extensively in Chapter 4.

Furthermore, in the *Encyclopedia on Indo-European Culture,* Mallory says the following:[37]

> *Clearly related in structure is the other IE creation myth that comprises a primeval sacrifice of "Twin" (*yemHos) by his brother "Man." The myth is seen in Indo-Iranian, Germanic, and Roman tradition. In the Indic sources, the figures are Yama (twin) and Manu (man). Yama is the first mortal to die and he establishes the otherworld. Manu is the ancestor of mankind, first king, originator of sacrifice, and legendary composer of the Manu smrti, the Tradition or Law of Manu. Yama is seen as the sacrificial victim of his "brother" Manu, which sets creation in motion. The Iranian equivalent of Yama was Yama Xsaeta who, after sinning, is deprived of his royal halo (xvarenah) which is then dispersed to the patrons of the three social classes and who is cut in half by his brother. The Germanic myth is preserved best in Tacitus' Germania, which records the origin of the Germans from a primeval Tuisto (from the root "two" and often taken to mean "twin" or perhaps "bisexual.") and his son Mannus (man - cognate with Old Indic Manu) who generate the three social classes of the Germans (as was also the case in Iran.) The Ymir (<Germanic *Yumiyaz) of the Norse creation myth noted above as an example of the cosmogonic myth also means "twin" and is cognate, some would argue, with the Old Indic "Yama."*

This should all sound familiar from Chapter 6. The fratricide motif in the Krakow foundation legend is therefore highly significant. The fact that the two sons of Krak are associated with the foundation of a city or settlement (Krakow) is rich with Indo-European symbolism. Additionally, as I have shown, the way in which the Wawel dragon is defeated (by drinking from the Vistula until it explodes) appears to link the narrative with the dragon-plowman legends involving two brother saints in East Slavic countries. But there is another striking piece of evidence that shows how extensively the sacrifice of *yemHos is connected with the dragon plowman motif. But in order to review that, we need to shift gears from Slavic folklore, and talk about an unlikely source of data; the Ob-Ugrians of western Siberia.

The Sons of Num-Torem: A Critical Parallel in Ugrian Mythology

You may have preconceptions about the relevance of Siberia. It seems like an unlikely place to find the secrets of Slavic paganism. After all, the Russians did not truly begin to dominate in Siberia until after the fall of Kazan in 1552. However, there are some indicators of a long-shared history between people on both sides of the Ural mountains (the dividing line between Eastern Europe and Siberia).

As I discussed in the opening chapter, there is significant linguistic evidence for contact between Uralic and Indo-European language speakers. For one, the Finnic languages (a branch of the Uralic language family) seem to have West Siberian origins, and yet they penetrated into the Baltic region sometime during the 1st millennium BCE. During this migration, they brought with them the Y-Chromosomal haplotype N. The Y-Chromosome is passed from father to son, which means that if you have Haplotype N in Europe, you almost certainly have some sort of Finno-Ugric language speaking ancestor through the paternal line. This is not a haplotype that was prevalent in Europe before the 1st millennium BCE, but it appears to have become prevalent at around the same time that the Finno-Ugric language speakers arrived from Siberia. Today, Haplotype N is found in about 20% of Russians, 9% of Ukrainians, and 4% of Poles. (Again, reference Chapter 1: The Ancient Origins of Europe up to the Early Slavs.)

However, the arrows of influence went both ways. The Proto-Finno-Ugric language appears to have already contained a number of Indo-Iranian loanwords. Some of these are still recognizable today. For instance, the Finnish word for hundred "Sata" is essentially identical to the Sanskrit word for hundred (Sata). That's because it is borrowed directly from an Indo-Iranian language!

Genetically, there is also something interesting going on in the Y-Chromosomal haplotypes of Ob-Ugrians (the Khanty and the Mansi). The haplotype R1a-Z280 is generally considered a typically "Slavic" haplotype. However, among the Mansi of the Konda River Basin, it reaches frequencies as high as 19%.[38] A full attempt to explain this would be beyond the scope of this book. Still, it does demonstrate very well that the Ural Mountains did not form an impenetrable barrier between Russia and Western Siberia. At some point, it seems likely that men carrying R1a-Z280 did bring a haplotype originating west of the Urals into Siberia.

Ancient DNA is increasingly showing that the origins of most Eurasian R1a seem to be rooted in the Bronze-Age Corded Ware culture, and perhaps its precursors - the Middle Dnieper and Late Sredny-Stog cultures. Therefore, almost all clades of this haplotype seem to be related to an expansion from the Indo-European language speaking world. We can dispense with the idea that Ob-Ugrians were somehow completely isolated from Balto-Slavic and Indo-Iranian populations. Any genetic analysis of the Ob-Ugrians seems to say otherwise. And that's part of a larger tendency that I intend to hammer home in this book; People have tended to vastly underestimate the interrelatedness of North Eurasian Mythologies. And that category includes Slavic mythology.

The Ob-Ugrians are not uniform. They are often seen as originating from a mixture of "Southern" and "Northern" elements. The southern elements are sometimes assumed to be from a "Proto-Finno-Ugric" population that was heavily influenced by Indo-Iranians from the steppe (perhaps even fully nomadic, like the Scythians). This idea is perhaps strengthened by the fact that the Magyars, who were steppe nomads, also spoke an Ugric language (Hungarian). Their migration into Central Europe from Siberia is still poorly understood - but many scholars suspect that a group of Ugrian peoples adopted the nomadic Scythian lifestyle at some point. The linguistic difference between Hungarian and Mansi indicates a split in the remote past, during the 1st millennium BCE.[39]

Therefore, linguistically, the Hungarian / Mansi split seems to have occurred during the period of Scythian dominance in much of Southern Siberia and Central Asia. Therefore, it's extremely tempting to see Scythian influence behind the apparent nomadic pastoralist lifestyle of the early Hungarians (aka Magyars).

All the more reason to closely examine the Ob-Ugrian horseman deity, Mir Susne Khum. Firstly, the very idea of horsemanship among the Ob-Ugrians is probably of Indo-Iranian origins. It's very unlikely that they were introduced to equestrian culture by anyone else. This deity, "Mir Susne Khum" has a number of names among the Ob-Ugrians. He can be called "Loven-Xu", or "Kon-Iki" (literally "Man on a Horse"). However, regardless of his name, he is recognizable as a distinct figure across all Ob-Ugrian cultures. For example, he is always the seventh and youngest son of Num-Torem (the Sky Father). He obviously rides a horse as well. These traits are consistent across the various Ob-Ugrian cultures.[40, 41, 42]

One of his most noteworthy functions is that some of the Ob-Ugrians claim him as their divine tribal ancestor. This requires some explanation, however. Among the Mansi, and some Khanty, there is a dual kinship system involving two clans or "phratries." These are known as the "Mos" and the "Por." The Mos claim descent from Mir-Susne-Khum / Loven-Xu / Kon-Iki. On the other hand, however, the Por Phratry claims descent from another son of Num-Torem; The Bear Spirit Kon-Pupi. This alone is fascinating enough. Recall that the divine twins are generally sons of the Sky Father in Indo-European mythologies, and they also are frequently associated with animal totems. They have a very clear association with divine ancestor myths across the Indo-European ethnic groups. (Refer to Chapter 6: Advanced Concepts in Indo-European Mythology.)

In Mansi *and Northern Khanty* mythology, there is a creature known as a Jalan. A Jalan is a kind of giant with multiple heads. Often with three, seven, or nine heads. This provides an interesting parallel to the Slavic dragon, which often has three, six, nine, or twelve heads.[43] Polycephaly is also a standard trait for dragons and various foes of the Gods in Indo-European mythology. As M.L. West notes, multiple heads are a common trait among many grotesque monsters of Indo-European mythology, including Norse giants, and dragons in Indo-Iranian mythologies.[44] Another very similar creature from a Finno-Ugric mythology is the figure "Gundir" which is referenced in the folklore of the Komi - the western neighbors of the Mansi. Like the Mansi Jalan, the Gundir is typically a giant with three, six, nine, or twelve heads. However, Komi folklore often conflates it with the Slavic dragon. Naposlkikh actually considers the name an Iranian loan (cognate to Ossetic kaf-qwndar, originally meaning "dragon").[45] Russian ethnographic research also indicates that the term "Jalan" denotes a kind of dragon or serpent in some Southern Siberian Altaic cultures.[46] Overall, the evidence supports the idea that a "Jalan" could be either a polycephalous giant or a polycephalous dragon. Furthermore, it should be noted that Slavic dragons frequently display "humanoid" characteristics, like being able to ride a horse. (Reference the Sample Tale "Ivan the Cow's Son" from the end of Chapter 3.)

To recap, the Khanty mythological figure, Loven-Xu (Also meaning "Horseman") flies around on his winged, white-horse. He is the seventh son of Num-Torem, the Sky Father. In one significant legend, he comes across a Jalan who is throwing giant stones into the Ob River, attempting to dam it up. And this is our second hint that we are dealing with an Ob-Ugrian version of a Zmey or Dragon. He not only has multiple heads, but he is also damming up a river to prevent people from having access to water. This is a classic motif in tales about dragon-slaying throughout Indo-European culture. (Reference Chapter 6: Advanced Concepts in Indo-European Mythology.)

Finally, the piece de resistance: Loven-Xu strikes the Jalan dead and drags his body. While the Jalan is being dragged, his giant toes puncture the earth, and they plow out the twin channels of the landmark known as "Jalan's Brook." This, of course, parallels the creation of the "Dragon's Banks" by the divine ploughmen saints, Boris and Gleb in Ukrainian dragon-slaying tales.[47] In both stories, the defeat of the polycephalous monster is associated with the creation of a landmark feature (e.g. a brook, furrow, or bank).

However, the Khanty episode of landscape creation doesn't end there. According to the Khanty myth, Loven-Xu then chopped up the Jalan's body. He threw the pieces all around him, and from those bloody pieces appeared forests, and cedar tree islands among the swamps, known as "hands", "legs", and "body." And opposite Kazym Cape, the Stony Cape appeared as well. And that concludes the story of Loven-Xu and the Jalan.[48]

The Khanty narrative clearly combines three motifs that I would argue are clearly of Indo-European origin.

1. The slaying of a water-blocking, polycephalous monster (A relative of the Slavic zmey or dragon) by a son of the Sky father.
2. The "ploughing out" of a landmark such as a brook, bank, or furrow.
3. The dismemberment of a primordial sacrifice, directly derived from the Proto-Indo-European *yemHos (twin) in the act of landscape creation.

This doesn't just present a connection with Slavic mythology. In Roman mythology as well, we have the motif of ploughing associated with the divine twins. Remus was killed because he jumped over the furrow that Romulus was ploughing around the foundations of Rome. Later, the legendary founder Romulus himself would be dismembered by the Senators. (Reference Chapter 6: Advanced Concepts in Indo-European Mythology.) Some scholars do indeed connect the name "Remus" with Proto-Indo-European *yemHos, meaning "twin."[49]

With all of that said, the Khanty myth does have some important differences from the Slavic narratives. We do not see any divine twin motif in this tale, even though one is heavily implied by the *yemHos dismemberment motif. However, in the Khanty myth, it is the polycephalous monster that is dismembered to create the landscape.

Secondly, the Slavic narratives make it completely clear that the dragon-slaying episode involves both twins, and the fratricide, if it occurs, takes place only later. Recall that the East Slavic twin saints work together to harness the dragon and force it to plow. Crucially, the Polish tale about the two sons of Krak places the fratricide only *after* they slay the dragon together. Therefore, if we were to reconstruct a Proto-Slavic version of this myth, the ritual dismemberment of *yemHos (Volos) would most likely take place only after he and Dazhbog slew the dragon together. Of course, this contradicts some assumptions that have held sway since Ivanov and Toporov. Namely, that all Slavic dragons are Volos, and Volos is always a dragon. Except that this is evidently not the case here.

In fact, there is not a single attested Indo-European mythology where the dragon adversary of the storm God is also the King of the Dead. There has never been a single Indo-European mythology (as far as we know) that combines these roles. Granted, the word "Velinas" has become a synonym for "Devil" in Lithuanian. Which means that some Lithuanian folklore about the devil fleeing from thunder (Also known in Russia) can be misconstrued in this way. But this reconstruction of Volos as a dragon was always fairly speculative. Far more so than some other ideas about Velinas, like for instance his role as an underworld deity. However, once Velinas was identified to Christians as the God of the underworld, he tended to become equated with the devil rather quickly, which made it difficult to gain any subsequent information about him that was trustworthy.

Granted, the conflation of the Jalan with *yemHos is apparent in the Khanty narrative, which means that an interpretation of Volos as the dragon may have existed. But the narratives that we have about Cosmas and Damian, about Boris and Gleb, and about the sons of Krak clearly attest to a divine twin/fratricide myth in which the conflict between brothers comes after the dragon-slaying episode. Which is what we should expect, because dragon-slaying is one of the basic functions of the divine twins in many Indo-European traditions. (Reference Chapter 6: Advanced Concepts in Indo-European Mythology.) As such, it's obvious why many Slavic narratives avoid erasing the participation of both brothers in the actual dragon-slaying episode.

We have spoken briefly about the two phratries or clans among the Ob-Ugrians. We have the Mos, who are descended from Loven-Xu / Mir-Susne Khum. We also mentioned the other group - the Por - who are descended from another of Num-Torem's sons: The Bear Spirit Kon-Pupi.

This is downright fascinating, because there is an extensive body of literature from Russia linking Volos with the cult of the bear. As many scholars have noted, the Slavic deity Volos tended to merge with the image of St. Nicholas, and also with the Volga Finnic bear-ancestor cult.[50] And for once, I have very little criticism about this research. They appear to be fundamentally correct; Volos was associated with the bear. It's worth noting that the bear-ancestor cult apparently dates back to Proto-Finno-Ugric times. The belief in a mythic bear-ancestor is attested among the Finns and Sami, as well as the Ob-Ugrians.[51]

However, among the Volga Finns and East Slavs, it appears that this tradition merged with the Indo-European divine twins tradition - which also tended to be closely connected with myths about clan or tribe origins.

And there is a certain degree of mythological "logic" in combining the Finno-Ugric bear ancestor cult with the cult of the divine twins - particularly with one of the twins being identified with *yemHos. We already discussed multiple generations of divine twins in Chapter 6. But that was Proto-Indo-European mythology. Here, we are discussing late Indo-European tradition being forcefully blended with Finno-Ugric tradition. The result was that the bear seems to have become *yemHos in some respects. It was logical enough; the divine twins were sons of the Sky Father, and the bear was the son of God in Finno-Ugric mythology. In Indo-European tradition, *yemHos becomes the first mortal, and after death became the lord of the dead. In Siberian / Finno-Ugric traditions, the bear is associated with the dead ancestors, and many Ob-Ugrian narratives describe how the bear asked his father to lower him down to earth after seeing its beauty from heaven. This essentially ends the "immortal" or heavenly existence of the bear in the abode of his father.[52] It's not hard to see how the bear's fall from heaven can easily become conflated with the Indo-European narrative about a divine son who accepts mortality to become a dead ancestor.

In fact, there are many parallels here to another Finno-Ugric mythology; I am speaking of Komi mythology. In Komi mythology, Joma (twin) and her brother Voipel lived with their father, the Sky God initially, but later ended up falling from heaven. This led to them becoming progenitors of mankind. Here we see the name for "twin" applied only to the sister, Joma, whereas her brother is called Voipel.[53] Indo-Iranian mythology would use approximately the same name for both figures (e.g. Old Indic Yama and his sister Yami).[54] But the idea is the same. Clearly, the bear-ancestor who fell from heaven in Finno-Ugric mythology could transform into a kind of "Yama" figure. And if we assume that this syncretism is the origin of the Slavic deity Volos, he begins to make a lot of sense.

Another interesting thing about the two Ob-Ugrian phratries or clans is that they tended to worship a son of Num-Torem (the one they claim descent from) as part of a domestic hearth ritual. Whether they are worshipping Kon-Pupi, the Bear Spirit, or Kon-Iki, the Man on a Horse, they seem to venerate their divine ancestor in a similar manner. The two rival sons of Num-Torem are apparently linked to wood or metal images of the clan spirits who protect the patriline. The images of the family patriline gods are sometimes brought out and treated as guests. They are served food and vodka, and the male head of the extended family serves as host. In their honor, a new fire is kindled in the seasonal home.[55] Here we see what looks like echoes of the divine twin hearth tradition, as attested among the East Slavs with the Saints Cosmas and Damian.

Seasonal Change and Wolf Shepherds

I was introduced to the concept of "wolf-shepherds" in Slavic folklore from a number of sources, but it was initially unclear what it meant, if anything. I believe that Monika Kropej has done a great job of bringing Slovenian folklore studies to the attention of the wider world, and in doing so, she has helped me to clarify its significance. There is also an excellent study on the Slavic Wolf Holidays by Mirjam Mencej.[56]

As Monika Kropej notes, Slovene folklore casts Zeleni Jurij and Jarnik as opposite twins who are associated with "mastery" over the wolves at different seasonal points of the year. Jarnik is the autumnal counterpart of Zeleni Jurij (Green George) who is clearly associated with Spring. She further observes that Radoslav Katicic placed the act of "closing" or locking the jaws of wolves on St. George's Day (April 23rd).[57]

Of course, Radoslav thought that Jarilo/ Jurij was a deity who married his sister, Marena, on Summer Solstice. As we have discussed, however, South Slavic folklore makes it very clear that this is a myth about the Sun marrying his sister. Hence, Katicic's "Jarilo" is totally indistinguishable from Dazhbog. (Reference Chapter 5: The Zoryas as Sea Maidens.)

And sure enough, in Serbia, we find that Dazhbog (Under the name "Dajbog") has become associated with the role of wolf shepherd.[58] This is one of the clearest cases in which Katicic has completely failed to construct Jarilo as a distinct Slavic deity. For the most part, we can assume that most of the narratives he examined were simply stories about Dazhbog. In fact, the sole piece of Pre-Christian evidence for a figure called "Jaro" comes from the Polabian God Gerovit. The defining symbol of Gerovit was a golden shield.[59] This is a likely solar symbol.

As mentioned in Chapter 6, St. George became the de-facto replacement of the divine twins in much of the Orthodox world, including Ossetia. Furthermore, when the Slavs flooded into the Balkans, they encountered a Saint named "George" who was honored in late April. This name "George" became "Yuri", which made for a nice homophone with Old Slavic "Yar" meaning "Spring."[60] Based on this, it's likely that "Jaro" could be an epithet of Dazhbog. However, it's noteworthy that this name is completely absent from the Kievan pantheon. Much of its popularity could in fact derive from conflation between Dazhbog and St. George. Prior to contact with the Christian Saint George, "Jaro / Juri" may not have been a primary name of the solar deity.

As Mencej recounts, the list of Saints involved in the shepherding of wolves is quite long. In Russia it tends to be St. George. In Poland, St. Nicholas. In Romania, St. Demetrios. In Serbia, it is often St. Martin (called Mrata). However, there are particular saints associated with "locking" the jaws of wolves in late Spring, and others associated with feast days in late Autumn / Early Winter who are said to unleash the wolves. Thus, as Katicic deduced, St. George's day in late April was the day for "locking" the jaws of wolves. Meanwhile, according to Serbian tradition, St. Mrata unleashes them to feed in November. In some places like Poland and Finland, St. Nicholas unleashes the wolves in early December.[61]

These are the same two seasonal turning points that we discussed earlier with the feast day of Boris and Gleb (May 3rd) and of Cosmas and Damien (November 1st). Six months apart. The Russian and Ukrainian traditions surrounding these Saints seems to indicate that both twins could be honored together on both days. Among the South Slavs, it tended to be one Saint assigned to each half of the year - but the two festival dates are almost the same.

These are also both days for honoring the dead ancestors in most of Eastern Europe.

The Lithuanian autumnal day of the dead was often just called "Velines." It often involved inviting the dead to a family feast at home. In fact, a cup full of offerings to the dead was poured into the hearth fire. The combination of harvest, hearth, and the dead seems to have been central to Velines. Straw was spread out over the table, along with bread and beer, and prayers to the dead were whispered over candlelight with the entire household present. Often taking place in late October, it was a feast following immediately after the harvest very much like Halloween or Samhain in the west. Much as in Slavic countries, the Lithuanians practiced two major days of the dead - one around Easter, and one around All-Souls Day. The one around Easter was called "Veliu Velykos" and it was characterized by families visiting cemeteries for outdoor veneration of the dead. They often left eggs as offerings during this time.[62]

So it seems we have two divine ancestors of the clan, two days for honoring the dead ancestors, and two sons of the Sky Father who are honored (together or separately) during two seasonal turning points at the end of Spring and the end of Autumn.

For the Lithuanian "Veli", offerings on Velines made directly to the hearth fire were common. We have already discussed the likely connection of Dazhbog to Safa - the Ossetian God of the hearth, and the hearth chain. We have discussed how the Saints Cosmas and Damian relate to these figures, and how they became the recipients of a Balto-Slavic autumnal rooster sacrifice to the fire. We have discussed how the Serbian "Dajbog" came to be remembered as a wolf-shepherd. There is one final piece of evidence that ties these elements together. A chain (in fact, a hearth chain) ties them all together.

The wolf-holiday rituals linked with Saint Martin (Mrata) in the Balkans are clearly linked with the hearth chain. Even the ritual slaughter of a rooster tracks here. In Crna Trava, families typically sacrificed a black hen on Mrata's day. Its head was then hung on the hearth chains above the fireplace. Eventually, the head fell into the fireplace to be burnt. This is done so wolves don't harm livestock.[63] Recall that in Ossetian mythology, the hearth / blacksmith deity Safa was the patron of the hearth chain.

It is tempting to interpret the wolf shepherd tradition as being related to the Proto-Indo-European Koryos ritual. This would especially correspond to the versions that place the Wolf Holiday on the day of Saint Nicholas during December. However, Saint Martin's Day (November) is equally prevalent as a "wolf-holiday" in Slavic countries. Generally, the winter is governed by a saint with a feast between late October and early December. By contrast, Saint George is almost always the bringer of Summer in Slavic folklore. In some regions of Romania and Ukraine, St. Demetrios may be treated as the "cold" brother of George who governs the dark half of the year.

In Hutsul folklore, Juri (St. George) demands that his brother Dmytro (Demetrios) hand over the keys of heaven in spring, so that he can usher in the warm season. In some parts of Ukraine, however, Dmytro is substituted with Mikula (Nicholas).[64] As in the rest of Eastern Europe, however, St. George (Juri) always embodies the warm half of the year in Ukrainian folklore.

That St. George is often indistinguishable from Dazhbog is evident perhaps most of all in Bulgarian folklore, where the personified male sun is common. In one Bulgarian legend, the personified sun fell in love with a mortal woman named Grozhdanka, and so he lowered a golden swing for her on St. George's day. She sat on it and was pulled up to heaven.[65]

I feel that at this point, most of the arguments in favor of linking the "warm season" twin with Dazhbog have been made. Anyone who wishes to see the evidence of it can confirm for themselves by reading everything written up to this point. But some might still question adding Volos as the twin brother of Dazhbog. Why Volos? Let's review the reasons.

Interpreting Volos as the "Other" Svarozhich

I have disagreed with a lot of respected Slavic scholars here, so perhaps it is time to praise one. Upenskij appears to have done a fantastic job of showing that the Cult of the Bear, the Leshi (forest spirit), and the Cult of St. Nicholas all underwent significant mixing with the Slavic pagan deity Volos in rural Russia.[66, 67] And in fact, his work was critical for helping me understand the parallels between the Slavic divine twin tradition, and the two divine ancestors of the Ob-Ugrian dual kinship system.

The fact that the Ob-Ugrian "Loven-Xu" represents Dazhbog seems obvious. The solar attributes of Num-Torem's youngest son were noted by Vladimir Toporov, who actually claimed that "Mir-Susne-Khum" was a solar divinity related to the Iranian Mithra.[68] And in this case, I would tend to agree with him.

We have established that in East Slavic lore, the twin Saints Cosmas and Damian engage in a similar "landmark plowing" episode, very reminiscent of the one carried out by Loven-Xu. This only strengthens Dazhbog's link with Num-Torem's many-named seventh son (Mir-Susne-Khum, Kon-Iki, Loven-Xu, etc.). To make matters even more clear, the Lay of Igor's Campaign actually calls the Russians "Grandchildren of Dazhbog"[69] thus implying a sort of phratry-ancestor relationship very similar to that of the Ob-Ugrian Mos Phratry with Mir-Susne-Khum.

This relationship is so clear and so strong, we must question who to "equate" or link the other phratry with. Namely, the Por Phratry bear spirit ancestor, often referred to as "Kon-Pupi." The work by Upesnkij goes a long way towards showing that Volos is the strongest candidate by far. And it is not only the connection with the bear that helps to demonstrate this. The connections explored by Upenskij with St. Nicholas and the Leshi (forest spirit) will also help to hammer this connection home. For one thing, we have already discussed the wolf shepherds of Slavic folklore. We know that "Dajbog" appears to be one of them in Serbian folklore.[70] On the other hand, there is abundant evidence that the Leshi or forest spirit could assume this role of "Master of Wolves."[71] Here again, Upenskij's research does a lot of my work for me. But the connection between Volos and the Forest spirit is not hard to elucidate.

The Leshi deserves some discussion. In many North Eurasian folk traditions, the Cult of the Bear is connected with the idea of a "Master of the Forest." In Ob-Ugrian mythology, Num-Torem's eldest son, the bear, ultimately becomes the "Master of the Forest" after he descends to earth.[72] Therefore, it can be argued that the divine ancestor of the Ob-Ugrian Por Phratry is actually a relative of the Russian Leshi.

Again - hardly surprising. The wolf shepherd symbolism in Slavic countries appears to clearly depict the "Leshi" and the solar deity "Dajbog" as the keepers of the two seasonal turning points, and the masters of wolves. And the linking of Volos with the wolf shepherd motif is actually fairly mainstream among South Slavic folklorists. Mirjam Mencej and Monika Kropej both voice support for the idea that, as the God of Cattle and beasts, Volos probably did play the role of wolf-shepherd. Mencej is quite supportive of the idea that the Leshi became a successor of Volos.[73, 74]

It is perhaps noteworthy that offerings of eggs were sometimes made to the Leshi to invoke his protection over cattle against wolves.[75] This provides a strong parallel to the widespread Eastern European custom of offering eggs to the dead around Easter. If you read Chapter 4: Untangling the Beard of Volos, this will be no surprise. Also, as mentioned in that chapter, the Volosatik was essentially a term for the Leshi, or Wood Goblin.

It should seem fairly clear that the Leshi is related to the wolf shepherd and the bear spirit, as well as the deity Volos. It's time to move on to St. Nicholas - another critical figure examined in the research done by Upenskij. To start things off, we can identify St. Nicholas as one of the major "wolf-shepherd" Saints. Particularly in Poland, and sometimes in Russia. One of the attributes of the East Slavic "Nicholas" was his association with the last patch of grain harvested from the field. Often called the "Beard of Volos" in Russia, it could also sometimes be called the "Beard of Nicholas."[76] However, the most strikingly pagan practice associated with St. Nicholas in Russia was perhaps the bull sacrifice on his feast day on December 6th.

The bull to be sacrificed was named *mikolets*, after the Saint himself. It was separated from the herd well in advance and fed a special ration of oats and malt. After being ceremoniously pampered, it was sacrificed and butchered on the feast of St.

Nicholas. A portion of the meat was brought to church as an offering, and the rest was consumed in a communal meal. After the feast of St. Nicholas, a priest would sprinkle holy water on all the cattle to bless them.[77] It's not hard to see how this could reflect a memory of the East Slavic "cattle God" Volos.

As discussed in Chapter 4, the tradition of leaving coins with the dead for the ferryman "Charon" actually penetrated into Slavic territory just ahead of Christianization. It actually began around the Viking period, when contact between the Slavic and Germanic worlds intensified. This appears to indicate pre-Christian familiarity with the ferryman of the dead, at least among some Slavs.

All the more interesting, therefore, that after Christianization St. Nicholas became the de-facto ferryman of the dead in East Slavic folklore.[78] We should also remember that Czech sources say Veles dwelt "across the sea."

And this is all critical for interpreting this chapter's Sample Tale. It is a story about the personified male Sun, and a ferryman. At the end of this tale, both figures marry a sea maiden. Recall from Chapter 5: The Zoryas as Sea Maidens, that the sea maiden often represents the dawn Goddess(es) in Slavic folklore. She typically has a romantic relationship with her brother, the Sun. In this narrative, it appears that the ferryman (Nicholas / Volos?) also marries a sea maiden.

Similarly, it has been noted that St. George and St. Nicholas came to be identified with the divine twins in Belarusian folklore. In particular, St. George and St. Nicholas formed a triad with the dawn Goddess Zaranica, as noted by the scholar Siarhei Sanko.[79]

The name Mykula or Nikita (Nicholas) is also applied to legendary ploughmen of East Slavic folklore, including Nikita the Tanner, who harnesses a dragon to a plow and uses it to carve out a furrow in one Russian legend.[80]

This should sound very familiar. In the bylina of Svyatogor, I have mentioned the nameless smith who forges the destinies of those who will be wed. The bylina also features a ploughman named Mykula (Nicholas). I would argue that Nikita is actually the smith's brother. I would submit that Nicholas the ploughman is essentially Volos, and the smith is his brother, Dazhbog / George. Together, these figures (ploughman and smith) have the exact same attributes as the twin brother saints Cosmas and Damian.

Dual Phratry Organization in Eastern Europe: A Late Successor to Tripartition?

The dual organization of kinship into two exogamous phratries or clans is the basis for the two Ob-Ugrian deities analyzed in this chapter. The Mos phratry is descended from one son of Num-Torem, called by various names. His distinguishing features are horsemanship, being the youngest of seven sons, and what Toporov finds to be an Iranian character inherited from a "solar" Mithra-like deity. The other phratry belongs to the Por - the descendants of the Proto-Finno-Ugric bear spirit. The merger of the Indo-European *Yemhos and Ugrian bear ancestor seems to have given rise to the Slavic Volos, whereas the ancestor of the Mos appears to be related to the Slavic Dazhbog.

These close analogies raise the question; Did the Slavs also have a system of kinship based around two clans or phratries? The basis for such social organization among the Ob-Ugrians appears to be from the nomads of the Eurasian steppe. A similar bipartite social organization is known to have existed among the Xiongnu, the precursors of the Huns, as well as the later Mongols. The origin story of the Magyars involves a very similar narrative about the two brothers Hunor and Magor, who go on to become progenitors of the Huns and Magyars respectively. A similar narrative is associated with the Avars.[81] However, the Altaic nomads of the Mongolian steppe may have derived their bipartite system from the Scythians. And the same probably holds true for the Ob-Ugrians. Granted, cultures displaying two different "phratries" or "moieties" are not unknown outside of Eurasia. For instance, there are parallels in the indigenous cultures of the Americas. It must be admitted that this could also potentially be a Paleosiberian concept. However, in the context of the Proto-Slavs, it is logical to conclude that the idea of bipartition arrived via the nomads of the steppe.

Recall that scholars like Toporov claimed that the divine ancestor of the Mos phratry - Mir-Susne-khum - reflected Iranian influence. I would take it a step farther. I would argue that this hints at steppe origins for the idea of bipartition (having two kinship groups) in itself.

At a glance. There does seem to be some textual evidence for a bipartite division among the Slavic tribes. In the 6th century CE, Byzantine sources divide the new barbarian menace into two tribes known as the "Sclavenes" and the "Antes." Obviously, the Sclavenes are Slavs. But who were the Antes? There is no such group around today, as far as we know. In theory, some Ukrainians and South Slavs could be their descendants, however.

According to Procopius, the Antes and Sclavenes both spoke the same "barbarous" tongue. He claims that they were both descended from a people known as the Sporoi.[82] This is very reminiscent of the Hungarian origin legend, which claimed that "Magor" and "Hunor" were originally brothers, and hence the Magyars and Huns shared common origins.

We know that "Slav" probably comes from "Slovo" meaning simply "Word." Therefore, a "Slav" probably originally referred to an ethnolinguistic identity. This explains the name "Sclavene" or "Slovene." Interestingly, the name "Ante" does not appear to be Slavic in its origins. The most prevalent theory - held by scholar George Vernadsky, is that the name "Ante" is of Iranian (Sarmatian) origins.[83] If so, it may well be that the bipartite social structure seen among the Slavs originated from the Antes - and perhaps Dazhbog was originally the patron hearth deity of the Antes. Meanwhile, Volos was regarded as the divine ancestor of the Sclavenes. This would make the Antes rough equivalents of the Ob-Ugrian "Mos" phratry, who claimed descent from a very "Iranian" deity with many names. He was described as a golden hero who rode a winged horse. By this logic, the so-called "Sclavenes" were the Slavic counterparts of the "Por" who retained the totemistic of belief in their descent from a bear spirit. This division may also be based on geography. The steppe nomads were obviously people of the endless grasslands or steppes found across north Eurasia. However, the Ob-Ugrians and Slavs were both from the steppe-forest zone directly north of the grassy plains. For a people associated with forests, a bear ancestor probably seemed very fitting. The bipartition seen in this region could therefore correspond to the north / south division between the Eurasian Steppe and the Forest-Steppe zone. This "north / south" division between forest and steppe peoples is shown below (drawn by the author with guidance from Renato Sala for ecological borders[84]) This is listed below as "Figure 4."

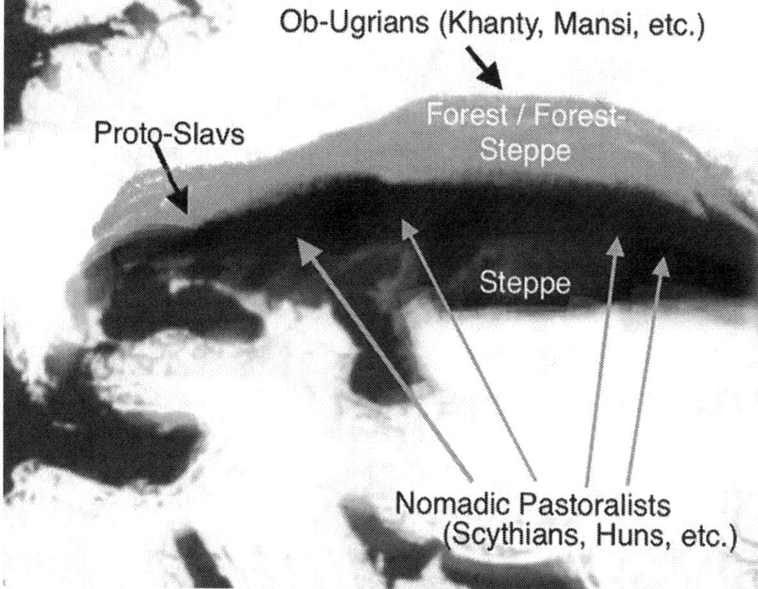

Figure 4: The north / south division between forest and steppe zones on the Eurasian continent.

If confirmed, this could also further demonstrate that the bipartite divisions seem among the Ob-Ugrians and Xiongnu are similarly of Iranian (Scytho-Sarmatian) origins. In any case, it seems likely that the Antes adopted this bipartite system of social organization, which seems to have its roots at the border between the steppe grasslands and the northern forests. The nomads of the steppe grasslands claimed descent from a golden horseman, one who often had solar characteristics, and the forest people of the north were possibly perceived (by the steppe nomads) as a single "other" ethnic group. Hence, the Proto-Slavs and Ob-Ugrians could both be generalized as "northerners" descended from the forest master - an ancestor-spirit who often took the form of a bear. It is likely that the Antes initially spoke an Iranian language, but Procopius confirms that they spoke a Slavic tongue by the 6th century. It would seem that the Antes were ultimately assimilated as one of the major "Slavic" tribes in the end.

It's not clear to what extent bipartition may have superseded the tripartite division of society that we associate with Proto-Indo-European culture. However, it may have gained priority over all other types of social division at the forest / steppe border.

Dazhbog seems especially difficult to classify according to the three functions, and in his case, it may be a moot point. He seems to have absorbed elements of the Balto-Slavic hearth cult, which probably belonged to the commoner class. However, his associations with the Scytho-Sarmatian sun cult were probably somewhat elitist. As such, Dazhbog may have been a fairly unique Slavic deity who broke many of the older rules governing a tripartite social division. Or alternatively, he may have merged all three functions, which is not without precedent in Indo-European cultures. His forging of the first plough to defeat a dragon (with Volos) certainly seems to combine motifs of all three functions. Blacksmithing appears to have had magical overtones in Slavic culture, but the plough is an agrarian symbol. However, the defeat of a dragon evokes warrior myths found in many Indo-European cultures. It's hard to say what produced this unique Slavic myth, but social bipartition may have been one of the underlying innovations that gave rise to this myth. It's possible that no other culture combined all three functions in such a distinct manner.

Evidently the dragon-slaying myth involving a third brother did survive in parts of Russia (Reference Chapter 3) but a very different tradition involving two brothers seems to have attached itself to the ruling dynasties of Krakow and Kiev. Finally, it's worth considering that the joint worship of two divine twins in the princely cult of Boris and Gleb (Patrons of the Rurikid dynasty) could indicate that by the 10th century CE, just before Christianization, the elites of Kievan Rus could no longer be identified with just one clan or phratry. Thus, state formation may have tended to dissolve the older bipartite division introduced by the Antes, facilitating the joint worship of the two brothers under one cult.

Conclusion: Dazhbog and Volos as Joint Hearth Deities

This concludes my analysis on the divine twins: Dazhbog, and Volos. Both appear to have been ancestral deities tied to the hearth and the cult of ancestors. Various Slavic tribes may have regarded themselves as their "grandchildren." They could also be venerated alongside the dead, on holidays dedicated to ancestor-worship. These appear to have been primarily in early May, and in early November. (With some variation depending on region.) Essentially, these correspond to the feast day of Cosmas and Damien in early November, and the feast day of Boris and Gleb in early May.

The two brothers could both function as wolf shepherds, but Dazhbog was probably the one invoked to restrain wolves in

May. In November, Volos unleashed the wolves on those who did not please him. Volos was a deity of the forest, the bear cult, the dead, and the otherworld. Dazhbog was a deity of sun, fire, blacksmithing, and marriage.

As discussed in Chapter 4, Volos was associated with the last patch of grain harvested from the field, called the "Beard of Volos." This links him with the Balto-Finnic Jumis, who was associated with virtually identical agrarian rituals in Balto-Finnic culture. The Balto-Finnic Jumis, in turn, was closely related to the Proto-Indo-European *yémHos, and the Indo-Iranian Yama/Yima. Any doubt of this should be dispelled by the brother / sister incest motif, well known from Indo-Iranian studies, and which also appears in Finno-Ugric and Latvian narratives surrounding Jumis and Joma. Yet there is also an apparent connection with the cult of Cosmas and Damian. The agrarian rituals associated with Jumis could often connect him to the threshing barn, which was the cult location for the twin brother Saints Cosmas and Damian. Additionally, the "mock" marriages performed for the Balto-Finnic Jumis find their closest Slavic parallels in the mock weddings performed for the effigy of "Kuzka" (Cosmas) in Russia.

In particular, Volos helps attest to a merger between the Paleosiberian bear ancestor cult and the Proto-Indo-European *yemHos - the twin dismembered by his brother as a primordial act of creation. He was the first man to die, and later the King of the Dead. However, as the Krakow foundation legend attests, this fratricide took place only after the two brothers conquered a dragon together, generally by causing it to drink water until it burst. In East Slavic folktales, this motif is associated with a tale in which the divine twins harness a dragon to a plow and force it to carve out a legendary landmark.

In the context of previous scholarship, this appears to contradict the idea that all dragons are "Volos", which has been prevalent since Ivanov and Toporov. This model also bears some resemblance to that of Marija Gimbutas, who identified the Saints Cosmas and Damian with Dazhbog and Stribog. Obviously, we are only half-way in agreement on that. Still, the parallels could indicate some similar reasoning on both sides.

Sample Tale: The Good Ferryman and the Water Nymph[85]

There was once an old man, very poor, with three sons. They lived chiefly by ferrying people over a river; but he had had nothing but ill-luck all his life. And to crown all, on the night he died, there was a great storm, and in it the crazy old ferry-boat, on which his sons depended for a living, was sunk.

As they were lamenting both their father and their poverty, an old man came by, and learning the reason of their sorrow said:

"Never mind; all will come right in time. Look! there is your boat as good as new."

And there was a fine new ferry-boat on the water, in place of the old one, and a number of people waiting to be ferried over.

The three brothers arranged to take turns with the boat, and divide the fares they took.

They were, however, very different in disposition. The two elder brothers were greedy and avaricious, and would never take anyone over the river, without being handsomely paid for it.

But the youngest brother took over poor people, who had no money, for nothing; and moreover frequently relieved their wants out of his own pocket.

One day, at sunset, when the eldest brother was at the ferry the same old man, who had visited them on the night their father died, came, and asked for a passage.

"I have nothing to pay you with, but this empty purse," he said.

"Go and get something to put in it then first," replied the ferry-man; "and be off with you now!"

Next day it was the second brother's turn; and the same old man came, and offered his empty purse as his fare. But he met with a like reply. The third day it was the youngest brother's turn; and when the old man arrived, and asked to be ferried over for charity, he answered:

"Yes, get in, old man."

"And what is the fare?" asked the old man.

"That depends upon whether you can pay or not," was the reply; "but if you cannot, it is all the same to me."

"A good deed is never without its reward," said the old man: "but in the meantime take this empty purse; though

it is very worn, and looks worth nothing. But if you shake it, and say:

'For his sake who gave it, this purse I hold,

I wish may always be full of gold;'

it will always afford you as much gold as you wish for."

The youngest brother came home, and his brothers, who were sitting over a good supper, laughed at him, because he had taken only a few copper coins that day, and they told him he should have no supper. But when he began to shake his purse and scatter gold coins all about, they jumped up from the table, and began picking them up eagerly.

And as it was share and share alike, they all grew rich very quickly. The youngest brother made good use of his riches, for he gave away money freely to the poor. But the greedy elder brothers envied him the possession of the wonderful purse, and contrived to steal it from him. Then they left their old home; and the one bought a ship, laded it with all sorts of merchandize, for a trading voyage. But the ship ran upon a rock, and everyone on board was drowned. The second brother was no more fortunate, for as he was travelling through a forest, with an enormous treasure of precious stones, in which he had laid out his wealth, to sell at a profit, he was waylaid by robbers, who murdered him, and shared the spoil among them.

The youngest brother, who remained at home, having lost his purse, became as poor as before. But he still did as formerly, took pay from passengers who could afford it, ferried over poor folks for nothing, and helped those who were poorer than himself so far as he could.

One day the same old man with the long white beard came by; the ferry-man welcomed him as an old friend, and while rowing him over the river, told him all that had happened since he last saw him.

"Your brothers did very wrong, and they have paid for it," said the old man; "but you were in fault yourself. Still, I will give you one more chance. Take this hook and line; and whatever you catch, mind you hold fast, and not let it escape you; or you will bitterly repent it."

The old man then disappeared, and the ferry-man looked in wonder at his new fishing-tackle—a diamond hook, a silver line, and a golden rod.

All at once the hook sprang of itself into the water; the line lengthened out along the river current, and there came a strong pull upon it. The fisherman drew it in, and beheld a most lovely creature, upwards from the waist a woman, but with a fish's tail.

"Good ferry-man, let me go," she said; "take your hook out of my hair! The sun is setting, and after sunset I can no longer be a water-nymph again."

But without answering, the ferry-man only held her fast, and covered her over with his coat, to prevent her escaping. Then the sun set, and she lost her fish-tail.

"Now," she said: "I am yours; so let us go to the nearest church and get married."

She was already dressed as a bride, with a myrtle garland on her head, in a white dress, with a rainbow-coloured girdle, and rich jewels in her hair and on her neck. And she held in her hand the wonderful purse, that was always full of gold.

They found the priest and all ready at the church; were married in a few minutes; and then came home to their wedding-feast, to which all the neighbours were invited. They were royally entertained, and when they were about to leave the bride shook the wonderful purse, and sent a shower of gold pieces flying among the guests; so they all went home very well pleased.

The good ferry-man and his marvelous wife lived most happily together; they never wanted for anything, and gave freely to all who came. He continued to ply his ferry-boat; but he now took all passengers over for nothing, and gave them each a piece of gold into the bargain.

Now there was a king over that country, who a year ago had just succeeded to his elder brother. He had heard of the ferry-man, who was so marvellously rich, and wishing to ascertain the truth of the story he had heard, came on purpose to see for himself. But when he saw the ferry-man's beautiful young wife, he resolved to have her for himself, and determined to get rid of her husband somehow.

At that time there was an eclipse of the sun; and the king sent for the ferry-man, and told him he must find out the cause of this eclipse, or be put to death.

He came home in great distress to his wife; but she replied:

"Never mind, my dear. I will tell you what to do, and how to gratify the king's curiosity."

So she gave him a wonderful ball of thread, which he was to throw before him, and follow the thread as it kept unwinding—towards the East.

He went on a long way, over high mountains, deep rivers, and wide regions. At last he came to a ruined city, where a number of corpses were lying about unburied, tainting the air with pestilence.

The good man was sorry to see this, and took the pains to summon men from the neighboring cities, and get the bodies properly buried. He then resumed his journey.

He came at last to the ends of the earth. Here he found a magnificent golden palace, with an amber roof, and diamond doors and windows.

The ball of thread went straight into the palace, and the ferry-man found himself in a vast apartment, where sat a very dignified old lady, spinning from a golden distaff.

"Wretched man! what are you here for?" she exclaimed, when she saw him. "My son will come back presently and burn you up."

He explained to her how he had been forced to come, out of sheer necessity.

"Well, I must help you," replied the old lady, who was no less than the Mother of the Sun, "because you did Sol that good turn some days

ago, in burying the inhabitants of that town, when they were killed by a dragon. He journeys every day across the wide arch of heaven, in a diamond car, drawn by twelve grey horses, with golden manes, giving heat and light to the whole world. He will soon be back here, to rest for the night... But here he comes; hide yourself, and take care to observe what follows."

So saying she changed her visitor into a lady-bird, and let him fly to the window.

Then the neighing of the wonderful horses and the rattling of chariot wheels were heard, and the bright Sun himself presently came in, and stretching himself upon a coral bed, remarked to his mother:

"I smell a human being here!"

"What nonsense you talk!" replied his mother. "How could any human being come here? You know it is impossible."

The Sun, as if he did not quite believe her, began to peer anxiously about the room.

"Don't be so restless," said the old lady; "but tell me why you suffered eclipse a month or two ago."

"How could I help it?" answered the Sun; "When the dragon from the deep abyss attacked me, and I had to fight him? Perhaps I should have been fighting with the monster till now, if a wonderful mermaid had not come to help me. When she began to sing, and looked at the dragon with her beautiful eyes, all his rage softened at once; he was absorbed in gazing upon her beauty, and I meanwhile burnt him to ashes, and threw them into the sea."

The Sun then went to sleep, and his mother again touched the ferry-man with her spindle; he then returned to his natural shape, and slipped out of the palace. Following the ball of thread he reached home at last, and next day went to the king, and told him all.

But the king was so enchanted at the description of the beautiful sea-maiden, that he ordered the ferry-man to go and bring her to him, on pain of death.

He went home very sad to his wife, but she told him she would manage this also. So saying she gave him another ball of thread, to show him which way to go, and she also gave him a carriage-load of costly lady's apparel and jewels, and ornaments—told him what he was to do, and they took leave of one another.

On the way the ferry-man met a youth, riding on a fine grey horse, who asked:

What have you got there, man?"

"A woman's wearing apparel, most costly and beautiful"—he had several dresses, not simply one.

"I say, give me some of those as a present for my intended, whom I am going to see. I can be of use to you, for I am the Storm-wind. I will come, whenever you call upon me thus:

'Storm-wind! Storm-wind! come with speed!

Help me in my sudden need!'"

The ferry-man gave him some of the most beautiful things he had, and the Storm-wind passed.

A little further on he met an old man, grey-haired, but strong and vigorous-looking, who also said:

"What have you got there?"

"Women's garments costly and beautiful."

"I am going to my daughter's wedding; she is to marry the Storm-wind; give me something as a wedding present for her, and I will be of use to you. I am the Frost; if you need me call upon me thus:

'Frost, I call thee; come with speed;

Help me in my sudden need!'"

The ferry-man let him take all he wanted and went on.

And now he came to the sea-coast; here the ball of thread stopped, and would go no further.

The ferry-man waded up to his waist into the sea, and set up two high poles, with cross-bars between them, upon which he hung dresses of various colours, scarves, and ribbons, gold chains, and diamond earrings and pins, shoes, and looking-glasses, and then hid himself, with his wonderful hook and line ready.

As soon as the morning rose from the sea, there appeared far away on the smooth waters a silvery boat, in which stood a beautiful maiden, with a golden oar in one hand, while with the other she gathered together her long golden hair, all the while singing so beautifully to the rising sun, that, if the ferry-man had not quickly stopped his ears, he would have fallen into a delicious reverie, and then asleep.

She sailed along a long time in her silver boat, and round her leaped and played golden fishes with rainbow wings and diamond eyes. But all at once she perceived the rich clothes and ornaments, hung up on the poles, and as she came nearer, the ferry-man called out:

"Storm-wind! Storm-wind! come with speed!

Help me in my sudden need!"

"What do you want?" asked the Storm-wind.

The ferry-man without answering him, called out:

"Frost, I call thee; come with speed,

Help me in my sudden need!"

"What do you want?" asked the Frost.

"I want to capture the sea-maiden."

Then the wind blew and blew, so that the silver boat was

capsized, and the frost breathed on the sea till it was frozen over.

Then the ferryman rushed up to the sea-maiden, entangling his hook in her golden hair; lifted her on his horse, and rode off as swift as the wind after his wonderful ball of thread.

She kept weeping and lamenting all the way; but as soon as they reached the ferry-man's home, and saw his wife, all her sorrow changed into joy; she laughed with delight, and threw herself into her arms.

And then it turned out that the two were sisters.

Next morning the ferry-man went to court with both his wife and sister-in-law, and the king was so delighted with the beauty of the latter, that he at once offered to marry her. But she could give him no answer until he had the Self-playing Guitar.

So the king ordered the ferry-man to procure him this wonderful guitar, or be put to death.

His wife told him what to do, and gave him a handkerchief of hers, embroidered with gold, telling him to use this in case of need.

Following the ball of thread he came at last to a great lake, in the midst of which was a green island.

He began to wonder how he was to get there, when he saw a boat approaching, in which was an old man, with a long white beard, and he recognized him with delight, as his former benefactor.

"How are you, ferry-man?" he asked. "Where are you going?"

"I am going wherever the ball of thread leads me, for I must fetch the Self-playing Guitar."

"This guitar," said the old man, "belongs to Goldmore, the lord of that island. It is a difficult matter to have to do with him; but perhaps you may succeed. You have often ferried me over the water; I will ferry you now."

The old man pushed off, and they reached the island.

On arriving the ball of thread went straight into a palace, where Goldmore came out to meet the traveller, and asked him where he was going and what he wanted.

He explained:

"I am come for the Self-playing Guitar."

"I will only let you have it on condition that you do not go to sleep for three days and nights. And if you do, you will not only lose all chance of the Self-playing Guitar; but you must die."

What could the poor man do, but agree to this?

So Goldmore conducted him to a great room, and locked him in. The floor was strewn with sleepy-grass, so he fell asleep directly.

Next morning in came Goldmore, and on waking him up said:

"So you went to sleep! Very well, you shall die!"

And he touched a spring in the floor, and the unhappy ferry-man fell down into an apartment beneath, where the walls were of looking-glass, and there were great heaps of gold and precious stones lying about.

For three days and nights he lay there; he was fearfully hungry. And then it dawned upon him that he was to be starved to death!

He called out, and entreated in vain; nobody answered, and though he had piles of gold and jewels about him, they could not purchase him a morsel of food.

He sought in vain for any means of exit. There was a window, of clearest crystal, but it was barred by a heavy iron grating. But the window looked into a garden whence he could hear nightingales singing, doves cooing, and the murmur of a brook. But inside he saw only heaps of useless gold and jewels, and his own face, worn and haggard, reflected a thousand times.

He could now only pray for a speedy death, and took out a little iron cross, which he had kept by him since his boyhood. But in doing so he also drew out the gold-embroidered handkerchief, given him by his wife, and which he had quite forgotten till now.

Goldmore had been looking on, as he often did, from an opening in the ceiling to enjoy the sight of his prisoner's sufferings. All at once he recognized the handkerchief, as belonging to his own sister, the ferry-man's wife.

He at once changed his treatment of his brother-in-law, as he had discovered him to be; took him out of prison, led him to his own apartments, gave him food and drink, and the Self-playing Guitar into the bargain.

Coming home, the ferry-man met his wife half-way.

"The ball of thread came home alone," she explained; "so I judged that some misfortune had befallen you, and I was coming to help you."

He told her all his adventures, and they returned home together.

The king was all eagerness to see and hear the Self-playing Guitar; so he ordered the ferry-man, his wife, and her sister to come with it to the palace at once.

Now the property of this Self-playing Guitar was such that wherever its music was heard, the sick became well, those who were sad merry, ugly folks became handsome, sorceries were dissolved, and those who had been murdered rose from the dead, and slew their murderers.

So when the king, having been told the charm to set the guitar playing, said the words, all the court began to be merry, and dance—except the king himself!... For all at once the door opened, the music ceased, and the figure of the late king stood up in his shroud, and said:

"I was the rightful possessor of the throne! and you, wicked brother, who caused me to be murdered, shall now reap your reward!"

So saying he breathed upon him, and the king fell dead—on which the phantom vanished.

But as soon as they recovered from their fright, all the nobility who were present acclaimed the ferry-man as their king.

The next day, after the burial of the late king, the beautiful sea-maiden, the beloved of the Sun, went back to the sea, to float about in her silvery canoe, in the company of the rainbow fishes, and to rejoice in the sunbeams. But the good ferry-man and his wife lived happily ever after, as king and queen. And they gave a grand ball to the nobility and to the people... The Self-playing Guitar furnished the music, the wonderful purse scattered gold all the time, and the king entertained all the guests right royally.

Endnotes

1. Rosik, Stanislaw, and Anna Tyszkiewicz. The Slavic Religion in the Light of 11th and 12th-Century German Chronicles (Thietmar of Merseburg, Adam of Bremen, Helmold of Bosau): Studies on the Christian Interpretation of Pre-Christian Cults and Beliefs in the Middle Ages. 2020. Page 111
2. West, Morris. Indo-European Poetry and Myth. Oxford: Oxford University Press, 2007. Page 197
3. Ivanits, Linda J. Russian Folk Belief. M E Sharpe Incorporated, 1989. Internet resource. Page 13
4. Образование древнерусского государства, Мавродин Владимир Васильевич. 1945. Page 312
5. Warner, Elizabeth. Russian Myths. London: The British Museum Press, 2002. Page 12
6. Greimas, Algirdas J. Of Gods and Men: Studies in Lithuanian Mythology. Bloomington: Indiana University Press, 1992. Pages 184-185
7. Chadwick, H M. The Origin of the English Nation. Cambridge: Cambridge University Press, 2013. Page 255

8. West, Morris. Indo-European Poetry and Myth. Oxford: Oxford University Press, 2007. Page 270
9. Nagy, Gregory. Greek Mythology and Poetics. 2018. Internet resource. Page 100
10. ФГБУНСеверо-Осетинский институт гуманитарных и социальных исследований им. В.И. Абаева ВНЦ РАН и Правительства РСО-Алания, Таказов Федар Магометович, МИФОЛОГИЧЕСКИЕ АРХЕТИПЫ МОДЕЛИ МИРА В ОСЕТИНСКОЙ КОСМОГОНИИ, Владикавказ 2014. Page 71
11. West, Morris. Indo-European Poetry and Myth. Oxford: Oxford University Press, 2007. Page 269
12. Общественный строй и быт осетин (ХУП-Х1Х вв.) 1974. Page 317
13. Gazdanova, Valentina Soltanovna. Традиционная осетинская свадьба: миф, ритуалы и символы. Russia, Иристон, 2003. Page 115
14. Uchenyiā̄zapiski Imperatorskago moskovskago universiteta: Otdīēl istoriko-filologicheskīĭ. Russia, Tip. F. B. Millera, 1882. Page 267
15. Більське городище в наукових працях Б. А. Шрамка: збірник наукових праць, присвячений 95-річчю від дня народження вченого. Ukraine, Алексей. Page 220
16. Vernadsky, George. Kievan Russia. New Haven [Conn.: Yale University Press, 1976. Page 51
17. Филологические науки. Вопросы теории и практики Philology. Theory & Practice 2021. Том 14. Выпуск 5. С. 1524-1528, 2021. Volume 14. Issue 5. P. 1524-1528
18. Reichelt, Hans. Avesta Reader: Texts, Notes, Glossary and Index. 2019. Internet resource. Page 277
19. Mallory, James P, and Douglas Q. Adams. Encyclopedia of Indo-European Culture. London: Fitzroy Dearborn, 1997. Page 458
20. Borissoff, Constantine L. "Non-Iranian Origin of the Eastern-Slavonic God Xursu/xors." Studia Mythologica Slavica. 17 (2014): 9-36.
21. Greimas, Algirdas J. Of Gods and Men: Studies in Lithuanian Mythology. Bloomington: Indiana University Press, 1992. Pages 184-185

22. Chadwick, H M. The Origin of the English Nation. Cambridge: Cambridge University Press, 2013. Page 255
23. Ivanits, Linda J. Russian Folk Belief. Armonk, N.Y: M.E. Sharpe, 1989. Page 61
24. Ivanits, Linda J. Russian Folk Belief. Armonk, N.Y: M.E. Sharpe, 1989. Page 32
25. Pronin, Alexander. Byliny; Heroic Tales of Old Russia. Frankfurt: Possev, 1971. Page 48
26. Bartlett, Robert. Why Can the Dead Do Such Great Things? Saints and Worshippers from the Martyrs to the Reformation. 2015. Internet resource. Pages 141-142
27. Warner, Elizabeth. Russian Myths. London: The British Museum Press, 2002. Page 72
28. Johns, Andreas. Baba Yaga: The Ambiguous Mother and Witch of the Russian Folktale. 2004. Page 172
29. Golema, Martin. "Medieval Saint Ploughmen and Pagan Slavic Mythology." Studia Mythologica Slavica. 10 (2007): 155-177.
30. Quaestiones Medii Aevi. Volume 10. Warszawa Ed. de l'Univ. de Varsovie. 2005. Page 386
31. Dabrowski, Patrice M. Poland: The First Thousand Years. DeKalb: Northern Illinois University Press, 2021. Page 7
32. Maczko, Stephen. "Boris and Gleb: Saintly Princes or Princely Saints?" Russian History, vol. 2, no. 1, 1975, pp. 68–80
33. Quaestiones Medii Aevi. Volume 10. Warszawa Ed. de l'Univ. de Varsovie. 2005. Page 386
34. Santos, Marinas E. "Reassessment, Unification, and Enlargement of the Sources of Slavic Pre-Christian Religion." Russian History. 40.1 (2013): 32.
35. Oinas, Felix J. "Jumi: A Fertility Divinity." Journal of the Folklore Institute, vol. 18, no. 1, Indiana University Press, 1981, Pages 69-70
36. Русский традиционный календарь: на каждый день и для каждого дома /Некрылова, А. РИПОЛ классик, 2017. Page 554

37. Mallory, James P, and Douglas Q. Adams. Encyclopedia of Indo-European Culture. London: Fitzroy Dearborn, 1997. Pages 129-130
38. Pamjav, Horolma & Dudás, Eszter & K, Krizsán & Galambos, A. (2019). A Y-chromosomal study of Mansi population from Konda River Basin in Ural. Forensic Science International: Genetics Supplement Series. 7.
39. Bakro-Nagy, et al. Oxford Guide to the Uralic Languages. S.l.:, 2022. Page 523
40. Stepanova, Eila. Mythic Discourses. Helsinki: Finnish Literature Society / SKS, 2012. Internet resource. Page 30-32
41. Mousalimas, S A. Arctic Ecology and Identity. Budapest: Akademiai Kiado, 1997. Page 196
42. Wiget, Andrew, and Olga Balalaeva. Khanty, People of the Taiga: Surviving the Twentieth Century. Fairbanks, Alaska: University of Alaska Press, 2011. Internet resource. Page 130
43. Propp, Vladimir I. A, and Sibelan E. S. Forrester. The Russian Folktale by Vladimir Yakovlevich Propp. Detroit: Wayne State University Press, 2012.
44. West, M. L. Indo-European Poetry and Myth. United Kingdom, OUP Oxford, 2007. Pages 299-300
45. Konakov, Nikolaj D, and Vladimir V. Napol'skich. Komi Mythology. Budapest: Akad. Kiado, 2003. Page 121
46. Ivanov, Sergeĭ Vasil'evich. Скульптура алтайцев, хакасов и сибирских татар: XVIII-первая четверть XX в. Russia, Наука, 1979. Page 168
47. Golema, Martin. "Medieval Saint Ploughmen and Pagan Slavic Mythology." Studia Mythologica Slavica. 10 (2007): 155-177.
48. Stepanova, Eila. Mythic Discourses. Helsinki: Finnish Literature Society / SKS, 2012. Internet resource. Page 30-32
49. Witzel, Michael. The Origins of the World's Mythologies. New York, NY: Oxford University Press, 2013. Page 168
50. Haney, Jack V. The Complete Russian Folktale: Volume 1. 2015. Page 67)

51. Stepanova, Eila. Mythic Discourses. Helsinki: Finnish Literature Society / SKS, 2012. Internet resource. Page 30-32
52. Stepanova, Eila. Mythic Discourses. Helsinki: Finnish Literature Society / SKS, 2012. Internet resource. Page 30-32
53. Indo-Iranian Elements in Fenno-Ugric Mythological Lexicon." Indogermanische Forschungen. 110.1 (2005): 163-164
54. Gamkrelidze, Thomas V, Vjaceslav V. Ivanov, Roman Jakobson, and Nichols Johanna. Indo-European and the Indo-Europeans: A Reconstruction and Historical Analysis of a Proto-Language and Proto-Culture. Part I: the Text. Part Ii: Bibliography, Indexes. 2010. Internet resource. Page 680
55. Wiget, Andrew, and Olga Balalaeva. Khanty, People of the Taiga: Surviving the Twentieth Century. Fairbanks, Alaska: University of Alaska Press, 2011. Internet resource. Page 112
56. Mencej, Mirjam. The Role of Legend in Constructing Annual Cycle. 2006. Internet resource.
57. Kropej Telban, Monika, Nives Sulič, and Valentina Batagelj. Supernatural Beings from Slovenian Myth and Folktales. Ljubljana: Založba ZRC, 2012. Page 55-56
58. Pettazzoni, Raffaele, Domenico Accorinti, and Herbert J. Rose. Raffaele Pettazzoni and Herbert Jennings Rose, Correspondence 1927-1958: The Long Friendship between the Author and the Translator of the All-Knowing God. Leiden: Brill, 2014. Page 326
59. Herbordus, and Charles H. Robinson. The Life of Otto Apostle of Pomerania 1060-1139. London: Society for promoting Christian knowledge, 1920. Page 134
60. Kocjubynski, Mychajlo M, and Bohdan Rubchak. Shadows of Forgotten Ancestors. Littleton, Co: Ukrainian Acad. Pr, 1981. Page 69
61. Mencej, Mirjam. The Role of Legend in Constructing Annual Cycle. 2006. Internet resource.
62. Trinkunas, Jonas. Of Gods & Holidays: The Baltic Heritage. Vilnius: Tverme, 1999. Page 119

63. Mencej, Mirjam. (2009). Wolf holidays among Southern Slavs in the Balkans. Acta Ethnographica Hungarica. 54. Page 339
64. Kocjubynski, Mychajlo M, and Bohdan Rubchak. Shadows of Forgotten Ancestors. Littleton, Co: Ukrainian Acad. Pr, 1981. Pages 69-70
65. Ralston, W R. S. Songs of the Russian People, As Illustrative of Slavonic Mythology and Russian Social Life. Forgotten Books, 2019. Internet resource. Page 171
66. Haney, Jack V. The Complete Russian Folktale: Volume 1. 2015. Page 67
67. Michael Shapiro, Neglected evidence of Dioscurism (Divine Twinning) in the Old Slavic pantheon" Journal of Indo - European Studies 10(1-2), 1982:137-166
68. Святость и святые в русской духовной культуре. Том I. Первый век христианства на Руси. Russia, ЛитРес, 2018. Page 572
69. Vernadsky, George. Kievan Russia. New Haven [Conn.: Yale University Press, 1976. Page 51
70. Pettazzoni, Raffaele, Domenico Accorinti, and Herbert J. Rose. Raffaele Pettazzoni and Herbert Jennings Rose, Correspondence 1927-1958: The Long Friendship between the Author and the Translator of the All-Knowing God. Leiden: Brill, 2014. Page 326
71. Mencej, Mirjam. The Role of Legend in Constructing Annual Cycle. 2006. Internet resource. Pages 108-109
72. Wiget, Andrew, and Olga Balalaeva. Khanty, People of the Taiga: Surviving the Twentieth Century. Fairbanks, Alaska: University of Alaska Press, 2011. Internet resource. Page 106
73. Kropej Telban, Monika, Nives Sulič, and Valentina Batagelj. Supernatural Beings from Slovenian Myth and Folktales. Ljubljana: Založba ZRC, 2012. Page 55
74. Mencej, Mirjam. The Christian and Pre-Christian Conception of the Master of the Wolves. 2005. Internet resource.
75. Биармия: северная колыбель Руси. Russia, Алгоритм, 2017.
76. Ivanits, Linda J. Russian Folk Belief. Armonk, N.Y: M.E. Sharpe, 1989. Page 12

77. Ivanits, Linda J. Russian Folk Belief. Armonk, N.Y: M.E. Sharpe, 1989. Page 25
78. Łukasz Miechowicz, Coins in the Western and Eastern Slavs burial practices in the Middle Ages – relicts of pagan beliefs or a sign of Christian traditions?, Rome, Constantinople and Newly-Converted Europe. Archaeological and Historical Evidence. Kraków – Leipzig – Rzeszów – Warszawa 2012, Pages 613-624
79. Sanko, Siarhei. (2018). Reflexes of Ancient Ideas about Divine Twins in the Images of Saints George and Nicholas in Belarusian Folklore. Folklore: Electronic Journal of Folklore. 72. 15-40.
80. Haney, Jack V. An Anthology of Russian Folktales. 2015. Internet resource. Page 27
81. Pohl, Walter. The Avars: A Steppe Empire in Central Europe, 567-822. Cornell University Press, 2018. Page 265
82. Basilevsky, Alexander. Early Ukraine: A Military and Social History to the Mid-18th Century. 2016. Internet resource. Page 56
83. Vernadski, Gueorgui V. A History of Russia. New Haven: Yale University Press, 1969. Page 22
84. Sala, Renato. (2018). Interaction of Climate, Environment and Humans in North and Central Asia during the Late Glacial and Holocene: Impacts and Human Adaptation. 10.1201/9781351260244-15.
85. Glinski, A J. Polish Fairy Tales, Trans. M.A. Biggs. London: John Lane, 1920. Page 53-68

Chapter 9

Death and the Soul in Slavic Paganism

We have talked a lot about deities. And that's a good thing, because deities are an important part of the spiritual life in most cultures. But there is something equally important that we haven't discussed in depth; We haven't covered beliefs about the soul and its fate after death.

To this end, I would like to start with a discussion of Navi Easter, the spring-time celebration of the dead. There is a fabulous passage referencing this custom in "*On the High Uplands: Sagas, Songs, Tales, and Legends of the Carpathians.*" Yet nestled within this passage is an offhand reference to two times of year in which the dead are honored. This is one of the main reasons that I have chosen to open with this passage, because it seems to get to the heart of the ritual observances. Throughout Eastern Europe, there is ample evidence for both a late spring and late autumn celebration in honor of the dead. The passage contains a footnote explaining that "Navi" is the Slavic pagan abode of the dead[1] and it reads as follows:

> *So there is also something quieter, though dear and native to us: the Navi Easter. This is a survival of ancient times, a spring festival of the dead for their own. It involves sacrifices, prayers, confessions, and the mutual renunciations of the dead and the living - all in silence. But even this is not enough: so five weeks after the Christian Easter we have the finale of the spring festivals, the Rachman Easter...*
>
> *The Rachman celebrations have long been known in all the Eastern areas of Poland and in the Black Sea basin, but undoubtedly have been preserved best of all here in our mountains. Possibly here they have even been developed still further. For long ages our*

> *Rus have believed that beyond the seas, far towards the sunrise, lives a virtuous and friendly tribe of Rachmans, who are related to us. They are separated from us by insuperable barriers. And yet by prayer, by incessant fasting, by lives filled with virtue and mysteries, they maintain and renew this our human world. It is thanks to them that we live in this world; to them we owe all that is good...*
>
> *With these distant beings we can communicate once a year, or perhaps twice a year. We send them the sign. In Holy Week, on the Friday or the Saturday - such is the custom - we throw the shells of Easter egg, or our decorated eggs that will float on water, into the rivers. Within five weeks those shells will be transformed into eggs and will have floated right to the Rachmans, so it is believed. And then they, the Rachmans, share out the eggs. They need so little and live in such harmony that one egg is sufficient for twelve of them. And then they celebrate Easter: their own, Rachman Easter And they in turn give us a sign: they ring the bells. On that day our people set their ears to the ground, and say they can hear bells ringing from over the seas.*

Readers may note that this is yet another fantastically rich relic of Slavic pagan customs from the Hutsuls of the Carpathians. It seems as though the Hutsuls may have been among the last practitioners of nearly "pure" Slavic paganism. Many of their Carpathian highland traditions appear to be incredibly well preserved, even compared with those of remote Russian provinces. I believe that study of their folklore and that of other Carpatho-Rusyn groups is instrumental to Slavic reconstructionism. However, I don't think the narrator in Stanislaw's book is wrong in attributing this belief to Eastern Poland as well. Residues of this practice show up in my sources on Polish tradition as well.

According to one source, the dead in Poland were believed to lie in the earth guarding the seeds. Twice a year, during the spring and fall, Poles would honor the dead by bringing food and drink to their graves. In Poland, there were the Zaduszki ceremonies which took place in November, as well as the April ceremonies which were closely tied to Easter. Polish priests routinely condemned "feeding" the dead, yet it seems the custom of bringing eggs, fruit, and bread to the cemetery on the third day of Easter continued nearly into the modern era. This corresponds fairly well with the Hutsul material mentioning two times of year in which the living may communicate with the dead.

Additionally, the people of Krakow evidently had a custom of gathering on a mound near a rocky cliff called Krzenmionek. This was thought to be the burial ground of the legendary dragon slayer "Krak" who founded Krakow, thus marking him as a kind of honored founder or ancestor. In ancient times, people gathered on the mound would throw down eggs and nuts left over from their own Easter feast to the poor waiting below at the foot of the mound as part of the rituals of "feeding the dead." Polish priests of the 15th century evidently disliked the custom, and clearly perceived it as pagan. Nevertheless, the custom continued into the 19th century. Similarly, the beggars would receive food during All Souls Night on November 1st, clearly "standing in" for the spirits of the deceased.[2] It's possible that the substitution of the beggars for the dead is Christian influence. On the other hand, it may have been thought that some of these beggars could really be from beyond the grave, much like the old Irish beliefs about spirits knocking on Halloween.

It is interesting that eggs are a recurring gift to the dead in Slavic and Baltic spring celebrations. This may have something to do with eggs being seen as an intermediary between worlds. From an ancient perspective, an egg is not quite dead and not quite alive either. Thus, it may have been thought of as an offering that was uniquely suitable for crossing the sea that separated this world from the afterlife.

Returning to the subject of "Navi" or the land of the dead, it's also extremely interesting that various nymphs and nature spirits are often associated with the term. For instance, the related word Niavka in the Hutsul dialect describes a type of forest nymph.[3] Alternatively, in Ukraine, the term Mavka can also refer to a type of Rusalka are water spirit. The Rusalki, for their part, are often thought to be the spirits of dead girls, often the "unclean" or restless dead. They are thought to dwell at the edge of the earth, and to fly on wings from across the sea to bring moisture and fertility. In Russia, Rusalki were said to leave the waters in spring to walk upon the Earth, thus bringing fertility to the vegetation.[4] Thus, the watery Rusalka is poorly differentiated from the terrestrial nymph, and may even be terrestrial for part of the year. Both were clearly associated with the spirits of the dead in recent times. The idea that Rusalki dwell across the sea and help sustain earthly life is actually quite consistent with the Rachmans mentioned above, who also appear to be deceased ancestors. On the other hand, the various nymphs of Slavic folklore could also be quite capricious, and a man could easily end up drowned or tickled to death if he ran afoul of them. It's likely that as with many pagan figures, the positive aspects of these beings were downplayed over time. Nevertheless, the Rusalki were honored in parts of Russia up into the 19th century for their role in ripening the corn fields.[5]

The Rusalki were thought to leave their riverbeds around April 10th, and later return around midsummer. However, if we equate the Rusalki with phantoms or maras, then things get complicated, because the Hutsuls believed that the maras spend much of the year roaming the upland pasture of the Carpathians. Specifically, they were thought to roam there from approximately fall to late April.[6] In short, the Maras actually vanish from the upland pasture at just around the time that the Rusalki appear on land. This makes them appear to be polar opposites, rather than close kin. On the other hand, a similar duality is observed between the beautiful appearance of the Rusalki in southern Russian folklore, and the hideous appearance attributed to them in the more severe climate of the far north. What we seem to have is a two-sided family of entities from the spirit world or underworld who manifest differently throughout the year, or based on the local climate.

The seasonal effigy traditions of Eastern Europe are almost certainly linked to Rusalka week. In Poland, for instance, the Marzanna effigy who is tossed into the water as a farewell to winter is clearly linked to the maras.

The gaik or green branch that is subsequently brought back to the village, representing spring clearly resembles similar traditions involving birch trees during the Russian holiday known as Rusalka week.[7, 8]

I have previously linked these effigy traditions to the Goddesses Mokosh (refer to Chapter 2) and I strongly believe they are related. Just as the maras have their queen in Mokosh, so too do the Rusalki have a mysterious "elder" whom they answer to, who is responsible for calling them back to the otherworld at the end of Rusalka week. This figure is probably also Mokosh.

When Rusalka week ended, the female spirits were thought to return back to where they came from. In theory, this meant that they returned to various bodies of water. However, in the Hutsul tradition of Rachman Easter it is quite clear that the land of the dead is not in the sea exactly, but beyond the sea. However, this simplistic view of the afterlife is contradicted by other narratives which appear to portray a legitimate lower world that exists beneath the earth. It should be noted that cosmological confusion exists even in well attested mythologies like Irish and Norse mythology.

No figure illustrates this confusion in Slavic folklore more so than Baba Yaga. In some tales, she may live beneath the earth. However, she may also appear as a forest spirit or forest mother.

She may also live by the sea or by a fiery river.[9] This fiery river has parallels in Komi mythology, from slightly northeast of historically East Slavic territory.

In Komi mythology, the burning river known as the Syr Yu or "River of Pitch" marks the boundary between this world and the underworld. It was believed that the bridge to the next world took the form of a wide pathway for the righteous, but for the evil it could be as thin as a cobweb.[10] Komi mythology therefore has notions of afterlife judgment that some would take for Christian influence. Regardless of the origins of the idea, this bridge seems to be referenced in some Russian tales about Baba Yaga. In one story in particular, the hero waves his handkerchief as Baba Yaga is crossing and causes the bridge across the fiery river to suddenly become narrow, causing her to fall to her death.[11]

In reality, this bridge is almost certainly an ancient concept. We also see it in Lithuania. To quote Jurate Baranova from his book "*Lithuanian Philosophy: Persons and Ideas*":

> *The cosmic mountain, on top of which Dievas or Perkunas lives, is the center of the afterlife. The heavenly abode of the dead is right behind it or at its top, where it is warm and light, a wonderful garden. Sometimes it is believed that in climbing that mountain souls have to use their own nails or that of predatory animals that are burnt on the funeral pyre. Sometimes a dragon is mentioned at the foot of the mountain. One rare belief asserts that there is a bridge leading to the top of the mountain; the souls of the righteous cross it very easily, bad ones, however, fall down and are taken by a dragon.*[12]

As discussed previously in this book, shared myths between Finno-Ugric, Slavic, and Baltic narratives are probably indicative of interactions from the distant past.

This is further attested by the presence of fingernails or animal claws in funerary rituals, to assist the dead in "climbing to the afterlife." This notion shows up in Komi paganism as well, where fingernails are saved to help the dead climb a slippery mountain which appears after they cross the previously mentioned bridge.[13]

In Slavic countries, the evidence for these beliefs is more circumstantial, but strong enough to point to continuity. In Russian folk belief, for example, it was thought that nail clippings or eagle claws could assist a buried person in climbing out of the grave on judgment day.[14] In one Polish folk tale, the hero uses the claws of a wildcat to ascend a glass mountain, where he discovers an otherworldly kingdom with a tree that bears golden apples.[15]

The use of lynx claws for climbing the cosmic mountain is also attested in Lithuanian funerary traditions, where they would typically be cremated with the body in the funeral pyre.[16]

We have already discussed the early Slavic attitude towards cremation and inhumation. So we can probably reconstruct a basic early Slavic funerary tradition involving cremation of the body with one's own trimmed nails, or with the claws of a wild animal. This is likely related to a broader Indo-European tradition involving trimming the nails of the dead. Another example of this would be the pagan Norse beliefs surrounding the Naglfar, the doomsday ship which was said to be constructed from the improperly disposed-of nails of the dead. The Persians also thought that failing to bury the nails of the dead properly would give rise to demons.[17]

At first glance, it seems confusing that the Rachmans of Carpathian tradition live "across the sea" whereas some East European narratives speak of a burning river. In some contexts, these two barriers may have been interchangeable. For instance, in one Ukrainian tale the magical bridge conjured up by a handkerchief spans a sea rather than a fiery river. In this story, the pursuer from the other side is not Baba Yaga, but a devious dragon, which recalls the dragon at the base of the cosmic mountain in Lithuanian tradition.

The land of the Rachmans is described as being across the sea, in the direction of the sunrise.[18] This probably connects it to the Island of Buyan in Russian folk belief. This mythical island shows up in Russian epic songs or bylinas, as well as zagovors which are a type of charm or prayer. The Isle of Buyan is the home of the maiden Zaria, the personified dawn. This is consistent with the way that the island of the Rachmani is described "in the direction of the sunrise." The island of Buyan often is the place of the mythical Alatyr or Latyr stone, out of which flow the waters or rivers that nourish the world. The island may also be home to a massive tree with a serpent dwelling beneath its roots[19] similar to the world tree in Norse mythology. However, the world tree sometimes seems to be replaced by a mountain.

One Russian bylina opens with the following passage:

> *To the sea, to the blue sea, to the blue and the cold sea, to the stone, to the Latyr stone, to that baba, to Zlatygorka.*[20]

Zlatygorka simply means "golden mountain" in Russian. The reference to the sea and the Latyr stone makes it clear the Zlatygorka is on the island of Buyan. Later we find out that the baba or woman is actually named "Golden Mountain." However, it's likely that the island of Buyan was thought to have a literal golden mountain. In one Russian folktale, there is a mysterious island with a literal golden mountain on it.[21] This appears to be identical to the cosmic mountain in Lithuanian mythology. In reality, the woman or "baba" of the golden mountain is probably just a ruler or inhabitant of the golden mountain.

Apparently, most of the otherworldly afterlife imagery in Lithuanian pagan beliefs is also found in Komi and Slavic mythology. None of this is terribly shocking, although it certainly was amazing when I first discovered the parallels. The idea that Balto-Slavic and Finno-Ugric cultures have a long history of interaction is not likely to draw objections from many scholars. However, there is one parallel that is kind of the elephant in the room here. That "elephant in the room" is Zoroastrianism. In Zoroastrianism, there is also a bridge of judgment which the dead must cross, known as the bridge of the separator[22] or "Chinvat Bridge." How did the Persians get this notion?

One explanation might be that these are all features of late (Satem) Indo-European tradition, and that it is the Komi who have borrowed elements from others. If so, then the Chinvat bridge / judgement motif in Zoroastrianism is no reform by Zoroaster, but a standard view of the afterlife among many Indo-European cultures.

There is one other interesting parallel which seems to link Zoroastrianism with the traditions of Eastern Europe. Zoroastrianism preserves traces of a belief in a composite soul. While the exact details are hard to pin down, we know that the Persians worshiped the souls (Fravashis) of the dead in Spring, much like the Slavs, whereas another entity known as the Urvan was thought to face judgment in the next world.[23, 24] A dual soul also shows up in Lithuania, where the Siela remains behind in the earthly realm, often reincarnating or inhabiting nature, whereas the Vele goes on to the next world.[25]

Uralic pagan beliefs often involve numerous soul components. The Nenets believed in two souls, which were very similar in nature to those of Lithuanian culture. According to the Nenets, one was the breath or "life force" and the other was the "shadow" which is capable of moving independently of the body.[26] In Finnish paganism, there are three elements of the human soul. They are the Itse, Henki, and Luonto.[27] The concept of multiple souls may seem odd, but in a way, it makes sense that one aspect of the soul is closely tied to the physical world. After all, physical things like drinking alcohol and getting clubbed in the head do impact our mental state. Today, we can even see how the brain is responsible for cognitive processing. Yet it seems that many Uralic and Balto-Slavic traditions have always acknowledged an aspect of the soul that is permanently bound to the physical world. Additionally, the aspect of our soul that does "move on" to the next world is not quite everything that we are currently. Under this model, there is indeed something of our identities that we leave behind when we die.

The evidence for beliefs in these compound souls is scant in Slavic countries. One folktale hints at "reincarnation" or transmigration of the soul[28] which is characteristic of the siela in Lithuanian paganism. Also, the word for "strength" in Slavic languages, often "sila" or something similar, is derived from the same root. This makes sense, given that this portion of the soul was associated with physical life-force or vitality. On the other hand, the typical Slavic word for soul, "dusa", is cognate to Lithuanian "dausos" which is the heavenly realm atop the cosmic mountain. Afterlife beliefs appear to have been remarkably conservative in Balto-Slavic cultures, and the Slavic beliefs had much in common with those of Baltic peoples.

The strong links to Uralic cultures probably suggest that there was a middle Bronze Age to early Iron Age convergence of spiritual beliefs in the general region of northeastern Europe, and Slavic paganism was a part of this cultural zone. To an extent, the Iranian peoples also partook of this development.

I have already written quite a bit on the household cult of the Slavs while trying to analyze the Goddess Mokosh, who is clearly closely associated with the household spirits. It is noteworthy that the Slavic word for "Lord"- "Gospodar" - literally means "guest-patron" or "master of guests." There is a near universal agreement that the Domovoi or house spirit is connected with the cult of ancestors. In general, the house spirit seems to have been a dead relative or ancestor. It was closely connected with the oven or hearth fire, which demonstrates once again the importance of the sacred flame in Slavic paganism. For instance, coals needed to be transferred from the hearth in order to ensure that the Domovoi followed you to a new home.[29] More generally, every location was thought to have a spirit of some kind in many Slavic countries. In Bulgaria, the guardian or stopan was thought to inhabit the household, but natural features like springs could also host a stopan. In fact, Bulgarians would engage in a kind of divination to ascertain the nature of a place spirit before building a house on a new site. One way of doing this was by leaving ashes out overnight and coming back to see if any kind of imprint was made in them the next day.[30]

Which begs the question; Are place spirits simply the spirits of the dead? I don't think it is truly possible to distinguish the two. In Lithuanian folklore, the transmigration of the siela often resulted in the siela dwelling in a tree. This appears to neatly bridge the gap between humans and the natural world, whereas the more insubstantial vele or dusa seems to return from the otherworld only periodically. Even then, these periodic visitors from the otherworld may appear as rusalki of the waters, maras of the upland pasture, or mavki of the forest.

In terms of relating this cosmology to our world, there are obviously some issues. As I have said though, these are not dissimilar to the issues involved in other mythic cosmologies like Norse or Finnish.

In Lithuanian paganism, the bridge or path to the afterlife is actually identified with the Milky Way.[31] Similar beliefs about the Milky Way actually show up in English and German folklore as well.[32]

Regarding the multiple souls found in Uralic lore, there is little evidence for more than two among the Balto-Slavs. One exception may be the "helper" spirit believed to enable shamans to take animal forms in Uralic paganism. With the aid of a helping spirit, a Uralic shaman may take the form of an iron reindeer or white eagle, or some other animal. Similarly, a banned book in medieval Russia known as the Charovnik supposedly gave instructions for leaving your body as though dead and flying as an eagle, crow, magpie, owl, etc. or else transforming into a wolf or a bear, or even "flying like a serpent." Ryan W.F. notes that this sounds very "shamanistic."[33]

Thus, it is possible that the tripartite or even more complex souls found in Finnish paganism and some other Uralic traditions may have had some analogues in East Slavic shamanism or sorcery. Perhaps the pagan priests known as Volkhvy, whose name seems to mean "Wolves", were the practitioners of this art, and were thought to utilize some other type of spirit akin to the Finnish luonto. However, this is perhaps better discussed in the context of Slavic magical practices, which is not the subject of this chapter.

In Norse mythology, the female luck spirit called the Hamingja functioned as a kind of guardian angel. Some Norse heathens actually regard luck as an aspect of the soul. The Slavic equivalent of this is probably the Dolya, a woman who lived behind the stove and personified the luck of the household. Her name, "dolya", literally means "lot" as in "my lot in life." Yet as mentioned in Chapter 2, the Dolya is a kind of household spirit, arguably associated with the fortune of the family or clan rather than the luck of the individual. While she may be analogous to the Hamingja, she probably was not regarded as a component of the individual soul. In fact, this seems to have been the case in some Norse beliefs as well. Icelandic sagas seem to imply that the Hamingja could belong to an entire family, and that their luck could be inherited across generations.[34] Likewise for the household spirit Dolya, who probably watched over the family but ultimately answered to fate and to the Queen of the spirit world (Mokosh).

I should probably use this chapter to discuss vampires briefly. These are best known thanks to Bram Stoker's Dracula, but the belief in vampires was widespread from Russia, to Poland, to Bulgaria. In the lay of Saint Gregory the Theologian, it is interesting that Bereginyas and Upyri are mentioned side by side as being worshiped by the Slavs. The term Bereginya is likely related to the Slavic word for "riverbank" which is "bereg." This leads many scholars to equate them with the water nymphs known as Rusalki. Additionally, Upyri are typically taken to mean "vampires."[35] This reference can be taken a number of different ways, but it's probably no coincidence that Rusalki and Vampires are mentioned together. As we have seen, Rusalki are also a type of Niavka, or spirit of the dead. Vampires may simply be another class of the Niavki.

Alternatively, these may be polar opposites. Bereginyas may be the "clean" dead who walk the land in springtime, whereas Vampires may refer to the "unclean" dead who often haunt Slavic folklore. The Slavs evidently believed that suicides, sorcerers, dead children, and a number of other groups became unclean spirits in death. Similarly, a corpse that had not been properly washed and keened over might become a vampire. In any case, it's clear that the upyri needed to be appeased. The maras who haunted the land during the dark months probably are synonymous with the unclean dead. In Bulgarian folklore, late December and early January were known as the "dirty days" and harmful "unclean" spirits were thought to wander around this time.[36]

Endnotes

1. Vincenz, Stanisław. On the High Uplands: Sagas, Songs, Tales and Legends of the Carpathians. London: Hutchinson, 1955. Page 326-327
2. Knab, Sophie H. Polish Customs, Traditions and Folklore. New York: Hippocrene Books, 2017. Pages 115, 225
3. Kotsiubyns'kyĭ, Mykhaĭlo, and Bohdan Rubchak. Shadows of Forgotten Ancestors. Littleton, Colo: Published for the Canadian

Institute of Ukrainian Studies by Ukrainian Academic Press, 1981. Page 51

4. Ivanits, Linda J. Russian Folk Belief. M E Sharpe Incorporated, 1989. Pages 78-79
5. Barber, Elizabeth W. The Dancing Goddesses: Folklore, Archaeology, and the Origins of European Dance. New York: W W Norton, 2014. Page 71
6. Kotsiubyns'kyĭ, Mykhaĭlo, and Bohdan Rubchak. Shadows of Forgotten Ancestors. Littleton, Colo: Published for the Canadian Institute of Ukrainian Studies by Ukrainian Academic Press, 1981. Page 51
7. Knab, Sophie H. Polish Customs, Traditions and Folklore. New York: Hippocrene Books, 2017. Page 86
8. Ivanits, Linda J. Russian Folk Belief. M E Sharpe Incorporated, 1989. Pages 78-80
9. Johns, Andreas. Baba Yaga: The Ambiguous Mother and Witch of the Russian Folktale. 2004. Page 298
10. Konakov, N D, Vladimir Napolskikh, Anna-Leena Siikala, and Mihaly Hoppal. Komi Mythology. Budapest: Akademiai, 2003. Pages 58, 204, 213
11. Haney, Jack V. An Anthology of Russian Folktales. 2015. Internet resource. Page 36
12. Baranova, Jurate. Lithuanian Philosophy: Persons and Ideas. Washington, D.C: Council for Research in Values and Philosophy, 2000.
13. Konakov, N D, V V. Napolskikh, Anna-Leena Siikala, and Mihály Hoppál. Komi Mythology. Budapest: Akadémiai Kiadó, 2003. Pages 205, 278
14. Ryan, W F. The Bathhouse at Midnight: An Historical Survey of Magic and Divination in Russia. Stroud: Sutton, 1999. Internet resource. Page 285
15. Kuniczak, W S, and Pat Bargielski. The Glass Mountain: Twenty-eight Ancient Polish Folktales and Fables. New York: Hippocrene Books, 1997. Internet resource. Pages 20-21

16. Katzel, Josef A. A Short History of Lithuania to 1569: Centennial Edition (1921–2021). N.P, Primedia eLaunch LLC, 2021.
17. Lincoln, Bruce. Religion, Culture, and Politics in Pre-Islamic Iran: Collected Essays. Netherlands, Brill, 2021. Page 274
18. Vincenz, Stanisław. On the High Uplands: Sagas, Songs, Tales and Legends of the Carpathians. London: Hutchinson, 1955. Page 326
19. Ralston, William R. S. Russian Folktales. London [England: Smith, Elder, 1873. Page 109
20. Bailey, James, and T G. Ivanova. An Anthology of Russian Folk Epics. 2015. Internet resource. Page 40
21. The Greatest Russian Fairy Tales & Fables (With Original Illustrations): 125+ Stories Including Picture Tales for Children, Old Peter's Russian Tales, Muscovite Folk Tales for Adults & Others (Annotated Edition). N.P, e-artnow, 2017.
22. Masumian, Farnaz. Life After Death: A Study of the Afterlife in World Religions. Los Angeles: Kalimat Press, 2002. Page 18
23. Rose, Jenny. Zoroastrianism: A Guide for the Perplexed. 2019. Internet resource. Page 157
24. Langton, Edward. Good and Evil Spirits: A Study of the Jewish and Christian Doctrine, Its Origin and Development. Eugene: Wipf and Stock Publishers, 2014. Internet resource. Page 128
25. Pennick, Jones, and Nigel Pennick. A History of Pagan Europe. London: Routledge, 1995. Page 176
26. Frog, Anna-Leena Siikala, and Eila Stepanova. Mythic Discourses: Studies in Uralic Traditions. Helsinki: Finnish Literature Society, 2013. Page 364
27. Lehmusto, Heikki. Juhana Vilhelm Snellman: ja hänen asemansa Hegelin koulukunnassa. Finland, Otava, 1923. Page 101
28. Sixty Folk-tales from Exclusively Slavonic Sources. United Kingdom, E. Stock, 1889. Page 161
29. Ivanits, Linda J. Russian Folk Belief. M E Sharpe Incorporated, 1989. Page 56
30. MacDermott, Mercia. Bulgarian Folk Customs. Philadelphia: Jessica Kingsley, 2010. Page 135

31. Aitamurto, Kaarina. Modern Pagan and Native Faith Movements in Central and Eastern Europe. 2014. Page 86
32. West, Morris. Indo-European Poetry and Myth. Oxford: Oxford University Press, 2007. Pages 350-351
33. Ryan, W F. The Bathhouse at Midnight: An Historical Survey of Magic and Divination in Russia. Stroud: Sutton, 1999. Internet resource. Page 76
34. Routledge Research Companion to the Medieval Icelandic Sagas.: Routledge, 2019. Page 204
35. Warner, Elizabeth. Russian Myths. London: The British Museum Press, 2002. Page 11
36. MacDermott, Mercia. Bulgarian Folk Customs. Philadelphia: Jessica Kingsley, 2010. Page 170

Chapter 10

Magical Traditions in Eastern Europe

Magic and witchcraft are a primary focus for many who research pre-Christian traditions, but it is not something that has been covered in depth so far. Many Slavic cultures are rich in folk magic traditions, even to this day. A lot of the folk-magic from Eastern Europe fits into the category of magical practices studied by Sir James Frazer in his 1890 comparative study of mythology and religion. In "*The Golden Bough*", Frazer begins by listing two common principles of magic; These are the law of similarity, and the law of contagion.

The law of similarity refers to the common belief that like produces like, or that an effect can be produced by imitating it.[1] A good example of this in Slavic folklore is the belief that rain can be produced by dumping water on a vegetation-covered girl. These practices are common among the South Slavs, where the ritual or the girl herself may be referred to as "Dodola". The ritual can be found throughout most of the Balkans.[2] In this case, the act of pouring water on a fertile young girl who wears vegetation is an imitation of the desired outcome (rain on plants!) This can also be referred to as homeopathic magic because the action (pathos) is thought to be similar (homo) to the effect.

The other principle commonly observed in magical traditions, according to Frazer, is the principle of contagion. This seems to be based on the idea that associated objects can act on one another at a distance. So, for example, we can observe this in the common Slavic practice of cursing or charming somebody using their footprint. This is a widespread pattern, but a specific example can be found in the bylina of Dobrynya and Marinka. In this song, the witch Marinka casts a love spell on

Dobrynya by lifting the mud of his footprints out of the ground and casting it into a fire.[3] By lifting a footprint, it was clearly imagined that a witch gained power over a man according to the laws of contagion. In a nutshell, because the mud is from Dobrynya's footprint, whatever is done to the footprint will impact Dobrynya. This example also involves homeopathic magic; Upon casting the soil into the fire, Marinka chants:

> *As this wood blazes, and this young man's footprint with it, so must the heart of young Dobrynya Nikitich catch fire.*

Neither is this the only charm where fire is thought to produce passion or love through homeopathic magic. In other chapters, I have mentioned a similar charm involving "77 Egi-Babas" who dwell upon 77 stoves. This charm utilizes similar language in the hopes of kindling passion in the heart of the target.[4]

Slavic magical traditions are actually not a difficult subject compared to the reconstruction of Slavic pagan theistic beliefs. Whereas the old pagan Gods of Eastern Europe were forgotten or carefully disguised, there is evidence that magic survived somewhat better in folk-tradition. Much as with other aspects of paganism, however, Slavic witchcraft survived better in the east, particularly in Orthodox Christian countries. This is partially because the Orthodox church was less zealous about rooting out witches than the Catholic church was.

In Russia, it appears that accusations of witchcraft were often a civil offense that would warrant a fine, and in some cases the Church would call for penance.[5] In the Orthodox Christian world, there was a certain tolerance for spells and charms, particularly if the overtly pagan elements could be removed and replaced with Christian symbols.

Excellent examples of this can be found in the Russian charms known as Zagovori. Some reference the mysterious white "stone of Alatuir" which lies on the blessed island of Buyan.

This island is said to reside far in the east, where Zaria the dawn herself lives. On this island is a damp oak, and beneath this oak is the chthonic serpent Garafina.[6] Suffice to say, the island of Buyan is rich in pagan imagery. However, many narratives Christianize the Alatuir stone by placing it near the River Jordan, or mentioning a golden church built upon it. In some charms, the Lord or the Virgin Mary occupies the Alatuir stone rather than a pagan figure like the personified dawn.

The stone of Alatuir is not always well defined, but its ubiquity in Russian charms is undeniable. One interesting charm for the protection of a child lists it at both the beginning and end, but never really says much about it:

> *Be thou, oh my never-enough-to-be-gazed-upon child, brighter than the brilliant sun, softer than a spring day, clearer than fountain water, whiter than virgin wax, firmer than the fiery stone Alatuir. I avert from thee the terrible devil, I drive away the fierce whirlwind, I keep away from thee the one-eyed Leshi, from the stranger Domovoy, from the evil Vodyany, from the witch of Kief, from her evil sister of Murom, from the beckoning Rusalka, from the thrice-accursed Baba Yaga, from the flying fiery snake.*[7]

All of the figures mentioned in this charm are familiar beings from Russian folktales, and often mentioned in this book. The leshi, for instance, is a wood spirit. The beckoning Rusalka is a water nymph. The fiery serpent has a close connection with Baba Yaga, the supernatural hag. The charm ends with another mention of Alatuir. This is an interesting charm, not just because of the emphasis on Alatuir, but also because it lists the many spirits that Russian peasants feared. Protection against supernatural beings is a common category of magic in Slavic folklore. The methods of repelling spirits often relied on charms. For instance, some invoke the dawn Goddess against the midnight demon to soothe a child.[8]

However, perhaps the most common weapons against the unclean forces of Slavic folk belief were botanical. Garlic was widely believed to repel the unclean dead such as vampires. Wormwood and garlic were both used as a ward against the Rusalki during Rusalka Week.[9] However, this was hardly the only use for garlic. Among the Carpatho-Rusyns, it was also used to ward off the child-stealing Bohynia[10] who was probably a darker aspect of Mokosh, or else one of her servants.

In Poland, Mugwort was gathered on St. John's Night and hung as a protective measure.[11] This is part of a much broader European practice of gathering herbs around Summer Solstice, one that can be found distributed from Spain to Russia. Herbs gathered on the night of Summer Solstice (St. John's Night) were thought to be especially potent. Girls of the Enisei region of Siberia would go out on this night to gather twelve herbs, which would be placed under their pillow to induce a prophetic dream. In other parts of Russia, a custom was observed on Summer Solstice of gathering herbs naked, and without being seen. The gatherer was supposed to ask Mat Syraia Zemlya (Moist Mother Earth) for her blessing beforehand.[12]

In Spain, herbs and flowers were similarly thought to be in full bloom and full power on this night. However, the power of the fairies was also thought to peak on St. John's Night. Therefore, herbs were gathered for protection against them. This is largely consistent with the Slavic practice. Similar parallels can be found in the Anglo-Saxon medical lore, as illustrated in the Lacnunga, which specifies that medicinal herbs should be gathered "three nights before Summer comes to town." i.e. before Midsummer.[13]

In Italy, the gathering of fern seeds on St. John's Night was condemned in the Synod of Ferrara in 1612.[14] In some Slavic countries, early summer was also a time for harnessing the powers of vitality and banishing sickness. In Bulgaria, girls would take two threads: a red one signifying health, and a yellow one signifying sickness. They would tie the yellow one to their own wrists overnight, while the red one was tied to a rose bush. The following day, they would switch the threads over in order to make the sickness "vanish into the forest."[15] Banishing that which was "unwanted" off to the forest appears to be a common formula, also seen in charms against sleeplessness.

There were numerous herbs thought to possess powers in Russia, and they were by no means limited to protection against spirits. Melampyrum Nemorosum could be used for anything from restoring marital harmony to warding off burglars. Plakun trava, probably Lythrum Salicaria was another protective plant, which had to be gathered with a non-ferrous implement. Crosses made from the flowers of the latter remained common in the Christian era but were also sometimes regarded as heretical.[16]

The significance of St. John's Night was manifold in the Slavic world. Not only were herbs thought to become potent, but it was also a night for purification by bonfires. The practice of leaping over the bonfire was practiced at this time in Russia. Additionally, St. John's Night was a special time for divination. Divination was also very common around Midwinter.[17]

Perhaps the most common means of divination was that involving molten materials, like molten lead or hot wax. This was dripped into water, and the shape was interpreted. Some of these are obvious, like a coffin meaning death or a church meaning a marriage. Others are specific to Russian culture, for instance, a stove means grief. (By pun: Pech is stove, Pechal is grief.) The times for these various divinations varied, but interestingly, the best place for divination seems to have been the bathhouse, a location deeply significant in Russian superstitions.[18]

It appears that the Slavic peoples engaged in divination for any number of occasions. Before building a house somewhere, it was a common practice in Bulgaria to attempt to divine the nature of any local spirits. This was done by scattering ashes, and searching for subsequent animal prints. However, a number of beliefs associated with major life events are what we might call "superstitions" rather than witchcraft proper. The distinction between the two is in the eye of the beholder. For instance, houses were typically built on an auspicious day like Wednesday or Monday, and during a full moon or new moon. The first spadeful of earth was dug before dawn on the eastern side of the house.[19] Weddings were similarly plagued by anxieties about the supernatural, particularly the evil eye. Protections against evil magic took a number of forms. Sometimes pins without eyes were inserted into the bridal gown. In some cases, a witch or magician would be invited to the wedding in the belief that they would protect it in return.[20]

Evil sorcerers and good ones are difficult to distinguish in Russian folklore, as in other cultures. There are numerous terms used for these practitioners of folk magic, although they each have their ambiguities. One of the most noteworthy figures in Russian magical beliefs is the Volkhv.

The Volkhvy were shaman-like figures of great social significance in pre-Christian Kievan Rus. These figures were not just magicians, but were also known to act as leaders and champions of the Slavic tribes. They often led revolts against Christianity, and evidently even the Varangian princes came into conflict with their political power.[21]

It's likely that the more "shamanistic", spiritual, and religious versions of Slavic magic were associated with the Volkhvy. For one, the term appears to come from the Russian word for "wolf" (Volkh). It is thus tempting to link them with the werewolves of European folklore. They may have been associated with the ability to send out their spirits in the forms of animals, which is an ability alluded to in reference to the Charovnik, a banned Russian book of magic. The idea of sorcerers turning into wolves in Eastern Europe has a long history, going all the way back to the Neuri mentioned by Herodotus, so this may have been a major element of the religion in Eastern Europe since ancient times.

Ultimately, humble folk magic practitioners long outlasted the Volhvy, who were evidently too prominent to avoid persecution. The Ved'ma or "learned witch" has a similarly telling name. Her name comes from vedat meaning "to know." This term differentiated her from an innate magical practitioner. The typical folk-magic practitioner was simply referred to as a koldun (male sorcerer) or koldun'ya (female sorcerer).[22]

By now it should be clear that "Slavic magic" as we know it was mainly folk magic. However, it is possible that more complex and esoteric beliefs existed at one time, particularly in the context of so-called "shamanistic practices." These would have been nearly obliterated with the elimination of the Volkhvy, however, who spearheaded the short-lived open resistance to Christianity in Russia. It is possible that South Slavic analogues of their shamanistic practices can be found in the zduhak, or kresniki, people whose spirits would take the form of a dragon, ox, or an eagle and leave their bodies in order to battle storm demons and even rival sorcerers with bad intentions for the community.[23]

Another esoteric element that has been added on top of Slavic folk magic is western esotericism. Byzantine magical traditions infiltrated Kievan Rus early on, as evidenced by parallels in their charms. Much later, Freemasonry, Rosicrucianism, and Martinism became moderately popular among the 18th and 19th century elites of Russia.

More recently, occultism tends to be a very Christian phenomenon in Russia. Some modern concepts have become prevalent in Russia as well, such as beliefs in "energy vampires." However, this belief, like many others, is typically interpreted within a fairly conservative and Christian-influenced framework. Wicca has not penetrated into Russia very much, partially due to lack of translation, and partially because of its heavily Celtic roots which are not widely understood in Russia. Thus, the common blending of occultism and paganism in the west is not quite as pronounced there. This appears to be less the case among West Slavic countries like Poland and the Czech Republic. In Poland, there has been some contact with Wicca, particularly since the mid-2000's when some Polish people were initiated into covens in the U.K. In these more western Slavic countries, western influence is having more impact. Rodnovery is common enough in Eastern Europe, but the relationship with magical practices still appears to be developing.

Endnotes

1. Frazer, James George. The Golden Bough: A Study in Magic and Religion. United Kingdom, Oxford University Press, 1998. Page 26
2. The Folk Arts of Yugoslavia: Papers Presented at a Symposium, Pittsburgh, Pennsylvania, March 1976. United States, Duquesne University Tamburitzans Institute of Folk Arts, 1976. Pages 99-100
3. Warner, Elizabeth. Russian Myths. Austin, Tex: Univ. of Texas Press, 2002. Page 64
4. Johns, Andreas. Baba Yaga: The Ambiguous Mother and Witch of the Russian Folktale. New York [etc.: Peter Lang, 2010. Page 59
5. Ivanits, Linda J. Russian Folk Belief. Armonk, N.Y: M.E. Sharpe, 1989. Page 91
6. Ralston, William Ralston Shedden. The Songs of the Russian People: As Illustrative of Slavonic Mythology and Russian Social Life. United Kingdom, Ellis & Green, 1872. Page 375
7. Ralston, William Ralston Shedden. The Songs of the Russian People: As Illustrative of Slavonic Mythology and Russian Social Life. United Kingdom, Ellis & Green, 1872. Page 373
8. Ryan, W F. The Bathhouse at Midnight: An Historical Survey of Magic and Divination in Russia. University Park, Pa: Pennsylvania State University Press, 1999. Page 178

9. Ivanits, Linda J. Russian Folk Belief. M E Sharpe Incorporated, 1989. Page 75
10. Kotsiubyns'kyĭ, Mykhaĭlo, et al. Shadows of Forgotten Ancestors. United States, Canadian Institute of Ukrainian Studies, 1981. Page 44
11. Knab, Sophie H. Polish Customs, Traditions and Folklore. New York: Hippocrene Books, 2017. Pages 136, 166
12. Ryan, W F. The Bathhouse at Midnight: An Historical Survey of Magic and Divination in Russia. University Park, Pa: Pennsylvania State University Press, 1999. Pages 47-48
13. Watts, Donald. Dictionary of Plant Lore. Amsterdam: Elsevier/AP, 2007. Page 339
14. Dillinger, J. Magical Treasure Hunting in Europe and North America: A History. United Kingdom, Palgrave Macmillan UK, 2011. Page 106
15. MacDermott, Mercia. Bulgarian Folk Customs. Philadelphia: Jessica Kingsley, 2010. Page 218
16. Ryan, W F. The Bathhouse at Midnight: An Historical Survey of Magic and Divination in Russia. University Park, Pa: Pennsylvania State University Press, 1999. Page 277
17. Ryan, W F. The Bathhouse at Midnight: An Historical Survey of Magic and Divination in Russia. University Park, Pa: Pennsylvania State University Press, 1999. Page 351
18. Ryan, W F. The Bathhouse at Midnight: An Historical Survey of Magic and Divination in Russia. University Park, Pa: Pennsylvania State University Press, 1999. Pages 7, 311
19. MacDermott, Mercia. Bulgarian Folk Customs. Philadelphia: Jessica Kingsley, 2010. Page 135-138
20. Ryan, W F. The Bathhouse at Midnight: An Historical Survey of Magic and Divination in Russia. University Park, Pa: Pennsylvania State University Press, 1999. Pages 75, 86
21. Ryan, W F. The Bathhouse at Midnight: An Historical Survey of Magic and Divination in Russia. University Park, Pa: Pennsylvania State University Press, 1999. Page 71-72

22. Ryan, W F. The Bathhouse at Midnight: An Historical Survey of Magic and Divination in Russia. University Park, Pa: Pennsylvania State University Press, 1999. Pages 72-78
23. Folk Belief Today. Estonia, Estonian Academy of Sciences, Institute of the Estonian Language & Estonian Museum of Literature, 1995. Page 366

Chapter 11

Chernobog and the Earth-diver Myth

This chapter deals with the extremely complex dilemma of Pre-Christian Slavic dualism. In fact, speaking more broadly, this chapter will explore the notion of Ancient North Eurasian dualism. In short, where do the dualist creation stories of North Eurasia and the Americas originate?

In Eastern European folklore, a common creation story begins with God and the Devil meeting on the primordial waters to create the earth. God orders the Devil to dive down to the bottom of the sea, and to retrieve sand from the sea floor. The Devil does so, and God inflates the sand to create all of the land on earth. The Devil in these stories is often said to have hidden some sand in his mouth so that he could have land for himself. However, when God causes the land to grow, the sand in the devil's mouth also grows, and he spits up all over the new earth, spoiling its smooth surface. Tales of this nature can be found in Russia[1] in Ukraine,[2] in Poland,[3] in Romania,[4] in Bulgaria,[5] in Lithuania[6] and really all throughout Eastern Europe.

It was once thought that these legends reflected the influence of the Balkan heretical movement known as Bogomilism. The Bogomils were a dualist heresy presumably related to Gnosticism and Catharism - but one that flourished in medieval Bulgaria from about the 10th to 13th centuries. Evidence of this link is seen in a medieval apocryphal religious text from Bulgaria known as "*The Tiberian Sea*." This medieval text, written in Old Bulgarian (a South Slavic language), appears to date to between the 11th and 13th centuries. In this text, we have one of the earliest examples of a creation narrative in which the "devil" takes the form of a duck or loon, and dives down to retrieve soil for God to create with.[7, 8]

While the Slavic variants are all fairly similar, some of them do stand out for the level of detail or unique elements they contain. One of the most intricate is probably the narrative surrounding the "Aridnyk" of Hutsul folklore. The Hutsuls were an East Slavic people of the Carpathians (Carpatho-Rusyns) who lived in modern day western Ukraine during pre-industrial times. According to them, the world was created by God, and his brother, the Aridnyk. Just as described previously, God ordered the Aridnyk to dive down below the sea to retrieve sand, and to obtain it in God's name. However, the Aridnyk hid some in his mouth without permission, and when the sand began to grow and expand, he spat it out. This led to the creation of mountains and swamps. This is the "Ukrainian" example cited previously.

With the land created, God decided to sleep. The Aridnyk tried to kill his "brother" God by rolling him into the sea. However, as he did so, the newly created land expanded, thus preventing the Aridnyk from reaching the edge. When God awoke, he remarked slyly that he dreamt about someone trying to kill him. The Aridnyk lied and said that he knew nothing about it, and that he himself had been asleep. From this first lie (according to Hutsul lore) was born all deception in the world, as well as dreams and poetry. The mystical significance of this "first lie" is obvious, although subject to interpretation. To punish the Aridnyk for his attempted murder, God threw him into the water and put a sheet of ice over him.

Before the distribution of these legends was well understood, people tried to argue that Bogomils carried dualist ideas to Bulgaria from Iran. However, as scholars like Yuri Stoyanov have noted, the basic legend is actually widespread throughout Eurasia, even as far east as Siberia and Mongolia.[9]

In Mongolian mythology, the creation narratives take many forms, but there are some which have many similarities to the Slavic variants described previously.

In the beginning, there was only water and the Sky Father, who had two sons, Ulgen Tenger and Erleg Khan. Sky Father gave Ulgen the space that would be the upper world, and Erleg the space that would be the lower world. To create his world, Ulgen sent the loon into the depths to bring up mud with which to form land. The loon failed. A duck was more successful and provided a bit of mud upon which Ulgen immediately fell asleep. Ulgen's brother Erleg, seeing this, tried to pull the land from under his brother. But this only made the land grow in all directions. Next, Ulgen woke up and created the animals and humans out of wet clay, and left them to dry. He assigned the dog to watch over them. Erleg tempted the dog by offering him a fur coat. The dog allowed Erleg to creep in and spit on the humans, condemning them forever to the diseases and pains that animals and humans are subject to. When he returned, Ulgen was furious and punished the dog by making him smelly and dependent on humans for survival.[10]

The legend above from Mongolia is clearly related to dualist creation legends from Eastern Europe. The only thing missing from the above example is the explicit identification of the "Devil" figure with the earth-diver. Instead, the diver in the above narrative is a duck who is totally distinct from the malevolent "Erleg." As we will see, this may be the more archaic version of the narrative. More on that later.

In other Turkic/ Mongol dualist legends, we do in fact see Erlik / Erleg acting specifically in the role of the earth-diver, much more in line with the East European variants.[11] Therefore, if you account for the full diversity of Turkic and Mongolian creation narratives, it's clear that all of the components of the Slavic narratives are found there - hidden among an even greater diversity of motifs than can be found in Eastern Europe. This is consistent with the idea that the Slavic versions originate from a subset of those found in Siberia.

It should be noted that Erlik is an ambiguous figure in some Altaic traditions. Even when he is portrayed as malevolent, he may still play a role in afterlife beliefs, and sacrifices to propitiate him are often considered an acceptable practice among Mongolian and Turkic peoples.[12]

The element of the dog as partial accomplice of Erleg / the devil is not very common in most of Europe. In Europe, the element of the dog seems to be mainly limited to East Slavic territories (Ukraine, Belarus, Russia) and some Balto-Finnic groups. The corruption of mankind by an evil demiurge figure also tracks in Europe. It can be found among the Southern Estonian language speaking group known as the Setu (near the Russian / Estonian border). A narrative from the Setu also talks about how the evil being "Vanapagan" corrupted mankind by spitting on the figure that the creator sculpted and left to dry. In a Setu variant of the tale, the devil poked the figure with his finger, making the human body sensible to pain.[13]

It is noteworthy that Finno-Ugric peoples like the Setu have a number of the same legends as the Mongols and Slavs. Another such narrative comes from the Komi-Zyrians, an ethnic minority in modern day Northern Russia. In one Komi-Zyrian creation narrative, creation started with the great mother duck Chezh who was gliding over the primordial waters. She laid the eggs of life-birth, but most of them sank to the bottom of the sea. Only two hatched; From one came Jen, the embodiment of Truth, and from the other came Omol, the embodiment of "the lie." Later in this narrative, Chezh smashes her body against the water and "dies" thus becoming the earth itself. She directs her two sons to dive down and retrieve her eggs from the bottom of the sea, which they then use to create the sun, the moon, attendant spirits, and life.

However, much like in the other legends, we see Omol try to kill his brother - in this case by freezing the surface of the water when he dives down. Later Jen creates man, and Omol tries to imitate him by creating women. However, only Jen is able to breathe a soul into the figure created by Omol.[14]

We know very little about the chronology of these myths as they were disseminating throughout the Slavic world. However, there are some medieval texts that probably place them squarely in Eastern Europe by the mid-1st millennium CE. As already discussed, the apocryphal Bulgarian text "Tiberian Sea" places the devil in the role of an earth-diving water bird, most likely sometime between the 11th and 13th centuries CE.[15] Additionally, the idea of "God' and the "Devil" quarreling over the creation of man shows up in one Russian text from the 11th century CE. According to two pagan sorcerers (Volchvy, Volkhvy) interrogated, tortured, and executed by the tax collector Jan Vysatic in Beloozero, mankind was created in the following manner.[16]

> *While God was bathing in the bathhouse, he sweated and wiped himself with a tuft of straw and dropped it from the sky onto the Earth. And there was a dispute between Satan and God, who will create from it. The devil created a man, and God put a soul in him. Therefore, when a man dies, the body goes to earth, but the soul goes to God.*

This has parallels to many of the dualist legends recounted here, including those of the Komi and of the Turkic nomads. A common theme in these tales is the inability of the Erlik or "the devil" to create the soul, as seen in the Komi legend where Omol's figure must be animated by Jen. Or alternatively, Erlik animates a human figure himself while the creator is away.[17]

In one narrative from the Mordvins (also known as the Moksha and the Eryza) Shaitan tells Cham Pas; "My breath is in him to a half, and thine to a half. Let us divide all mankind; let half be thine, and half mine." On the other hand, another Mordvin creation narrative from Nizhni-Novgorod is nearly identical to that of the Slavic Volkhvy in Beloozero; According to them, God dried himself with a towel while at the bathhouse, and Shaitan then used the towel to make man's body, while God animated it with his breath. According to this narrative, the soul therefore goes back to God, and the body to Shaitan.[18]

There is no consistent doctrine or philosophy here, just a general North Eurasian myth type that deals with the dual origins of man. However, the myths vary greatly in how they describe humankind's dual origins. As the examples show, even a single cultural group (the Mordvins) may not have a single cohesive doctrine expressed in their various creation myths - yet the dualist element is still present across multiple versions.

Based on the narrative from Beloozero, we can say this concept of a dualist struggle behind man's creation was probably prevalent among the East Slavs by the 11th century CE. However, this was well after the period of peak influence of Altaic peoples upon the East Slavs. The period of maximum influence from the Altaic nomads on Old East Slavic culture probably would have been at least a couple of centuries earlier.

Finally, it should be noted that dualist elements and earth-diving episodes do show up in the Americas, most likely indicating common roots in paleolithic Siberia. However, with a few exceptions, dualist struggles between benevolent and malevolent deities are not consistently linked to earth-diver creation myths in the Americas. Rather, most earth-diver myths in the Americas simply portray an animal such as a spider or muskrat that dives down to the sea-floor to retrieve soil for creating all land on earth.

However, the Iroquoian legends are one case in which the earth-diver scenario is followed by a struggle between two rival "creator" Gods who are sons of the Earth Mother. According to one version, the Muskrat dives down to bring soil from the bottom of the sea, and the daughter of Sky Woman lies down on the land to give birth to two twin boys. One is said to be benevolent, and creates good things. The other twin is malevolent.[19] The malevolent brother is said to have killed his mother by bursting out of her body, and he later creates things that are considered "bad" like poisonous plants. However, this conflict only comes after an animal dives to create the earth. The so-called "Crow" (Absarko) Indians also have a near-dualist juxtaposition between "Old Coyote" and "Little Coyote" in their creation story, which is also preceded by an earth-diver episode performed by water birds.[20]

This ordering of the two episodes (Earth-diving followed by dualist conflict) can be found in Eurasia as well - for instance, the Mongolian narrative (previously recounted) also does not introduce the conflict between Ulgen and Erleg until after a duck dives down to create the earth.

However, a number of Turkic narratives and essentially all Slavic versions seem to come from a version that identifies the "Erlik" or the "Devil" figure with the earth-diver itself.[21] The Uralic peoples are divided on whether or not they adopt this arrangement - the Mordvins do[22] but the Mansi, Khanty, and Komi typically do not.[23, 24, 25] In the latter Uralic cultures, the earth-diving water bird is not demonized. Much has been said about the supposed "Uralic" nature of the Slavic earth-diver myths. But this is far from clear.

However, all of these mythological traditions have a near-dualist conflict of some sort, including that of the Khanty in Siberia, who feared and placated the underworld deity Kul, the bringer of death and disease. Kul was often considered the brother to Num Torum the Sky Father.[26]

As we will see, this "diving devil" version can probably be traced back to the Turkic migrations of the Mid - 1st millennium CE - whereas the narrative that distinguishes "Diver" from "Devil" is probably an incredibly archaic North Eurasian myth. However, it should be stressed that Native American creation myths are incredibly diverse, and the same should probably be assumed for paleolithic Siberia. Therefore, this article does not posit any single unified mythology or doctrine shared throughout Paleolithic Siberia.

Instead, the "archaic" narrative reconstructed here was probably one of many creation narratives in Paleolithic Siberia, but one that happened to survive extremely successfully into the modern era in North Eurasia. This was probably due in large part to the dualist or near-dualist elements, and to its perceived compatibility with the "civilized" religious traditions further south, in Sogdia and Bactria, during the time of the Silk Road. This contact is difficult to date but was undoubtedly significant by the 6th century CE if not earlier. Within the framework of the Turkic migrations, this narrative seems to have displaced much of the diversity of creation stories that can be presumed to have existed in Paleolithic Siberia. This theory requires some clarification, however, about who the Old Turkic peoples actually were. For one thing, they weren't from Turkey!

Interactions and Distribution of Balto-Slavic, Uralic, and Altaic Cultures

A few notes belong here regarding the three categories of language families involved in the review thus far; They are Balto-Slavic, Uralic, and Altaic. The Balto-Slavic languages include Russian, Bulgarian, Polish, Lithuanian, and many others in Eastern Europe. There are actually only two Baltic languages surviving today as a subgroup within this family (Lithuanian and Latvian). The other sixteen languages of the Balto-Slavic group are Slavic.

The Uralic languages may be harder to explain to the average person. Their distribution bridges the gap between "European" Russia in the west, and Siberia in the east. The traditional Europe / Asia divide therefore cannot be applied to the Uralic peoples as a whole. The majority of Uralic language speakers can also be referred to as "Finno-Ugric" language speakers - the only Uralic groups outside of this category are the Samoyedic people of the Arctic circle. It is noteworthy that the Setu people, mentioned previously, speak a South Estonian language, and therefore belong to the Finno-Ugric group. Likewise for the Komi-Zyrians. The origins of Uralic languages are hazy, but their region of origin is generally thought to be up around the Volga and Kama rivers. A 2018 study found that most members of this language family share a Siberian ancestral component.[27]

The Altaic languages include Mongolian, and also the Turkic languages which originated from Central Asia - probably not far from Mongolia. This is confusing for many, because some Turkic tribes migrated to Anatolia, in the Middle East, which led to the Anatolian peninsula being renamed "Turkey" in the Middle Ages. The Mongolian languages are mainly limited to Mongolia. The Turkic languages are widespread throughout Northeast China, Turkmenistan, Kazakhstan, and Turkey. Tungusic is mainly limited to isolated regions of Siberia.[28]

The Korean affiliation with the Altaic languages is uncertain. Likewise for Japanese. Linguists also don't agree that the other three groups are descended from a single ancestor language. Rather, it may just be that they have mixed with each other since prehistoric times. But there is no definite "family tree" pattern with a single trunk - instead, it looks more like at least three trees that eventually got tangled together.[29]

When we speak about Altaic nomads who invaded Eastern Europe, we are generally talking about Turkic tribes like the Bulgars - or groups like the Huns who were probably Turkic, but cannot be conclusively categorized based on language. That generalization largely holds true from the 4th century CE (with the Huns) all the way up to the 13th century CE (when the Mongols finally arrived in Europe for the first time in recorded history).

The interaction between the Turkic tribes and the Finno-Ugric peoples is particularly evident with the Ugric branch of Finno-

Ugric languages. The Khanty, Mansi, and Hungarian languages belong to this group. Evidently a subset of the Ugric peoples adopted the Turkic nomadic lifestyle, and horse-based methods of warfare, and the Magyars essentially became indistinguishable from Turkic nomads to many medieval European chroniclers. This horse-based military culture in large part contributed to the Magyar success in conquering the Pannonian basin in 895 CE, and defeating many European armies in the 10th century. Yet linguistically, the closest relatives of Hungarian are the Khanty and Mansi languages, which are associated with a traditionally hunter-gatherer / reindeer herding people.[30]

Comparative linguistics tells us the original Magyar / Hungarian language probably came from somewhere close to the Khanty and Mansi homeland in Siberia. Later, they would migrate westward as the "Magyars" eventually joining the Khazar Khaganate (Khazar Empire). When the Magyars migrated even further west to found Hungary, it's said that they took three Khazar (Turkic) tribes with them.[31]

Another interaction between the Altaic and Finno-Ugric groups can be seen in Volga Bulgaria. Even before the Khazars arrived on the Pontic Steppe, a previous group of Turkic peoples called the Bulgars lived there. When the Khazars arrived in the 7th century CE, the Bulgars split into two groups; One group of Bulgars went north to found Volga Bulgaria, right in the heart of historical Finno-Ugric territory. This could be why the Mordvins (aka the Moksha and Eryza) have a legend in which the "devil" is ordered to dive down and retrieve soil for creation of the world.[32] Earth-diving and the diabolical rivalry against the creator are two elements that many Finno-Ugric mythologies actually avoid combining, despite often having both elements independently. But in the case of the Mordvins, close contact with the Turkic Volga Bulgars is a tempting explanation for this exception. The region would also later be within the Khazar sphere of influence.

A second group of Bulgars fled southwest into the Balkans, founding the First Bulgarian Empire in 681 CE. This was the predecessor state to modern day Bulgaria. The Bulgars were a Turkic elite surrounded by Europeans, and consequently they eventually adopted Slavic as their primary language. Interestingly, however, the Slavic Bulgarian language would eventually be used to write the apocryphal medieval text "The Sea of Tiberias" which also portrays Satan in the role of an earth-diving water bird. If this narrative was introduced to the Balkans with the arrival of the Bulgars in 681 CE, then it would predate the Christianization of most Slavic tribes.

Meanwhile, further east, in modern day Southwest Russia and Eastern Ukraine, the Khazars brought Turkic influence to a different region as well. During the 8th and 9th centuries CE, an archaeological culture known as the Volyntsevo culture thrived in Northeastern Ukraine (Just East of the Dnieper.) In many respects, it was a typical East Slavic culture, and the people are presumed to be ancestors of modern-day Ukrainians and Russians. However, Khazar influences are also significant in this region at the time. This includes not only Khazar pottery, but also the flow of silver coins from the Arab world, apparently indicating that they were economically connected to the Middle East via the Khazar Empire. The Russian Primary Chronicle of the Middle Ages corroborates this to some extent, listing the Slavic tributaries of the Khazar Khaganate. These apparently included the East-Slavic tribes known as Severiane, Vyatichi, and Radimichi.[33] Considering that the Volyntsevo culture dates at least to the 8th century CE, this is another an example of "Pre-Christian" contact between the Slavic tribes and the Turkic peoples.

When interpreting the story about the creation of man from 11th Century CE Beloozero[34] it is tempting to see it as a sign of Khazar influence upon the East Slavs. Much in the same way that the occurrence of the same legend among the Mordvins probably represents Khazar or Volga Bulgar influence. In particular, the Mordvins are known to have been under strong Volga Bulgar influence.[35]

However, in order to understand the history of Altaic nomads in Europe, we need to go back even further than the 7th century CE. Before the Bulgars arrived in the Balkans, there was already a Khaganate (A domain ruled by a "Khagan", which was essentially a "Khan.") in the Balkans known as the Avar Khaganate. This state was founded in the 6th century CE.

The Avars may have exercised an even more profound influence on the Slavic tribes than the Bulgars. The Byzantines described them as fighting side by side with one another, and there's evidence of a hybrid Slav-Avar culture in the Pannonian Basin by the 7th century CE.[36] There are also descriptions of the Slavs rebelling against the Avars - for instance, Samo's Empire in the 7th century CE arose from such a revolt against Avar rule. According to historical records, the Avars would take Slavic women and produce offspring with them. However, the sons born from these unions often empathized with the native Slavs and helped facilitate the rebellion against the Avars.[37]

The difference between the rebellious Slavs of Samo's Empire and the coexisting Avar-Slav community of the Pannonian basin is interesting. It's not clear why the relationship with the Avars varied in different locations, but one clear conclusion is that the Slavs living closest to the Avar center of power (the Pannonian basin) were more likely to be incorporated into the "core" of the Avar state than those on the periphery of Avar rule.

Interestingly, pottery styles from the region of Avar influence would later expand outward, into modern day Southwest Ukraine, Southern Poland, Czechia, and Lusatia.[38] Some of the earliest archaeological evidence of Slavic social organization above the tribal level appears to arise from this hybrid Avar-Slavic culture, which spurred the development of denser and more permanent variants of the Early Slavic settlement model.[39]

This could explain the diffusion of pottery styles from the same region, and could indicate that the Pannonian basin was a cultural hub during the Common Slavic Period (When all Slavic language was mutually intelligible.) It is considered likely by many scholars that Old Slavic eventually became the lingua franca of the Avar Khaganate. Unlike the Bulgars and Khazars, we don't have a clear idea of what type of language the Avars spoke. They are almost unanimously considered to have been Altaic nomads, but theories of Turkic and Mongolian linguistic identity both seem equally plausible to scholars.

Interestingly, however, the Avars, Bulgars, and Khazars were all (In their own way) products or "offshoots" of the Gokturk Khaganate in Central Asia. This massive empire, founded in the 6th century CE, apparently helped drive the Avars westward. The Gokturk Empire would later get angry with the Byzantines for making deals with the Avars, calling the latter "escaped subjects" of the Gokturk Empire in Central Asia. For the Khazars and Bulgars, it is equally clear that they were splinter groups from the same Gokturk Empire, and both spoke Oghuric Turkic languages that were probably closely related to the native tongue of the Gokturk empire elites. Therefore, all three groups could be considered to have common origins, at least as former subjects of the same empire.[40]

Going back even further, to the migration period, the Roman writer, Jordanes, mentions that Atilla the Hun's funeral feast was referred to as a "strava." This is often taken by scholars as a Slavic word for a feast.[41] Even today, it should be noted that the same word denotes a "dish" or "fare" in Ukrainian and Czech. Later, in 537 CE, the Roman writer Procopius writes of "Hun and Slav horsemen" fighting as mercenaries in the imperial army.[42]

This latter example is slightly after the collapse of the Hunnic empire, so it's not clear who these post-empire "Huns" are, who are riding beside Slavs as Roman mercenaries. Perhaps they were actually Kutrigurs - another Turkic group, more recently arrived from Central Asia. Still, it is highly suggestive of continued contact with the Steppe nomads of the region. Prior to the Huns, there is no evidence for Altaic language speaking nomads in Europe. Or indeed, throughout most of the historical records of Eurasian civilizations other than China.

In theory, the Proto-Slavs would not have experienced much direct contact with the Uralic peoples, but it is plausible that they could have been influenced by them indirectly through the assimilation of Baltic peoples to their north. Still, the evidence for such "Uralic" influence on the early Slavs is weaker than for Altaic influence in the historical record. Alternatively, it could be a combination of both, with the Huns, Avars, Bulgars, and Khazars all "amplifying" an already existing North Eurasian mythological component among the Balto-Slavic peoples.

Non-Earth-diver Dualist Creation Legends

As argued previously, the Bogomils are an unlikely candidate for being the ones who single handedly spread dualistic mythology in North Eurasia. Their influence was mainly limited to the Balkans. The Bogomil heretics may have influenced other Orthodox Christian Slavs, like those of Kievan Rus. However, there is some debate about this.

The Russian and Ukrainian folktales about God and the Devil creating the world may have Balkan influences. However, the idea that this East Slavic folktale single-handedly introduced dualist tendencies to Mongolian, Korean, Turkic, Tungusic, Khanty, Mansi, Mari, Mordvin, Komi-Zyrian, and Nenets creation narratives seems more than unlikely.

The dualist creation narratives are too widespread, and found in too many distinct cultures of the region for all of them to be explained by a single non-canonical folktale that circulated among the Russian peasantry. Neither are the other North Eurasian variants simple "copies" of the East Slavic narratives. On the contrary, the narratives from farther east share details that are largely missing from the Slavic variants, thus implying that the Slavic variants are a simplification of a more diverse cultural tradition that was transmitted from the east. For instance, most Slavic variants portray God and the Devil as existing at the beginning of creation. However, many narratives often portray the two rival demiurges as brothers, and children of a mutual parent deity.[43, 44]

This appears to be something which was "lost" in Christian folklore due to the inherent problems with giving God and the Devil a single parent figure. However, if this concept was erased from East Slavic folk tradition, then East Slavic peoples like the Russians could not subsequently have transmitted it further east.

The Bogomils of Bulgaria may have originally conceived of Jesus and the Devil as two sons of God,[45] but it's unlikely that non-Bogomil Russian peasants would have preserved or transmitted this idea during their expansion into Siberia many centuries later. Giving the two demiurges a parent figure is not typical of East Slavic legends.

Another important motif associated with dualist legends in northern Asia is the flower contest. Many of these flower contest myths also feature a conflict between two brothers who are sons of a Heavenly Father. Stories of this nature show up as Far East as Korea. One narrative from Cheju (aka Jeju) island off the coast of South Korea exemplifies the dualist tendencies in some of these narratives. Manabu Waida has brilliantly summarized the distribution and probable origin of these myths.[46]

In one flower contest story, the heavenly father, Chonju-wang and the Earth Mother give birth to two sons, Great Star (Taebol-wang) and Little Star (Sobeol-wang). The heavenly father ascended to heaven after they were born. Subsequently, Great Star and his younger brother Little Star grew up and ascended to heaven to meet their father face to face. The heavenly father assigned his elder son to govern this world, and his younger son to rule over the next world. However, the greedy Little Star was not satisfied. He challenged his elder brother to the flower contest. They agreed that the one in whose vase a flower would grow should govern the world. The youngest brother, by exchanging his own vase having no flower in it with that of his brother's showing a blossoming flower, took possession of the world. Later, Little Star found that the world is full of evil deeds such as killing, rebellion, theft, adultery, and so forth. He asked his brother to help correct these evils, but Great Star refused. Consequently, this world remains flawed as it is.

A very similar story can be found in North Korea. Here, however, the two brothers are called "Sokka" and "Miruk." It is noteworthy that these are Korean versions of the names of two Buddhist figures, namely the Boddhisattva's Sakyamuni and Maitreya. In this story, "Sokka" waits until his brother is sleeping during the flower contest, and plucks the first flower that blooms, secretly placing it on his knees.

The flower contest narratives are found in Korea, some Japanese islands, and also in Mongolia. In Mongolia, however, they overlap with some of the dualist earth-diver narratives described previously. In one Mongolian narrative, the two brothers engage in an earth-diving scenario together. Later, they craft the human body out of clay, and the devil (Shulmus) sneaks in to animate the bodies. Later, in order to determine who will rule over humans, the two engage in a flower contest. In Mongolia as well, these two brothers are sometimes named after the same two Buddhist figures "Shaktshi-Toba" [Sakyamuni] and "Maidari" [Maitreya].

The flower contest succession myths in Mongolia do not always just involve two brothers. As shown in the previous example, the devil (Shulmus) may even appear as a "third" figure. Indeed, one narrative does have Khan Churmas Tengri (King Ahura Mazda Tengri) trying to resolve a dispute among his three sons with a flower contest. The story ends with Tolty Khan declaring to his brother;

> *You have stolen the flowers. Now you should rule over the world, and I, as there is nothing else, will be Erlik. But in protest, I will say that your people will live no longer than 100 years...*

This is reminiscent of a number of Korean variants. For instance in North Korea, this narrative is similarly used to explain the short life-span of flowers. In one Korean flower contest involving two Goddesses, the loser is transformed into the Goddess of death and the underworld. This parallels the transformation of Khan Churmas Tengri's son, Tolty Khan, into the figure known as "Erlik."

The flower contest is also sometimes an explanation for the origins of dishonesty, and it is here that the strongest parallels are found with more western narratives like that of the Hutsuls in Ukraine. In Central Asian flower contest narratives, Maitreya declares that (because of his brother's deception) "Thieves shall be in the world forever and ever!"

The motif of a greedy brother cheating in a flower contest while "Maitreya" sleeps parallels many Slavic narratives where the devil tries to kill God. For instance, in Hutsul lore, in southwestern Ukraine, where the Aridnyk (devil) tries to push his brother "God" into the water as he sleeps. This does not succeed, because the earth expands as the Aridnyk pushes God towards the sea. According to Hutsul lore, the Aridnyk later told the first lie when God asked him about the attempted murder - thus introducing deceit into the world.[47]

It's noteworthy that this motif of "stretching the earth", common to many Slavic narratives, also shows up in the Mongolian narrative recounted at the beginning of the article, with Erleg Khan trying to pull the earth out from under the sleeping Ulgen Khan, causing the land to grow.[48] Like the flower contest, this "land stretching" narrative describes the "devil" figure's attempt to seize sovereignty from his sleeping brother, and subsequently introducing dishonesty or thievery to the world at the beginning of creation.

The northern Korean narrative, "Song of the Creation of the Universe" also credits Seokga's "unjust" victory over Mireuk in the flower contest with introducing "unjust elements" to the world.[49] Therefore, if we draw parallels from Eastern Europe to Korea, the flower contest should not be seen as a substitute for the earth-diver myth itself, but rather a variant of the later episode in which the "devil" tries to kill God and tells the first lie.

Overall, the weight of the evidence seems to suggest that the dualistic "Flower Contest" narrative originates in Central Asia, not far from modern day Mongolia. However, there are many similarities to Iranian dualist traditions like Classical Zoroastrianism and Zurvanite Zoroastrianism. The latter has a very similar tradition in which the elder deity "Zurvan" has two children named Ohrmazd and Ahriman. The latter (Ahriman) is evil, and competes for rule over the world - which he temporarily wins. Additionally, the name of the father in one Mongolian narrative is "Khan Churmas Tengri" which is clearly a compound of Tengri (the Mongolian Sky Father God) and "Hormusta" - an apparent Central Asian loan word derived from the Zoroastrian God Ahura Mazda.[50, 51]

Going back to the Flower Contest myths, it should be noted that the Tungus of the Transbaikal region tell a very similar story about a kind of "Tree Contest" between Buga (God) and Buninka (the devil). in this story, Buninka creates a small and crooked tree, whereas Buga succeeds in creating a strong and tall one, thus proving himself the better creator. This narrative is not an earth-diver myth, although there are parallels to the earth-diver myth; Instead of seeking sand from the bottom of the sea, Buga creates a fire and evaporates some of the water away to create dry land.[52]

One such story in the Americas is that of the Quechan (Not to be confused with Quechuan), or "Yuma Indians" native to Arizona. Below is a summary of their creation story.[53]

> *At first there was only water and emptiness. Then mist from the waters became sky. Then the creator, who lived without form deep in the maternal waters, was born of those waters as the twins, Kokomaht, the good one, and Bakotahl, the evil one... -*
>
> *... - Kokomaht set about making the four directions, taking four steps on the water in each direction, and pointing and announcing the names: north, south, east, and west. Now Kokomaht said he would make the earth, but Bakotahl doubted his twin's power. "Let me try first." he said. "No" said Kokomaht, and he stirred up the waters so much that they brought up land. Kokomaht sat on the land.*
>
> *Bakotahl was angry at his twin, but sat down next to him. Secretly, he made a little human figure out of mud, but it was imperfect, to say the least. Kokomaht himself decided to make a new being, and he made a perfect man, who got up and walked. Then he made a perfect woman.*

This episode is almost identical to many North Eurasian dualist legends, except that the earth diving element is replaced with a scene where the "Good" brother simply creates land by stirring up the water. Additionally, the "Good" Kokomaht later has a son named Komashtam'ho, who continues with the work of creation after his father dies. Interestingly, Coyote steals the heart of Kokomat from his funeral pyre. Because of this, Coyote was condemned to be a wild man and a thief. Later, the earth is destroyed by Komashtam'ho who creates a massive flood. He then creates a huge fire and dries the sea water away, so that dry land can re-appear.

This strongly parallels the Tungusic myth where the "Good" creator deity Buga dries up the sea and reveals the earth using fire. However, the Quechan narrative arguably combines the earth-diver with the sea-boiler imagery by having the "first" world get flooded, and then having the earth re-emerge from the sea once again. So the Quechan myth combines two types of myths found in Siberia to explain the emergence of land. What's more, it combines this with a dualist conflict between two brothers - and it has preserved this narrative in Arizona of all places, in North America.

This should make us hesitate to ascribe Iranian origins to all dualist myths among the Mongols, Koreans, and Tungus - and if you can't tell, I am strongly arguing against this interpretation. The majority of elements in these East Asian narratives clearly date back to Paleosiberian times, as evidenced by the fact that they appear in the Americas. The Iranian influence may be apparent in certain names, like the name for God "Chormus" that shows up in some Mongolian stories. However, this Iranian influence should not be mistaken for the actual origin of the stories.

In any case, most of the details in this North American story should sound familiar at this point. If you have been very attentive, you may even think to yourself "Hey, the part about Coyote sounds familiar." If so, then congratulations. You are right!

The Coyote and the Dog

Coyote is an interesting and ambiguous figure in Native American mythology. He can be helpful, wise, foolish, funny - or even immoral. The Quechan myth above depicts him as a thief who is punished for stealing the heart of the creator, and is therefore condemned to live as a scavenger or thief in the wilderness.[54]

This is such a small element of the Quechan myth (at least the one referenced here) that you could almost miss it. To understand Coyote better, it is worth looking to some similar creation narratives that give him a larger role. In particular, the theft episode of the Quechan myth greatly resembles the Caddo legend describing the origin of death.

According to the Caddo, people used to live forever. It was decided one day that death was necessary because the earth was too full of people. A debate arose as to whether or not death should be permanent. Most felt that people should only die temporarily, and then be resurrected in a medicine house. Only Coyote said that death should be permanent because otherwise there would not be food enough for all.

Later, when the medicine men try to call the spirit of the first dead man into the medicine house, Coyote sneaks over and closes the door of the medicine house. The spirit of the first dead man passes the house by, thus "mythologically" making death permanent. The story ends saying: "Coyote was afraid after he saw what he had done. He ran away and never came back. Since then he has run from one place to another, always looking over his shoulders to see if anyone is pursuing him. And ever since then, he has been starving, because no one will give him anything to eat."[55]

This has parallels to the Mongolian creation stories in which Erleg / Erlik bribes the guard dog to let him spit on the clay figures of the newly created humans. The one recounted previously ends as follows;

> *The dog allowed Erleg to creep in and spit on the humans, condemning them forever to the diseases and pains that animals and humans are subject to. When he returned, Ulgen was furious and punished the dog by making him smelly and dependent on humans for survival.*[56]

There are very similar themes here, regarding the punishment of a canine figure for a primordial crime. The idea of blaming a canine figure or spirit for death and disease is therefore a plausible Paleosiberian tradition. Additionally, it is clear that this figure is sometimes combined with near-dualist Earth-diver Creation Myths. This holds true even in the Americas. Particularly, the so-called "Crow Indians" or Absarkoes have a narrative that demonstrates this:[57]

> *Once there was only water and Old Man Coyote, the Creator. "I wish I had someone to talk to." He said, and when he turned around he found two red-eyed ducks. "How about diving down to see if there is anything under the water." He said to them. The first duck dove and stayed under for so long that Coyote thought he was dead. After a while, though, he came back and said he had hit bottom. On a second dive he found a root; on a third dive he found a lump of earth. Coyote was pleased and announced that he would make a place to live using the mud. When he breathed on it, it grew and grew until it was the Earth. Coyote then planted the root that the duck had brought up, and this started the plants and trees growing.*

This first part of the Absarko narrative shows that the earth diving episode once again precedes the introduction of dualist tension. This is in keeping with the tendency seen in Iroquoian tradition as well, where the two "creator" brothers engage in conflict only after the earth diving animal creates land. Interestingly, while this arrangement is far from universal in Eurasia, examples like the Mongolian narrative listed at the beginning agree with this sequence remarkably well. Likewise for one Samoyed myth among the Uralic peoples, which also places the creation of land before the introduction of two adversarial creators. Why change this incredibly archaic sequence to make the "devil" the creator of the earth itself? This is something that will need to be discussed later, on the topic of Iranian influence.

If we were to try to reconstruct a "Proto-myth" in Paleolithic Siberia, it would probably follow more-or-less this pattern. In the Absarko narrative, the dualist or near-dualist tension is not yet evident until Old Man Coyote encounters "Little Coyote." This episode unfolds as follows:

> One day Old Man Coyote came across a little version of himself, Little Coyote. Where did you come from, Little Brother? He asked.
>
> *"I don't know, Big Brother, Little Coyote answered. I'm just here." "Well Little Brother, I am Old Man Coyote, and I made everything you can see."*

The narrative still is not dualistic in this phase, however. Creation proceeds for some time before we catch a glimpse of the "bad" side of Little Coyote;

> *Then Little Coyote did something bad. He suggested to Old Man Coyote that he give the people different languages so they would misunderstand each other and use their weapons in wars. He convinced the creator that people would thrive as warriors, horse thieves, and woman thieves. He talked about heroism, war dances, and songs of heroic deeds; he talked of honor. Old Man Coyote did what Little Coyote said, and the people had different languages and made war on each other. Some became heroes and chiefs, and some became horse thieves and woman thieves.*

This last part may be pretty self-explanatory. Once again, we see an etiological myth for something "bad" like death or theft. (i.e, why a specific bad thing exists.) It's noteworthy that this narrative has no explicit philosophy or doctrine attached to it. It simply shows that one of the two primordial "Coyote" figures did something "bad" to humans. But it does not tell us explicitly that Little Coyote personifies evil, or even that he only does evil. It is noteworthy that only one specific bad thing is created in this narrative. We cannot extrapolate that all bad things were created by Little Coyote, so the near-dualist elements are still fairly ambiguous.

This ambiguity was probably the norm throughout Eurasia as well until at least the time of Iranian influence. That brings us to one of the most challenging dilemmas: Iranian influence. And the connection with Iranian dualism in general.

The Iranian Background: From the Avesta to Mani

The parallels between the Absarko Coyote and the Mongolian dog are noteworthy. It turns out that a late Zoroastrian tradition has recorded a similar narrative about the guard dog appointed to guard mankind at the beginning of creation - albeit with significant differences. It is not attested in the Avesta, but could reflect an older tradition:

> *After creating the first man Gaiomard, Ohrmazd commissioned seven sages to guard him from Akhriman but they could not fulfill the task. So Ormuzd put the dog Zarrīngoš ("yellow ears") as a guard and since then this dog protects from demons the souls who go to the Beyond.*[58]

One possibility that can probably be rejected outright is that the concept of dualism was introduced to the Mongols and Turkic nomads by Iranian culture. This fits well with our modern biases, which tell us that good / evil dualism is an element of civilized culture, and that more "primitive" people are incapable of formulating such concepts on their own. However, this simplistic scenario can probably be rejected, simply on the grounds that Native American stories seem to have inherited similar dualist or near-dualist creation stories from their Paleosiberian ancestors.

There is some evidence that Iranian religious traditions are somehow related to the dualist myths found in Siberia and Mongolia. There are a number of striking parallels, and these seem even more significant when one considers the appearance of the name "Ahura Mazda" (The Iranian / Zoroastrian Good deity) as a title for the Sky Father in Mongolian mythology, albeit in the form of "Hormusta."[59]

The researchers who have studied the flower contest in Mongolia and Korea seem to agree that it displays Iranian influences. Specifically, the concept of two rival brothers embodying the principles of Good and Evil, and vying for rule of the world. This seems to be related to Zurvanite Zoroastrianism, which was a widespread heretical version of Zoroastrianism in the Persian Empire. The Zurvanite idea of the two brother Gods having a father figure, called Zurvan, seems to be reflected in Mongolian and Korean narratives.[60]

Also present in the Zurvanite tradition is the reliance of the "Good" brother Ohrmazd on his evil counterpart Ahriman for the creation of light. In Zurvanite tradition, Ohrmazd sends a spirit to spy on Ahriman to obtain the secret of creating light. The spirit eventually overhears Ahriman speaking the secret out loud and reports it back to Ohrmazd. This is paralleled in Korea and Mongolia, where the secret of creating fire is obtained by the good creator from an intermediary, such as a hedgehog.[61] As we will see, the Slavic parallels to this narrative are also very compelling.

The Zurvanite myth also states that Ahriman gained temporary control over this world, and that Ohrmazd will only triumph over him after Ahriman has reigned on earth for 9,000 years. This is reflected in the succession narrative of the flower contest in East Asia, which often depicts the "bad" brother as gaining rule over the human world.

While Zurvanite cosmology does not necessarily demonize the material world altogether, the "pessimistic" view of the world as being temporarily ruled by an evil deity probably did set the stage for anti-materialist forms of dualism like Manichaeism. Manichaeism is a later development of Iranian religion which took this to an even more ideological extreme; For the Manichaeans, the material world itself was a prison ruled by the devil, which the light of the soul needed to escape from.[62]

Turkic nomads like the Uyghurs apparently adopted Manichaeism from Sogdians via the Silk Road. We have no evidence of this prior to the 8th century[63] but it's likely that religious influence from Sogdia on the Turkic peoples is as old as the northern Silk Road itself. If so, then the arrival of Manichaeism in Central Asia would indeed have been preceded by Sassanid Persian Zurvanism.

Zurvanism was widespread throughout the Sassanid Persian empire for much of the early 1st millennium CE.[64] This would have coincided with the participation of Sogdian traders in the northern Silk Road during the 4th to 7th centuries CE. The earliest evidence of an extensive network of Sogdian traders connecting the Persian and Chinese worlds is probably from the Sogdian letters of the 4th century, discovered in the ruins of a tower west of Dunghuang in China. One such letter discusses (in Sogdian) the trade prospects in the region, and the impact of the "Xwn" (Huns) who had just destroyed the Chinese city of Luoyang - until then the capitol of the Jin Dynasty. This apparently dates the letter to 311 CE, or shortly thereafter. Thus, 60 years before the arrival of the Huns in Eastern Europe, the Sogdian merchants and the Chinese were beginning to come into intense contact with a related group of nomads.[65]

The Sogdians for their part had practiced Zoroastrianism since the time of the Achaemenid Persian empire, starting in the 6th century BCE according to many scholars. As a people living just north of Persia, they were culturally and linguistically close relatives to the Persians. Their ties to Central Asia increased greatly after the Huns destroyed Luoyang in 311 CE. In 350 CE, the same "Huns" or "Chionites" are said to have invaded Sogdia and Bactria. The Sassanid Persian emperor Shapur II was forced to go to war with them to defend his eastern and northern provinces. By 360 CE, however, at least some of these "Hun" nomads from central Asia were fighting as mercenaries for Shapur II. Ten years later, in 370 CE, it seems a second branch of the same migration appeared in Eastern Europe as the "Huns" from Roman sources.[66]

Thus, from their earliest appearance in Eastern Europe in the 4th century CE, the Altaic nomads have long had ties to the Persian / Sogdian cultural sphere as well. However, it is not clear whether the European Huns themselves ever saw Sogdia or Persia. Possibly, they were from a separate branch that never made contact with the realm of Shapur II. They may have split from the Eastern "Xionites" prior to 350 CE for all we know. For later influxes of nomads in Eastern Europe, however, the ties to the Silk Road become more undeniable.

Following the arrival of the Xionites, a more significant empire seems to have been carved out by the Kidarites around Transoxiana in the 5th century CE. It seems clear that they absorbed influence from the former Silk Road populations like the Bactrians and the Yuezhi. It would be very surprising if the Kidarites were not familiar with Manichaeism and Zoroastrianism, at least superficially. Certainly, after the Kidarites and their relatives, the Hephthalites, conquered Bactria and Sogdia, it seems that East Iranian languages continued to be the languages of the state, and the primary religions practiced continued to be Buddhism and Zoroastrianism.[67]

It is likely that the Wusun and the Kangju - two Indo-European language speaking ethnic groups closely involved in the Silk Road, were at least partially absorbed into these eastern "Huns" at some point.[68] The Kangju were probably close relatives of the Sogdians, or a subset of Sogdians. The Wusun may have been Iranian or Tocharian language speakers - but even if they spoke Tocharian, they had likely adopted the religious traditions of the Silk Road long ago. (That is, mainly Buddhism, but also perhaps Manichaeism, and / or Zoroastrianism.)

With the rise of the Gokturk Khaganate in the 6th century, Sassanid Persian influence on the Eurasian steppe reaches its zenith. The Gokturk Khaganate adopted the Sogdian writing system for government administration, and the only Sogdian marriage contract we have attests to a Turkic/Sogdian mixed marriage.[69] Zoroastrianism was undoubtedly a major religion of the Gokturk Khaganate, especially among the predominantly Sogdian merchant class. However, it's believed that some Turkic elites adopted Zoroastrianism during this time as well.[70] It is worth noting that this all slightly predates the rise of Islam in the 8th century. It is from this setting of the Gokturk Khaganate that the Khazars, Bulgars, and Avars all migrated into Eastern Europe. There is even evidence of Zoroastrian style fire-temples built by the Bulgars in Europe.[71] So if we're talking about Silk Road influences on the Altaic people who entered Eastern Europe, and the impact on dualist belief systems, that's basically the whole story - as well as I can summarize here.

It essentially looks like Silk Road influences amplified and augmented an already existing "implicit" or near-dualist tradition in North Eurasia. Non-dualist creation stories probably coexisted with dualist creation stories in pre-Silk road Siberia, much as in the pre-Colombian Americas. With the influence of the Gokturk Khaganate, however, it looks like the mythological format for creation myths became more "standardized" throughout North Eurasia than in the Americas.

The number one case-in-point example of this is probably the tendency for North Eurasian myths to identify the "devil" with the earth-diver, thus making him the creator of the earth. This is totally unlike anything in the American myths listed thus far, and probably influenced by Sogdian Manichaeism. These Manichaean influences were probably disseminated throughout North Eurasia with the help of the Turkic migrations.

By contrast, the Paleosiberian "Proto-Myth" best reconstructed from North Eurasian and Native American creation stories probably had some kind of conflict between rival creators after the initial earth diving episode. Additionally, the "evil" figure may have been blamed for only one negative aspect of the world, like death or war. (e.g. as seen with "Little Coyote") Not necessarily all evil in existence. The "evil" nature of said deity may have been implicit at times, but the myth did not necessarily have an explicit doctrine or philosophy to guide the listener in judging the dispute. Therefore, the effect of Iranian influence may have been threefold;

- Standardization - a decrease in the diversity of North Eurasian creation stories, with dualist variants clearly being favored.
- A shift from implicit or ambiguous dualism to explicit moral dualism.
- In some cases, there was also a more pessimistic view of the world as something that the "evil" God now ruled over, or had even created.

But is that the whole story of Iranian dualism? This relates to a question many ask about Slavic paganism. Could the Iranian nomads of the classical world - the Scytho-Sarmatians, have introduced dualism to Eastern Europe earlier than the Huns? Or, is it possible at least that the Avestan tradition was part of a broader religious reform among Iranian peoples?

This is difficult to rule out. However, like with a lot of questions, there is a spectrum. The most extreme position would be that Zoroastrian style dualism is Proto-Iranian. This is not supported, however, by what little we know of the Ossetians or the Scythians.

We don't know a lot about the Scythian religion. Were they dualists like their fellow Iranian language speaking kin, the Zoroastrians? The one "reform" that can probably be substantiated is the rejection of the term "Daeva" (Cognate to

Sanskrit "Deva" meaning deity.) We do in fact see this among the Iranian nomads, much like in the Persian and Bactrian languages. In Slavic languages, the Iranian word for deity, "Bog" was borrowed from the Eurasian steppe.[72]

Another term used for deity was "Yazata." Specifically, in Zoroastrianism, these were the Good lesser deities ranking under Ahura Mazda. They were the exact opposite of the Daevas, who were considered unworthy of worship. This is paralleled in Khotanese Saka - an eastern Scythian language recorded in the Silk Road city of Khotan. In Khotanese Saka, "dyu" meant "demon" and "jasta" meant "deity."[73] Interestingly, in Saka Khotanese, "Urmaysde" is translated as "sun."[74]

This is a lot to unpack. It confirms that the Scythians, like the Avesta, probably conceived of the "Daeva" as an unworthy category of Gods. However, the fact that Ahura Mazda (Urmaysde) is a word for "sun" is not suggestive of Zoroastrianism. Rather, it probably shows that Ahura Mazda is a pre-Zoroastrian solar, day, or sky deity. Probably the same solar deity venerated as the supreme being by the Massagetae, another Iranian nomadic group. According to Herodotus, the Massagetae worshipped the Sun through horse sacrifice.[75] This parallels a Persian tradition, in which Ahura Mazda was thought to accompany the Persian army in an empty chariot drawn by white horses.[76]

The Zurvanite conception of Ahura Mazda as one of two divine brothers under the divine father might reflect the earlier, pre-Iranian conception of the deity. Specifically, it may show Zoroastrian dualism to be derived from the Indo-European concept of the divine twin horsemen. The exact same concept seems to be preserved in the Zoroastrian myth about the good horse deity Tishtrya and his adversary, the demonic horse Apaosha. These two battled in the forms of a white horse and black horse respectively.[77]

Interestingly, the Saka and Avestan languages seem closer to one another on religious terminology than to Ossetian in the west.

This could indicate that Avestan culture was most strongly linked to eastern, not western Scythian cultures. Certainly the pantheon of seven deities described by Herodotus among the western Scythians in Eastern Europe does not seem to indicate any break from traditional Indo-European polytheism. The Scythian pantheon appears fairly simple and polytheistic, with emphasis on natural forces like the sun, earth, and sea.[78] If we are talking about the Scythians living in Eastern Europe during the time of Herodotus, a dualist reform seems very doubtful for the culture described.

On the other hand, Herodotus's description of the Massagetae further east as a people who… "-only worship the sun" could in fact be interpreted as a Zoroastrian-like religious tradition.[79] It also differs greatly from Herodotus's description of the Pontic Scythian religion. This could indicate a religious reform of some kind taking place among the Scythians of Central Asia, but not yet influential in the Pontic region during the Classical period.

The evidence is scant, but it appears to indicate that the reforms of the Proto-Iranian religion were mainly concerned with the rejection of the "Daevas" as unworthy Gods. However, this parallels other Indo-European traditions like Norse and Indian mythology, which also speak of a conflict between two tribes or families of Gods.[80] This does not necessarily imply reform to the extent seen in Zoroastrianism, or even reform towards dualism.

More compelling is the idea of Zoroastrian-like ideas as being limited mainly to the Central Asian part of the Iranian world. This may have included Bactria during the time the Avesta was composed there, or somewhere very near to it. It may also have included the Saka and Massagetae to an extent.

It is worth noting that burial of bodies was anathema to the Zoroastrians[81] but archaeologists do see it being widely practiced in all the regions of Scythia. It seems that there is very little evidence for Zoroastrianism proper among the Scythians, although the possibility of a related tradition is hard to rule out.

The general consensus seems to be that the "Saka" Scythians around Khotan were not Zoroastrians. On the other hand, one suspects that at least the Scythian groups immediately bordering the Achaemenid empire were familiar with some aspects of Persian culture. The Dahae are one such group who were apparently subjects of the Achaemenid Empire, and even fought with Darius III against Alexander the Great.[82]

It may be that Zoroastrianism developed independently from North Eurasian near-dualist traditions, but then later syncretized with them. A second major possibility is that the Iranian nomads in Siberia actually came under North Eurasian influence. This could potentially have helped catalyze some religious reforms evident in the Avesta.

With so little historical data, it is possible that ancient DNA can shed some light on the historical migrations. Thankfully, we do now have a detailed picture of gene flow on the Eurasian steppe.

This somewhat augments the scarce historical data from the region. The most recent study from 2021, "*Ancient genomic time transect from the Central Asian Steppe unravels the history of the Scythians*" provides insight into the gene flow of the Central Asian steppe from 2,000 BCE up to the late 1st. Millennium CE.[83]

In short, the study by Gnecchi-Ruscone says that we do see significant admixture between the Central Asian pastoralist nomads of the bronze age, and Mongolian Steppe people from about 1400 BCE, up to 900 BCE. Over the same period, Middle Eastern gene flow from the south also enters the Central Asian Steppe. Interestingly, this fits fairly well with the time in which the Zoroastrian Avesta is thought to have been composed. The dating of both the Avestan language, and the first shift in central Asian DNA are imprecise- but it is noteworthy that they are within spitting distance of one another.

This makes a lot of sense, because we would expect religious reform to be the result of social and cultural change in Central

Asia. Admixture with three different cultural groups would provide a compelling reason for such cultural change. And clearly, periods of cultural admixture can be indirectly attested by gene flow.

The same study also shows that the final period of 600 BCE to 500 CE shows a "Persian-related influx" from the south, which is in line with the gradual development of northern silk-road contacts. This period of contact between the steppe and the Persian empire has already been discussed, and it's obvious that the same contacts are detectable in the form of gene flow.

However, this scenario would also imply that the dynamic period of cultural admixture came slightly after the split of Proto-Indo-Iranian (generally considered to be prior to 1400 BCE among linguists). Therefore, the admixture shown in the study probably does not represent the ethnogenesis of the Proto-Iranians themselves. Rather, it seems more like a period of rapid social development among the already slightly differentiated steppe Iranians of Central Asia. If we consider Zoroastrianism a reform of the Indo-Iranian religion under multiple foreign influences (or as a response to them) then we would still expect these reforms to be an eastern or southeastern phenomenon during the 2nd millennium BCE. In short, this would not apply to the entire Iranian world.

Interestingly, the gene flow does appear to confirm that later Iranian groups from Central Asia were pushed even farther west into Europe throughout the 1st millennium BCE. This was the beginning of the westward "tide" of migration that would culminate with the Huns from even farther East.

The Central Asian Scythian familiarity with Bactrian or Sogdian dualism is not impossible, but we have little evidence of it. Likewise for the admixture originating from the Mongolian steppe, which could have introduced some Paleosiberian influences to the Saka (Eastern Scythian) religion. However, if Iranian nomads did bring these ideas into Europe, it would be most likely with the latest "wave" (Sarmatians) some of whom had remained in Central Asia until about 100 BCE. It is also likely that the Huns absorbed significant elements of the easternmost Iranian nomads, like the Saka. For our purposes, that is significant, because the religious vocabulary of Khotanese Saka may suggest that the Easternmost Scythian cultures had greater affinity with Zoroastrian beliefs than those further west.

Thus, even if some Iranian nomads did have dualist ideas, these "dualist" Iranian nomads may have been herded into Europe by the Huns relatively late - perhaps not until the 4th century CE. Certainly, the 4th Century seems to mark a turning point in which the entire Eurasian Steppe became "Orientalized" or culturally more eastern than it had been previously. One suspects that elements of the easternmost Scythians were absorbed directly into the Hunnic horde. Even if "eastern" Scytho-Sarmatian groups like the Alans brought dualist ideas from Central Asia, this did not automatically mean that there was transmission to the Proto-Slavs. Even in this instance, it might only be with the Slavic expansion of the 6th century that large swaths of foreign peoples (and their ideas) were assimilated into the early Slavic culture. Additionally, the fact that Slavic dualist legends appear to all be associated with the earth-diver creation myth (A distinctively non-Iranian creation story) hints that they may all come from an Altaic source, like the Huns. The earth-diver myth is not attested in any known Iranian culture.

Overall, it doesn't seem far-fetched that the Alans were familiar with some elements of Persian culture. On the other hand, the Scythian nomads who inhabited the Pontic region in the time of Herodotus are not described as having any kind of reform from traditional polytheism, and there are historical reasons why this group, in particular, may have been insulated against cultural changes taking place on the Mongolian steppe and on the northern frontier of Middle Eastern agrarian society

- both of which could have introduced more "Zoroastrian-like" beliefs to the steppe Iranians.

Neither is this to say that Zoroaster "stole" or borrowed from other cultures in a direct sense. This is simply to say that religions are more likely to undergo reform when cultural change is occurring. Exposure to two different waves of foreign people could have therefore created the "demand" for religious reform, simply by causing a shift in lifestyle and / or values - particularly on the southern and eastern frontiers of the Iranian-speaking world.

It seems tempting to say that agricultural civilizations like Bactria and Margiana influenced the reforms of Zoroaster. In many of his teachings, the traditional values of nomadic pastoralism are challenged - which may imply that the old nomadic lifestyle was no longer as universally embraced. On the other hand, it is not until the Younger Avesta that we see clear evidence of an agrarian development in Iranian culture. The Older Avesta seems to portray a culture that is still highly nomadic.[84] Still, this does not contradict the evidence of early gene flow from neighboring farming populations in the south, which could have arrived from exogamous marriage or other practices that did not immediately impact local lifestyles.

Similarly, if we accept the dog / coyote narrative about the origin of death as Paleosiberian, there is some late evidence that a revised form of this narrative entered into Zoroastrianism, as mentioned previously. We might take this as an indication that the influence of the Mongolian steppe played a greater role in the Iranian religion than is often appreciated. Interestingly, researchers have determined that the East-Asian related ancestry prevalent in the Central Asian steppe from ~1700 BCE onward was not prevalent among the steppe nomads who contributed to Indian / South Asian populations.[85] Note that this pushes the admixture date back even further than the previously cited paper. Yet the absence of such ancestry among early Indian populations may suggest East-Asian like ancestry played a role in the differentiation of steppe Iranian and Indo-Aryan language speakers.

Slavic Background: From Chernobog to Hyssop Flowers

When examining the topic of dualism among the pagan Slavs, many have chosen to focus on a medieval manuscript written by the German missionary, Helmold, and to examine it in isolation. The reference, which dates to the 12th century CE is interesting, although in my opinion it can be considered of secondary importance to the earth-diver myth itself. The passage reads as follows:

> *There exists among the Slavs a strange delusion. At their feasts and carousals they pass around a drinking bowl over which they utter words, not of consecration but of execration, in the name of the gods – of the good one, as well as of the bad one – professing that all propitious fortune is arranged by the good god, adverse, by the bad god. This is why in their language they call the bad god Diabol or Zcerneboch, which means the black god."*[86]

The reference to the devil "Diabol" has led many to dismiss this as Christian influence. And it definitely does illustrate that the Pagan Polabian Slavs of the 12th century were fairly familiar with Christianity. Still, if these Polabians were still polytheistic, as Helmold says, one wonders why they would adopt the "Devil" as an isolated element of Christianity while continuing to fight against the religion itself.

Furthermore, the name "Chernobog" (rendered "Zcerneboch") is a native Slavic name meaning "Black God" just as Helmold claims it does. If nothing else, linguists agree his translation is correct. This name is clearly heretical from the Christian standpoint, because it actually acknowledges the devil as a "God" which would be anathema to Christianity.

Interestingly, Helmold describes a belief in a Deus Otiosus among the Polabian Slavs. That is, a belief in a Heavenly Father who does not intervene in worldly affairs, letting his divine children govern in his name.[87] This strengthens the case that the Polabian pagan cosmology had analogies to Uralic and Altaic cultures, where this concept is common. It often coincides with dualistic creation myths. For example, in the mythology of the Komi and of the Altaians. The Altaian creation myth cited below begins with a dualist struggle between "God" and his evil counterpart Erlik. Near the end, it contains the following passage:[88]

> *God then told the man he had made cattle, food, and good water for him; that he would soon go away not soon to return. Before doing so he gave directions to Yapkara, Mandy Shire, and Shal Yime to look after mankind in various ways.*

The concept of "Black Gods" does show up in Siberia as well, although typically it refers to a collection of deities or spirits. In Khanty mythology, there is a division between the "White Gods" of the upper world, and "Black" deities associated with disease and death in the underworld. This has been proposed as an archaic shared feature of Uralic mythologies.[89] The malevolent Khanty God of the underworld and disease, Kul, is sometimes referred as "Pykht Iki" which literally means "Black Man."[90]

Similar ideas are found in Mongolia. According to the Buryats, the 55 Gods of the West are good and referred to as "white." Those of the East are wicked and are referred to as "black."[91] All in all, the description of the Polabian religion by Helmold conforms quite well to a description of a religious tradition with ties to the rest of North Eurasia. This includes the famous reference to Chernobog, which appears very credible when placed in context.

The question of Altaic influence on the Polabian Slavs is tricky, because this is a group of Slavs that probably could not have been influenced by the Khazars or the Bulgars - not even indirectly. The Polabians lived far to the west, in what is today Northeast Germany. In this case, Uralic / Baltic influence may be plausible. However, we also should not rule out the fact that the Proto-Slavs fought alongside the Huns during the migration period, in which case we should not rule out Hunnicized Slavs reaching even as far west as Germany by the 12th Century. The Huns predated the Slavic migrations themselves, so any Hunnic influence on Slavic culture could in theory have spread to all Slavic tribes. The hybrid Avar-Slav culture of the Pannonian basin may also have influenced the Polabians, as shown by the diffusion of Danubian pottery styles from Pannonia to eastern Germany in the 7th century CE. As discussed previously, the impact of the Avar Khaganate on "Common Slavic" culture is not to be underestimated, even as far west as Polabia.

Of the Slavic creation myths found in folklore, it would seem that one from Bulgaria provides the richest example. This narrative is provided at the very end because it combines many of the elements discussed thus far, including the idea of God sending a spy to obtain a secret from his adversary (as seen in Zurvanite myth, with the creation of light). There is also a hint of a flower contest in this one. Both of these elements are covered in depth by Waida, Manabu's previously cited (and fantastic) article "The Flower Contest between Two Divine Rivals. A Study in Central and East Asian Mythology."

The Bulgarian myth, first recorded by Obst Trud II in 1868[92] is summarized below as follows:

At first there was no earth and no people. Everywhere was water. There was only the Lord and the devil. Once the Lord said to the devil: "Let us make the earth and people." The devil agreed, but asked how.

"There is dirt under the water," said the Lord; "go down and get some. But before you go down, say 'With God's power and mine!" Then you will reach the bottom and find dirt."

The devil went down but he did not say first "With God's power and mine!" Therefore he did not reach the bottom. He tried again and did not reach the bottom. Finally, the third time, he said "With God's power and mine!" and then he reached the bottom and grasped a little dirt. God took the dirt and put it on the water, and created a little dry land.

When the devil saw that, he thought up this piece of deceit: he proposed that they sleep; then, when the Lord had fallen asleep, he would push him into the water, and thus he (the devil) would be left alone, and he could take credit for having made the earth. The devil took the Lord in his hands, and started for the water, but the earth grew. As he did not reach the water, he turned in the other direction, but again he could not reach the water. Then he turned in the third direction, and when he did not reach the water, he put the Lord down and lay down also. When he slept a bit, it occurred to him that there was still a fourth direction. He picked up the Lord and carried him down toward the water, but still he could not reach it.

Then the devil roused the Lord: "Get up Lord, let us bless the earth!" But the Lord replied that he had already blessed it when the devil carried him in all four directions, and made a cross with him. The devil got mad and left. When the Lord was left alone and the earth had grown so big that the sun could not cover it, he created the bee, and sent it to spy on the devil.

The bee lit on the devil's should, and heard him saying, "Huh, what a stupid Lord!" He does not know enough to take a stick and make the sign of a cross to the four directions, and say "That is enough earth," but instead he wonders what to do!" When the bee heard that, she buzzed away.

The devil heard her and shouted "May he who sent you eat your excrement." Thus the Lord learned how to stop the earth from growing, and henceforth declared that no excrement should be sweeter than the bee's!"

After creating man, God invited the devil to live with him, but the devil insisted that he would do so on one condition: that the living people belong to the Lord, but the dead ones be his. The Lord agreed to this. After much time, the Lord saw that the dead were becoming more numerous than the living, and that the devil had more people than he did.

Eventually, God discovered another secret from the devil; That he could rescind the contract only in the following manner.

The Lord made a bouquet of flowers of hyssop, and put it on his bosom. He slept with it one night while thinking that he wished a son to be born from the spirit of God. He sent the angel Gabriel to bring the bouquet to the Virgin Mary. The angel said to her, "I bring you from God a gift of lovely flowers; smell it, and see how lovely it smells." She took the bouquet and smelled it. After two- or three-days Mary became pregnant.

Later Jesus Christ was born, and declared to the devil that he was taking the dead souls of man back from him. When the devil asked "How will you do that, when I have a contract with your father that the living shall be his, and the dead mine?" Jesus simply replied "You have a contract with my father, but not with me." The devil could do nothing. Thus ended 800,000 years of companionship between God and the Devil.

Conclusion: Summary on Chernobog

The genesis of the classic "Slavic type" of the dualist earth-diver creation myth seems to date back to the Bulgars and the Khazars, both offshoots of the Gokturk khaganate which was ruled by the Ashina clan. The Ashina clan aristocracy traced their roots back to the Turkic nomads of central Asia - close relatives of the Mongolians. However, at its full extent, the Gokturk Khaganate ruled over much of the Silk Road running through Sogdia, thus providing a link between China and Persia. As such, their empire was a meeting place of Central Asian Tengrist beliefs, Zoroastrianism, Buddhism, Manichaeism, and to a lesser extent probably Nestorian Christianity as well.

The specific narrative in which the devil is the one who dives for the earth seems to be a recent permutation of the narrative, one that post-dates many Central Asian narratives which explicitly avoid equating the earth-diver with the devil. Native American legends also tend to avoid equating the Earth-diver with a malevolent figure. The most tempting explanation is that this motif reflects Manichaean influences, specifically the Manichaean belief that the material world is a creation of the devil. This is further substantiated by the documented fact that one Turkic group - the Uyghurs - temporarily adopted Manichaeism via their Silk Road contacts in Sogdia. It is worth noting that this happened in the 8th Century CE - too late to impact the Bulgars or the Khazars. Still, one suspects this was not the first time Turkic nomads encountered Sogdian preachers or proselytizers. This had probably been happening since at least the Gokturk khaganate - in the 6th Century CE.

On the other hand, the Native American narratives do sufficiently show evidence of a struggle between rival creators - one of whom is malevolent towards humans or even treacherous towards his own family. Even in the Americas, it seems this often coincides with earth-diver and what I have dubbed "sea-boiler" myths, just as seen in Eurasia. Therefore, the paleolithic Siberian traditions that gave rise to these myths probably did have a hint of dualism, or something close enough to dualism to independently develop in that direction more than once on both sides of the Pacific.

The evidence for Manichaean influence on Altaic tradition is probably mired among many other layers as well. In addition to this, there may have been a Zurvanite Zoroastrian layer, as reflected in the flower succession motif illustrated by Manabu Waida.

At the same time, however, we should not ignore the possibility that Zoroastrianism was itself born out of a mixture of influences, as represented in ancient genomic data: specifically, the three-way mixture of Bactria-Margianan, Proto-Indo-Iranian, and Mongolian steppe populations that intermingled from about 1700 BCE up to about 900 BCE at the end. This range plausibly includes the time in which the religious reformer Zoroaster is thought to have lived, and possibly a couple of centuries before it as well. Therefore, the chronology fits quite well if we see this mixture as reflecting a period of cultural (as well as genetic) change which laid the foundations for religious reform.

The Manichaean variant of the earth-diver myth is distinctly un-pagan, and probably thousands of years more recent than North Eurasian dualism itself. In the archaic or ancient form of the myth, the diver was a water bird independent of Erlik, Chernobog, or the Devil - and the struggle between the two "creators" only came after the earth-diving episode. This non-Manichaean version is probably reflected in the Polabian mythology around Chernobog. This is consistent with the idea that Bulgars and Khazars brought the Manichaean variant into Europe, because the Polabians had probably not had contact with Altaic nomads since the time of the Huns. The only indirect Altaic influence they might have more recently come under is probably from the Avar-Slavic hybrid culture of the Pannonian basin, which did have a significant impact on the material culture of the Elbe Slavs (in what is today eastern Germany). Alternatively, this Polabian "Black God" could reflect Baltic influence absorbed into early Slavic culture. Baltic mythology may have been influenced by Finno-Ugric elements as much as it was influenced by Indo-European ones. As P.M. Barford attests, the Slavic migrations undoubtedly led to the assimilation of many Baltic peoples.

The narrative from the Southern Estonian people, the Setu, in which the "devil" figure "Vanapagan" pokes a hole in the body of the first human, making it susceptible to pain[93] raises some questions about the extent of these myths. It does seem to imply that some version of the dualist North Eurasian tradition was known to certain Finnic groups. This narrative could be indigenous to the Balto-Finnic region. In Finnish mythology, the underworld is portrayed negatively, but often in association with a frightening Goddess like the Finnish Louhi or Loviatar. According to Finnish mythology, Loviatar birthed eight boys named Consumption, Colic, Gout, Rickets, Ulcer, Scab, Cancer, and Plague, and they represented all ills and plagues of the Northland.[94] Although distinguished from Louhi in many tales, it seems Loviatar was originally interchangeable with her.[95] Certainly if you remove the "-tar" ending, meaning lady, "Lovi" and "Louhi" do not seem to have different etymologies.

This idea of a set number of plague spirits who are all siblings does show up in Russian folklore. However, in Russian folklore they are obviously not referred to as the sons of Loviatar. Rather, Russian folklore has it that the daughters of Herod (from the Bible) were swallowed up by hell. They supposedly became the personifications of the twelve "fevers" or twelve "convulsions." Their new "father" Satan was believed to dispatch them to cause suffering on earth, and many Russian healing charms were designed to expel them.[96] The inclusion of the Biblical "Herod" is obviously Christian. However, the choice of name could be related to the Hutsul "Aridnyk", and / or "Ordog" the Hungarian word for devil.

The Norse Loki, and his mother Laufey, may be relatives of the Finnish Louhi and Loviatar.[97] This would fit very well, because Loki engages in arguably "immoral" behavior, and was imprisoned in the underworld. According to Norse mythology, Loki will not break free until the fated time of Ragnarok (the end of the world) thus precipitating the final battle with the Gods and giants.

Similar stories were told by the Hutsuls about the Aridnyk - their folkloric "devil" figure. They believed the Aridnyk was imprisoned after participating in the creation of the world, and that he would break free to battle with the thunder-wielding Saint Elijah at the world's end. In much of Ukraine, it was common to say that making Easter Eggs tightened the chains of an evil monster, and that the monster would destroy the world if lots of Easter Eggs were not made.[98] Similar stories were told about the Altaian "devil" figure Erlik, and his role in bringing about Armageddon. In particular, one Altaian prophecy is remarkably close to the Norse description of Ragnarok:

> *Then will Erlik arise with Karan and Kerei, and will come to earth to fight with the heroes of Ülgen, Mandy-Shire and Mai-Tere, and the blood of Mai-Tere will burn the earth, and that will be the end of the world.*[99]

Interestingly, the Hutsuls of western Ukraine believed that the final battle between St. Elijah and the Aridnyk would have a similar outcome. According to Hutsul lore, the thundering saint's spilt blood will cause a conflagration that consumes the earth.[100]

Based on the evidence, the link between the Norse Loki and the Altaic Erlik is not quite as far-fetched as it may seem. When we speak of parallels between Mongolia and Scandinavia, however, we are probably speaking (in part) of Indo-European influences brought to Mongolia by the Indo-Iranians. The end-of the-world battle known as Ragnarok among the Norse is probably a reflex of a Proto-Indo-European myth. However, the "doomsday" monster archetype may have been a convenient scaffold for later dualistic influences to attach to in multiple IE cultures.

It seems likely that much of the character of "Loki" in Norse mythology reflects Finno-Ugric influence in Scandinavia. The tendency of Finno-Ugric mythology to denigrate the ruler of the underworld (Loki / Louhi) seems like Ancient North Eurasian residue, and it may have rubbed off in the depiction of the Norse Loki as well. In fact, even Loki's role as a "mother" of beasts may reflect conflation with the Finnish underworld Goddess Louhi / Loviatar. In Norse mythology, Loki plays "mother" to the monstrous serpent Jormungandr. Similarly, in Finnish folktales, Loviatar's eldest son is presented as a monstrous three-headed serpent or dragon.[101] It's not clear how Loviatar / Louhi may have morphed into Laufey and her son Loki. It's also unclear why the Norse Goddess of the underworld, Hel, is portrayed as Loki's daughter. Still, the connection seems very plausible overall.

In Finnish paganism, an entity called Lempo is also held responsible for diseases. Finnish healing charms often implore a figure called "Lempo" or "Piru" to extract his "arrow" from those who are afflicted with illness.[102] Recall also that in Mongolian mythology, diseases are introduced to man by Erleg Khan's spit.

The narratives around Lempo in Finland may be related to the Estonian (Setu) legend about Vanapagan introducing pain to humankind by spitting on the first human bodies, or "piercing" them with his finger. In the mythology of the Khanty (a Siberian Finno-Ugric people) the creator's adversary Kul is clearly associated with the underworld and with diseases.[103]

Finnish healing charms may refer to diseases as "Tuoni's grub." Disease in Finnish charms could also be called "Lempo's dog" or "Tuoni's dog."[104] Interestingly "Tuoni", "Lempo", or "Mana" can also refer to the primary male God of the underworld, and father of Loviatar. He is depicted as a frightful personage with three pointed iron fingers on each hand.[105] This is reminiscent of the Estonian Vanapagan, who pokes the human body with his finger and makes it sensible to pain for the first time.

It's likely that the Norse and Finnic people were familiar with a kind of North Eurasian "Loki" figure like Loki, Louhi, Tuoni, Kul, and Vanapagan; One who, if not morally "evil" was at least responsible for pain, death, and disease, and who was prophesied to bring about the end of the world. Additionally a monstrous snake or dragon like Jormungandr may have been "birthed" or created by this deity or by his daughter. This reconstruction may also summarize the oldest and most "primitive" layer of near-dualist tension involving a Loki / Tuoni / Louhi figure in early Balto-Slavic mythology. When combined with Avar or Hunnic influence, this could easily mutate into a more explicit dualism.

The most archaic dualist tradition in North Eurasia seems to be the one with emphasis on an agent of human suffering, and definitely not originally anti-materialist dualism, which had hostility to the material world. This version definitely seems more compatible with paganism.

Or so you would think. However, it's clear the pagan sorcerers of Beloozero in the 11th century were familiar with the more "Manichaean" style of dualism, in which the body goes to the devil and the soul to God. As we have seen, one Mordvin narrative is almost identical to the one from Beloozero, where mankind was created from a towel. This strengthens the case that the narrative springs from the former territory of Khazaria. However, it would be a mistake to see Manichaeism as more than just one shade of the many dualist or near-dualist schools of thought hidden within North Eurasian mythology.

Manichaean attitudes are probably reflected in Bulgarian apocrypha like "The Sea of Tiberias" which depicts the devil as the earth-diver, and therefore the first actor in the creation of the world. Once again, it seems the Bulgars and Khazars were especially successful in promoting legends that reflected this Manichaean philosophy.

However, we do not always see this in dualist legends of North Eurasia - for instance, one can find a Samoyed narrative that avoids this approach by making the adversary of the creator separate from the earth-diver.[106] The same distinction appears in some Mongolian myths.[107]

Among the Lebed Tatars as well, the earth diving episode happens independently of the dualist struggle.[108] Similarly, none of the Native American myths cited here identify the malevolent figure with the earth-diver itself. Therefore, the foundations of this legend are incredibly ancient, even paleolithic, but the "Diving Devil" variant probably is a product of the Gokturk Khaganate, and thus of the 6th or 7th century CE.

It is worth noting, however, that this is still early enough to belong to the Pre-Christian layer of Slavic culture. The Bulgars conquered the Balkans in the late 7th century CE, and Bulgaria was not Christianized until the 9th century CE.[109, 110] Likewise, the peak of Khazar influence on the East Slavs was probably the 8th - 9th centuries[111] whereas the baptism of Kiev took place at the end of the 10th century. Therefore, all of the myths recounted here can be considered "Pre-Christian" from the perspective of the Slavs. Personally, however, as a Slavic pagan, I strongly tend towards the more archaic (but still dualist) interpretation, one that rejects any Manichaean influences that are hostile to the material world.

Slavic Pagan Opinions and Author's Philosophy

My favorite North Eurasian creation narrative is probably the Komi-Zyrian one. The Komi-Zyrian narrative discusses the mother duck Chezh, who glides over the primordial waters and lays four eggs. Two eggs fall under the water, but two hatch into the rival demiurges; Jen and Omol. The truth and the lie. Later, she smashes her body on the waters, creating the earth. Jen and Omol dive to retrieve her eggs, not the earth. By smashing the eggs on the Earth Mother's body, they create the Sun and Moon.

This story brings a lot of balance to the philosophy of the narrative. We have a common parent figure to the two "Gods" and she is a goddess - not a father figure. This complements the Slavic narratives, which tell us nothing about the origins of the two male figures. It even provides balance in terms of the inclusion of a feminine figure. Like with Zurvanism, there is a monist implication that good and evil can be reconciled, or at least have been reconciled in the past. Yet they still exist independently in this world.

The mother figure in this narrative has many parallels to Ilmatar, the archaic Finnish Goddess of creation. In Finnish mythology, a duck nests in her lap to lay eggs. When Ilmatar moves, the eggs fall from her lap into the water, and the breaking of the eggs creates the earth, sky, and heavenly bodies.[112] Later her son Vainamoinen continues with the creation of the world, with help from various other figures like the "Great Bear" in the sky.

Additionally, however, the narrative has striking similarities to Iroquoian mythology in the Americas. For example, among one Iroquoian group (The Tuscarora) the twins Good Mind and Bad Mind are born of Sky Woman. She later dies, and her son Good Mind uses her head to create the sun. The other heavenly bodies are created with the rest of her body. This narrative also features an Earth Diving episode. This could indicate that elements of the Komi-Zyrian myth are incredibly archaic echoes of Paleosiberian culture.

It's difficult to square all of this with the parallels to Zurvanism, however. Zurvanite mythology has many parallels to the myths described just above, even to the extent that Ahriman is said to have killed his parent (Zurvan) by bursting out of his body violently, thus marking him as the 'bad" twin, and Ohrmazd as the good one. Zurvan is said to have pledged that the first-born son would claim kingship after "him." Consequently, Ahriman burst out of the womb early, ripping through Zurvan, in order to claim his right to rule.[113] Similarly, in some Iroquoian myths (e.g. that of the Oneida) the wicked brother forces his way out from his mother's armpit, and kills his mother. Later, he lies, telling his grandmother that his innocent brother is the one who killed their mother.[114] I won't try to prove that these are examples of cultural diffusion. For one, I'm not certain to what extent Zurvanite theology is North Eurasian - it may not be. However, if it isn't, then this is surely a remarkable convergence of dualist mythologies, and probably represents a universal truth; Evil can be part of a greater system, but rarely respects the value of preserving the system it is a part of.

The emphasis on lying is also a consistent part of the "evil" creator twin's mythology in many stories. In the case of the flower contest, we clearly see that the evil brother claims mastery of the universe (in a very Zurvanite manner) through deception. This primordial act of deception is said to have introduced unjust elements to the world. Similarly, in some East Slavic narratives[115] the evil one may be blamed for introducing deceit to the world by trying to kill "God" as he sleeps, and then denying it. This murder attempt is mirrored in one Mongolian creation story, although not necessarily as an explicit explanation for the origins of deceit. The identification of Jen and Omol with the "Truth" and the "Lie" also shows up in Komi mythology.[116] This may reflect "late" or "intermediate" influences from Zoroastrianism, which was frequently concerned with the struggle between "Truth" and "Untruth."[117]And from my own perspective, it is this obsession with "truth" that seems to be the most profound manifestation of dualist thinking. In my view, it is the struggle against untruth that provides the most compelling foundation for a dualist philosophy.

Zoroastrian influences in North Eurasia may have included, but were not necessarily limited to, Zurvanite theology. Again, the most plausible link is the Northern Silk Road, and the Turkic nomads who cooperated with Sogdian traders to bridge the two regions of North Eurasia and Iran. But we also cannot rule out older connections altogether.

Among Altaic cultures like the Mongols and Turks, we rarely see the prominence of a mother Goddess like the Finnish Ilmatar and the Komi-Zyrian Chezh. Altaic cultures are much more patriarchal in this respect, generally emphasizing a heavenly father figure (Tengri, Tengere) as the parent of the two rival creation deities. Even here, however, we see a balanced and nuanced view of dualism. In particular, with Buryat mythology, where the heavenly father presides over 55 "White Gods" and 44 "Black Gods."

This 55:44 formula may reflect a sophisticated dualist philosophy. And it illustrates how much more nuanced the Altaic dualist tradition was than, say Christianity. The implication is that the highest divinity has appointed both black and white deities. However, in "his" wisdom, he has appointed only slightly more benevolent than malevolent powers. There is some realism to this; Total good is unachievable and would likely sow the seeds of its own destruction. The next time you consider the question of good and evil, consider the balanced approach of achieving "good" in a 5 to 4 ratio, or something close to it. As human beings, it's likely that we will always have some preference for the things that bring us joy. Yet even our preferences must be moderated at times.

As the examples provided show, dualism divested of Abrahamic monotheism can be quite syncretic and pagan. The champions of Altaian mythology who will battle Erlik and his kin at the end of the world, Maitere, Mandyshire, are among the same divinities appointed by the creator before he retired from the world. As mentioned elsewhere, Maitere (or "Maitreya") is actually a Buddhist Boddhisattva! Another figure of Altaian mythology is Shal-Yime, an apparent form of the Indo-Iranian underworld God Yima / Yama. Shal-Yime is also appointed by a retired creator in Altaian mythology.[118, 119] The German missionary Helmold paints a very similar picture of the Slavic creator as a retiree with many divine children.

Another point worth raising is the divine twins - obviously, the Indo-European mythological motif of the divine twins could be interwoven into this narrative. However, the Khanty and Mansi probably got it right by separating the two. According to them, the founders of the two paternal clans or phratries of Ugric peoples were sons of the Sky Father, Num Torum. These two brothers were both seen as distinct from Num Torem's malevolent adversary, Kul.[120] The Komi-Permyaks also believed they were descended from the two brothers Osjas and Ozjas, whom they did not conflate with the dualist adversaries Jen and Omol.[121]

It is possible that these dualist ideas could be grafted onto the cult of the divine twins described in Chapter 8. I am speaking of Dazhbog and Volos. However, it may also have been obvious that these traditions had separate origins. The cult of the divine twins is Indo-European, whereas the north Eurasian Dualist tradition has Paleosiberian origins. And if the Uralic peoples are any indication, this distinction was not entirely lost with time. Furthermore, as discussed in Chapter 6: Advanced Concepts in Indo-European Mythology, the Proto-Indo-Europeans may have believed in multiple generations of divine twins. If that's the case, then the dualistic pair of brothers could easily be inserted into an older generation preceding Dazhbog and Volos. As sons of Svarog, Dazhbog and Volos may have been assigned the roles of second-generation divine twins. In fact, this may be similar to what happened with many Uralic peoples like the Khanty. It's noteworthy that the Altaians also spared "Shal-Yime" (Yama) from demonization, and preserved him as an honorable mythological figure distinct from Erlik. Shal-Yime is an Altaian survival of the Indo-Iranian Yama / Yima, who was the God of the Underworld initially. Yet it is noteworthy that even in modern times, Altaians have tended to identify him with the Biblical

Adam rather than Satan.[122] This speaks to his early integration as a positive figure within a dualist framework. In Zoroastrianism as well, Yima was remembered as the first man and first King, who reigned over a period of prosperity. It is noteworthy that he was especially venerated by Iranian peoples in Central Asia.[123]

We also know that the Persians were remarkably syncretic and tolerant of many religions until the rise of Christianity. It's no coincidence that the modern Farsi word for the planet Venus (Nahid) comes from the Persian Goddess Ardvi Sura Anahita! This tradition apparently coexisted with Zoroastrianism. Her name seems to have originally referred to the Indo-Iranian Goddess Sarasvati.[124]

Neopagans in the West tend to assume dualism would have vanished without Christianity. However, many of the dualist traditions that developed across Asia might still have remained far more "pagan" than monotheistic. This idea of a dualist struggle seems to have been historically compatible with polytheism. Only in its Abrahamic monotheistic form would the dualist emphasis on morality be conflated with adherence to a strictly monotheistic orthodoxy.

It is possible that Manichaeism also acted as an intermediary for Iranian dualism in some cases - however, it seems doubtful that hordes of Hunnic and Turkic nomads became ascetics who shunned the material world. Therefore, even where Manichaean influence did reach Altaic peoples, it's likely that the borrowing was highly selective. The true nature of North Eurasian dualism was not hostile to the material world, and rightly regarded it as holy. Indeed, anti-materialist dualism encouraged a cowardly retreat from the world's problems, which was quite contrary to the heroic values of our Pre-Christian ancestors.

Endnotes

1. Ivanits, L. J. (1989). Russian folk belief. Armonk, N.Y. M.E. Sharpe. Page 41

2. Kotšîûbyns'kyĭ, Mykhaĭlo, et al. Shadows of Forgotten Ancestors. United States, Canadian Institute of Ukrainian Studies, 1981. Pages 47-48
3. Gieysztor, Aleksander. Mitologia Slowian. Warszawa: Wydawn. Uniw. Warszawskiego, 2006.
4. Costin, Claudia. Folkloric Aspects of the Romanian Imaginary and Myth. United Kingdom, Cambridge Scholars Publishing, 2018. Page 88
5. Nicoloff, Assen. Bulgarian Folklore. United States, A. Nicoloff, 1983. Page 31
6. Tautosakos darbai. Lithuania, Academia, 1996. Page 56
7. Stoyanov, Yuri, and Yuri Stoyanov. The Other God: Dualist Religions from Antiquity to the Cathar Heresy. New Haven: Yale Nota Bene, 2000. Page 133
8. Acta Ethnographica Hungarica. Hungary, Akadémiai Kiadó, 2006. Page 315
9. Stoyanov, Yuri, and Yuri Stoyanov. The Other God: Dualist Religions from Antiquity to the Cathar Heresy. New Haven: Yale Nota Bene, 2000. Pages 132-136
10. Leeming, David Adams. Creation Myths of the World: An Encyclopedia. Ukraine, ABC-CLIO, 2010. Page 195
11. Stoyanov, Yuri, and Yuri Stoyanov. The Other God: Dualist Religions from Antiquity to the Cathar Heresy. New Haven: Yale Nota Bene, 2000. Page 135
12. The Cambridge Medieval History: The Christian Roman empire and the foundation of the Teutonic kingdoms. United Kingdom, Macmillan, 1911. Pages 345-346
13. Berezkin, Y. "The Dog, the Horse and the Creation of Man." Folklore (Estonia). 56 (2014): 25-46.
14. Konakov, Nikolaj D, Vladimir V. Napol'skih, Anna L. Siikala, Mihály Hoppál, and Sergej Belyh. Komi Mythology. Budapest: Akadémiai Kiadó, 2003. Page 371
15. Acta Ethnographica Hungarica. Hungary, Akadémiai Kiadó, 2006. Page 315

16. Dynda, Jiří. "Slavic Anthropogony Myths. Body and Corporeality in the Slavic Narratives about the Creation of Man." New researches on the religion and mythology of the Pagan Slavs (2019): n. pag.
17. Leeming, David A, and David A. Leeming. Creation Myths of the World: An Encyclopedia. Santa Barbara, Calif: ABC-CLIO, 2010. Page 38
18. The Folk-lore Journal. United Kingdom, Folk-lore Society, 1889. Pages 76-77
19. Graymont, Barbara. The Iroquois. United States, Facts On File, Incorporated, 2009. Page 7
20. Leeming, David A, and David A. Leeming. Creation Myths of the World: An Encyclopedia. Santa Barbara, Calif: ABC-CLIO, 2010. Pages 91-92
21. Stoyanov, Yuri, and Yuri Stoyanov. The Other God: Dualist Religions from Antiquity to the Cathar Heresy. New Haven: Yale Nota Bene, 2000. Pages 132-136
22. The Folk-lore Journal. United Kingdom, Folk-lore Society, 1889. Pages 75-76
23. Gemuev, I N, and Vladimir Napolskikh. Mansi Mythology. Budapest: Akademiai Kiado, 2008. Page 160
24. Wiget, Andrew, and Balalaeva, Olga. Khanty, People of the Taiga: Surviving the 20th Century. United States, University of Alaska Press, 2011. Page 105
25. Konakov, Nikolaj D, Vladimir V. Napol'skih, Anna L. Siikala, Mihály Hoppál, and Sergej Belyh. Komi Mythology. Budapest: Akadémiai Kiadó, 2003. Page 371
26. Wiget, Andrew, and Balalaeva, Olga. Khanty, People of the Taiga: Surviving the 20th Century. United States, University of Alaska Press, 2011. Pages 106-107
27. Tambets, K. Yunusbayev, B. Hudjashov, G. et al. Genes reveal traces of common recent demographic history for most of the Uralic-speaking populations. Genome Biol 19, 139, 2018.
28. Kassian, A. Starostin, G. Egorov, I. Logunova, E. & Dybo, A. (2021). Permutation test applied to lexical reconstructions partially

supports the Altaic linguistic macrofamily. Evolutionary Human Sciences, 3, E32.

29. Dalby, Andrew. Dictionary of Languages: The Definitive Reference to More Than 400 Languages. United Kingdom, Bloomsbury Publishing, 2015. Page 18
30. Forsyth, James. A History of the Peoples of Siberia: Russia's North Asian Colony 15811990. Brazil, Cambridge University Press, 1994. Page 12
31. Zhirohov, Mikhail, and Nicolle, David. The Khazars: A Judeo-Turkish Empire on the Steppes, 7th–11th Centuries AD. United Kingdom, Bloomsbury Publishing, 2019. Page 8
32. The Folk-lore Journal. United Kingdom, Folk-lore Society, 1889. Pages 75-76
33. Barford, Paul M. The Early Slavs: Culture and Society in Early Medieval Eastern Europe. United Kingdom, Cornell University Press, 2001. Pages 99, 238
34. Dynda, Jiří. "Slavic Anthropogony Myths. Body and Corporeality in the Slavic Narratives about the Creation of Man." New researches on the religion and mythology of the Pagan Slavs (2019): n. pag.
35. Cole, Jeffrey. Ethnic Groups of Europe: An Encyclopedia. United Kingdom, ABC-CLIO, 2011. Page 269
36. Bulletin. United Kingdom, The Society, 1982. Page 24
37. Pukanec, Martin. The Kiev Leaflets as Folia Glagolitica Zempliniensia. United Kingdom, Cambridge Scholars Publishing, 2020. Page 9
38. Barford, Paul M. The Early Slavs: Culture and Society in Early Medieval Eastern Europe. United Kingdom, Cornell University Press, 2001. Pages 67, 77-78, 96
39. Zaroff, Roman. "The Avar Impact on Socio-Political Developments Among the Western and Southern Slavs." Proceedings of The University of Queensland History Research Group 10 (1999): 1–10.
40. Crossley, Pamela Kyle. Hammer and Anvil: Nomad Rulers at the Forge of the Modern World. United States, Rowman & Littlefield Publishers, 2019. Pages 58-59

41. Barford, Paul M. and Barford, Paul M. The Early Slavs: Culture and Society in Early Medieval Eastern Europe. United Kingdom, Cornell University Press, 2001. Page 43
42. Zaroff, Roman. "The Avar Impact on Socio-Political Developments Among the Western and Southern Slavs." Proceedings of The University of Queensland History Research Group 10 (1999): 1–10.
43. Konakov, Nikolaj D, Vladimir V. Napol'skih, Anna L. Siikala, Mihály Hoppál, and Sergej Belyh. Komi Mythology. Budapest: Akadémiai Kiadó, 2003. Page 371
44. Leeming, David Adams. Creation Myths of the World: An Encyclopedia. Ukraine, ABC-CLIO, 2010. Page 195
45. Stoyanov, Yuri, and Yuri Stoyanov. The Other God: Dualist Religions from Antiquity to the Cathar Heresy. New Haven: Yale Nota Bene, 2000. Page 161
46. Waida, Manabu. "The Flower Contest between Two Divine Rivals. A Study in Central and East Asian Mythology." Anthropos, vol. 86, no. 1/3, 1991, pp. 87–109
47. Kots͡iu͡byns'kyĭ, Mykhaĭlo, et al. Shadows of Forgotten Ancestors. United States, Canadian Institute of Ukrainian Studies, 1981. Pages 47-48
48. Leeming, David Adams. Creation Myths of the World: An Encyclopedia. Ukraine, ABC-CLIO, 2010. Page 195
49. Encyclopedia of Korean Folk Literature. South Korea, National Folk Museum of Korea, 2014. Page 85
50. Waida, Manabu. "The Flower Contest between Two Divine Rivals. A Study in Central and East Asian Mythology." Anthropos, vol. 86, no. 1/3, 1991, pp. 104-106
51. Balzer, Marjorie M. Religion and Politics in Russia: A Reader, 2015. Internet resource. Page 249
52. Waida, Manabu. "The Flower Contest between Two Divine Rivals. A Study in Central and East Asian Mythology." Anthropos, vol. 86, no. 1/3, 1991, pp. 102) As we will see, a "sea boiler" myth can also be found in the Americas.

53. Leeming, David Adams. Creation Myths of the World: An Encyclopedia. Ukraine, ABC-CLIO, 2010. Pages 291-292
54. Leeming, David Adams. Creation Myths of the World: An Encyclopedia. Ukraine, ABC-CLIO, 2010. Pages 291-292
55. American Indian Myths and Legends. Toronto: Random House, 1984. Pages 470-471
56. Leeming, David Adams. Creation Myths of the World: An Encyclopedia. Ukraine, ABC-CLIO, 2010. Page 195
57. Leeming, David Adams. Creation Myths of the World: An Encyclopedia. Ukraine, ABC-CLIO, 2010. Pages 91-92
58. Berezkin, Y. "The Dog, the Horse and the Creation of Man." Folklore (Estonia). 56 (2014): 25-46.
59. Balzer, Marjorie M. Religion and Politics in Russia: A Reader. 2015. Internet resource. Page 249
60. Waida, Manabu. "The Flower Contest between Two Divine Rivals. A Study in Central and East Asian Mythology." Anthropos, vol. 86, no. 1/3, 1991, pp. 104-105
61. Waida, Manabu. "The Flower Contest between Two Divine Rivals. A Study in Central and East Asian Mythology." Anthropos, vol. 86, no. 1/3, 1991, pp. 105-106
62. Stoyanov, Yuri, and Yuri Stoyanov. The Other God: Dualist Religions from Antiquity to the Cathar Heresy. New Haven: Yale Nota Bene, 2000. Pages 108-113
63. Stoyanov, Yuri, and Yuri Stoyanov. The Other God: Dualist Religions from Antiquity to the Cathar Heresy. New Haven: Yale Nota Bene, 2000. Page 116
64. Stoyanov, Yuri, and Yuri Stoyanov. The Other God: Dualist Religions from Antiquity to the Cathar Heresy. New Haven: Yale Nota Bene, 2000. Pages 99-101
65. Vaissière, Étienne. Sogdian Traders: A History. 2017. Internet resource. Pages 40-46
66. Kim, Hyun Jin. The Huns, Rome and the Birth of Europe. United Kingdom, Cambridge University Press, 2013. Pages 36-37

67. Wink, André. Al-Hind: Early medieval India and the expansion of Islam, 7th-11th centuries. Netherlands, Brill, 2002. Page 110
68. Kim, Hyun Jin. The Huns, Rome and the Birth of Europe. United Kingdom, Cambridge University Press, 2013. Page 42
69. de la Vaissière, Étienne. Sogdian Traders: A History. Netherlands, Brill, 2018. Pages 200-201
70. Great Journeys Across the Pamir Mountains: A Festschrift in Honor of Zhang Guangda on His Eighty-fifth Birthday. Netherlands, Brill, 2018. Page 124
71. Stoyanov, Yuri, and Yuri Stoyanov. The Other God: Dualist Religions from Antiquity to the Cathar Heresy. New Haven: Yale Nota Bene, 2000. Page 384
72. Vernadsky, George. Kievan Russia. United Kingdom, Yale University Press, 1973. Page 50
73. History of Civilizations of Central Asia. India, Motilal Banarsidass, 1999. Page 316
74. Boyce, Mary. A History of Zoroastrianism: The Early Period. Germany, E.J. Brill, 1989. Page 39
75. Nomads of the Eurasian Steppes in the Early Iron Age. United States, Zinat Press, 1995. Page 249
76. Urban, Thomas G. and Burgan, Michael. Empires of Ancient Persia. United States, Facts On File, Incorporated, 2009. Page 105
77. Journal of the American Oriental Society. United Kingdom, American Oriental Society. 1917. Page 313
78. Jacobson, Esther. The Art of the Scythians: The Interpenetration of Cultures at the Edge of the Hellenic World. Germany, E.J. Brill, 1995. Page 53
79. Alemany, Agustí. Sources on the Alans: A Critical Compilation. Germany, Brill, 2000. Page 298
80. Cahill, Michael A. Paradise Rediscovered: The Roots of Civilisation. Australia, Glass House Books, 2012. Page 848
81. Encyclopedia of Death and Dying. United Kingdom, Taylor & Francis, 2003. Page 67

82. Sidnell, Phil. Warhorse: Cavalry in Ancient Warfare. United Kingdom, Bloomsbury Publishing, 2007. Page 108
83. Ancient genomic time transect from the Central Asian Steppe unravels the history of the Scythians, By Guido Alberto Gnecchi-Ruscone, Elmira Khussainova, et al. Science Advances 26 MAR 2021: EABE4414
84. The Cambridge History of Iran. United Kingdom, Cambridge University Press, 1985. Page 662
85. Narasimhan, Vagheesh & Patterson, Nick & Moorjani, Priya & Rohland, Nadin & Bernardos, Rebecca & Mallick, Subhashis & Lazaridis, Iosif & Nakatsuka, Nathan & Olalde, Iñigo & Lipson, Mark & Kim, Alexander & Olivieri, Luca & Coppa, Alfredo & Vidale, Massimo & Mallory, James & Moiseyev, Vyacheslav & Kitov, Egor & Monge, Janet & Adamski, Nicole & Reich, David. (2019) The formation of human populations in South and Central Asia. Science. 365.)
86. On the Concept of Chernebog and Bielbog in Slavic Mythology. Collegivm Slavicvm Academiae Hokkaido, n.d. Internet resource.
87. Europe's Centre Around AD 1000. Germany, Theiss, 2000. Page 158
88. Drahomaniv, Mykhailo Petrovych, et al. Notes on the Slavic Religio-ethical Legends: The Dualistic Creation of the World. Netherlands, Indiana University, 1961. Pages 46-47
89. Leete, Art. (2017). Landscape and Gods Among the Khanty. Journal of Ethnology and Folkloristics. 11. 19-38. 10.1515/jef-2017-0003.
90. Balalaeva, Olga, and Wiget, Andrew. Khanty, People of the Taiga: Surviving the 20th Century. United States, University of Alaska Press, 2011. Page 107
91. Czaplicka, Marie Antoinette. The Collected Works of M.A. Czaplicka: The Turks of Central Asia. United Kingdom, Curzon Press, 1999. Page 283

92. Drahomanov, M P, and Earl W. Count. Notes on the Slavic Religio-Ethical Legends: The Dualistic Creation of the World. Bloomington: Indiana Univ, 1961. Pages 1-5
93. Berezkin, Y. "The Dog, the Horse and the Creation of Man." Folklore (Estonia). 56 (2014): 25-46.
94. Comparetti, Domenico. The Traditional Poetry of the Finns. India, Longmans, Green and Company, 1898. Page 201
95. Comparetti, Domenico. The Traditional Poetry of the Finns. India, Longmans, Green and Company, 1898. Page 200-201
96. Ivanits, Linda J. Russian Folk Belief. United Kingdom, Taylor & Francis, 2015. Page xxxiv
97. Haavio, Martti. Suomalainen mytologia. Finland, Werner Söderström Osakeyhtiö, 1967. Page 393
98. Surmach, Yaroslava. Ukrainian Easter Eggs. United States, Surma, 1957. Page 4
99. Zhirmunsky, Victor, et al. Oral Epics of Central Asia. United Kingdom, Cambridge University Press, 2010. Page 168
100. Koenig, Samuel. Cosmogonic Beliefs of the Hutsuls. 1936.
101. Scandinavian Folk & Fairy Tales: Tales from Norway, Sweden, Denmark, Finland, Iceland. Norway, Avenel Books, 1984. Pages 565-567
102. Abercromby, John. Finnish Magic Songs. 2018. Internet)
103. Wiget, Andrew, and Balalaeva, Olga. Khanty, People of the Taiga: Surviving the 20th Century. United States, University of Alaska Press, 2011. Page 90
104. Magic Songs of the West Finns: The Pre and Proto Historic Finns (Complete). N.p. Library of Alexandria, 2020.
105. Lönnrot. The Kalevala: The Epic Poem of Finland. N.p. Lulu.com, 2016. Page 9
106. Stoyanov, Yuri, and Yuri Stoyanov. The Other God: Dualist Religions from Antiquity to the Cathar Heresy. New Haven: Yale Nota Bene, 2000. Page 132
107. Leeming, David Adams. Creation Myths of the World: An Encyclopedia. Ukraine, ABC-CLIO, 2010. Page 195

108. Eliade, Mircea. History of Religious Ideas, Volume 3: From Muhammad to the Age of Reforms. United States, University of Chicago Press, 2013. Page 9
109. The Other Europe in the Middle Ages: Avars, Bulgars, Khazars, and Cumans. Netherlands, Brill, 2008. Pages 137
110. Obolensky, Dimitri. The Bogomils: A Study in Balkan Neo-Manichaeism. United Kingdom, Cambridge University Press, 2004. Page 71
111. Sdobnikov, IŪriĭ Andreevich, and Grekov, Boris Dmitrievich. Kiev Rus: Transl, from the Russian by Y. Sdobnikov. Russia, Foreign Languages Publishing House, 1959. Page 49
112. Leeming, David Adams. Creation Myths of the World: An Encyclopedia. Ukraine, ABC-CLIO, 2010. Page 109
113. Zaehner, Robert Charles. Zurvan: A Zoroastrian Dilemma. United Kingdom, Biblo and Tannen, 1972. Page 66
114. Leeming, David Adams. Creation Myths of the World: An Encyclopedia. Ukraine, ABC-CLIO, 2010. Page 21
115. Kotsiubyns'kyĭ, Mykhaĭlo, et al. Shadows of Forgotten Ancestors. United States, Canadian Institute of Ukrainian Studies, 1981. Pages 47-48
116. Konakov, Nikolaj D, Vladimir V. Napol'skih, Anna L. Siikala, Mihály Hoppál, and Sergej Belyh. Komi Mythology. Budapest: Akadémiai Kiadó, 2003. Page 371
117. Redner, Harry. Ethical Life. United Kingdom, Rowman & Littlefield, 2001. Page 118
118. Zhirmunsky, Victor, et al. Oral Epics of Central Asia. United Kingdom, Cambridge University Press, 2010. Page 168
119. Drahomaniv, Mykhailo Petrovych, et al. Notes on the Slavic Religio-ethical Legends: The Dualistic Creation of the World. Netherlands, Indiana University, 1961. Pages 46-47
120. Balalaeva, Olga, and Wiget, Andrew. Khanty, People of the Taiga: Surviving the 20th Century. United States, University of Alaska Press, 2011. Pages 106-108

121. Konakov, Nikolaj D, Vladimir V. Napol'skih, Anna L. Siikala, Mihály Hoppál, and Sergej Belyh. Komi Mythology. Budapest: Akadémiai Kiadó, 2003. Pages 239-240
122. Chadwick, Nora K. et al. Oral Epics of Central Asia. United Kingdom, Cambridge University Press, 2010. Page 168
123. Kuz'mina. The Origin of the Indo-Iranians. Netherlands, Brill, 2007. Page 190
124. An Introduction to Ancient Iranian Religion: Readings from the Avesta and Achaemenid Inscriptions. United States, University of Minnesota Press, 1983. Page 119

Chapter 12

Vaguely but Firmly Attested Deities

Unfortunately, not every deity in the Slavic pantheon can have a 20-page chapter. There are some Slavic deities who can be discussed fairly briefly. They appear in this chapter because they are well-substantiated, but the details on them are limited. This is more or less how a lot of scholars treat Slavic deities in general. I hope I have shown that there is legitimate detail to be explored behind some Slavic Gods. In particular, Mokosh, Perun, Volos, the Zoryas, and Dazhbog can all be connected to a detailed network of Eurasian mythological traditions. The dualist narratives of Slavic folklore are also deeply rooted in Eurasian tradition. The following deities are a legitimate part of the Slavic tradition, but it would be difficult to expound upon them in detail.

Cult of the Mountain God: Svyatogor

Perhaps the most detailed analysis in this chapter will be related to the cult of the mountain God. There is some pervasive evidence that such a deity (or class of deities) was widespread among the Slavic tribes. We don't see an abundance of evidence for a Mountain God in the Russian Primary Chronicle, and there's not much indication of one among the Polabian Slavs either. However, that's not entirely surprising, because one would expect that Mountain God cults would be restricted mainly to mountainous regions. Perhaps this is why the evidence is so patchy. However, there are some fragments that attest to vigorous Mountain God cults among some Slavic groups.

One such figure is the giant "Svyatogor" from the Russian epic songs, or byliny. One bylina about Svyatogor has already been mentioned briefly in Chapter 8: Svarozhichi - Sons of Svarog. I argued previously that the ploughman Mykula and the mysterious "Blacksmith of Destinies" in this song correspond to Volos and Dazhbog respectively. In this bylina, the giant Svyatogor appears in the same narrative as the smith and the plowman, and Svyatogor is actually the main character.[1] The fact that he seems to appear beside two major Slavic divinities (the plowman and smith) could indicate that Svyatogor was also an important mythological figure at one time. It is extremely noteworthy that the name "Svyatogor" means "Holy Mountain."

In the narratives of the byliny, Svyatogor ultimately ends up dying. He comes across a glass coffin and lies down in it. When the coffin is sealed, he finds that he can no longer escape, and he accepts his death. This reads very much like a eulogy to paganism. Yet ironically, this narrative also preserves no less than three Slavic divinities - so it has also helped keep them alive, in a sense. In order to pass the torch to the new hero, Illya of Muromets, Svyatogor gives up a portion of his strength, and his magnificent sword.[2] As we will see, this is not the only Slavic narrative in which a giant associated with mountains passes away, or in which he gives up a magical sword.

There is a story in the folktale collection from Antoni Jozef Glinski which also features a giant "mountain-head" who gives up a magical sword to the hero. The title of this tale is "The Whirlwind."[3]

However, many scholars write this off as a rip-off of Pushkin's "Ruslan and Ludmila", which has the exact same episode of a giant mountain head yielding up a magical sword to a hero.[4] Regardless of the origins of the tale, however, it can be regarded as an independent corroboration that adds to the evidence of Svyatogor. (Or a figure from which Svyatogor was derived.) Pushkin's "Ruslan and Ludmila" was actually published in 1820. That's significant because the bylina tradition surviving in the far north of Russia was not widely known until at least 1861 - that's when Rybnikov published his first samples of byliny from the Olonec region.[5] In short, the giant head who gives up his magical sword in Pushkin's "Ruslan and Ludmila" actually predates widespread awareness about the bylina of Svyatogor, and therefore the bylina was probably not an influence on Pushkin. It's unclear what folk traditions Pushkin drew upon for this book, which is ultimately a literary creation, but some basis in Russian folklore is almost certain.

But there is another odd element in Glinski's tale, which I have not been able to corroborate from any literary Russian source. That's the idea of the giant mountain-head having "basilisk-eyes" that will turn hapless adventurers into stone. From what I can tell, the giant head from Pushkin's tale actually does not have this attribute. It's not clear to me where Glinski got the idea of a mountain-head with "basilisk-eyes." And that's fairly bizarre because there is an Ob-Ugrian mountain God who has the exact same ability. Specifically, the Mansi mythological figure Nor-Ojka is a mountain deity who has the ability to turn adversaries to stone with his gaze. He is one of the sons of the Sky Father, Num-Torem.[6] As we have seen, the Slavic deities Dazhbog and Volos may have had counterparts among the sons of Num-Torem. As I argue in Chapter 8: Svarozhichi - Sons of Svarog, these two sons of Svarog may have corresponded to the two divine ancestors of the Mos and Por phratries among the Ob-Ugrians. If Num-Torem had a mountain deity son, then it's quite possible that the Slavic Svarog did as well.

Poland is a long way from the Mansi of western Siberia. Overall, the most likely explanation is that the motif of "basilisk-eyes" was borrowed by Glinski from an East Slavic folktale of some sort. We know that many of his tales were actually of Belarusian origin, rather than Polish. If that's the case, then this may yet be another corroboration of a connection between Ob-Ugrian and East Slavic folklore.

If we look to the South Slavs, we find a relative of the severed-Giant head in another tale from Slovenia. It is interesting that this tale has so many parallels to Pushkin's story. All in all, it seems unlikely that this element of Pushkin's story was a literary creation. He must have heard some type of Slavic folktale that led to the creation of his "giant head."

In Slovenia, it was said that a giant named Robavs lived in Borovlje and a giant named Rogovilez lived in Mojstrana. One day the Fates (Zark Zene) set a giant snake on Rogovilez, which killed him. His head was taken by the shepherds to the top of Mt. Zolozen, where it turned to stone. Legend says the head remains there to this day.[7]

I would be remiss if I did not mention the evidence for a mountain cult among the Western Slavs. During a visit to Niemcza in Southwest Poland, Thietmar mentions that the Sleza mountain (from which we get the region name Silesia) was once worshipped in pagan times. Similarly, Cosmas of Prague spoke of Czech peasants making offerings to hills and mountains even in the 12th century.[8]

Interestingly, it seems there is a modest cult of Svyatogor among Russian Rodnovers.[9] This was a pleasant surprise to me because I hadn't thought there would be. Based on this brief analysis, it would seem they are on the right track. In short, the tale of Svyatogor reflects some kind of Pre-Christian Slavic deity.

Cult of Dodola

The Cult of Dodola is attested mainly in the Balkans. Also known as "Perperuna", she was worshipped for her ability to provide rain in Bulgaria and Macedonia. Water was poured over a youth playing the part of the goddess, and wine was drunk in honor of the deliverer of rain. Old Russian sermons condemning the "whirling" dancers who honor Pereplut might be related as well. It's commonly thought she was a consort of Perun, and that her name is related to Lithuanian Dundulis (Thunder, rumbling).[10]

There are Polish clerical texts that talk about "Dziedzielelya" who is identified with Venus.[11] In Poland, the name Gromnica comes from the Slavic word for thunder (Grom). It refers to a Holiday dedicated (allegedly) to St. Mary on February 2nd. Candles that are blessed on this day are called gromnicy, since these candles are lit during thunderstorms.[12] It is tempting to link this tradition with Dodola as well.

Cult of the Lunar Svarozic

For some time, I struggled with the question of who the main brother of Dazhbog was. I needed a deity who could act as his counterpart, and a divine twin. In Ossetian mythology, the sun and moon act as brothers who participate in creation of the earth.[13] There is also an interesting division of solar and lunar dynasties in Indian culture.[14] This resembles the bipartite division in Chapter 8: Svarozhichi - Sons of Svarog.

Indeed, if we were discussing a purely Indo-Iranian mythology, a solar and lunar pair of Gods might reflect the two progenitor ancestors. But there was never much evidence a strong lunar cult among the Slavs. Certainly not on the order of Volos or Dazhbog or Perun. There are just a few exceptions, which might hint at a lunar cult surviving in a few pockets. Some Croatian folk songs contain the refrains "Lunaj!" And "Lunajilje! Along with "Moj Bozicu Svarozicu. (My God, the moon, son of Svarog.)[15] It's noteworthy that the moon is addressed as "father" or "grandfather" in some Slavic prayers to obtain health and prosperity.[16]

In some folktales, the moon seemingly appears along with the sun and wind as a son of Baba Yaga. She is not called "Baba Yaga" in the story, but she seems to be indistinguishable from Baba Yaga based on her description.[17]

Cult of Stribog

The sole pieces of evidence for Stribog that mention him by name are the Russian primary chronicle and the Lay of Igor's campaign. The Russian Primary chronicle confirms that Stribog's idol was among those erected by Prince Vladimir in Kiev.[18]

In the Lay of Igor's Campaign, the winds are poetically referred to as "Grandchildren of Stribog."[19] The Lay of Igor's Campaign is usually not terribly useful for determining functions of deities, simply because of the poetic ways in which deity names are used. However, this may be the sole exception. If the winds were his progeny, it seems there is little reason to deny that Stribog was a wind deity.

Some shockingly prominent scholars have claimed Stribog means "Apportioner of Wealth." Just as they have claimed Dazhbog means "giver of wealth."[20] However, "Bog" simply means "deity" in all Slavic languages. To force it to mean anything else is an incredible contortion, not supported by any extant Slavic language. A derived term like Russian "Bogatstvo" can mean wealth. But we are talking about Stribog... not Stribogatstvo.

The personified wind occasionally shows up in Slavic folktales. One Ukrainian tale introduces him as follows:[21]

> *He went on farther and farther till he saw before him a forest, and on the borders of that forest stood a hut on hens' legs. The man went into this hut and was filled with astonishment, for there lay on the floor a huge, huge old man, as grey as milk. He lay there stretched at full length, his head on the seat of honour, with an arm and leg in each of the four corners, and all his hair standing on end. It was no other than the Wind himself. The man stared at this awful ancient with terror, for never in his life had he seen anything like it. "God help thee, old father!" cried he.—"Good health to thee, good man!" said the ancient giant, as he lay on the floor of the hut. Then he asked him in the most friendly manner, "Whence hath God brought thee hither, good man?"*

It is interesting that he appears to be in the house of Baba Yaga. Not unlike the moon in the previous section. This probably shows that Stribog, like Myesats (Moon) and Dazhbog, could be a son of the Great Mother Goddess Mokosh. In the quoted story above, the wind appears as a kindly figure who bestows gifts like a money-making Ram and a magical sack of plenty.

Cult of Tsar Morskoi

As with Svyatogor, the strongest evidence for a Tsar Morskoi (Tsar of the Sea) is from the Epic Russian Songs or byliny. Specifically, I am speaking of the bylina about the merchant Sadko, who in the song is cast into the sea from a ship. He ends up stranded beneath the sea with the Sea Tsar, where he performs on a gusli to entertain his host. The dancing of the Sea Tsar causes storms, and the pleasure he brings to Tsar Morskoi ultimately leads to him being allowed to go home.[22]

Interestingly, one known function of the songs known as byliny is that they were sometimes sung aboard ships in order to calm the sea.[23] It is tempting to see the Song of Sadko as originating from this tradition of calming the sea with Epic Songs, or with music in general. This appears to follow a magical rationale; The sailors sang a song about a merchant who pleased the Sea Tsar with his music in order to mollify the Sea Tsar, and ensure calm seas. This seems to almost follow the model of sympathetic magic, in which like produces like. Essentially, the bylina of Sadko could have been a song intended to produce the outcome of its own narrative.

In many Slavic folktales, the water-man or Tsar Morskoi forces a King to promise or ransom their infant son. Sometimes the King makes this promise will full knowledge, other times he simply promises to give the Tsar Morskoi "That which he does not know he has." In some stories, the King only discovers later that he has inadvertently promised his infant to the Tsar Morskoi. In other cases, he is coerced with full knowledge of what he is offering up to the Sea Tsar.[24] This agreement is strikingly similar to the deal made between Cian and the Sea

God in one Irish folktale, which leads to Cian's son (Lugh) being fostered by the Sea God Manannan Maclir.[25]

As we have discussed in Chapter 5: The Zoryas as Sea Maidens, there are also some fascinating connections between the daughters of Tsar Morskoi and the daughters of the Sea God Donbettyr from Ossetian Mythology. In all likelihood, the ferocious warrior maiden of Russian folktale, Maria Morevna, (Literally meaning "Maria Sea-Daughter") represents a Dawn-Goddess who is the daughter of Tsar Morskoi.

Cult of Simargl

The deity Simargl is another one that can be extrapolated mainly from the name. Simargl was the name of yet another idol that was erected by Vladimir in Kiev.[26] The main means of interpreting this deity comes from the conclusion that his or her name "Simargl" is cognate to Persian "Simurgh", a fabulous winged dog from Iranian mythology. According to Iranian mythology, the seeds of crops are distributed whenever Simurgh shakes her wings. A 12th to early 13th century silver pendant from Kievan Rus showing a similar creature is sometimes thought to represent Simargl. Therefore, it is often thought that the East Slavic Simargl was a theriomorphic fertility deity.[27]

Few conclusions can be drawn about this deity outside of the Iranian connection. Although the presence of a "Simargl" in Vladimir's pantheon is highly suggestive that many East Slavic deities could have had Iranian (Scytho-Sarmatian) origins.

Endnotes

1. Pronin, Alexander. Byliny; Heroic Tales of Old Russia. Germany, Possev, 1971. Pages 43-50
2. Pronin, Alexander. Byliny; Heroic Tales of Old Russia. Germany, Possev, 1971. Pages 51-57

3. Biggs, Maude Ashurst, and Gliński, Antoni Józef. Polish Fairy Tales: Translated from A.J. Gliński. United States, Folcroft Library Editions, 1920. Page 44
4. Thomas, D. M. Ruslan and Ludmila. United Kingdom, Scribner UK, 2019.
5. The Study of Russian Folklore. Germany, De Gruyter, 2019. Page 2
6. Gemuev, Izmail Nukhovich. Mansi Mythology. Finland, Akadémiai Kiadó, 2008. Page 136
7. Kropej, Monika. Supernatural Beings from Slovenian Myth and Folktales. Slovenia, Scientific Research centre of the Slovenian Academy of Sciences and Arts, 2012. Page 136
8. Thietmar of Merseburg, Adam of Bremen, Helmold of Bosau: Studies on the Christian Interpretation of Pre-Christian Cults and Beliefs in the Middle Ages. Netherlands, Brill, 2020. Pages 149, 152
9. Русское родноверие. Неоязычество и национализм в современной России. Russia, ББИ, 2020.
10. Jakobson, Roman. Selected Writings. Germany, Mouton, 1985. Pages 23-24
11. Roczniki Towarzystwa Naukowego w Toruniu. Poland, Nakl. Towarzystwa Naukowe, 1925. Page 49
12. Mary and Mariology. N.p. PediaPress. Pages 159-160
13. ФГБУНСеверо-Осетинский институт гуманитарных и социальных исследований им. В.И. Абаева ВНЦ РАН и Правительства РСО-Алания, Таказов Федар Магометович, МИФОЛОГИЧЕСКИЕ АРХЕТИПЫ МОДЕЛИ МИРА В ОСЕТИНСКОЙ КОСМОГОНИИ, Владикавказ 2014. Page 47
14. Bowles, Adam. Dharma, Disorder, and the Political in Ancient India: The Āpaddharmaparvan of the Mahābhārata. Netherlands, Brill, 2007. Page 377
15. Pet stoljeća hrvatske knjizevnosti. Croatia, n.p, 1968. Page 22
16. Eliade, Mircea. History of Religious Ideas, Volume 3: From Muhammad to the Age of Reforms. United States, University of Chicago Press, 2013. Page 33

17. Cossack Fairy Tales and Folk-tales. United Kingdom, A. H. Bullen, 1902. Pages 191-200
18. Ivanits, Linda J. Russian Folk Belief. United Kingdom, Taylor & Francis, 2015. Page 13
19. Religious Systems of the World: A Contribution to the Study of Comparative Religion: a Collection of Addresses Delivered at South Place Institute. United Kingdom, S. Sonnenschein, 1901. Page 267
20. Jakobson, Roman. Selected Writings. Germany, Mouton, 1985. Page 30
21. Cossack Fairy Tales and Folk Tales. United Kingdom, G.G. Harrap & Company, 1916. Pages 27-32
22. Ralston, William Ralston Shedden. The Songs of the Russian People: As Illustrative of Slavonic Mythology and Russian Social Life. United Kingdom, Ellis & Green, 1872. Page 178-179
23. Handbook of Russian Literature. United Kingdom, Yale University Press, 1985. Page 69
24. Ralston, William Ralston Shedden. The Songs of the Russian People: As Illustrative of Slavonic Mythology and Russian Social Life. United Kingdom, Ellis & Green, 1872. Page 179
25. Squire, Charles. The Mythology of the British Islands: An Introduction to Celtic Myth, Legend, Poetry, and Romance. Kiribati, Blackie and son, limited, 1905. Page 237
26. Ivanits, Linda J. Russian Folk Belief. United Kingdom, Taylor & Francis, 2015. Page 13
27. Warner, Elizabeth. Russian Myths (Legendary Past Series). Austin, University of Texas Press, 2002. Page 17

Chapter 13

Slavic Holidays

We have discussed remarkably few actual holidays, and it honestly seems that there are only four main ones that recur with great regularity in Slavic folklore. Those that can be best reconstructed from an academic or folkloric standpoint are as follows.

- **Early March** - New Year. A day of Marena / Mokosh (see Chapter 2).
- **Early May -** A Day for honoring the dead ancestors, as well as the Gods Dazhbog and / or Volos (see Chapters 4, 8, and 9).
- **Midsummer - Late June.** A day for honoring Zorya Utrennyaya and Dazhbog (see Chapter 5).
- **Early November** - A Day for honoring the dead ancestors, and the Gods Dazhbog and / or Volos (see Chapters 4, 8).

Additionally, I would recommend a few other holidays based on personal preference - not necessarily an abundance of research. Although one of these (Perun's Day) is in agreement with Rybakov's work. I would submit that Early February is a logical enough day for a festival of Zorya Utrennyaya since it marks the end of winter. I also prefer to honor Mokosh on Winter Solstice (around December 20th) by telling a story of Aarne-Thompson-Type 480. And that's a great ritual tip in general - tell a story! There are plenty referenced in this book. A Mokosh day in November would also make sense, but as mentioned, November is already very busy. A winter solstice date is associated with Frau Holle and Ange Patyai, so I apply it for Mokosh as well. I also unashamedly reflect on the creator

Svarog / Belobog around Christmas time. Call it my one exercise in Dvorverie, or Christian-influenced syncretism. Below I list the holidays that I observe based on personal preference.

- **Early February** – Zorya Utrennyaya
- **Early August -** Perun's Day
- **December 20th-22nd**: Mokosh's Night (see Chapter 2)
- **December 25th** - A Day to Honor Svarog

This is more of an intermission than a chapter. I tend to be very private about these matters, but I wanted to illustrate how a series of pagan Slavic holidays could look in practice. Furthermore, a full exploration of the Slavic holidays would deserve a book of its own.

Chapter 14

Closing Statements

It is difficult to describe what has driven me to delve into this topic so deeply. Why have I used my skills to study Slavic Paganism? For a man living in Texas and a Bachelor of Science, this might seem like a bizarre choice. And it is.

My roots as a half-Polish-American and half-Jewish man are not any less confusing. And my parents did not exactly promote the Polish heritage to me. If anything, Judaism is what first gave me a taste of an identity beyond the mainstream. The idea of people having distinct origins and cultures, going back much further than the modern mainstream culture of white America was fascinating for me. My mother and her family were fairly intellectual and educated, which gave me a further reach in processing the nuances of cultural identity. Yet it was the Polish side of my ancestry that gave me the most complex feelings. From the beginning, I struggled to process what "Polish" identity even meant. I knew who the Jewish people were (more or less), but who on earth were the Poles?

In no small part due to my mother, I was exposed to Indo-European studies at an early date. I recall reading an overview of the topic from *Mysteries of the Past*, by Lionel Casson, which was published in 1978.[1] This book has sat upon my mother's bookshelf since at least the early 1990's. I was in Middle School, probably not more than 13 years old, when I was introduced to the concept of an Indo-European language family, and a people living before 3,000 BCE who created this massive language family. Considering the obscurity of the topic, and my ignorance at the time, it was a fine introduction. In many ways it inspired me, and it left a lasting impression about the cultural interconnectedness of billions of people worldwide.

Even then, the notion of a "Slavic" identity did not even fully form in my brain until High School. It was then that I discovered a branch of the Indo-European language family that was called the "Slavic" branch, and which included the Polish language that two of my grandparents had been familiar with. Like many westerners, I had vague notions of a Classical Greco-Roman and even a vague "Germanic" culture that stretched back to ancient times. But to truly understand that there used to be an ancient "Proto-Slavic" people took at least until I was about 17 years old.

As I have stated, my only formal higher education was in the pursuit of a Bachelor of Science in Biology. While the eclecticism of my personal studies should be obvious, it's worth noting that this did play a role in my return to Indo-European studies. In 2015, Haak published his groundbreaking genetic study on the Corded Ware Culture, showing a massive genetic contribution from the Eurasian Steppe. Far more so than proponents of the Steppe model had dared dream of. In some ways, this makes the topic more intoxicating than ever. For decades, the biggest issue people have had with Indo-European studies has been the level of abstraction. The linguists were absolutely right, of course, but it's hard to explain to people how an entire language and culture can be constructed through comparative analysis. Very much like with comparative mythology! With the new genetic data showing the Proto-Indo-Europeans of the Pontic steppe were indeed a real people who migrated and became (to a large extent) our ancestors, the significance of this field has never been less abstract than it is today. This is a golden opportunity to explain to the world that this field represents the search for a very real culture that we know existed.

This road is littered with dangers. As a half-Jewish man myself, I know very well how the Nazi's co-opted the so-called "Aryan" identity of the Proto-Indo-Europeans. However, as a man who lived through 2016 and 2020 in the United States, I also know that a vacuum of identity is not necessarily a good thing. On the contrary, it is precisely when people feel a gaping void of identity that they reach most desperately for a delusion to fill that emptiness. That aptly describes large swaths of the United States right now. The void of an identity has caused a desperate search for something meaningful. And that does not always have good consequences. It can be quite dangerous, especially when bad actors step in to provide people with a toxic delusion that will make them feel better.

This book is not that. Rather, I am arguing that the earnest search for an identity is a good thing when based on truth, solid principles, and a desire to build a happier world. The early Slavs, for example, did not see themselves as "White." They probably fought alongside the Huns as readily as the Goths, if not more-so. They did not artificially orient themselves more closely to other "Europeans" than to so-called "Asiatic" nomads. Thus, in some ways, the honest search for ancient origins is threatening to the cultural status quo and does not necessarily just reinforce conservative identities in the mainstream culture. On the contrary, the honest study of the ancient world has long been a way of transforming such clear-cut preconceptions about who we are.

I'll admit that interest in my own ancestry was a gateway to this topic. But on its own, I sincerely doubt if that would have gotten me so deeply involved in reconstructing Slavic culture. One of the things that has propelled me so furiously into the study of this topic is that, in my opinion, it is incredibly neglected. If I am right about the many points I make in this book, then the obvious implication is that the field has been allowed to fall behind and decay over the past few decades. How else could an amateur like me make so many observations about it? The only explanation is that I come from a unique vantage point.

Unlike most Westerners, I do have an intense interest in the early Slavic cultures. That is a rare enough quality in the

English-speaking world! However, the English-speaking world is the global hub of Indo-European studies. Indeed, the barrier between English scholarship and the scholarship of the former Soviet world remains enormous. As of 2022 it does not appear that the chasm between cultures will be fully closed any time soon. For comparison, the impact of this cultural divide on Mayan studies is well known. In 1952, the Soviet scholar Yuri Knorozov published his seminal work Drevnyaya pis'mennost' Tsentral'noy Ameriki, or *Ancient Writing of Central America* which revolutionized our understanding of the Mayan writing system. However, Western Scholarship did not fully begin to adopt his methods until at least 1975, when his noted Western critic John Thompson died.[2]

Reconstructing Slavic mythology, from the perspective of academia, is not equivalent to cracking the Mayan writing system. I am not trying to equate the two. Reconstructing a writing system would be infinitely more difficult than anything accomplished here. At the same time, however, it demonstrates the principle of how cultural divides can delay the progress of a field. Particularly in the study of cultures with incomplete records. This can be for a number of reasons. For one, cultures that are poorly understood are difficult for just one culture to reconstruct. In the case of Mayan studies, Knorozov had a broad base of knowledge that was unusual in the West. He also paid greater attention to the European corpus of material, specifically the Spanish material recorded by Friar Diego De Landa during his book-burning crusade in the Yucatan. And so it is with many reconstructions of lost cultures; The different pieces of the puzzle lie in different parts of the world.

In the case of the study of Slavic Pre-Christian beliefs, I would argue that a similar delay has taken place. The divide between Knozorov and Western Scholarship seems to have led to something like a 20-year delay in his recognition. I would argue that the geopolitical upheavals that have wracked Slavic countries have had an even more profound impact. Where the West has pioneered the advancement of Indo-European studies, the scholarship on the Eastern European and Russian Federation traditions (Slavic, Uralic, Turkic, Romanian, and North Caucasian) seems to have lagged behind by about 50 years in comparison. Which means that most of the world still has an extremely outdated view of Slavic Paganism. One that any J.P. Mallory or Dumezil could probably have improved considerably if they considered it worth their time.

In folklore studies, many scholars have acknowledged the need to study motifs from across a wide area. For instance, the tales of Aarne-Thompson-Type 480 (The Kind Girl and the Unkind Girl) are widespread. They can be found across Eurasia and the Americas. However, in order to truly reconstruct the genealogy or phylogeny of these tales, we must begin with a broad (international) analysis of them. And in many respects, folklorists like Warren Roberts have already pioneered this type of phylogenetic analysis with particular folktale types. Roberts has neatly summarized the application of this method for Aarne-Thompson type 480. He explains, for example, how if we see a motif in just two isolated "pockets" like Japan and the Middle East (and none of the adjoining regions) we can make inferences about its antiquity. In such a scenario, we can say that the motif was fairly widespread in the distant past.[3] It is precisely this phylogenetic or integrative approach which has been lacking in the reconstruction of Slavic mythology. Ivanov and Toporov specialized in Belarusian and Russian folklore.[4] Meanwhile, Katicic and Belaj openly admitted their goal of reconstructing a distinctive "Croatian" mythology, with emphasis on the folklore of their homeland.[5] Consequently, their insights have been as narrow as their specialties.

Ivanov and Toporov believed that Belarusian material was the most archaic out of East Slavic folk traditions. Without a doubt, the northern periphery of East Slavic territory retained many archaisms. That's why the byliny were preserved in Karelia. At the same time, latitude is not the only factor in the archaism of East Slavic folklore. Industrialization was also a critical factor in eliminating folk tradition throughout Europe. The East Slavic peoples who came under industrialization last were probably the Carpathian-Rusyns. And one can hardly read about the folklore of the Hutsuls (A Carpatho-Rusyn people) without concluding that it was one of the most "archaic" in Europe. As Bohdan Rubchak notes, however, Ivanov and Toporov were likely unfamiliar with Hutsul ethnographic material. He writes;[6]

> *The first part of this excellent structuralist-semiotic study examines the many variations of the duel between Perun and Veles, which put Hutsul legends of Saint Elias and the Aridnyk into a wider Slavic context. Despite their staggering erudition, the authors do not seem to be aware of this cycle of Hutsul legends, which could have provided them with excellent illustrations of their central thesis. When they do cite examples from Ukrainian mythology, they tend to regard them as Russian, probably governing themselves by the principle that it is better to risk one's scholarly responsibility than one's freedom.*

In my experience, nobody will tell you the truth about Russia like a Ukrainian. (And to be fair, the same could be said for the USA and Mexico.) I can clearly recall that this passage was shocking to me when I first read it, over a decade ago. How could the renowned scholars Ivanov and Toporov be unfamiliar with Carpatho-Rusyn folklore in their own backyard? Actually, Soviet scholars often had very little knowledge about cultures in their own backyard. Or if they did, they often wrote very little about them. Not out of negligence, but simply because of the times they lived in. It was a terrible environment for this type of research. It's clear that the stifling atmosphere of Russian domination has set Slavic studies back considerably.

In general, Russian scholarship has had a strong political incentive to de-emphasize the native culture of Ukraine. And it's hard not to see this as a motive in their research, particularly where they assume that only "Northern" regions of East Slavic territory harbored archaic traditions. In fact, the Carpathians of western Ukraine had a 19th century folk-tradition that was at least as "archaic" as that of Belarus and the Russian north. Like the Hutsuls, the people of the Balkans were also among the last to industrialize in Europe[7] and this is evident in the obvious archaism of early 20th century Balkan culture. Like the culture of Ukraine, however, the native cultures of the Balkans were also often de-emphasized in Soviet Scholarship. Meanwhile, as I show in Chapter 1, a number of Polish scholars stubbornly resisted Soviet scholarship showing that the Proto-Slavic homeland lay in the east, in modern day Ukraine. In short, the study of the early Slavs is plagued by division from all sides. However, I believe that this book advances a fairly objective review of the Pre-Christian Slavic culture that avoids any real bias for any one nation.

In short, there are historical and political reasons why this field is fragmented. And these explain why I am apparently the one to put many of these pieces together. I don't apologize for my audacity, however. This should have been done at least a decade ago. And by someone who had the resources to do it far more easily.

As a Biology major writing about Slavic mythology, I can honestly say that specialization has never been one of my failings. But on this topic, that may be for the best. I would argue that this topic is particularly suited to a broad, integrative approach. When it comes to reconstruction, one of the few strengths of Slavic paganism (and there are few!) is that we have thirteen Slavic countries to draw folklore from. And the folklore motifs of these countries are intertwined with other Eastern European ethnic groups as well. It's time we started pressing our one advantage - namely, the sheer quantity of interrelated cultures in Eastern Europe (and even east of the Urals). Most of these cultures do not have traditions that are well-attested individually, but together they constitute a significant sample of data.

As a non-specialist, I cannot write the "final word" on Slavic mythology. Or even a complete study. However, here is my outline for future researchers; begin by reconstituting the folklore of the Common Slavic period. Prior to about 1,000 CE the Slavic language dialects across Eastern Europe were basically mutually intelligible with each other. We can infer that there was a vigorous cultural exchange during this time. Create an international study that seeks to find the common elements, scattered throughout various countries, that point to this period. That will push your reconstruction back to the medieval period. For those in Eastern Europe, it may be challenging. But please, for once, set aside your divisions and reconstruct the Common Slavic elements in your folklore. There has been some speculation about this, but in general, there still is no comprehensive reconstruction of Common Slavic folklore elements. This book identifies only a handful. That is the necessary first step.

Next, seek analogies with "Slav-adjacent" cultures that appear to be closely related. (Balts, Ossetians, Romanians, Komi, Mordvins, Karelians. Mansi, etc.) Do not try to interpret the Common Slavic folklore as mythology until you do this! Some elements of Common Slavic folklore will be impossible to interpret otherwise. Simply list out the motifs and find the parallels. Then consider the implications for Slavic mythology.

If you follow this methodology, it will push your reconstruction back from medieval times all the way into the migration period or earlier. Obviously, Proto-Indo-European mythology (as reconstructed by scholars) should be treated as one of the related mythologies in this analysis. I can't do all of this. But as I hope to show in this book, this is how it should be done. And it may well be that a Russian or Ukrainian or Polish scholar is best qualified to do this. But we all need a little good advice from an outsider sometimes. Perhaps that is my role.

The methodical approach I have described has been applied to Indo-European studies for ages. It is absolutely applicable to the ethnographic material on various Eastern European ethnic groups, if applied properly. In some cases, the Eastern European proto-myths you reconstruct may not be distinctively "Slavic" in their origins. Sometimes they may be Scythian, or even "Late Indo-European" residue from the "Satem" group of the Eastern Corded Ware Culture. Some elements, particularly those relating to dualism, could have been introduced to the Slavs only during the Common Slavic period. Even in these instances, however, it will often be possible to demonstrate that some Slavic tribes preserved a variant of the myth in question. Thus, under that definition, it will still constitute a kind of "Slavic paganism." It is not necessarily the origin of the narrative that matters here, only whether it survived up to the Common Slavic period in a form that was independent of Christianity. And this is another stance that might be politically problematic in Eastern Europe – to say that Slavic mythology was influenced by migration period borrowings from others could obviously be unpopular in some countries. However, I don't care very much about this. The environment of the late migration period was hardly a recipe for cultural purity.

I should stress that not everyone in this field of research has been a disappointment. Upenskij did a thorough job of exploring the connections between Volos, the bear, and St. Nicholas. Rybakov and Shapiro deserve credit for some of my own reconstructions here. In particular, Rybakov's reconstruction of Mokosh is perhaps perfect as it is, and I am heavily indebted to him. Likewise for Shapiro, who has further explored the connections with Mokosh and Frau Holle. Furthermore,

Stanislaw Rosik has recently published a great analysis of the Polabian Slavic religion, which reaffirms the often-neglected significance of Svarog among the Pre-Christian Slavs. Also, my observations about the Earth-diver Creation Myth are not at all new. But the field of Slavic studies is still in need of critical attention.

However, I would argue that this is a loss for comparative studies in the West as well. Indo-European mythology is indeed reconstructable with great precision and detail. Still more so now that we have the genetic data showing that the culture existed. However, it seems likely that a significant portion of the necessary data is still concealed behind the barrier of "niche culture" studies. If all of the relevant material on Slavic, Uralic, Turkic, East Iranian, and North Caucasian traditions were translated, and widely circulated, the field of Indo-European Comparative Mythology would probably experience a renaissance.

This book just represents a small trickle of the relevant material that probably could be yielded from such a project. However, I feel this analysis has been thorough enough that most of my main observations on Slavic mythology would still stand.

During my analysis of the Earth-diver Creation myth, I encountered some similar implications for the study of indigenous American mythologies. This field will be just fine without me, however. I don't presume to egg it along. Rather, it is the study of Eastern Europe that has sputtered and floundered well behind where it should be in 2022. So much so that even someone like me can critique it – and that's really saying something!

I wrote this book first and foremost for people who are interested in Slavic paganism, however, and not necessarily for scholars (though I think they would benefit from the analysis). The reasons are many. For one, I don't believe most scholars will care what I write (at first). I suspect that sufficient popularity could bring this book to the attention of scholars, but it would need to become very popular first. On the other hand, I do think that a lot of Slavic pagans could do with better guidance – and it seems that many will listen to me. I was deeply disappointed by the resources available on this topic. But I hope that others may be less disappointed, thanks to this book.

And ultimately, this gets to the core reason of why I have chosen to gravitate to the early Slavic culture; We have been robbed. As I state at the beginning of this book, culture and a sense of identity are the birthright of all human beings. Many people have lost this in the modern world. I would list indigenous people of the Americas as being some of the foremost examples of this. Many even now are trying to regain what was taken from them. And just to be clear- they have lost far more than I have.

However, they are not the only ones whose ancestors have been written out of the spotlight of history. The truth is that most of the world is not descended from people like the Greeks and Romans who take the "leading roles" in official historical records. Most of us are descended from those little-known cultures that are scarcely mentioned during ancient times. And it's time we came to appreciate the scale of that theft. Not just the Slavs, but much of humanity has lost its archaic or" primitive" roots. And while I'm definitely not calling for a return to the ancient way of life, I do think that there is much that modern human beings can learn from those roots as we move forward into the future.

In short, it seems to me that being a custodian of the early Slavic culture is something that I am obligated to do. I value it for religious reasons, because I do believe in a creator, and in his children, the Gods. I believe in a Pre-Christian (Probably Altaic) doctrine involving a dualist struggle between Good and Evil. The Truth and the Lie, as Zoroaster would have called it. And I believe that monotheism has more often served Evil than Good. In fact, the selfishness and egotism implied by monotheism is an excellent portrait of true evil. Conveniently enough, it also grants an implicit license to believers to engage in cultural imperialism.

Thus for me, polytheism embodies the inherent plurality of goodness. Goodness is incredibly varied and diverse. There are many ways to be good. As strange as it may sound, the marriage between dualism and polytheism is an incredibly beautiful one, because the veneration of diversity is an excellent example of moral goodness. And let us not forget that Zoroastrianism was not a monotheistic religion, even though it stressed moral goodness. The Zoroastrians did worship the Wise Lord, Ahura Mazda, but they also blatantly worshiped the Yazata's (deities) appointed by him. This did not precipitate a fit of jealous rage from the creator. Why? Because the Zoroastrian God is not a jealous tyrant. Contrary to popular belief, there is no contradiction between moral dualism and polytheism. A better question might be how mandatory monotheism can be considered compatible with a "moral" religion.

Yet ultimately, it must be admitted that the pursuit of goodness that permeates Christianity comes from the same source (culturally or spiritually) as Zoroastrianism. Likewise for the dualist traditions explored in Chapter 11: Chernobog and the Earth-diver Myth. Ultimately, all traditions can be taken in a positive direction, and nobody can really say that all followers of a particular faith (or of no faith) are all "lost" or unworthy of praise. There are indeed some wonderful people on all sides, regardless of belief. And my message to good Christians would be this; You have more in common with good people of other faiths than you do with the bad people in your own. We might have some different values, but we welcome you to join us in the fight against those who have no values at all.

Furthermore, even "Good" and "Evil" may be brothers of the same womb. (Mother Chezh, as the Komi would call her.) As a Slavic pagan, I tend to refer to her simply as "Boginya." (Goddess) This maternal kinship between good and evil is a mystery worth reflecting on.

Finally, the awe that we feel at the beauty of nature, and the simple folklore of our ancestors comes from the same part of the human psyche as our sense of right and wrong. The ability to feel adoration towards a vast mountain or river is not the same as moral goodness, obviously. But as many Greek philosophers noted, the ability to appreciate these things is not unrelated to goodness. The two impulses are deeply connected and should be cultivated together. Ultimately, they both spring from the fiery and irrational human heart. And by the same logic, we can say that those who have no regard for nature are missing that inner fire and sense of goodness. The same holds true for those who would carelessly obliterate ancient monuments of our human heritage. Or the intangible treasures of human culture.

These are my beliefs.

On the other hand, belief is pleasant, but certainty is absurd. Anybody who has 100% certainty on religion is lying or insane. But that uncertainty is a part of the mystery of life. Even in the absence of theistic beliefs, however, I believe that it is still possible to honor our ancestors who lived and died to bring us to this point in time. Even as an atheist, I still would study this topic, simply because it is a golden treasure trove of human heritage. I know this because I have been an atheist, and my deep adoration for our ancient ancestors never abated. In much the same way that the curator of a museum loves his artifacts, I discovered that I still loved the traditions of our ancient ancestors- even in the absence of faith.

So religious belief is only a portion of my passion for this topic - although it is an important part. And in some ways, this makes my spirituality even more profound. If you wish to know more about the ancient beliefs of the Slavs, then this book is your rightful inheritance. It is my duty to pass it on to you, as completely as I can.

Endnotes

1. Casson, Lionel. Mysteries of the Past. London: Mitchell Beazley, 1978.
2. Johnson, Scott A. J. Translating Maya Hieroglyphs. Norman: University of Oklahoma Press, 2014. Page 10
3. Roberts, Warren E. The Tale of the Kind and the Unkind Girls: Aa-th 480 and Related Tales. Detroit: Wayne State University Press, 1994.
4. Bojtar, Endre. Foreword to the Past: A Cultural History of the Baltic People. New York: Central European University Press, 2000. Internet resource. Page 249
5. Marjanic, Suzana. "A Review of Contemporary Research on Croatian Mythology in Relation to Natko Nodilo." Traditiones. 47.2 (2018): Pages 15-31
6. Kotsiubinsky, Mykhail, and Bohdan Rubchak. Shadows of Forgotten Ancestors. Littleton, Colo: Published for the Canadian Institute of Ukrainian Studies by Ukrainian Academic Press, 1981. Internet resource. Pages 125-126
7. "Building a Continental Area: Identities, Differences and Urban Developments in Europe." 1 (2000): Pages 114-142

About the Author

T.D. Kokoszka lives in Austin, Texas. He holds a B.S. in Microbiology, and currently writes in addition to pursuing other career goals. He is a member of the Hearthstone Grove in Austin, which is affiliated with the pagan organization ADF (Ar nDraiocht Fein). This group is mainly Celtic-oriented, but it also provides a haven for people of various spiritual paths. He can be found attending many of the major events associated with this group. The author can also be reached by email. Streptomycetacea@gmail.com

MOON
BOOKS

PAGANISM & SHAMANISM

What is Paganism? A religion, a spirituality, an alternative belief system, nature worship? You can find support for all these definitions (and many more) in dictionaries, encyclopaedias, and text books of religion, but subscribe to any one and the truth will evade you. Above all Paganism is a creative pursuit, an encounter with reality, an exploration of meaning and an expression of the soul. Druids, Heathens, Wiccans and others, all contribute their insights and literary riches to the Pagan tradition. Moon Books invites you to begin or to deepen your own encounter, right here, right now.

If you have enjoyed this book, why not tell other readers by posting a review on your preferred book site.

Recent bestsellers from Moon Books are:

Journey to the Dark Goddess
How to Return to Your Soul
Jane Meredith
Discover the powerful secrets of the Dark Goddess and transform your depression, grief and pain into healing and integration.
Paperback: 978-1-84694-677-6 ebook: 978-1-78099-223-5

Shamanic Reiki
Expanded Ways of Working with Universal Life Force Energy
Llyn Roberts, Robert Levy
Shamanism and Reiki are each powerful ways of healing; together, their power multiplies. *Shamanic Reiki* introduces techniques to help healers and Reiki practitioners tap ancient healing wisdom.
Paperback: 978-1-84694-037-8 ebook: 978-1-84694-650-9

Pagan Portals – The Awen Alone
Walking the Path of the Solitary Druid
Joanna van der Hoeven
An introductory guide for the solitary Druid, *The Awen Alone* will accompany you as you explore, and seek out your own place within the natural world.
Paperback: 978-1-78279-547-6 ebook: 978-1-78279-546-9

A Kitchen Witch's World of Magical Herbs & Plants
Rachel Patterson
A journey into the magical world of herbs and plants, filled with magical uses, folklore, history and practical magic. By popular writer, blogger and kitchen witch, Tansy Firedragon.
Paperback: 978-1-78279-621-3 ebook: 978-1-78279-620-6

Medicine for the Soul

The Complete Book of Shamanic Healing

Ross Heaven

All you will ever need to know about shamanic healing and how to become your own shaman...

Paperback: 978-1-78099-419-2 ebook: 978-1-78099-420-8

Shaman Pathways – The Druid Shaman

Exploring the Celtic Otherworld

Danu Forest

A practical guide to Celtic shamanism with exercises and techniques as well as traditional lore for exploring the Celtic Otherworld.

Paperback: 978-1-78099-615-8 ebook: 978-1-78099-616-5

Traditional Witchcraft for the Woods and Forests

A Witch's Guide to the Woodland with Guided Meditations and Pathworking

Mélusine Draco

A Witch's guide to walking alone in the woods, with guided meditations and pathworking.

Paperback: 978-1-84694-803-9 ebook: 978-1-84694-804-6

Wild Earth, Wild Soul

A Manual for an Ecstatic Culture

Bill Pfeiffer

Imagine a nature-based culture so alive and so connected, spreading like wildfire. This book is the first flame...

Paperback: 978-1-78099-187-0 ebook: 978-1-78099-188-7

Naming the Goddess

Trevor Greenfield

Naming the Goddess is written by over eighty adherents and scholars of Goddess and Goddess Spirituality.

Paperback: 978-1-78279-476-9 ebook: 978-1-78279-475-2

Shapeshifting into Higher Consciousness

Heal and Transform Yourself and Our World with Ancient Shamanic and Modern Methods

Llyn Roberts

Ancient and modern methods that you can use every day to ansform yourself and make a positive difference in the world.

Paperback: 978-1-84694-843-5 ebook: 978-1-84694-844-2

Readers of ebooks can buy or view any of these bestsellers by clicking on the live link in the title. Most titles are published in paperback and as an ebook. Paperbacks are available in traditional bookshops. Both print and ebook formats are available online.

Find more titles and sign up to our readers' newsletter at http://www.johnhuntpublishing.com/paganism

Follow us on Facebook at https://www.facebook.com/MoonBooks and Twitter at https://twitter.com/MoonBooksJHP